Lecture Notes in Computer Science 2319

Edited by G. Goos, J. Hartmanis, and J. van Leeuwen

Springer
Berlin
Heidelberg
New York
Barcelona
Hong Kong
London
Milan
Paris
Tokyo

Cristina Gacek (Ed.)

Software Reuse: Methods, Techniques, and Tools

7th International Conference, ICSR-7
Austin, TX, USA, April 15-19, 2002
Proceedings

 Springer

Series Editors

Gerhard Goos, Karlsruhe University, Germany
Juris Hartmanis, Cornell University, NY, USA
Jan van Leeuwen, Utrecht University, The Netherlands

Volume Editor

Cristina Gacek
University of Newcastle, Department of Computing Science
Centre for Software Reliability
Newcastle upon Tyne NE1 7RU, UK
E-mail: cristina.gacek@ncl.ac.uk

Cataloging-in-Publication Data applied for

Die Deutsche Bibliothek - CIP-Einheitsaufnahme

Software reuse: methods, techniques, and tools : 7th international
conference ; proceedings / ICSR-7, Austin, TX, USA, April 15 - 19, 2002.
Cristina Gacek (ed.). - Berlin ; Heidelberg ; New York ; Barcelona ; Hong
Kong ; London ; Milan ; Paris ; Tokyo : Springer, 2002
  (Lecture notes in computer science ; Vol. 2319)
  ISBN 3-540-43483-6

CR Subject Classification (1998): D.2, K.6, D.1, J.1

ISSN 0302-9743
ISBN 3-540-43483-6 Springer-Verlag Berlin Heidelberg New York

Springer-Verlag Berlin Heidelberg New York
a member of BertelsmannSpringer Science+Business Media GmbH

http://www.springer.de

© Springer-Verlag Berlin Heidelberg 2002
Printed in Germany

Typesetting: Camera-ready by author, data conversion by Steingräber Satztechnik GmbH, Heidelberg
Printed on acid-free paper   SPIN: 10846652   06/3142   5 4 3 2 1 0

Message from the Program Chair

As the years have passed, much progress in the field of software reuse has been made. Many of the early ideas in this area have already become embedded in everyday software development practices, and many of its sub-areas have gained enough recognition to be discussed as relevant topics of their own, with their own clear sub-community. These developments could imply a fragmentation of the software reuse community and a decline in interest in software reuse in general. Fortunately, as reflected by the program of ICSR-7, both academic and industrial reuse communities realize that there are many advantages to holding discussions in a broader forum, adding to the diversity of experiences and ideas shared.

ICSR-7 is privileged to have a very prestigious and dedicated program committee, with all members having embraced an electronic review process that was demanding and time-consuming. I would like to thank them for their excellent performance and dedication towards making the conference a success.

In times when many conferences are observing a decreasing number of sub-missions, ICSR-7 has been very fortunate to have received a large number of good quality submissions originating from several continents: America (North and South), Asia, Europe, and Oceania. This has resulted in a set of papers, tutorials, and workshops that should enlighten and deepen the knowledge of readers and conference participants with varying backgrounds and interests. I believe Austin (Texas-USA) will prove to be *the* place to be during the ICSR-7 timeframe. I hope you enjoy the conference and the surrounding environment to the fullest!

April 2002   Cristina Gacek

Message from the General Chair

This is the seventh International Conference in Software Reuse and the second time it has been held in the United States. The conference has matured and stands as an important forum for the academic world as well as an important technology transfer gate to the software industry. Our main focus is the leverage of productivity in software production by means of reusing processes and artifacts previously built. It is a simple idea, but with huge challenges, of both a technical and a social nature. Our conference, by means of its workshops, tutorials, keynotes (Jay Misra and Roger Sessions), and a program with the best submitted papers, aims at the presentation and discussion of new ideas and new results permeating the topic of reuse.

We are very happy to be in Austin this time. Austin has been an important center for research and development in the software industry and has focussed on aspects related to software reuse. We are very glad and grateful that Don Batory accepted to be our host, taking care of the local arrangements. I am certain that ICSR-7 in Austin will be a great conference.

I have to thank the excellent team that brought us ICSR-7. Cristina Gacek has done an amazing job as program chair. It was not easy handling the large number of mails that were necessary to coordinate a virtual program committee meeting and dealing with the submission and review web system. Peter Knauber, the tutorial chair, successfully put together eight tutorials for the conference. Krzysztof Czarnecki managed to bring together five workshops that deal with specific topics related to reuse and the first young researchers' workshop that aims to attract the graduate students to discuss their topics of research. We are all grateful to each one of the workshop chairs. Their work was most appreciated, as we widened the conference scope with their workshops. We thank Giancarlo Succi, who was responsible for our marketing. He managed and sponsored the ICSR-7 web site. As mentioned before, Don Batory took care of local arrangements, and I thank him for this. Many thanks to Ira Baxter, responsible for corporate donations and Ernesto Guerrieri the financial and registration chair. The steering committee (Biggerstaff, Favaro, Frakes, and Guerrieri) was of fundamental importance for their guidance and support. Of course, we extend our thanks to the institutions that host the members of our team, without whose support it would be impossible to put forward such a conference. We also would like to thank Sodalia and BigLever Software for their support.

I, myself, would like to thank Peter A. Freeman, responsible for the UCI Reuse Project, with whom I first learned about reuse. Many years have passed, but I can still remember the great times of the early findings in the reuse area. I also wish to thank the Departamento de Informática , PUC-Rio, and CNPq for their continuing support.

April 2002   Julio Cesar Sampaio do Prado Leite
                                                      www.inf.puc-rio.br/~julio

Committees

General Chair	Julio Cesar Leite	**Financial and Registrations Chair**	Ernesto Guerrieri
Program Chair	Cristina Gacek	**Workshop Chair**	Krzysztof Czarnecki
Local Chair	Don Batory	**Tutorial Chair**	Peter Knauber
Corporate Chair	Ira Baxter	**Publicity Chair**	Giancarlo Succi

Program Committee

S. Bandinelli (Spain)
L. Bass (USA)
D. Batory (USA)
I. Baxter (USA)
L. Benedicenti (Canada)
P. O. Bengtsson (Sweden)
T. Biggerstaff (USA)
B. Boehm (USA)
C. Boldyreff (UK)
J. Bosch (The Netherlands)
P. Clements (USA)
S. Cohen (USA)
K. Czarnecki (Germany)
P. Devanbu (USA)
J. C. Dueñas (Spain)
W. Emmerich (UK)
J. Favaro (Italy)
B. Frakes (USA)
C. Gacek (UK)

H. Gomaa (USA)
E. Guerrieri (USA)
J. Jourdan (France)
K. Kang (Korea)
P. Knauber (Germany)
C. Krueger (USA)
J. C. Leite (Brazil)
F. Linden (The Netherlands)
J. Llorens (Spain)
C. Lucena (Brazil)
J. A. McDermid (UK)
N. Maiden (UK)
M. Mannion (UK)
M. Marchesi (Italy)
M. Matsumoto (Japan)
A. Mili (USA)
M. Morisio (Italy)
H. Muller (Canada)
D. Musser (USA)

J. Neighbors (USA)
J. Ning (USA)
W. Pedrycz (Canada)
J. Penix (USA)
J. Poulin (USA)
W. Pree (Germany)
R. Prieto-Diaz (USA)
A. Romanovsky (UK)
B. Scherlis (USA)
K. Schmid (Germany)
M. Sitaraman (USA)
D. Smith (USA)
I. Sommerville (UK)
G. Succi (Canada)
B. Weide (USA)
D. Weiss (USA)
C. Werner (Brazil)

External Reviewers

Delano Beder
Rodrigo Cerón
Jilles van Gurp
Michel Jaring
Greg Kulczycki
Marcos Mangan

Jason Mansell
Eduardo Saenz Matallana
Michael Mehlich
Dirk Muthig
Ted Pavlic
Panos Periorellis

Serge Salicki
Iratxe Gómez Susaeta
Ian Welch
Juan C. Yelmo

Sponsors and Supporters

BigLever Software, Inc.

Dep. de Informática of PUC-Rio

Fraunhofer IESE

Generic Programming

Op40, Inc.

Semantic Designs, Inc.

Sodalia

Univ. of Alberta Dep. of Electrical and Computer Eng.

Univ. of Newcastle upon Tyne, CS Dept.

Univ. of Texas, Computer Science Dept.

Table of Contents

Integrating and Reusing GUI-Driven Applications

Mark Grechanik, Don Batory, and Dewayne E. Perry

UT Center for Advanced Research In Software Engineering (UT ARISE)
University of Texas at Austin, Austin, Texas 78712
{grechani,perry}@ece.utexas.edu, batory@cs.utexas.edu

Abstract. *Graphical User Interface (GUI) Driven Applications (GDAs)* are ubiquitous. We present a model and techniques that take closed and monolithic GDAs and integrate them into an open, collaborative environment. The central idea is to objectify the GUI of a GDA, thereby creating an object that enables programmatic control of that GDA.

We demonstrate a non-trivial application of these ideas by integrating a stand-alone internet application with a stand-alone Win32 application, and explain how *PDAs (Personal Digital Assistants)* can be used to remotely control their combined execution. Further, we explain how *Integrated Development Environment (IDEs)* may be extended to integrate and reuse GDAs using our approach. We believe our work is unique: we know of no other technology that could have integrated the GDAs of our example.

1 Introduction

Graphical user interface (GUI) driven applications (GDAs) are ubiquitous and provide a wealth of sophisticated services. Spread sheets, for example, provide general-purpose computational capabilities and web sites provide internet browser access to data stores. *Mega-applications* — programs that manipulate different data and computational resources by integrating different applications — are both common and important. For example, using spread sheets and databases to perform calculations on data harvested from different web sites is an increasingly common task.

Building mega-applications from GDAs is a challenging and fundamental problem of reuse. GDAs should be black-box components that are easy to integrate. Unfortunately, the opposite is true. Integration is extremely difficulty because GDAs are often distributed as binaries with no source. Further, the *Application Programmer Interfaces (APIs)* of GDAs are often not published or don't exist, and the only way to access their services is through their GUI. Internet applications are a special case. They are even more challenging because their binaries aren't available; clients can only invoke methods on remote servers through interactions with web pages or web services.

Conventional component technologies are focussed on *interface-centric programming* where components expose well-known APIs to allow clients to invoke their services.

C. Gacek (Ed.): ICSR-7, LNCS 2319, pp. 1–16, 2002.

COM, DCOM, COM+, CORBA, JavaBeans, and Enterprise JavaBeans are typical of this paradigm: they rely on explicitly defined interfaces with public methods. GDAs can be different from traditional components because they expose only GUIs or web-interfaces to their clients, "interfaces" that are not recognizable as COM, CORBA, etc. interfaces. For example, imagine an application that harvests data from `amazon.com` and summarizes data in a *Quicken ExpensAble (QE)* application. What is the programmable "interface" to `amazon.com`? What is the programmable "interface" to QE's GUI? It is easy to imagine how data could be harvested and summarized manually, but how a mega-application could be written that programmatically calls these "interfaces" to perform these tasks automatically is not obvious. The only solutions that we are aware involve hard and tedious work: they require a high-degree of software interoperability, say using COM or CORBA, coupled with sufficient engineering knowledge and a mature and stable domain. Many GDAs do not satisfy such constraints.

In principle, invoking the services of a GDA through its GUI or web-interface should be no different than invoking services through an API. We know GUIs and web-interfaces are indeed "interfaces", but what is lacking is a technology that allows us to access these applications programmatically through their GUIs. Outlining the principles of this technology and demonstrating a non-trivial application built using them is the contribution of this paper.

We begin with an explanation of instrumented connectors, the central concept that underlies our work. We review prior work and explain that programmatic interaction with GDAs is a special case with unusual properties that are not handled by traditional approaches. Next we present novel techniques to instrument GDAs and web-browser interfaces, and outline how our ideas can be added to *Integrated Developoment Environments (IDEs)* to provide tool support to integrate and reuse GDAs in an open and collaborative environment. We demonstrate a non-trivial application of these ideas by integrating a stand-alone internet application with a stand-alone Win32 application, and show how *PDAs (Personal Digital Assistants)* can be used to remotely control their combined execution. We believe our work is unique: we know of no other technology that could have integrated the GDAs of our example.

2 Connectors and Related Work

Classical models of software architecture [16][9] use connectors as an abstraction to capture the ways in which components interact with each other (Figure 1a). Connectors can be simple (component C calls component B directly via procedure calls) or complicated (C calls B remotely through CORBA, DCOM, or RMI). Connectors explicitly use APIs — the ends of a connector present the same interface; a client calls an API and server (at the other end of the connector) implements the API.

Instrumented connectors are connectors whose message traffic is observed by an intermediary component (Figure 1b).[1] An intermediary can record message traffic for later play-back (e.g., to simulate actual usage), analysis (e.g., to determine message invocation frequency), or to act as a transducer that modifies message traffic to achieve a par-

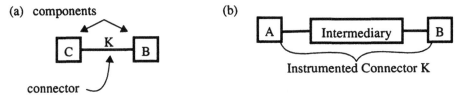

Fig. 1. Connectors and Instrumented Connectors

ticular purpose [11]. As a general rule, instrumented connectors are non-invasive and idempotent. *Non-invasive* means that their presence in a connector's implementation is undetectable; *idempotent* means that any number of intermediaries can be chained because their import and export interfaces are the same and that they are non-invasive.

Balzer was among the first to explore the use of coordinative connectors and their benefits [1]. The techniques that he used for realizing intermediaries relied on standard debugging concepts. Instead of placing breakpoints at the entries of the functions to be monitored, detours were used. A *detour* is a code fragment that is executed immediately prior to a function call and is unobtrusively injected like a breakpoint into the process space that contains the target function [12][13]. The detour encapsulates the actions of an intermediary — e.g. call monitoring code. Upon execution of the monitoring code, the execution of the target function resumes. Although initially demonstrated on Windows platforms (and tool support for detours is available for Windows [14]), the technique is applicable to all operating systems.

A common technique in Windows platforms is *emulation* [15]. Each COM component (or *dynamically linked library (DLL)*) has a *GUID (Globally Unique IDentifier)*. The Windows registry is a database of DLLs organized by GUIDs. A client loads a DLL by invoking a system call with the DLL's GUID; the registry is searched for the location of that DLL. Emulation is a registry technique that replaces an existing DLL with an intermediary DLL that implements the same COM interfaces but has a different GUID. When a client requests a particular DLL, the intermediary is loaded instead. In turn, the intermediary loads the shadowed DLL and acts as a "pass-through" for all client requests. Thus the intermediary can monitor call traffic for a COM interface unobtrusively.

A result that is directly relevant to our paper is the reuse of legacy *command-line programs (CLPs)*, i.e., programs whose functionality is accessible only through command-line inputs [21]. The idea is to place a wrapper around a CLP to programmatically invoke its commands. This part is simple: invoking a method of the wrapper causes specially-formatted (i.e., command-line) text to be sent to the program to invoke a specific CLP functionality. The CLP responds by outputting text that represents the result of the command. This text can be returned directly to the client, but it burdens the client to parse the returned text to decipher the output. A better way, as

---

1. For a discussion of the various types of instrumented connectors, see [17].

detailed in [21], is to have the wrapper parse the generated output and return a semantically useful result (an integer, an object, etc.) that can be more easily consumed by a calling program. Parsing is complicated by the possibility that the CLP can report events prior to reporting the result of a method call. For example, if the CLP is a debugger, the debugger can report that a breakpoint has been reached. The parser must be smart enough to recognize the semantics of the CLP response (i.e., to distinguish breakpoint event announcements from results of CLP method calls) and report events to the client. The technique used in [21] relies on CORBA for interoperability between a client and the CLP wrapper. Further, the CORBA Event Service is used to report events generated by the CLP. A wrapper specification language was used to simplify the development of parsers for CLP responses.

Also related to our paper is a set of general concepts and algorithms that trigger external services automatically when certain events occur in an application. Schmidt calls this the *interceptor pattern* [20]. The pattern is a framework with call-backs associated with particular events. A user extends the framework by writing modules that register user-defined call-backs with the framework. When a framework event arises, the registered methods are invoked thereby alerting the user to these events.

3 GDA Interception Concepts

In this paper, we deal with a special case of connectors where the connector interface is a GUI or web-page (Figure 2). Normally, the calling "component" is a person where the connector is materialized by hardware peripherals, such as a mouse and keyboard. We want to replace the client in Figure 2 with a program (component) C as in Figure 1a, so that application B can be programmatically manipulated by C. This requires that the GUI of B (somehow) be *objectified* — i.e., the GUI of B becomes an object and its sub-objects are its constituent GUI primitives. Further, we want to instrument this connector so that interactions between a client and a GDA (component) can be replayed and analyzed (e.g., Figure 1b). COM emulation, detours, and wrapping CLPs can't be used in this situation: GDAs might not be written in COM, GDAs might not have published APIs to instrument via detours, and GDA functionality is accessible through GUIs, not command lines.

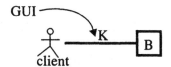

Fig. 2. "Connector" between Client and Application (Component) B

Although the concept of intercepting events for GUIs is identical to that of events for web-browsers, it turns out that different implementation techniques are used. In the following sections, we explain techniques that we have developed for both.

Consider how keyboard inputs to a program can be intercepted for subsequent playback. Suppose **incr** is a process that takes integers from a keyboard prompt and prints their incremented value. We want to record an interactive session with **incr** to replay the input of this session (and recompute **incr**'s response) at a later time. This can be done with the Unix **tee** operator, where > is the command-line prompt:

```
> tee file_input | incr
```

tee redirects standard input to one or more files (above, file "**file_input**") and this input is passed onto **incr** for execution. We can then replay this interaction via indirection:

```
> incr < file_input
```

This is an elementary example of interception: the binary application **incr** is unchanged, but its external events (i.e., keyboard input) have been captured for later replay. The process structure used above is important: the controlling process (**tee**) forks the controlled process (**incr**), much like a debugger (a controlling process) forks an instance of the (controlled) process to be debugged. Interception of GUI inputs uses similar but much more sophisticated techniques as the following sections reveal.

3.1 Injecting an Agent into a Controlled Process

Let B be a GDA whose services are invocable only through a GUI. Let C be the controlling client process that is to invoke the services of B programmatically. Because B has no capabilities to communicate with C, it is necessary to inject an intercepting program called an *agent* into the address space of B. The agent has its own thread of execution that can send and receive messages from C using standard interprocess communication mechanisms. In particular, the agent has two responsibilities: (1) to report to C selected events that occur within B and (2) to trigger events and invoke methods in B as instructed by C. Readers will recognize that (1) targets the reporting of a sequence of GUI events within B and (2) targets the playback of GUI events within B. In this section, we outline a general technique, called *code patching* [10][18][19][4], for introducing an agent into B. In the next section, we explain how an agent intercepts and injects GUI events.

Recall how debuggers work. To debug a process B, a debugger creates B as a slave (child) process. Doing so allows the debugger to read and write memory locations within B as well as manipulate its register set, and to enable the debugger to stop and continue B's execution. We use a similar technique to introduce an agent into B. The controlling process C creates B as a slave process. C interrupts B's execution and saves its context, which includes the *program counter (PC)* (Figure 3a). C reads a block of instructions starting from the PC in B's memory and saves these instructions. C then overwrites these instructions in B's space with code (Figure 3b) that:

- spawns a thread to load and execute the agent program,
- loads the agent program as a *dynamically-linked library (DLL)* into B's address space,

- jumps to the original breakpoint when the above two tasks have been completed. The PC now equals the value it had at the original interrupt.[2]

Next, C allows process B to continue execution. B runs the injected code, thus creating a thread to activate the agent and loading the agent DLL (Figure 3c). When B signals that the breakpoint has been reached, process C:

- restores the original block of code,
- restores the original context, and
- lets B continue (Figure 3d).

As far as process B is concerned, it has executed normally. B is unaware that it has been infiltrated by an agent that has its own thread of execution and whose purpose is to intercept and replay GUI events.

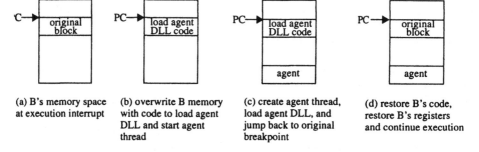

(a) B's memory space at execution interrupt

(b) overwrite B memory with code to load agent DLL and start agent thread

(c) create agent thread, load agent DLL, and jump back to original breakpoint

(d) restore B's code, restore B's registers and continue execution

Fig. 3. "Code Patching" an Agent into Binary B

3.2 Intercepting and Replaying GUI Events

Our agent (i.e., GUI interceptor) relies on deep knowledge of the structure of operating systems and how they process GUI interrupts and interact with GUI programs. Although our discussion and implementation focusses on Windows platforms, essentially the same concepts are used in other operating systems, so our technique is general. To avoid confusion in the following discussions, we capitalize the term "Windows" to denote the operating system, and the lowercase "window" to denote a GUI window created by a program.

Every GUI primitive (e.g., button, text field) and GUI window (i.e., a container of GUI primitives) created by a program is registered with the Windows operating system. Windows maintains for each primitive and window at least an identifier, its type, and the screen coordinates that it occupies. Each window additionally has a corresponding

---

2. The reason is that the contents of the PC cannot be altered by a "debugging" program, unlike other registers.

thread that runs an event loop, which receives and processes messages intended for the window and its embedded GUI primitives. We call this thread the *window thread*.

When a mouse is moved or clicked, Windows uses this information to (a) determine which GUI element the mouse is over and (b) which window thread is to be notified of the mouse interrupt. Thus, Windows translates low-level mouse hardware interrupts into an *Internal Windows Message (IWM)* that is delivered to the window thread whose window contains the mouse-referenced GUI element. The IWM contains the identifier of the referenced element, and the screen coordinates of the mouse's position. Other input (e.g., keyboard, tablet) is analogous; Windows stores the input in an IWM along with the identifier of the receiving GUI element.

Windows delivers an IWM to a windows thread via the thread's *Virtualized Input Queue (VIQ)*. Every window thread has a loop, often called the *event loop*, which periodically polls the VIQ for messages. When an IWM is dequeued, the thread uses the identifier in the IWM to deliver the message to targeted GUI element. Once delivered, the GUI element translates this message into a familiar GUI event (click, mouseUp, focus, mouseDown, etc.). Figure 4 depicts the above sequence of steps that translate mouse hardware interrupts to GUI events.

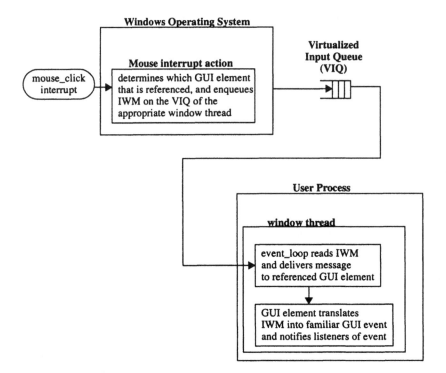

Fig. 4. Translation of Mouse Inputs into GUI Events

As mentioned above, Windows maintains a list of all GUI elements and windows. Further, it makes all this information accessible through system calls. These calls make it possible for an agent to determine what GUI primitives and windows a GDA has created; the agent can essentially recreate all of the data structures used by the Windows operating system and thus have its own copy. This capability is essential in monitoring and replaying GUI events, and objectifying a GDA GUI interface.

GUI programmers aren't typically aware of the above details; GUIs are designed to hide such details. GUI programs are designed only to react to GUI events, not translate IWM messages into GUI events. IWM to GUI event translations are performed by primitive GUI components that belong to *Windows Foundation Classes (WFC)*. User-defined GUIs are normally constructed from WFC primitives; only rarely are new primitive GUI elements implemented. Agents exploit this key fact.

Given the above, we can now explain how GUI events are intercepted. Recall that an agent can discover all GUI primitives of a program through system calls. To intercept a particular event is simple: like any other GUI program, an agent registers with a GUI primitive as a listener for that event. Readers familiar with GUI programming know that although there is a standard way to register for GUI events, different GUI primitives use different registration methods. So the question arises: for each GUI primitive, which of its methods should be called for event registration?

The agent relies on the fact that there are a small number of primitive GUI elements from which most, if not all, GUI programs are constructed: these are the elements in WFC (buttons, text areas, trees, etc.). We know the interface of each primitive GUI type, and thus we know what events they throw and what method to call to register for an event.

Once registered, every time an event is raised, the agent will receive the event, unobtrusively as all other listeners. At this point, the agent sends the event immediately back to the controlling client. For example, if a client wants to "see" what input was typed into a GDA GUI text field, the client instructs the agent to register for the event (e.g. **textChanged**) that is thrown by the text field to notify its listeners that its value has changed. When the client is notified of a **textChanged** event, it can request the agent to return the contents of the text field.

To playback a text field update, the agent simply invokes the **setText** method with the new string on that text field. The text field component, in turn, notifies all listeners that its content has changed. These listeners cannot tell, nor do they care, if the text field was updated from the keyboard or by the agent.

Other events are harder to replay. For example, there is no direct way (e.g., a method) to have a GUI element raise a button-click event. The only way to replay such events is indirect: the agent must create an IWM that will be translated into the desired GUI event. The agent has all the information to do this: it knows the identifier of the GUI element, it knows the screen coordinates of that element to provide the appropriate screen coordinates of a mouse click, and it knows the target window thread. Thus, the replay of events is sometimes accomplished by having the agent send a series of synthetic IWMs to the window thread. Because a windows thread cannot distinguish IWMs created by Windows and those created by the agent, an exact sequence of events can be replayed.

3.3 Intercepting and Replaying Web Browser Inputs

In principle, web browsers are just another class of GUI applications that are amenable to the GUI interception techniques of the previous section. The primary differences are that primitive GUI components on web pages are typically not the same as those used in GUI programs: there are indeed primitive text fields, buttons, combo-boxes etc. on web pages, but these components often have different implementations than their GUI program counterparts. All this means is that a different agent, one that understands web-components, needs to be written. But web browsers are a special class of applications that provide a wealth of support for interception that typical GUI programs don't have. Thus, using our techniques in Section 3 is by no means the easiest way to intercept and replay web browser input.

The document content shown in a browser's GUI is internally represented by the *Document Object Model (DOM)*. DOM level 2 is a specification that defines a platform- and language-neutral interface that allows programs and scripts to dynamically access and update the content, structure, and style of web documents [7]. Almost all commercial browsers use DOM to internally represent document content. Using DOM, software developers can access any component of a web application GUI using well-defined set of interfaces. The DOM event model, defined in [7], allows developers to intercept and replay any event in a web application GUI.[3]

There are two different ways in which DOM information can be accessed. One approach is to use the *Internet Explorer (IE)* web browser ActiveX Control. It provides a COM interface (i.e., **IWebBrowser2**) that can be instantiated and controlled directly by an external application [2][3]. This interface provides a wealth of services that support and extend the DOM services and makes it possible for developers to control and access every aspect of web-based applications.

---

3. While DOM support is a standard part of almost all commercial browsers, historically other techniques have been used. *Screen-scrapers* are programs designed to harvest and replay GUI information from web pages; they are essentially scaled-down web browsers. Other programs have used *Dynamic Data Exchange (DDE)*, which is a form of interprocess communication that uses shared memory to exchange data between applications. A client application can control a browser object, for example Netscape or *Internet Explorer (IE)* to get web documents and to reproduce desired actions. This approach is difficult and has a number of limitations. For example, a controlling application using DDE can only receive a very limited number events from IE. This makes it difficult to record sequence of IE events. Using DOM is the preferred way today to intercept and replay web-GUI events.

A better opportunity is presented by IE and to some degree by the open-source Mozilla browser. Starting version 4.0, IE introduced a concept called the *Browser Helper Object (BHO)*. A BHO is a *user-written* dynamic link library that is loaded by IE whenever a new instance of the browser is started. This library is attached to the IE process space and is implemented in COM. In effect, a BHO provides the perfect scaffolding that is needed to introduce agents — the BHO *is an agent* that is automatically loaded with IE, and the actions of this agent are not fixed by Microsoft, but are under user-control. Moreover, every BHO is given a pointer to the `IWebBrowser2` interface, which allows it to have full access to DOM information and events specifically for the task of intercepting and replaying web-GUI events.

Interception of GUI events for browsers or applications written in Java is harder. Our prototype was developed on a Windows platform, which provides OS support for GUI interception. Java GUI components rely on the *Java Virtual Machine (JVM)* for their implementation, and thus discovering what GUI components are present in a Java program or applet might not be accomplished through OS API calls. We believe that instrumentation and augmentation of the JVM is required to support Java GUI interception.

4 A Design for an Interception IDE

An *Interception IDE (I^2DE)* is an IDE that has the capabilities of a standard GUI builder (e.g., Visual C#, Visual Age) and the capability of integrating GDAs. To understand how an I^2DE might work, consider the following problem which illustrates the integration of two GDAs. GDA1 presents a GUI interface that contains text field **x** (Figure 5a). GDA2 presents a different GUI interface that contains text field **y** (Figure 5b). We want to build a GUI application **MyApp** that has a single text field **z** and button **add** (Figure 5c). When **add** is pressed, the contents of fields **x** and **y** are retrieved and their sum displayed in **z**. Assume **x** and **y** are variables that **MyApp** can access. The obvious event handler for clicking **add** is shown in Figure 5d.

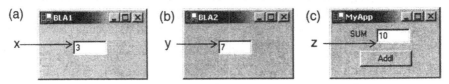

```
(d)  void add_Click(object sender, System.EventArgs e)
     {
         int xval = (int) x.getText();
         int yval = (int) y.getText();
         z.setText( xval + yval );
     }
```

Fig. 5. A GUI that Integrates Two GDAs

From this example and the discussions of the previous section, it becomes clear how an I^2DE can work. The **MyApp** GUI of Figure 5c is constructed in the usual way. (A button, text field, and label are dragged from a toolbox of primitive GUI elements onto a form, and their properties are modified to give the visual appearance of Figure 5c). Next, GDA1 is activated and an agent injected. The agent informs the I^2DE of each GUI element used by GDA1. In turn, the I^2DE creates a unique variable to reference each element. The same process is applied to GDA2. The set of these variables, which represents the set of all GUI elements used in all activated GDAs, is made accessible to the author of **MyApp**, so that s/he could write event handlers like Figure 5d. *These event handlers define how GDAs are integrated.* That is, each GDA is objectified as a local object whose data members are its constituent GUI elements. The event handlers define the relationships — a.k.a. business logic — between GDA objects that integrate them into a coherent application (i.e., **MyApp**).

When **MyApp** is compiled, the properties of the GDA GUI primitives are serialized or initialization code is generated, so when **MyApp** is executed, the properties of GUI variables can be reconstituted. (We currently write the values to a database, and when **MyApp** begins execution, the contents of the database are read). At **MyApp** startup, **MyApp** activates each GDA that it references and injects an agent into each GDA. Whenever a method of a GDA GUI variable is invoked, the identifier of that GUI element, the method and its parameters are transmitted to the agent for execution. The agent returns the result of that method invocation[4]. Similarly, to register for a GDA GUI event is method call on the event source. The agent invokes the registration method to receive event notifications. When an event occurs, the agent notifies **MyApp** of the event. Because event delivery from an agent is asynchronous, inside **MyApp** is a separate thread that executes an event loop that processes events from GDA agents. Using the same techniques that agents use to replay events, agent-posted events are delivered to the **MyApp** GUI.

There are, of course, other details to consider. For example, after an agent has been injected into a GDA, the set of primitive GUIs that define the GDA must be verified with the set that is expected by **MyApp**. (A new version of the GDA might have been installed since **MyApp** was created, and this new version may have changed the GDA's GUI, possibly invalidating the business logic of **MyApp**). There is also the matter of not displaying GDA GUIs during execution. Normally, when a GDA executes, its GUI is visible on the console monitor. While it is instructive to see the GUI of **MyApp** and its "slave" GDAs executing in concert, in general it is distracting and also a source of error (e.g., a client of **MyApp** could invoke inputs on a GDA GUI, disrupting its state). In Windows, there are system calls that can be invoked to disable the display of a GUI so that it is invisible. This is the normal mode in which agent-injected GDAs are activated. And just like any normal GUI, **MyApp** can have many different GUI forms/frontends, each defining a specific interaction among GDAs.

---

4. Readers will recognize these ideas as standard distributed object concepts, where **MyApp** references a remote application (agent) through a stub and the agent implements a skeleton for remote method invocation [8].

The above describes the essential concepts behind an I^2DE. However, there are other ideas worth mentioning. An I^2DE must display a list (or tree) of all primitive GUI elements of a GDA. This list (tree) informs authors of **MyApp** of the variables of a GDA GUI that can be accessed. The types of these variables are typically the same types as those offered by the GUI builder of the I^2DE. For example, variables **x**, **y**, **z** in Figure 5 might be instances of the same GUI element type. Even so, GDA GUI variables *cannot* be used in the construction of the **MyApp** GUI. The reason is that these variables are *remote stubs* to GDA components, and these components are visible only to the GDA GUI, and not to the **MyApp** GUI. It is easy enough to create a corresponding **MyApp** GUI variable and have its properties match those of a GDA GUI. This requires some programming, but conceptually is straightforward.

5 An Example From E-procurement

A spectacular illustration of an I^2DE application is the use of a *Personal Digital Assistant (PDA)* to remotely control an integrated set of GDAs. The architecture of such an application is simple (Figure 6): the I^2DE is used to define a **server** that has no GUI. The **server** interface exposes to remote clients a set of methods whose bodies invoke methods of GDA GUI primitives. The I^2DE also can be used to define a GUI program that will execute in the restricted confines of a **PDA** — small screen, limited graphics display capabilities, etc. The event handlers of this GUI invoke methods of the server. This is the basis of the e-procurement example described below that we have implemented and demonstrated in numerous forums.

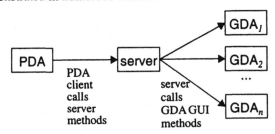

Fig. 6. PDA Remote Access of GDA GUIs

staples.com is well-known e-business retailer of office supplies, furniture, and business technology. Its customers are home-based businesses and Fortune 500 companies. **staples.com** provides on-line services for managing business transactions. One of these web-based services is a database where procurement requests of employees are recorded. A manager of a business can access a **staples.com** web-page to review the requests of his/her employees and can approve or reject requests individually.

To maintain a history, suppose a manager uses the *Quicken ExpensAble (QE)* accounting capabilities to keep track of expenses. QE is a proprietary Windows-based application that has no published APIs. It does not use COM or CORBA components, and the only way to use it is through its GUI.

A manager performs the following typical interaction: he logs into **staples.com** to review the list of employee purchase requests. Each request could be approved, denied, or a decision could be delayed until later. All requests of the displayed list are entered into QE, where previously existing elements are simply updated (instead of being replicated). Prior to our work, a manager would have to copy and merge lists into QE manually, a slow, tedious, and error-prone task. More over, the manager would have to run QE locally, as there is no facility to remotely access to QE. Using the ideas we discussed in this and in previous sections, we not only automated these tasks, we also created a PDA application so that managers could invoke these updates remotely.

The layout for this project is shown in Figure 7. Three computing platforms were used: PDA Palm OS 3.1, Internet Explorer web browser, and Windows 2000. A wireless PDA runs the I^2DE custom e-procurement client and is connected to **Palm.net** that uses Southwestern Bell as a wireless connectivity provider. Our PDA application communicates with our I^2DE **server** that, in turn, communicates with QE and **staples.com** via injected agents. The server uses the agent technology of Section 3 to intercept and replay QE events. It uses the DOM event interception mechanism discussed in Section 3.3 for accessing and controlling **staples.com**.

The manager initially sends a request to retrieve the approval list from **staples.com**. The server executes the request based on predefined business logic and retrieves data from the manager's **staples.com** approval queue. When the manager connects to the server the next time s/he receives the requested data back on the PDA. This time s/he approves or rejects items and sends the transaction request to the server. The server analyzes the request and applies the update to both **staples.com** and QE.

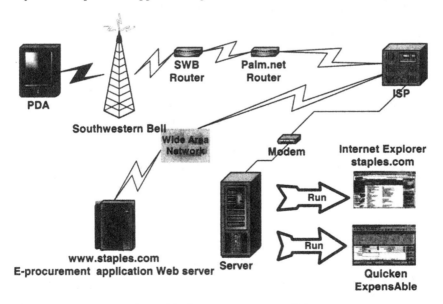

Fig. 7. The E-procurement example layout

6 Discussion

The reaction that we have received when giving live demonstrations of the application in Section 5 has been one of audience amazement and confusion. Interception of GDA GUIs prior to our work was limited to specialized applications (e.g., screen scrapers) that relatively few people knew about. Of course, even those technologies were not general enough to perform the GDA integration that we described above. So the element of surprise is understandable. At the same time, the techniques that we use are not immediately obvious to most people, and it takes time to fully understand how all they work cooperatively together to produce this result. Hence the other reaction.

Never-the-less, we believe an I^2DE has enormous potential. It could be used for data integration, GDA reuse, collaborative computing, and application migration to new platforms. Its key advantage is that all these uses involve minimal development efforts. Architects will not disrupt their organizations by recoding existing interfaces in order to add new functionality. It offers, for example, an attractive alternative to the way legacy applications are currently migrated to PDAs. And it abolishes the need for any programming changes to the existing legacy applications in order to integrate them.

Of course, there are limitations. It is not clear how our ideas could apply to legacy daemon or console applications. If an application has intensive graphic front end (e.g., a game), then our approach may not be able to cope with the speed at which data is updated. Further, legacy applications (and especially web pages) do change over time. These changes can impact an application created with our technology, requiring changes to be propagated to our application. For Win-32 and Unix GDAs, modifications of GUIs tend to be rare, whereas for web-pages, changes occur more often. In such cases, additional approaches such as information extraction technologies may be of help [5].

7 Conclusions

The reuse of binary legacy applications (GDAs) that can only be accessed through GUIs is both a difficult and fundamental problem of software reuse. We have shown that its solution is a special case of intercepting architectural connectors where a human is at one end of a connector and a GDA is at the other. By instrumenting this connector, we have demonstrated the ability to capture and replay inputs and GUI events, and more importantly, to write programs that integrate GDAs into mega-applications.

Our solution hinges on the ability to objectify GDA GUIs — treating a GDA GUI as an object and its constituent GUI elements as sub-objects. This required the use of agent processes to be injected into GDAs. These agents collect information on all GUI elements that are used by a GDA, monitor events that are generated, and trigger GUI input events. An agent presents an object (representing an objectified GDA GUI) to a controlling program. This program can then invoke methods on specific GDA GUI elements and replay GUI inputs with the support of the agent.

We illustrated our ideas by creating a server application that integrates (1) a proprietary Win32 application with (2) an Internet application. Further, we explained how a PDA, with a simple GUI application, could remotely access our server to invoke its capabilities. Doing so, we demonstrated capabilities that no other technology that we are aware can provide — GDA GUI integration and remote access to proprietary Win32 applications.

Our technology, as presented as an Interception IDE (I^2DE), can form the basis of a new class of IDEs. We believe that I^2DEs have great potential for opening up a new class of applications that, prior to our work, were difficult or impossible to create.

8 References

[1] R. Balzer and N. Goldman. "Mediating Connectors", *Proc. 19th IEEE International Conference on Distributed Computing Systems Workshop*, Austin, TX, June 1999, pp. 73-77.

[2] K. Brown. "Building a Lightweight COM Interception Framework, Part I: The Universal Delegator". *Microsoft Systems Journal*, Vol. 14, January 1999, pp. 17-29.

[3] K. Brown. "Building a Lightweight COM Interception Framework, Part II: The Guts of the UD". *Microsoft Systems Journal*, Vol. 14, February 1999, pp. 49-59.

[4] B. Buck and J. Hollingsworth. "An API for Runtime Code Patching". *International Journal of High Performance Computing Applications*, 2000.

[5] M. Califf, R. Mooney. "Relational Learning of Pattern-Match Rules for Information Extraction", *Working Notes of AAAI Spring Symposium on Applying Machine Learning to Discourse Processing*, 1997.

[6] D. Chappel, *Understanding ActiveX and OLE: A Guide for Developers and Managers*, Microsoft Press, 1996.

[7] *Document Object Model (DOM) Level 2 Specification*. W3C Working Draft, 28 December, 1998.

[8] W. Emmerich. *Engineering Distributed Objects*. John Wiley & Sons, 2000.

[9] D. Garlan and D. Perry. "Introduction to the Special Issue on Software Architecture", *IEEE Transactions on Software Engineering*, April 1995.

[10] S. Gill. "The Diagnosis of Mistakes in Programmes on the EDSAC". Proc. of the Royal Society, Series A, 206, May 1951, pp. 538-554.

[11] M. Gorlick and R.Razouk "Using Weaves for Software Construction and Analysis". *Proc. 13th International Conference on Software Engineering*, Austin, Texas, May 1991.

[12] G. Hunt and M. Scott. "Intercepting and Instrumenting COM Applications", *Proc. 5th Conference on Object-Oriented Technologies and Systems (COOTS'99)*, San Diego, CA, May 1999, pp. 45-56.

[13] G. Hunt. "Detours: Binary Interception of Win32 Functions". *Proc. 3rd USENIX Windows NT Symposium*, Seattle, WA, July 1999.

[14]P. Kessler. "Fast Breakpoints: Design and Implementation". *Proc. ACM SIGPLAN Conference on Programming Language Design and Implementation*, White Plains, NY, June 1990, pp. 78-84.

[15]MSDN Library. "Class Emulation", Microsoft Corporation, 2001.

[16]D.Perry and A.Wolf, "Foundations for the Study of Software Architectures", *ACM SIGSOFT Software Engineering Notes* 17(4), 1992, pp. 40-52.

[17]D.Perry, "Software Architecture and its Relevance for Software Engineering", *Keynote at Coordination 1997*, Berlin, September 1997.

[18]Matt Pietrek. "Learn System-level Win32 Coding Techniques By Writing an API Spy Program". *Microsoft Systems Journal*, 9(12), 1994, pp. 17-44.

[19]Matt Pietrek, "Peering Inside PE: A Tour of the Win32 Portable Executable Format", *Microsoft Systems Journal*, Vol. 9, No. 3, March 1994, p. 1534.

[20]D. Schmidt, M.Stal, H. Rohnert, F.Buschman. *Pattern-Oriented Software Architecture: Volume 2*, John Wiley & Sons, 2001.

[21]E. Wohlstadter, S. Jackson, and P. Devanbu. "Generating Wrappers for Command Line Programs", *International Conference on Software Engineering*, Toronto, Ontario, May 2001.

Source Tree Composition*

Merijn de Jonge

CWI, P.O. Box 94079, 1090 GB Amsterdam, The Netherlands
http://www.cwi.nl/~mdejonge/

Abstract. Dividing software systems in components improves software reusability as well as software maintainability. Components live at several levels, we concentrate on the implementation level where components are formed by source files, divided over directory structures.
Such source code components are usually strongly coupled in the directory structure of a software system. Their compilation is usually controlled by a single global build process. This entangling of source trees and build processes often makes reuse of source code components in different software systems difficult. It also makes software systems inflexible because integration of additional source code components in source trees and build processes is difficult.
This paper's subject is to increase software reuse by decreasing coupling of source code components. It is achieved by automized assembly of software systems from reusable source code components and involves integration of source trees, build processes, and configuration processes. Application domains include *generative programming*, *product-line architectures*, and *commercial off-the-shelf (COTS)* software engineering.

1 Introduction

The classical approach of component composition is based on pre-installed binary components (such as pre-installed libraries). This approach however, complicates software development because: (i) system building requires extra effort to configure and install the components prior to building the system itself; (ii) it yields accessibility problems to locate components and corresponding documentation [23]; (iii) it complicates the process of building self-contained distributions from a system and all its components. Package managers (such as RPM [1]) reduce build effort but do not help much to solve the remaining problems. Furthermore, they introduce version problems when different versions of a component are used [23, 29]. They also provide restricted control over a component's configuration. All these complicating factors hamper software reuse and negatively influence granularity of reuse [28].

We argue that *source code components* (as alternative to binary components) can improve software reuse in component based software development. Source code components are source files divided in directory structures. They form the implementation of subsystems. Source code component composition yields self-contained source trees with single integrated configuration and build processes. We called this process *source tree composition*.

---

* This research was sponsored by the Dutch Telematica Instituut, project DSL.

C. Gacek (Ed.): ICSR-7, LNCS 2319, pp. 17–32, 2002.

The literature contains many references to articles dealing with component composition on the design and execution level, and with build processes of individual components (see the related work in Sect. 9). However, techniques for composition of source trees of diverse components, developed in different organizations, in multiple languages, for the construction of systems which are to be reusable themselves and to be distributed in source, are underexposed and are the subject of this paper.

This paper is organized as follows. Section 2 motivates the need for advanced techniques to perform source tree composition. Section 3 describes terminology. Section 4 describes the process of source tree composition. Section 5 and 6 describe abstraction mechanisms over source trees and composite software systems. Section 7 describes automated source tree composition. It discusses the tool `autobundle`, online package bases, and product-line architectures. Section 8 describes experiences with source tree composition. Related work and concluding remarks are discussed in Sect. 9 and 10.

2 Motivation

In most software systems the constituent source code components are tightly coupled: the implementation of all subsystems is contained in a single source tree, a central build process controls their build processes, and a central configuration process performs their static (compile-time) configuration. For example, a top-level Makefile often controls the global build process of a software system. A system is then built by recursively executing `make` [15] from the top-level Makefile for each source code component. Often, a global GNU `autoconf` [24] configuration script performs system configuration, for instance to select the compilers to use and to enable or disable debugging support.

Such tight coupling of source code components has two main advantages: (i) due to build process integration, building and configuring a system can be performed easily from one central place; (ii) distributing the system as a unit is relatively easy because all source is contained in a single tree (one source tree, one product).

Unfortunately, tight coupling of source code components also has several drawbacks:

- The composition of components is inflexible. It requires adaption of the global build instructions and (possibly) its build configuration when new components are added [23]. For example, it requires adaption of a top-level Makefile to execute `make` recursively for the new component.
- Potentially reusable code does not come available for reuse outside the system because entangled build instructions and build configuration of components are not reusable [28]. For example, as a result of using `autoconf`, a component's configuration is contained in a top-level configuration script and therefore not directly available for reuse.
- Direct references into source trees of components yield unnecessary file system dependencies between components in addition to functional dependencies. Changing the file or directory structure of one component may break another.

To address these problems, the constituent source code components of a system should be isolated and be made available for reuse (*system decomposition*). After decomposition, new systems can be developed by selecting components and assembling them together (*system composition*). This process is depicted in Fig. 1.

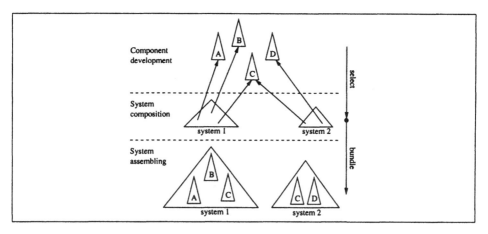

Fig. 1. Component development, system composition, and system assembly with source code component reuse. Components are developed individually; compositions of components form systems, which are assembled to form *software bundles* (self-contained software systems).

For system composition not only source files are required, but also all build knowledge of all constituent source code components. Therefore, we define *source tree composition* as the composition of all files, directories, and build knowledge of all reused components. To benefit from the advantages of a tightly coupled system, source tree composition should yield a self-contained source tree with central build and configuration processes, which can be distributed as a unit.

When the reuse scope of software components is restricted to a single Configuration Management (CM) [3] system, source tree composition might be easy. This is because, ideally, a CM system administrates the build knowledge of all components, their dependencies, etc., and is able to perform the composition automatically.[1]

When the reuse scope is extended to multiple projects or organizations, source tree composition becomes harder because configuration management (including build knowledge) needs to be untangled [7, 28]. Source tree composition is further complicated when third party components are reused, when the resulting system has to be reusable itself, and when it has to be distributed as source. This is because: i) standardization of CM systems is lacking [28, 32]; ii) control over build processes of third party components is restricted; iii) expertise on building the system and its constituent components might be unavailable.

Summarizing, to increase reuse of source code components, source tree composition should be made more generally applicable. This requires techniques to hide the decomposition of systems at distribution time, to fully integrate build processes of (third party) components, and to minimize configuration and build effort of the system. Once generally applicable, source tree composition simplifies assembling component based software systems from implementing source code components.

---

[1] Observe that in practice, CM systems are often confused with version management systems. The latter do not administrate knowledge suitable for source tree composition.

Suppliers of Commercial Off-The-Shelf (COTS) source code components and of Open Source Software (OSS) components can benefit from the techniques presented in this paper because integration of their components is simplified, which makes them suitable for widespread use. Moreover, as we will see in Sect. 7.3, product-line archi- tectures, which are concerned with assembling families of related applications, can also benefit from source tree composition.

3   Terminology

System building is the process of deriving the targets of a software system (or software component) from source [9]. We call the set of targets (such as executables, libraries, and documentation) a *software product*, and define a *software package* as a distribution unit of a versioned software system in either binary or source form.

A system's *build process* is divided in several steps, which we call *build actions*. They constitute a system's *build interface*. A build action is defined in terms of *build instructions* which state how to fulfill the action. For example, a build process driven by make typically contains the build actions all, install, and check. The all action, which builds the complete software product, might be implemented as a sequence of build instructions in which an executable is derived from C program text by calling a compiler and a linker.

System building and system behavior can be controlled by *static configuration* [11]. Static configurable parameters define at compile-time which parts of a system to build and how to build them. Examples of such parameters are debug support (by turning debug information on or off), and the set of drivers to include in an executable. We call the set of static configurable parameters of a system a *configuration interface*.

We define a *source tree* as a directory hierarchy containing *all* source files of a soft- ware (sub) system. A source tree includes the sources of the system itself, files containing build instructions (such as Makefiles), and configuration files, such as autoconf con- figuration scripts.

4   Source Tree Composition

Source tree composition is the process of assembling software systems by putting source trees of reusable components together. It involves merging source trees, build processes, and configuration processes. Source tree composition yields a single source tree with centralized build and configuration processes.

The aim of source tree composition is to improve reusability of source code compo- nents. To be successful, source tree composition should meet three requirements:

Repeatable. To benefit from any evolution of the individual components, it is essential that an old version of a component can easily be replaced by a newer. Repeating the composition should therefore take as little effort as possible.

Invisible. A source distribution of a system for non-developers should be offered as a unit (one source tree, one product), the internal structuring in source code compo- nents should not necessarily be visible. Integrating build and configuration processes of components is therefore a prerequisite.

```
package
identification
        name=CobolSQLTrans
        version=1.0
        location=http://www.coboltrans.org
            info=http://www.coboltrans.org/doc
    description='Transformation framework for COBOL with embedded SQL'
      keywords=cobol, sql, transformation, framework
configuration interface
    layout-preserving    'Enable layout preserving transformations.'
requires
    cobol 0.5 with lang-ext=SQL
    asf    1.1 with traversals=on
    sglr   3.0
    gpp    2.0
```

Fig. 2. An example package definition.

Due to lacking standardization of build and configuration processes, these requirements
are hard to satisfy. Especially when drawing on a diverse collection of software components, developed and maintained in different institutes, by different people, and implemented in different programming languages. Composition of source trees therefore
often requires fine-tuning a system's build and configuration process, or even adapting
the components themselves.

To improve this situation, we propose to formalize the parameters of source code
packages and to hide component-specific build and configuration processes behind interfaces. A standardized *build interface* defines the build actions of a component. A
configuration interface defines a component's configurable items. An integrated build
process is formed by composing the build actions of each component sequentially. The
configuration interface of a composed system is formed by merging the configuration
interfaces of its constituent components.

5   Definition of Single Source Trees

We propose *source code packages* as unit of reuse for source tree composition. They help
to: i) easily distinguish different versions of a component and to allow them to coexist;
ii) make source tree composition institute and project independent because versioned
distributions are independent of any CM system; iii) allow simultaneous development
and use of source code components.

To be effectively reusable, software packages require abstractions [22]. We introduce
package definitions as abstraction of source code packages. We developed a Domain
Specific Language (DSL) to represent them. An example is depicted in Fig. 2. It defines
the software package CobolSQLTrans which is intended to develop transformations for
Cobol with embedded SQL.

Package definitions define the parameters of packages, which include package identification, package dependencies, and package configuration.

Package identification. The minimal information that is needed to identify a software package are its name and version number. In addition, also the URL where the package can be obtained, a short description of the package, and a list of keywords are recorded (see the identification section of Fig. 2).

Package configuration. The configuration interface of a software package is defined in the configuration interface section. Partial configuration enforced by other components and composition of configuration interfaces is discussed in Sect. 6. For example, in Fig. 2, the configuration interface defines a single configuration parameter and a short usage description of this parameter. With this parameter, the CobolSQLTrans package can be configured with or without layout preserving transformations.

Package dependencies. To support true *development with reuse*, a package definition can list the packages that it reuses in the requires section. Package definitions also allow to define a (partial) static configuration for required packages. Package dependencies are used during *package normalization* (see Sect. 6) to synthesize the complete set of packages that form a system. For example, the package of Fig. 2 requires at least version 0.5 of the cobol package and configures it with embedded SQL. Further package requirements are the Algebraic Specification Formalism (asf) as programming language with support for automatic term traversal, a parser (sglr), and pretty-printer (gpp).

6   Definition of Composite Source Trees

A *software bundle* is the source tree that results from a particular source tree composition. A *bundle definition* (see Fig. 3) defines the ingredients of a bundle, its configuration interface, and its identification. The ingredients of a bundle are defined as composition of package definitions.

A bundle definition is obtained through a process called *package normalization* which includes package dependency and version resolution, build order arrangement, configuration distribution, and bundle interface construction.

Dependency resolution. Unless otherwise specified, package normalization calculates the transitive closure of *all* required packages and collects all corresponding package definitions. The list of required packages follows directly from the bundle's package dependency graph (see Fig. 4). For instance, during normalization of the package definition of Fig. 2, dependency upon the aterm package is signaled and its definition is included in the bundle definition. When a package definition is missing (see the dashed package in Fig. 4), a configuration parameter is added to the bundle's configuration interface (see below).

Version resolution. One software bundle cannot contain multiple versions of a single package. When dependency resolution signals that different versions of a package are required, the package normalization process should decide which version to bundle.

Essential for package normalization is compatibility between different versions of a package (see [31, 9, 32] for a discussion of version models). In accordance with [27],

```
bundle                                      package
 name=CobolSQLTrans-bundle version=1.0       name=aterm version=1.6.3
 configuration interface                      configuration
  layout-preserving
    'Enable layout preserving transformations.'  package
  boxenv                                       name=asf version=1.1
    'Location of external boxenv package.'      configuration traversals=on
 bundles
  package                                    package
   name=sdf version=2.1                       name=sglr version=3.0
   configuration                              configuration

  package                                    package
   name=sql version=0.2                       name=gpp version=2.0
   configuration                              configuration

  package                                    package
   name=cobol version=0.5                     name=CobolSQLTrans version=1.0
   configuration lang-ext=SQL                 configuration
```

Fig. 3. Bundle definition obtained by normalizing the package definition of Fig. 2. This definition has been stripped due to space limitations.

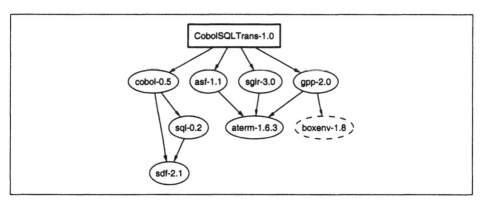

Fig. 4. A package dependency graph for the Cobol transformation package of Fig. 2. The dashed circle denotes an unresolved package dependency.

we require *backwards compatibility* to make sure that a particular version of a package can always be replaced by one of its successors. When backwards compatibility of a package cannot be satisfied, a new package (with a different name) should be created. Our tooling can be instantiated with different version schemes allowing experimenting with other (weakened) version requirements.

Build order arrangement. Package dependencies serve to determine the build order of composite software systems: building a package should be delayed until all of its required packages have been built. During package normalization, the collected package definitions are correctly ordered linearly according to a bottom up traversal of the dependency graph. Therefore, the cobol package occurs after the sql package in the bundle definition of Fig. 3. Circular dependencies between packages are not allowed. Such circularities correspond to bootstrapping problems and should be solved by package developers (for instance by splitting packages up or by creating dedicated bootstrap packages).

Configuration propagation. Each package definition that is collected during package normalization contains a (possible empty) set of configurable parameters, its configuration interface. Configurable parameters might get bound when the package is used by another which imposes a particular configuration. During normalization, this configuration is determined by collecting all the bindings of each package. For example, the CobolSQLTrans package of Fig. 2 binds the configurable parameter lang-ext of the cobol package to SQL, the parameter traversals of the asf package is bound to on (see Fig. 3). A conflicting configuration occurs when a single parameter gets bound differently. Such configuration conflicts can easily be detected during package normalization.

Bundle interface construction. A bundle's configuration interface is formed by collecting all unbound configurable parameters of bundled packages. In addition, it is extended with parameters for unresolved package requirements and for packages that have been explicitly excluded from the package normalization process. These parameters serve to specify the installation locations of missing packages at compile time. The configuration interface of the CobolSQLTrans package (see Fig. 3) is formed by the layout-preserving parameter originating from the CobolSQLTrans package, and the boxenv parameter which is due to the unresolved dependency of the gpp package (see Fig. 4).

After normalization, a bundle definition defines a software system as collection of software packages. It includes package definitions of all required packages and configuration parameters for those that are missing. Furthermore, it defines a partial configuration for packages and their build order. This information is sufficient to perform a composition of source trees. In the next section we discuss how this can be automated.

7   Performing Automated Source Tree Composition

We automated source tree composition in the tool `autobundle`. In addition, we implemented tools to make package definitions available via *online package bases*. Online package bases form central meeting points for package developers and package users, and provide online package selection, bundling, and contribution via Internet. These techniques can be used to automate system assembling in product-line architectures.

7.1   Autobundle

Package normalization and bundle generation are implemented by `autobundle`.[2] This tool produces an software bundle containing top-level configuration and build procedures, and a list of bundled packages with their download locations (see Table 1).

---

[2] `autobundle` is free software and available for download at `http://www.cwi.nl/~mdejonge/autobundle/`.

Table 1. The following files are contained in a software bundle generated by autobundle.

Makefile.am	Top-level automake Makefile that integrates build processes of all bundled packages.
configure.in	An autoconf configuration script to perform central configuration of all packages in a software bundle.
pkg-list	A list of the packages of a bundle and their download locations.
collect	A tool that downloads, unpacks, and integrates the packages listed in pkg-list.
README	A file that briefly describes the software bundle and its packages.
acinclude.m4	A file containing extensions to autoconf functionality to make central configuration of packages possible.

Table 2. These are the actions of the standardized build interface required by autobundle. In addition, autobundle also requires a tool configure to perform static configuration.

all	Build action to build all targets of a source code package.
install	Build action to install all targets.
clean	Build action to remove all targets and intermediate results.
dist	Build action to generate a source code distribution.
check	Build action to verify run-time behavior of the system.

The generated bundle does not contain the source trees of individual packages yet, but rather the tool collect that can collect the packages and integrate them in the generated bundle automatically. The reason to generate an empty bundle is twofold: i) since autobundle typically runs on a server (see Sect. 7.2), collecting, integrating, and building distributions would reduce server performance too much. By letting the user perform these tasks, the server gets relieved significantly. ii) It protects an autobundle server from legal issues when copyright restrictions prohibit redistribution or bundling of packages because no software is redistributed or bundled at all.

To obtain the software packages and to build self-contained distributions, the generated build interface of a bundle contains the actions collect to download and integrate the source trees of all packages, and bundle to also put them into a single source distribution.

The generated bundle is driven by make [15] and offers a standardized build interface (see Table 2). The build interface and corresponding build instructions are generated by autoconf [24] and automake [25]. The tool autoconf generates software configuration scripts and standardizes static software configuration. The tool automake provides a standardized set of build actions by generating Makefiles from abstract build process descriptions. Currently we require that these tools are also used by bundled packages. We used the tools because they are freely available and in widespread use. However, they are not essential for the concept of source tree composition. Essential is the availability of a standardized build interface (such as the one in Table 2); any build system that implements this interface would suffice. Moreover, when a build system does not implement this interface, it would not be difficult to hide the package specific configuration and build instructions behind the standardized build interface.

After the packages are automatically collected and integrated, the top-level build and configuration processes take care of building and configuring the individual components in the correct order. The build process also provides support for generating a self-contained source distribution from the complete bundle. This hides the structuring of the system in components and allows a developer to distribute his software product as a single unit. The complete process is depicted in Fig. 5.

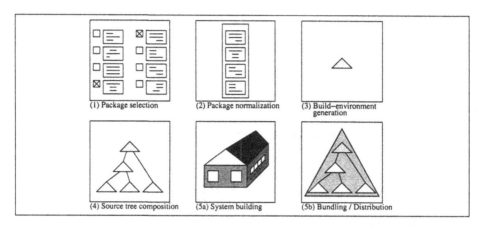

Fig. 5. Construction and distribution of software systems with source tree composition. (1) Packages of need are selected. (2) The selected set of packages is normalized to form a bundle definition. (3) From this definition an empty software bundle is generated. (4) Required software packages are collected and integrated in the bundle, after which the system can be built (5a), or be distributed as a self-contained unit (5b).

7.2 Online Package Bases

Dependency resolution during package normalization is performed by searching for package definitions in *package repositories*. We developed tools to make such repositories browsable and searchable via Inter/Intranet, and we implemented HTML form generation for interactive package selection. The form constitutes an *online package base* and lists packages and available versions together with descriptions and keywords. The form can be filled out by selecting the packages of need. By pressing the "bundle" button, the `autobundle` server is requested to generate the desired bundle. Anyone can contribute by filling out an online *package contribution form*. After submitting this form, a package definition is generated and the online package base is updated. This is the only required step to make an `autoconf/automake` based package available for reuse with `autobundle`.

Online package bases can be deployed to enable and control software reuse within a particular *reuse scope* (for instance, group, department, or company wide). They make software reuse and software dependencies explicit because a distribution policy of software components is required when source code packages form the unit of reuse.

7.3   Product-Line Architectures

Online package bases allow to easily assemble systems by selecting components of need. An assembled system is partly configured depending on the combination of components. Remaining variation points can be configured at compile time. This approach of system assembly is related to the domain of product-line architectures.

A Product-Line Architecture (PLA) is a design for families of related applications; application construction (also called product instantiation [17]) is accomplished by composing reusable components [2]. The building blocks from which applications are assembled are usually abstract requirements (consisting of application-oriented concepts and features). For the construction of the application, corresponding implementation components are required. To automate component assembly, *configuration knowledge* is required which maps between the *problem space* (consisting of abstract requirements) and the *solution space* (consisting of implementation components) [10].

We believe that package definitions, bundle generation, and online package bases serve implementing a PLA by automating the integration of source trees and static configuration. Integration of functionality of components still needs to be implemented in the components themselves, for instance as part of a component's build process.

Our package definition language can function as *configuration DSL* [11]. It then serves to capture configuration knowledge and to define mappings between the problem and solution space. Abstract components from the problem space are distinguished from implementation components by having an empty location field in their package definition. A mapping is defined by specifying an implementation component in the requires section of an abstract package definition.

System assembling can be automated by `autobundle`. It normalizes a set of abstract components (features) and produces a source tree containing all corresponding implementation components and generates a (partial) configuration for them. Variation points of the assembled system can be configured statically via the generated configuration interface. An assembled system forms a unit which can easily be distributed and reused in other products.

Definitions of abstract packages can be made available via online package bases. Package bases then serve to represent application-oriented concepts and features similar to feature diagrams [21]. This makes assembling applications as easy as selecting the features of need.

8   Case Studies

System development. We successfully applied source tree composition to the ASF+SDF Meta-Environment [4], an integrated environment for the development of programming languages and tools, which has been developed at our research group. Source tree composition solved the following problems that we encountered in the past:

- We had difficulties in distributing the system as a unit. We were using ad-hoc methods to bundle all required components and to integrate their build processes.
- We were encountering the well-known problem of simultaneously developing and using tools. Because we did not have a distribution policy for individual components, development and use of components were often conflicting activities.

– Most of the constituent components were generic in nature. Due to their entangling in the system's source tree however, reuse of individual components across project boundaries proved to be extremely problematic.

After we started using source tree composition techniques, reusability of our components greatly improved. This was demonstrated by the development of XT [20], a bundle of program transformation tools. It bundles components from the ASF+SDF Meta-Environment together with a diverse collection of components related to program transformation. Currently, XT is assembled from 25 reusable source code components developed at three different institutes.

For both projects, package definitions, package normalization, and bundle generation proved to be extremely helpful for building self-contained source distributions. With these techniques, building distributions of the ASF+SDF Meta-Environment and of XT became a completely automated process. Defining the top-level component of a system (i.e., the root node in the system's package dependency graph) suffices to generate a distribution of the system.

Online Package Base. To improve flexibility of component composition, we defined package definitions for all of our software packages, included them in a single package repository and made that available via Internet as the Online Package Base[3] (OPB).

With the OPB (see Fig. 6), building source distributions of XT and of the ASF+SDF Meta-Environment becomes a dynamic process and reduces to selecting one of these packages and submitting a bundle request to the autobundle server. The exact contents of both distributions can be controlled for specific needs by in/excluding components, or by enforcing additional version requirements of individual components. Similarly, any composition of our components can be obtained via the OPB.

Although it was initiated to simplify and increase reuse of our own software packages, anyone can now contribute by filling out a *package contribution form*. Hence, compositions with third-party components can also be made. For example, the OPB contains several package definitions for GNU software, the graph drawing package graphviz[4] from AT&T, and components from a number of other research institutes.

Stratego compiler. Recently, the Stratego compiler [30] has been split up in reusable packages (including the Stratego runtime system). The constituting components (developed at different institutes) are bundled with autobundle to form a stand-alone distribution of the compiler. With autobundle also more fine-grained reuse of these packages is possible. An example is the distribution of a compiled Stratego program with only the Stratego run-time system. The Stratego compiler also illustrates the usefulness of *nested* bundles. Though a composite bundle, the Stratego compiler is treated as a single component by the XT bundle in which it is included.

Product-line architectures. We are currently investigating the use of autobundle and online package bases in a commercial setting to transform the industrial application DocGen [14] into a product-line architecture [12]. DocGen is a documentation generator which generates interactive, hyperlinked documentation about legacy systems.

---

[3] Available at http://www.program-transformation.org/package-base/
[4] Available at http://www.research.att.com/sw/tools/graphviz/

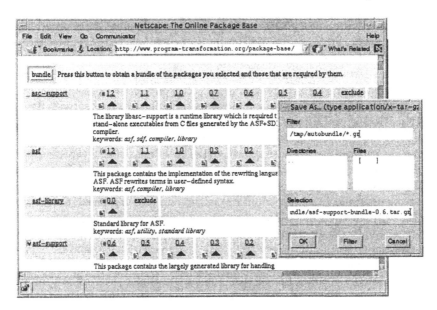

Fig. 6. Automated source tree composition at the Online Package Base. The Online Package Base is available at `http://www.program-transformation.org/package-base/`.

Documentation generation consists of generic and specific artifact extraction and visualization in a customer-specific layout. It is important that customer-specific code is not delivered to other customers (i.e., that certain packages are *not* bundled).

The variation points of DocGen have been examined and captured in a Feature Description Language (FDL) [13]. We are analyzing how feature selection (for instance the artifacts to document and which layout to use) can be performed via an online package base. Package definitions serve to map selected features to corresponding implementing components (such as specific extractors and visualizers). Such a feature set is normalized by `autobundle` to a bundle of software packages, which are then integrated into a single source tree that forms the intended customer-specific product.

9   Related Work

Many articles, for instance [6, 5, 8] address build processes and tools to perform builds. Tools and techniques are discussed to solve limitations of traditional `make` [15], such as improving dependency resolution, build performance, and support for variant builds. Composition of source trees and build processes is not described.

Gunter [16] discusses an abstract model of dependencies between software configuration items based on a theory of concurrent computations over a class of Petri nets. It can be used to combine build processes of various software environments.

Miller [26] motivates global definition of a system's build process to allow maximal dependency tracking and to improve build performance. However, to enable composition of components, independence of components (weak coupling) is important [31]. For source tree composition this implies independence of individual build processes and therefore contradicts the approach of [26]. Since the approach of Miller entangles all components of the system, we believe that it will hamper software reuse.

This paper addresses techniques to assemble software systems by integrating source trees of reusable components. In practice, such components are often distributed separately and their installation is required prior to building the system itself. The extra installation effort is problematic [29], even when partly automated by package managers (like RPM [1]). Although source tree composition simplifies software building, it does not make package management superfluous. The use of package managers is therefore still advocated to assist system administrators in installing (binary) distributions of assembled systems.

The work presented in this paper has several similarities with the component model Koala [28, 27]. The Koala model has a component description language like our package definition language, and implementations and component descriptions are stored in central repositories accessible via Internet. They also emphasize the need for backward compatibility and the need to untangle build knowledge from an SCM system to make components reusable. Unlike our approach, the system is restricted to the C programming language, and merging the underlying implementations of selected components is not addressed.

In [18, 19], a software *release management* process is discussed that documents released source code components, records and exploits dependencies amongst components, and supports location and retrieval of groups of compatible components. Their primarily focus is component release and installation, not development of composite systems and component integration as is the case in this paper.

10   Concluding Remarks

This paper addresses software reuse based on source code components and software assembly using a technique called source tree composition. Source tree composition integrates source trees and build processes of individual source code components to form self-contained source trees with single integrated configuration and build processes.

Contributions. We provide an abstraction mechanism for source code packages and software bundles in the form of package and bundle definitions. By normalizing a collection of package definitions (package normalization) a composition of packages is synthesized. The tool `autobundle` implements package normalization and bundle generation. It fully automates source tree composition. Online package bases, which are automatically generated from package repositories, make package selection easy. They enable source code reuse within a particular reuse scope. Source tree composition can be deployed to automate dynamic system assembly in product-line architectures.

Future work. We depend on backwards compatibility of software packages. This requirement is hard to enforce and weakening it is an interesting topic for further research. The other requirement that we depend on now, is the use of `autoconf` and `automake`, which implement a standard configuration and build interface. We have ideas for a generic approach to hide component specific build and configuration procedures behind standardized interfaces, but this still requires additional research. The research in using autobundle for the construction of product-line architectures is in an early phase. Therefore, we will conduct more case studies in autobundle-based product-line architectures.

Acknowledgments

We thank Arie van Deursen, Paul Klint, Leon Moonen, and Joost Visser for valuable discussions and feedback on earlier versions of the paper.

References

1. E. C. Bailey. *Maximum RPM*. Red Hat Software, Inc., 1997.
2. D. S. Batory, C. Johnson, B. MacDonald, and D. von Heeder. Achieving extensibility through product-lines and domain-specific languages: A case study. In *International Conference on Software Reuse*, volume 1844 of *LNCS*, pages 117–136. Springer-Verlag, 2000.
3. R. H. Berlack. *Software Configuration Management*. Wiley and Sons, New York, 1991.
4. M. van den Brand, A. van Deursen, J. Heering, H. de Jong, M. de Jonge, T. Kuipers, P. Klint, L. Moonen, P. Olivier, J. Scheerder, J. Vinju, E. Visser, and J. Visser. The ASF+SDF Meta-Environment: a component-based language development environment. In *Compiler Construction 2001 (CC 2001)*, volume 2027 of *LNCS*. Springer-Verlag, 2001.
5. P. Brereton and P. Singleton. Deductive software building. In J. Estublier, editor, *Software Configuration Management: Selected Papers of the ICSE SCM-4 and SCM-5 Workshops*, number 1005 in LNCS, pages 81–87. Springer-Verlag, Oct. 1995.
6. J. Buffenbarger and K. Gruel. A language for software subsystem composition. In *34th Annual Hawaii International Conference on System Sciences (HICSS-34)*. IEEE, 2001.
7. M. Cagan and A. Wright. Untangling configuration management. In J. Estublier, editor, *Software Configuration Management: Selected Papers of the ICSE SCM-4 and SCM-5 Workshops*, number 1005 in LNCS, pages 35–52. Springer-Verlag, 1995.
8. G. M. Clemm. The Odin system. In J. Estublier, editor, *Software Configuration Management: Selected Papers of the ICSE SCM-4 and SCM-5 Workshops*, number 1005 in LNCS, pages 241–2262. Springer-Verlag, Oct. 1995.
9. R. Conradi and B. Westfechtel. Version models for software configuration management. *ACM Computing Surveys*, 30(2):232–282, June 1998.
10. K. Czarnecki and U. W. Eisenecker. Components and generative programming. In O. Nierstrasz and M. Lemoine, editors, *ESEC/FSE '99*, volume 1687 of *LNCS*, pages 2–19. Springer-Verlag / ACM Press, 1999.
11. K. Czarnecki and U. W. Eisenecker. *Generative Programming. Methods, Tools, and Applications*. Addison-Wesley, 2000.
12. A. van Deursen, M. de Jonge, and T. Kuipers. Feature-based product line instantiation using source-level packages. submitted for publication, january 2002.
13. A. van Deursen and P. Klint. Domain-specific language design requires feature descriptions. *Journal of Computing and Information Technology*, 2001.
14. A. van Deursen and T. Kuipers. Building documentation generators. In *Proceedings; IEEE International Conference on Software Maintenance*, pages 40–49. IEEE Computer Society Press, 1999.
15. S. I. Feldman. Make – A program for maintaining computer programs. *Software – Practice and Experience*, 9(3):255–265, Mar. 1979.

16. C. A. Gunter. Abstracting dependencies between software configuration items. *ACM Transactions on Software Engineering and Methodology*, 9(1):94–131, Jan. 2000.
17. J. van Gurp, J. Bosch, and M. Svahnberg. On the notion of variability in software product lines. In R. Kazman, P. Kruchten, C. Verhoef, and H. van Vliet, editors, *Proceedings of the Working IEEE/IFIP Conference on Software Architecture*, pages 45–54. IEEE, 2001.
18. A. van der Hoek, R. S. Hall, D. Heimbigner, and A. L. Wolf. Software release management. In M. Jazayeri and H. Schauer, editors, *ESEC/FSE '97*, volume 1301 of *LNCS*, pages 159–175. Springer / ACM Press, 1997.
19. A. van der Hoek and A. L. Wolf. Software release management for component-based software, 2001. (In preparation).
20. M. de Jonge, E. Visser, and J. Visser. XT: a bundle of program transformation tools. In M. van den Brand and D. Parigot, editors, *Proceedings of Language Descriptions, Tools and Applications (LDTA 2001)*, volume 44 of *Electronic Notes in Theoretical Computer Science*. Elsevier Science Publishers, 2001.
21. K. Kang, S. Cohen, J. Hess, W. Novak, and A. Peterson. Feature-oriented domain analysis (FODA) feasibility study. Technical Report CMU/SEI-90-TR-21, Software Engineering Institute, Carnegie Mellon University, Pittsburgh, Pennsylvania, november 1990.
22. C. W. Krueger. Software reuse. *ACM Computing Surveys*, 24(2):131–183, June 1992.
23. Y.-J. Lin and S. P. Reiss. Configuration management in terms of modules. In J. Estublier, editor, *Software Configuration Management: Selected Papers of the ICSE SCM-4 and SCM-5 Workshops*, number 1005 in LNCS, pages 101–117. Springer-Verlag, 1995.
24. D. Mackenzie and B. Elliston. Autoconf: Generating automatic configuration scripts, 1998. http://www.gnu.org/manual/autoconf/.
25. D. Mackenzie and T. Tromey. Automake, 2001. http://www.gnu.org/manual/automake/.
26. P. Miller. Recursive make considered harmful, 1997. http://www.pcug.org.au/~millerp/rmch/recu-make-cons-harm.html.
27. R. van Ommering. Configuration management in component based product populations. In *Tenth International Workshop on Software Configuration Management (SCM-10)*, 2001. http://www.ics.uci.edu/~andre/scm10/papers/ommering.pdf.
28. R. van Ommering, F. van der Linden, J. Kramer, and J. Magee. The Koala component model for consumer electronics software. *IEEE Computer*, 33(3):78–85, March 2000.
29. D. B. Tucker and S. Krishnamurthi. Applying module system research to package management. In *Tenth International Workshop on Software Configuration Management (SCM-10)*, 2001. http://www.ics.uci.edu/~andre/scm10/papers/tucker.pdf.
30. E. Visser. Stratego: A language for program transformation based on rewriting strategies. System description of Stratego 0.5. In A. Middeldorp, editor, *Rewriting Techniques and Applications (RTA'01)*, volume 2051 of *LNCS*, pages 357–361. Springer-Verlag, May 2001.
31. D. Whitgift. *Methods and Tools for Software Configuration Management*. John Wiley & Sons, 1991.
32. A. Zeller and G. Snelting. Unified versioning through feature logic. *ACM Transactions on Software Engineering and Methodology*, 6(4):398–441, Oct. 1997.

Layered Development with (Unix) Dynamic Libraries

Yannis Smaragdakis

College of Computing,
Georgia Institute of Technology, Atlanta, GA 30332
yannis@cc.gatech.edu

Abstract. Layered software development has demonstrably good reuse properties and offers one of the few promising approaches to addressing the *library
scalability problem*. In this paper, we show how one can develop layered software
using common Unix (Linux/Solaris) dynamic libraries. In particular, we show
that, from an object-oriented design standpoint, dynamic libraries are analogous
to components in a mixin-based object system. This enables us to use libraries
in a layered fashion, mixing and matching different libraries, while ensuring that
the result remains consistent. As a proof-of-concept application, we present two
libraries implementing file versioning (automatically keeping older versions of
files for backup) and application-transparent locking in a Unix system. Both libraries can be used with new, aware applications or completely unaware legacy
applications. Further, the libraries are useful both in isolation, and as cooperating
units.

1 Introduction

Factored libraries have long been considered one of the most promising approaches to
software reuse. Factored libraries are motivated by what Biggerstaff [7] calls the *verti-
cal/horizontal scaling dilemma*. According to this dilemma, libraries should incorporate significant parts of functionality to be worth reusing, but then they become very
specific and, hence, less reusable. A factored (or *layered* [3]) library attempts to
address the problem by encapsulating a number of distinct components, each implementing a different axis of functionality. These components can then be put together in
an exponential number of legal configurations. The selection of components adapts the
library functionality to the needs of a specific application.

Several concrete technologies for implementing factored libraries have been proposed
in the past. Application generators [2][5], template libraries [21], and binary components are among them. In this paper, we show that standard Unix dynamic libraries are
a good architecture for factored or layered development. Using dynamic libraries to
represent library components has the advantages of language independence (components can be created from distinct languages), intellectual property protection
(dynamic libraries are binary components), and load-time configurability (combining
different dynamic libraries is done at application loading time, not at compile time).

C. Gacek (Ed.): ICSR-7, LNCS 2319, pp. 33–45, 2002.

The basis of our argument is the observation that a dynamic library model can be viewed as an object system.[1] That is, a dynamic library architecture supports all the standard properties required to identify a system as object oriented: inheritance, encapsulation, and overriding. Furthermore, as we will show, other common features of object models can be identified in dynamic libraries: a library can choose to call functionality of its parent library ("super" call) and can choose to call functionality in another named library (call through a reference). Indeed, even some not-too-conventional features of object systems are supported by the dynamic library model: "inheritance" is done late (at load time), making the dynamic library model resemble a "mixin-based" [8] object system. Furthermore, different copies of a library can participate in the same inheritance hierarchy.

The conceptual mapping of dynamic libraries to object-like entities is one of the contributions of this paper. Based on this, we translate well-known techniques for layered design in object-oriented languages into analogous techniques for dynamic libraries. The result is a style of dynamic library development that is very useful but unconventional: it requires constant consideration of whether a call should be dispatched "dynamically" (i.e., could be allowed to be overridden by child libraries in the inheritance hierarchy), "statically" (within the current library), or "by chaining" (by forwarding to the parent library in the hierarchy). Dynamic libraries that are designed with the understanding that they can be used in a layered fashion are modular and can be used in many combinations with other libraries. Conventional (*legacy*[2]) Unix dynamic libraries are rarely careful to cooperate with other libraries that may be overriding some of their symbols.

We should point out early on that the term "library" is overloaded in our discussion. When we talk of a "dynamic library", we mean a single file implementing a collection of routines. When we talk of a "layered" or "factored library" we mean a collection of components that are designed to be composed together in many configurations. Under the methodology we are proposing, a single "dynamic library" is just one of the components in a "layered library".

As a proof of concept for our approach, we present two dynamic libraries that can be viewed as different components of a factored library for file operations. The two libraries are designed to be used either together or in isolation. Both libraries perform system-level tasks, that are, however, commonly handled at the application level in Unix. The first library performs transparent file versioning: every time an "interesting" file is modified or erased, its old version is saved for backup. The second library performs file locking, so that inconsistent file editing is prevented. Both libraries can be used either with new applications, or with legacy applications. In the latter case, they can

---

1. For readers familiar with Unix dynamic libraries, a clarification and forward pointer is in order: our arguments are based on the use of the LD_PRELOAD technique instead of the more conventional path-based approach to using dynamic libraries.
2. We will use the term "legacy" to denote pre-existing Unix libraries and applications (i.e., binary objects that were not developed following the style of programming described in this paper). We do not assign any negative connotation to the term.

provide backup and locking functionality for existing executables (i.e., without re-compilation). Source code for both libraries is available at our web site.

The rest of this paper is structured as follows. Section 2 introduces Unix dynamic libraries and shows how they can be viewed in object-oriented terms. Section 3 discusses our two example applications and their structure as layers of a consistent library. Section 4 presents related work and Section 5 offers our conclusions.

2 Dynamic Libraries

In this section we introduce dynamic linking/loading, with special emphasis to the (not too common) use of the LD_PRELOAD environment variable in modern Unix variants. We then show how this technique supports layered software development, by enabling us to simulate a flexible object-oriented programming model.

Our examples have been tested on Linux and Solaris using several different versions of these operating systems over the past 2 years. Hence, reasonable stability can be expected. Most other modern Unix variants (e.g., FreeBSD/OpenBSD/NetBSD, AIX, Mac OS X) support dynamic libraries, but we have not personally tested them.

2.1 Background

Dynamic linking/loading is a common technique in modern operating systems. Under dynamic linking, an executable program can call routines whose code exists in a dynamic library. The dynamic library is loaded at execution time into the address space of the program. Routines from a dynamic library are identified by symbols and it is the responsibility of the dynamic linker to match the symbols referenced in the executable to the symbols exported from a dynamic library. The main advantage of dynamic libraries is that the executable does not need to be burdened by including common library code. This results into smaller executables, thus saving disk space. More importantly, it also enables keeping a single copy of the library code in the system memory during run-time, even though the code may be used by multiple executable files (or even by the OS kernel itself).

Another advantage of dynamic libraries is that they avoid hard-coding dependencies on library code. Instead of statically linking to a certain version of the code, which prevents exploiting future improvements, dynamic linking takes place at program load time. Thus, different libraries (possibly newer and improved or just alternative implementations) can be used. This enables modularity and it has been one of the main reasons why dynamic libraries are the technology of choice for binary object systems, like Microsoft's COM (e.g., see [9]). It is worth mentioning that this flexibility of dynamic libraries has also been the source of problems when library versioning is not managed carefully—the term "DLL hell" has become standard terminology.

Typically the search for libraries is path based: the name of the library exporting a certain symbol is fixed at build time, but by changing the lookup path for the library file, different dynamic libraries can be linked. For example, in Unix systems, an executable program calling routine `rout`, implemented in library `libroutines.so`, can be built with the `-lroutines` flag to signify that dynamic linking should be done to a file called `libroutines.so`. The user can then influence the process of finding the file by changing the environment variable `LD_LIBRARY_PATH`, which lists directory paths to be searched by the linker in order to find `libroutines.so`.

A very powerful feature of Unix dynamic libraries is the ability to interpose implementations of routines *before* the actual path based symbol lookup takes place. This is done by using the `LD_PRELOAD` environment variable. `LD_PRELOAD` can be set to a list of dynamic library *files* (not directory paths) that are linked before any other dynamic libraries. Effectively, symbols from the libraries in the `LD_PRELOAD` variable take precedence over any normal dynamic library symbols. We show examples of the use of `LD_PRELOAD` in the following section.

2.2 Dynamic Libraries and the Object-Oriented Model

The common attributes of an object-oriented (OO) system are encapsulation, inheritance, and overriding. As we will see, all of these and more are supported by dynamic library technology.[3]

The object model supported by dynamic libraries is not exactly like that of mainstream OO languages like C++ and Java: such languages are class-based, while the object model we discuss here is not. Instead, the dynamic library object model is closer to a delegation-based binary object model, like COM [9]. The use of the `LD_PRELOAD` variable is particularly interesting, as it enables late composition of dynamic modules.

Encapsulation. Dynamic libraries offer encapsulation: they contain the implementations of multiple routines that can be handled as a single unit. Data hiding is supported: routines are distinguished into those that are exported (*external symbols*) and those that are not.

The default resolution of symbols is to routines in the library itself. Thus, if a dynamic library references symbol `sym` and provides an implementation of `sym`, the library's own implementation will be used. Binary code can call the routines encapsulated in a different dynamic library, as long as a "reference" to the library exists. The reference can be obtained using the library pathname. For instance, calling routine `f` of library `lib` is done by explicitly opening the library and looking up the appropriate routine:

```
libhandle = dlopen("lib", RTLD_LAZY);
meth = (methtype *) dlsym(libhandle, "f"); // cache it in meth
meth(arg1); //or whatever is the regular signature of "methname"
```

---

3. Unix dynamic libraries are commonly also called "shared objects" (hence the `.so` file suffix). This is a fortunate coincidence, since, to our knowledge, the term "object" was not used in the object-oriented sense.

Inheritance. Dynamic libraries support inheritance:[4] a library can behave as if it were automatically "inheriting" all symbols exported by ancestor libraries in a hierarchy. A hierarchy is formed by putting the dynamic libraries in sequence in the value of LD_PRELOAD. For instance, consider setting LD_PRELOAD to be (csh syntax):

```
setenv LD_PRELOAD "$DLIBHOME/C.so $DLIBHOME/B.so $DLIBHOME/A.so"
```

This establishes a linear hierarchy of libraries, each having a notion of a "next" library in the hierarchy. In terms of inheritance, library C.so inherits from library B.so, which inherits from library A.so. All symbols of A.so can be referenced by code in B.so, etc.

Overriding. A dynamic library automatically overrides symbols from ancestor libraries in the hierarchy. "Dynamic" dispatch (really a misnomer, since the resolution occurs at load time) is effected by looking up a symbol using the RTLD_DEFAULT flag in the dlsym call:

```
virt_meth = (methtype *) dlsym(RTLD_DEFAULT, "methname");
virt_meth(arg1); // call the most refined method
```

This ensures that the lookup for the symbol proceeds through the dynamic libraries in order, beginning at the final node of the hierarchy. Thus, the overriding method is retrieved, not any overridden versions.

As usual in an OO hierarchy, code in one node can explicitly call code in the next node of the hierarchy (instead of calling its own "overridden" version of the code). Such "parent" calls are effected by looking up the symbol using the RTLD_NEXT specifier in the dlsym call:

```
super_meth = (methtype *) dlsym(RTLD_NEXT, "methname");
super_meth(arg1); // call the method
```

2.3 Layered Development with Dynamic Libraries

Dynamic libraries form an excellent platform for layered software development. This has already been exploited in limited ways. Windows dynamic libraries are the technology that supports Microsoft's COM. In Unix, there are some applications that extend their capabilities using dynamic loading (e.g., the Apache web server [1]). Nevertheless, to our knowledge, there is no factored library with its components implemented as dynamic libraries. That is, although large, monolithic dynamic libraries have been used successfully, no consistent array of functionality has been implemented as a collection of small dynamic libraries *all designed to cooperate* using load-time inheritance hierarchies.

---

4. The term "aggregation" would perhaps be more appropriate than "inheritance", since the latter is used to describe relationships between classes. Nevertheless, we prefer to use the term "load-time inheritance" or just "inheritance" to appeal to the reader's intuition.

The technology for such a coordinated interaction is already there. Indeed, the object model offered by dynamic libraries is close to a *mixin-based* model—a technology that has been used in layered libraries in the past, most notably in the GenVoca methodology [2]. *Mixins* [8] are classes whose superclass is not specified at mixin implementation time, but is left to be specified at mixin use time. The advantage is that a single mixin can be used as a subclass for multiple other classes. This is similar to what we obtain with dynamic libraries using the LD_PRELOAD variable. A single library can refer to "parent" functionality and to "overriding" functionality, but it is not aware of the exact hierarchy in which it participates. The same library can be used in many different hierarchies. The same symbols will be resolved to refer to different code depending on the exact hierarchy.

Consider, for instance, a factored library containing 6 dynamic library components, named A.so to F.so. Each of these components can encapsulate a different feature, which may be present or absent from a given component composition. All components should be designed with interoperability in mind. Thus, every call to a routine f should be carefully thought out to determine whether it should be a call to a routine in the same library (calling known code), a call to the parent library's routine (delegating to the parent), or a call to the overriding version of the routine (allowing the interposition of functionality by all other libraries in the hierarchy). This is the same kind of analysis that goes into the implementation of a mixin-based library.

The advantage of factored libraries is that they can be used to implement a number of combinations that is exponential in the number of components in the library. Each of the combinations is not burdened by unneeded features, yet can be as powerful as needed for the specific application. For instance, a composition of components A, B, and E (henceforth denoted A[B[E]], using GenVoca layer notation [5]) is effected by appropriately setting the LD_PRELOAD variable:

```
setenv LD_PRELOAD "$DLIBHOME/A.so $DLIBHOME/B.so $DLIBHOME/E.so"
```

The order of composition could also be important: compositions of the same components in a different order could result into different, but equally valid implementations.

In earlier work [22], we have shown the reuse advantages of layered libraries compared to other object-oriented technologies. Compared to OO application frameworks [15], for instance, layered libraries offer a much more compact representation of feature sets of similar complexity. In our experience, dynamic library technologies can offer full support for layered development. For instance, some important issues in layered development can be handled as follows:

- A major issue in layered libraries is ensuring that a composition is valid. Components commonly have requirements from other components participating in a composition. For instance, in a data structure factored library (like DiSTiL [20]) we can require that a storage policy component be at the root of the component hierarchy. Such requirements are often expressed in a component-centric way: each component exports some boolean flags asserting or negating certain (library-specific) properties. At the same time, components can enforce requirements on the union of all properties of components above them or below them in a component hierarchy [4]. For instance, component A can require that some component above it implement the storage property. If component B exports the property, then composition A[B] is valid.

Dynamic libraries can support automatic checking of properties at load time. By convention, the library can contain a special initialization function called _init. This function is called by the dynamic loader to perform library-specific initialization. Properties can be exported by libraries as symbols. For instance, a simple requirement can be expressed as:

```
void _init() {
  assert(dlsym(RTLD_NEXT, "property1"));
}
```

This ensures that a library above the current one in the component hierarchy exports a symbol called "property1". Using this technique, a factored library developer can add complex restrictions on what compositions are valid. The restrictions are checked early: at application (and library) load time, and not when the library functionality is called. It is the responsibility of the layered library author to express the dependencies among components as restrictions of the above form.

- A common feature of layered libraries is that layers can be instantiated multiple times in a single composition. At first, this may seem paradoxical: why would the same code be included more than once in a composition? Nevertheless, the code is actually parameterized by all the components above the current one in a component hierarchy. Thus, multiple copies of the same code can be specialized to perform different functions. Consider, for instance, a multi-pass compiler, where one of the passes is implemented as a component called process_tree. If the typechecking phase must be completed before reduction to an intermediate language takes place, then a reasonable composition would be:
process_tree[typecheck[process_tree[reduce]]] .

Dynamic libraries can handle multiple instances of a library in the same composition. In the worst case a brute-force approach (which we had to use in Solaris) is needed: the dynamic library file needs to be copied manually. In Linux, however, the same library can be used multiple times in an LD_PRELOAD hierarchy without problems.

- Layered library development requires a composition mechanism that imposes a low performance penalty for calling code in different layers. Indeed, Unix dynamic libraries have emphasized fast dispatch. A typical Unix loader will resolve symbols at load time and employ binary rewriting techniques to ensure that future invocations are performed at full speed, instead of suffering lookup cost dynamically on every invocation [17]. Although, there is still overhead from employing layering (e.g., routines from different layers cannot be inlined) the overhead is kept reasonably small. Additionally, the expected granularity of components developed using dynamic library technology is large: for fine-grained components, a source-code-level technique is more advantageous. Therefore, the overhead of layering using dynamic libraries is negligible.

Based on the above observations, we believe that dynamic libraries are a good technology for implementing layered libraries. The question that arises is why one should prefer dynamic libraries over other layering technologies. Compared to source code component technologies, dynamic libraries have the usual advantages of binary level components. First, dynamic libraries are language-independent: they can be created in many languages and used by code in other languages. Second, dynamic libraries are binary components, offering intellectual property protection. Furthermore, dynamic libraries have a unique feature compared to all other component technologies (binary or source level): their ability for load-time configurability. This ability yields a lot of flexibility in future updates, but also in operation with legacy code. For instance, dynamic libraries interposing on well-known symbols (e.g., from the `libc` library) can be used with completely unsuspecting pre-compiled applications.

3 Example Applications

To demonstrate the potential for layered development using dynamic libraries, we will discuss two libraries that we designed as parts of a transparent "file operations" layered library. We should point out that our code is not yet a mature and feature-rich layered library. In fact, our two libraries are not an ideal example of layered library components, as they are only loosely coupled. Nevertheless, our libraries are actual, useful examples. They serve as a basic proof-of-concept by demonstrating almost all of the techniques described in Section 2. Our source code can be found in:

> `http://www.cc.gatech.edu/~yannis/icsrcode.tar.gz` .

3.1 Versioning Library Overview

Typical Unix file systems do not offer automatic backup capabilities. Unix programs commonly resort to application-level solutions when they need to keep older versions of files when these are modified. For instance, the Emacs text editor and the Framemaker word processor both automatically create a backup file storing the previous version of an edited file. Advanced and general solutions have been proposed at the kernel level—for example, see the report on the Elephant file system [18] and its references. Nevertheless, it is relatively easy to come up with a good, quite general, and fairly OS-neutral solution at the user level using dynamic libraries. Our versioning dynamic library interposes its own code to the symbols wrapping common system calls, like `open`, `creat`, `unlink`, and `remove`. By setting LD_PRELOAD to point to the library, we can use it with completely unsuspecting legacy applications. The library recognizes "interesting" file suffixes and only acts if the file in question has one of these suffixes. Any attempt to modify (as opposed to just read) a file through one of the calls implemented by the library will result in a backup being created. Thus, unlike the usual "trash can" or "recycle bin" functionality, our library protects both against deletion and against overwriting with new data. Backup versions of files are stored in a "`.ver`-

sion" subdirectory of the directory where the modified file exists. We have put this library to everyday use for source code files (.c, .h, .cpp, .hpp, .cc, .hh, and .java suffixes) text files (.txt), etc.

An interesting issue in versioning functionality is which of the older versions are worth keeping. The Elephant file system [18] allows users to specify policies for keeping older versions. Our library is primitive in this respect: it only keeps a fixed number of the most recent back versions (currently only one, but this can easily change). An interesting future improvement might be to provide versioning policies as other components in our factored library—that is, as dynamic libraries. Then, the user will be able to select the right policy at load time, by composing the versioning library with policy libraries through an LD_PRELOAD component hierarchy.

3.2 Locking Library Overview

File locking is another piece of functionality that (although to some extent supported by Unix file systems) is commonly left for the application to provide. (File locking in Unix is a big topic—e.g., see Ch. 2 of the Unix Programming FAQ [11]—and our homegrown implementation is certainly not a general solution.) File locking intends to protect files from concurrent modification and to protect applications from inconsistent file views. Application-specific locking protects against access to a file by different instances of the same application, but does not prohibit access by different applications. The Emacs text editor and the FrameMaker word processor are, again, good examples of applications that provide their own locking implementation.

It should be noted that most text-oriented Unix applications do not operate by keeping files open for long periods of time. Instead, applications processing a file first make a temporary copy of the file, on which all modification takes place. Eventually, the temporary file is copied over the original, to reflect the changes. This upload/download-like approach provides some protection against inconsistent modification, but is not feasible in the case of large files (e.g., multimedia files).

Our file locking library works by overriding file operations like open, close, and creat. Just like our versioning library, the interposed code checks if the file in question is an "interesting" file. The library implements a readers/writers locking policy: multiple open operations are allowed on a file, as long as they are all read-only accesses. Any other concurrent access is prohibited. Thus, our locking is "mandatory" (but only for applications executing with our library in the LD_PRELOAD path) while common Unix locking mechanisms are "advisory" (i.e., they require application participation). Normally, our locking policy would perhaps be too strict. Nevertheless, it only becomes restrictive in the case of large files that are opened "in place". (The only other reasonable alternative in this case would be no locking whatsoever.) For the common case when a temporary copy of the file is created, our locking policy just prevents inconsistent write-backs (interleaved write operations by different processes to different parts of a file).

Locks and shared data (e.g., number of readers/writers) are stored in the file system, as files under a .lock subdirectory of the directory where the interesting file is found.

3.3 Implementation and Discussion

The locking and versioning libraries described above employ most of the techniques discussed in Section 2. Although the libraries are loosely coupled, they are designed to cooperate, as they interpose on many of the same symbols. Thus, they can be regarded as components in a simple layered library. The two libraries can be used together or individually on an application.

The main difficulty during library development has to do with identifying which procedure calls should conceptually refer to potentially "overridden" functionality, which should refer to functionality in the same library, and which should just be delegated to the parent library in the component hierarchy (or any other dynamic library through normal, path-based lookup).

To facilitate programming in this way, each library initializes a set of "super" implementations for all the symbols it overrides. For instance, the locking library contains initialization code like:

```
super_open = (Openfn) dlsym(RTLD_NEXT, "open");
super_close = (Closefn) dlsym(RTLD_NEXT, "close");
super_creat = (Creatfn) dlsym(RTLD_NEXT, "creat");
...
```

The super_open, etc., function pointers are static global variables, accessible from all the library routines. They are often used when normal, non-layered code would just call open, close, etc. For instance, the locking library creates a "pre-locking" file using a Unix exclusive file creation operation. The "pre-locking" file serves to ensure that no two processes try to access the locking shared data (i.e., numbers of readers/writers) at the same time. The code for that operation is:

```
lock_fd = super_open(extended_path, O_WRONLY | O_CREAT | O_EXCL,
                     S_IRUSR | S_IWUSR | S_IXUSR);
```

The most interesting interaction between layers is the one that occurs when a library calls a routine that is potentially overridden. Recall that this is analogous to a "dynamically bound" call in the object-oriented model. A good example of such a use can be found in the finalizer routine of the locking library. Since many processes do not explicitly close files before they exit, we tried to approximate the correct functionality by calling close on all open files when the library is finalized. This will ensure that the locking library correctly updates its locking information. Nevertheless, the call to close does not only concern the locking library, but also any other dynamic libraries loaded in the process. Thus, the call to close should be to the overriding method of the close routine. A slightly simplified version of our finalizer code is shown here:

```
void _fini() {
  Closefn virt_close = (Closefn) dlsym(RTLD_DEFAULT, "close");
  while (open_files != NULL) {
    open_file_data *next = open_files->next;
    virt_close(open_files->open_fd);
    open_files = next;
  }
}
```

(As can be seen in the above, the locking library has state: it keeps track of what files are open at any point.)

Finally, we should give a warning. Both the locking and the versioning libraries are based on interposing code on symbols used by existing programs. The disadvantage of this approach is that completeness is hard to guarantee. It is easy to miss a symbol that offers a different way to access the same core functionality. Even in the case of well-defined OS interfaces, there is potential for surprise: our first implementation of the versioning library missed the open64 symbol, used in Solaris as part of a transitional interface to accessing large files. Executables compiled to use the open64 symbol circumvented that early version of our library.

4 Discussion and Related Work

There has been a lot of research work presenting advanced techniques for software reuse. This includes work on generators and templates [10], transformation systems [6][16], language-level component technologies [19], module and interconnection languages [12][23], and much more. Our emphasis in this paper was not on proving that an overall approach to software design has good reuse properties. Instead, we adapted the existing approach of scalable libraries and layered designs to a different technology. The benefits of scalable libraries are well established [3][21]. We argued that most of these benefits can be obtained when Unix dynamic libraries are used as the underlying concrete technology.

Despite the emphasis on Unix systems throughout this paper, dynamic libraries are part of all modern operating systems. It may be feasible, for instance, to use some of our ideas in a Windows environment. Nevertheless, our emphasis was on the use of the LD_PRELOAD variable, which allows (even a third-party user) to specify compositions simply and concisely. No analogous mechanism exists on Windows systems. The difference between using LD_PRELOAD and using a path-based lookup mechanism (not only in Windows, but also in Unix variants) is in convenience and transparency. With path-based lookup, libraries need to have specific names, already known by the pre-compiled executables. Directories have to be set up appropriately to enforce a search order. Finally, to our knowledge, in Windows systems, there is no way to separate the lookup path for dynamic libraries from the search path for executables.

We should also mention that interposing dynamic libraries through the LD_PRELOAD variable raises some security concerns. For instance, there are commonly restrictions on what libraries can be dynamically linked to set-user-ID or set-group-ID executables. All of these restrictions, however, are orthogonal to the work presented in this paper: they have to do with the general issue of trust of binary programs. Linking a dynamic library is certainly no more dangerous than running an executable program.

Although only tangentially related, we should mention that a lot of work has been done over the years on layered operating system development. The *microkernel* approach is the best known representative of such research, and several object-oriented microkernels (e.g., Spring [14] and recently JX [13]) have been developed. Although conceptually related, the operating systems modularization work deals with completely different concerns (performance and hardware resource management) from this paper.

5 Conclusions

In this paper we argued that Unix dynamic libraries (or "shared objects") are a good platform for implementing layered designs. The basis of our argument is the observation that dynamic libraries offer exactly analogous mechanisms for interaction between libraries in a library hierarchy, as those offered for interactions between classes in an object-oriented inheritance hierarchy. Furthermore, the establishment of a dynamic library hierarchy is done at load time, allowing great configurability.

We believe that the dynamic library technology can form the basis for mature, industrial-strength factored libraries. Although many factored libraries have been produced so far, few are used in practical settings and most could benefit from the unique features of dynamic library technology (e.g., binding with legacy programs without recompiling). Similarly, although many mature dynamic libraries are in use, no consistent collection of cooperating dynamic libraries, allowing mix-and-match configurability, has been developed. Our work makes a first step in this promising direction.

Acknowledgments. This work was partially supported by DARPA/ITO under the PCES program.

6 References

[1]   Apache HTTP Server Documentation Project, "Version 2.0: Dynamic Shared Object (DSO) Support", available at
       `http://httpd.apache.org/docs-2.0/dso.html` .

[2]   D. Batory and S. O'Malley, "The Design and Implementation of Hierarchical Software Systems with Reusable Components", *ACM TOSEM*, October 1992.

[3]   D. Batory, V. Singhal, M. Sirkin, and J. Thomas, "Scalable Software Libraries", *ACM SIGSOFT* 1993.

[4]   D. Batory and B.J. Geraci, "Component Validation and Subjectivity in GenVoca Generators", *IEEE Trans. on Softw. Eng.*, February 1997, 67-82.

[5]   D. Batory, "Intelligent Components and Software Generators", *Software Quality Institute Symposium on Software Reliability*, Austin, Texas, April, 1997.

[6] I.D. Baxter, "Design maintenance systems", *Communications of the ACM* 35(4): 73-89, April 1992.

[7] T. Biggerstaff, "The Library Scaling Problem and the Limits of Concrete Component Reuse", *1994 International Conference on Software Reuse*.

[8] G. Bracha and W. Cook, "Mixin-Based Inheritance", *ECOOP/OOPSLA 1990*, 303-311.

[9] K. Brockschmidt, Inside OLE (2nd. ed.), Microsoft Press, 1995.

[10] K. Czarnecki and U. Eisenecker. *Generative Programming: Methods, Techniques, and Applications*. Addison-Wesley, 2000.

[11] A. Gierth (ed.), *Unix Programming FAQ*, available at http://www.erlenstar.demon.co.uk/unix/faq_toc.html .

[12] J. Goguen, "Reusing and interconnecting software components", *IEEE Computer*, February 1986, 16-28.

[13] M. Golm, J. Kleinoeder, F. Bellosa, "Beyond Address Spaces - Flexibility, Performance, Protection, and Resource Management in the Type-Safe JX Operating System", *8th Workshop on Hot Topics in OS* (HotOS-VIII), 2001.

[14] G. Hamilton, P. Kougiouris, "The Spring Nucleus: A Microkernel for Objects", *Sun Microsystems Laboratories Tech. Report*, TR-93-14.

[15] R. Johnson and B. Foote, "Designing Reusable Classes", *Journal of Object-Oriented Programming*, 1(2): June/July 1988, 22-35.

[16] J. Neighbors, "Draco: a method for engineering reusable software components", in T.J. Biggerstaff and A. Perlis (eds.), *Software Reusability*, Addison-Wesley/ACM Press, 1989.

[17] C. Phoenix, "Windows vs. Unix: Linking dynamic load modules", available at: http://www.best.com/~cphoenix/winvunix.html .

[18] D. Santry, M. Feeley, N. Hutchinson, A. Veitch, R. Carton, and J. Ofir, "Deciding when to forget in the Elephant file system", *17th ACM Symposium on Operating Systems Principles* (SOSP'99).

[19] M. Sitaraman and B.W. Weide, editors, "Special Feature: Component-Based Software Using RESOLVE", *ACM Softw. Eng. Notes*, October 1994, 21-67.

[20] Y. Smaragdakis and D. Batory, "DiSTiL: a Transformation Library for Data Structures", *USENIX Conference on Domain-Specific Languages (DSL 97)*.

[21] Y. Smaragdakis and D. Batory, "Implementing Reusable Object-Oriented Components", *5th Int. Conf. on Softw. Reuse (ICSR '98)*, IEEE Computer Society Press, 1998.

[22] Y. Smaragdakis, *Implementing Large Scale Object-Oriented Components*, Ph.D. Dissertation, University of Texas at Austin, December 1999.

[23] W. Tracz, "LILEANNA: A Parameterized Programming Language", in Ruben Prieto-Diaz and William B. Frakes, editors, *Advances in Software Reuse: Selected Papers from the Secomd Int. Work. on Softw. Reusability*, 1993, IEEE Computer Society Press, 66-78.

Early-Reply Components:
Concurrent Execution with Sequential Reasoning

Scott M. Pike and Nigamanth Sridhar

Computer and Information Science, Ohio State University,
2015 Neil Ave, Columbus OH 43210, USA
{pike,nsridhar}@cis.ohio-state.edu

Abstract. Generic software components have a reputation for being inefficient. Parallel implementations may improve performance, but can thwart reuse by being architecture-dependent or by exposing concurrency to client-side reasoning about component interactions. To address performance, we present Early-Reply as an alternative to blocking method invocations. Component operations can be partitioned into a *material computation* required to satisfy the postcondition, and a *residual computation* required to reëstablish the component invariant, optimize its representation, etc. Early-Reply exploits opportunities for parallelism by forwarding final parameter values to the caller as soon as the material computation completes, thereby offloading the residual computation to execute in parallel with subsequent client activities. Proof obligations for Early-Reply support a synchronous calling model, so clients can still reason sequentially about component behavior. Also, since Early-Reply components do not depend on system-wide support for component synchronization, they can be deployed incrementally. Finally, Early-Reply can improve the response time of idle components by orders of magnitude; when composed hierarchically, performance benefits are magnified by the potential fan-out of concurrently executing components.

1 Introduction

Mature engineering disciplines are witness to the fact that component-based development is fundamental to the construction of scalable systems. Despite the benefits of componentry, however, modularization techniques for software suffer from a perceived view of being inefficient. This reputation derives from two primary factors. First, when encapsulation and information hiding are observed, executing component code requires invocations which introduce synchronization costs and calling overhead. Second, reusable components should be applicable to a wide variety of contexts, a desideratum that precludes many domain-specific and architecture-dependent optimization techniques [8]. Calling overhead and context independence are certainly performance factors, but are generic components inherently inefficient, or is their reputation for inefficiency an artifact of current practice? We examine this question under the following two-fold thesis: synchronous software components can be implemented to execute concurrently

C. Gacek (Ed.): ICSR-7, LNCS 2319, pp. 46–61, 2002.

(1) without compromising sequential reasoning about component behavior, and
(2) without presupposing system-wide support for runtime synchronization.

Components typically adhere to a synchronous calling model, where a client *blocks* for the duration of an invocation, until the method body completes by returning control and results (if any). Strangely, the common-case implementation of a synchronous calling model is with synchronous calling conventions. This practice is somewhat daft, given that a calling model is just that: a *model*. As such, this abstraction can be implemented in many ways. We present Early-Reply as a construct that supports concurrent component execution in a synchronous calling model. We develop Early-Reply to exploit the performance benefits of concurrency, *without* compromising the reasoning benefits of synchronous calls.

Component methods can be partitioned into *material* and *residual* segments, corresponding to the initial computation required to satisfy the postcondition, and subsequent computation required to complete the operation, respectively. In a naïve implementation of a synchronous calling model, the caller blocks during the residual computation, even though the results of the invocation are already available. This is analogous to read-after-write data hazards in pipelined architectures, where future instructions may stall due to dependencies on earlier instructions in the pipeline. A well-known technique for minimizing pipeline stalls is to forward results to future instructions as soon as they become available. This increases both instruction-level parallelism and overall resource utilization.

In this paper, we extend the idea of result forwarding to software components. In Section 2, we introduce Early-Reply as an abstract construct to decouple data flow from control flow in sequential programs. Further characterization of Early-Reply is presented in Section 3. In Section 4, we use a Set component as an example to show how the response time of idle components can be optimized. Section 5 analyzes the worst-case response time of Early-Reply components. An approach to further minimizing the amount of client blockage time is described in Section 6. We show how Early-Reply can be used as a lightweight approach to transforming off-the-shelf components into Early-Reply implementations in Section 7. Some directions of related research are listed in Section 8. We summarize our contributions, outline areas of future work and conclude in Section 8.

2   Decoupling Data Flow from Control Flow

The common-case implementation of a synchronous calling model couples the flow of data to the flow of control. As such, component implementations cannot return parameter values to the caller without relinquishing control to execute further statements in the method body. Entangling data with control precludes many implementations that can improve performance by exploiting parallelism. To separate these concerns, we present Early-Reply as an abstract construct for decoupling data flow from control flow.

As a motivating example, we consider the implementation of a parameterized Stack component. We model the abstract value of type Stack as a mathematical string of Item, where the parameter Item models the type of entry in the Stack.

Furthermore, we assume that any variable x is created with an initial value for its type, which we specify using the predicate Initial(x). The initial value for a variable of type Stack is the empty string, denoted by <>. The operator $*$ denotes string concatenation; the string constructor <x> denotes the string consisting of the single item x; the length operator |s| denotes the length of string s; and x :=: y denotes the swap operator, which exchanges the values of x and y. Figure 1 gives specifications of basic stack operations, where #x in a postcondition denotes the incoming value of x, and x denotes its outgoing value. By convention, we view the left-most position of a string as the top of the Stack it models. Also, we use the distinguished parameter self to denote the component instance through which methods are invoked, which, in this example, is a component of type Stack.

```
op Push (Item x)
precondition: true
postcondition: Initial(x) and (self = <#x> * #self)

op Pop (Item x)
precondition: self ≠ <>
postcondition: #self = <x> * self

op Length (): int
precondition: true
postcondition: Length = |self|
```

Fig. 1. Specification of basic Stack operations

Figure 2 shows a common linked-list representation of Stack. Each **Node** n contains two fields: n.data of type **Item**, and n.next which points to the next node in the linked list. Each Stack instance has two data members: self.top (which points to the first **Node** in the linked list), and self.len (which denotes the current length of the Stack). Figure 3 shows the representation invariant and abstraction function. The former defines the state space of valid representations. The later defines how to convert such representations into their abstract Stack values.

Figure 4 shows common implementations of **Push** and **Pop**, in which the flow of data is coupled to the flow of control. That is, the formal parameter values of each method invocation are returned to the caller only upon relinquishing control

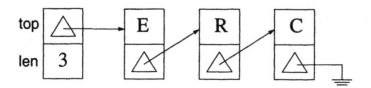

Fig. 2. Representation of a Stack<char> with abstract value < E, R, C >

Representation Invariant: self.len $\geq$ 0 **and** self.top points to the first node of a singly-linked list containing self.len nodes of type Node, and where the next field of the final node is Null.

Abstraction Function: AF (self) =
the string composed of the data fields of the first self.len nodes in the singly-linked list pointed to by self.top, concatenated together in the order in which they are linked together.

Fig. 3. Representation Invariant and Abstraction Function for Stack

```
op Push (Item x)
begin
1:    Node p;
2:    p := new Node;
3:    x :=: p.data;
4:    p.next := self.top;
5:    self.top := p;
6:    self.len++;
end
```

```
op Pop (Item x)
begin
1:    x :=: self.top.data;
2:    Node p := self.top;
3:    self.top := p.next;
4:    delete p;
5:    self.len−−;
end
```

Fig. 4. Blocking implementations of Push and Pop

at the termination of each method. These are *blocking* implementations, in the sense that caller activities are suspended for the duration of the method body. The Length operation, which we omit for brevity, simply returns the current value of the member variable self.len.

Consider the implementation of Push. The first two statements declare and allocate a Node variable p. Recall that the Item field p.data is created with an initial value so that Initial(p.data) holds. The third statement swaps the formal parameter x with p.data, after which the postcondition for Push is satisfied with respect to x, since Initial(x) now holds. At this point, we claim, it is unnecessary for the client to continue blocking in the following sense: there is no *client-observable* difference between returning the value of x now – rather than when the method terminates – so long as the Stack instance defers additional method invocations until the remainder of the Push operation completes. Similar remarks apply to the implementation of Pop, but even earlier: the postcondition of Pop is satisfied with respect to the formal parameter x after the first statement, whereupon x = #self.top. Again, we claim, the client should not have to block for the remainder of the method body. But why should this be the case?

A key insight of the foregoing remarks is that the final (i.e., postconditional) value of the parameter x in each method is produced early on, *and is never changed thereafter*. Moreover, the fact that the parameter x is never even *used* after its final value is determined underscores the independence between subsequent client activities and the residual computations of Push and Pop. To exploit this independence, we must decouple the link between data flow to the client and control flow in the method body. Accordingly, we present Early-Reply as an abstract construct for returning final parameter values to the caller without relinquishing local control to complete the method body. Figure 5 shows implementations of Push and Pop that use Early-Reply to reduce response time and to increase the potential for overlapping client and method computations.

```
op Push (Item x)          op Pop (Item x)
begin                     begin
1:    Node p;             1:    x :=: self.top.data;
2:    p := new Node;            Early-Reply;
3:    x :=: p.data;       2:    Node p := self.top;
      Early-Reply;        3:    self.top := p.next;
4:    p.next := self.top; 4:    delete p;
5:    self.top := p;      5:    self.len−−;
6:    self.len++;         end
end
```

Fig. 5. Early-Reply implementations of Push and Pop

In Figure 5, statements preceding each Early-Reply represent *material* computations, insofar as they establish the postcondition for the formal parameters. Statements subsequent to each Early-Reply represent *residual* computations, insofar as they: (1) maintain the postcondition with respect to the formal parameters; (2) establish the postcondition with respect to the distinguished parameter self; and (3) reëstablish the representation invariant for the Stack instance.

3   A Silhouette of Early-Reply

The Stack example above is essentially straight-line code. As such, it motivates the distinction between material and residual computations in software components. A formal characterization of this distinction is beyond the scope of this paper, but an in-depth analysis is not essential to understanding the fundamental insights developed herein. This section sketches a silhouette of Early-Reply, postponing advanced formalisms for special treatment in future work.

The operational semantics of Early-Reply are characterized informally as follows: executing an Early-Reply statement causes a *logical fork* in the flow of control, with one branch returning the current values of the formal parameters to the caller (excluding the distinguished parameter self), and the other branch completing execution of the residual method body. Early-Reply "locks" the component instance self for the residual computation. An invocation on self during this period blocks the caller until the current invocation completes, whereupon self becomes "unlocked" and handles the next method. Local locking enforces mutual exclusion, however, so the component represented by self can be *passed as a parameter* to another component without blocking the caller.

For each invocation, we define the *material computation* as the sequence of statements executed up to, and including, the first executed Early-Reply, if any. We define the *residual computation* as the sequence of statements executed after the first Early-Reply up to method termination. Obviously, material and residual computations depend on the implementation. As a boundary case, method bodies that do not use, or execute, an Early-Reply statement have empty residual computations. Also, due to branching control structures, the same implementation may, or may not, execute an Early-Reply statement depending on the formal parameter values. Finally, Early-Reply is idempotent; that is, any Early-Reply statement encountered during a residual computation is executed as a no-op.

But when is it safe to Early-Reply? That is, when can a method return parameter values to the caller without compromising the client-side *view* that the method has completed? To ensure design-by-contract [6] in a synchronous calling model, we must encapsulate residual computations from client observability. At a minimum, this requires the formal parameter values to satisfy the method's postcondition when replied to the caller. An eager interpretation of this requirement could reply each parameter as soon as its final value was obtained, but this approach complicates reasoning about component correctness, and typically requires system-wide support such as data-driven synchronization [2]. We adopt a more conservative interpretation; namely, a method can Early-Reply only once *all* of its formal parameters satisfy the method's postcondition. We amend this policy to exclude the distinguished parameter self, which can use a local locking mechanism to synchronize itself without system-wide support.

As an example, recall the Early-Reply implementation of Push in Figure 5. Upon invocation, the component instance self becomes locked. After swapping the formal parameter x with p.data in the third statement, x satisfies the postconditional requirement that Initial(x) holds. At this point, it is safe to Early-Reply, despite the fact that the distinguished parameter self has not yet satisfied its part in the postcondition. In particular, the value of self.len is wrong, and the representation invariant is broken with respect to linking in the new top Node of the list. Early-Reply ensures that these aspects are not observable by the client because self is locked during the residual computation of Push. Upon termination, however, we must dispatch proof obligations that the representation invariant is true, and that the postcondition holds for every parameter, *including self*.

To preserve sequential client-side reasoning about component behavior, we add the following proof obligation; namely, residual computations cannot change the values of parameters that were already replied to the caller. This protects the client in two ways. First, it prevents a method from violating its postcondition *ex post facto*. Second, it prevents potential inconsistencies arising from relational specifications, where a method could maintain its postcondition even while surreptitiously changing its replied parameter values.

A final proof obligation to protect implementations from subsequent client activities is that residual computations should not use *aliased* parameter values after an Early-Reply. After Early-Reply, the caller views the method as having completed. This fact is essential to supporting the abstraction of a synchronous calling model, but component correctness may be compromised if aliased parameters are altered by the caller during a residual computation. Consider, for instance, the effect of changing a key value while it is being inserted into a binary search tree! To avoid aliasing, a method can deep-copy parameter values that are needed during its residual computation. This is potentially expensive, especially when data needs only to be *moved* rather than *copied*. For brevity and efficiency, we use swapping in this paper as the primitive data-movement operator, since it can be implemented to execute in constant time without creating aliases [4].

4 Reducing the Response Time of Idle Components

A component is said to be *idle* if it has completed its most recent invocation; that is, it is not currently executing any residual (or material) code that would defer the immediate execution of subsequent methods. Note that blocking components satisfy this criterion trivially: since the caller blocks for the entirety of each method, the residual computation is always empty, and so the component immediately transits back to idle. Early-Reply components can reduce response time by offloading the work of non-empty residual computations. For idle components, Early-Reply can deliver order-of-magnitude improvements in response time. We substantiate this claim in the context of search-and-query components such as symbol tables and databases. For simplicity, we present a parameterized Set component in Figure 6 as a representative of this class of components. We represent the Set using a standard binary search tree (BST) [3]. The sole member variable of the component instance self is self.tree, which denotes the BST.

Set is modeled by finite set of Item initialization ensures: self = {}	**op** Remove_Any (Item x) **precondition:** self $\neq$ {} **postcondition:** x $\in$ #self **and** $\qquad$ self = #self $-$ {x}
op Add (Item x) **precondition:** x $\notin$ self **postcondition:** Initial(x) **and** $\qquad$ self = #self $\cup$ {#x}	**op** Is_Member (Item x): boolean **precondition:** true **postcondition:** Is_Member = (x $\in$ self)
op Remove (Item x, Item x_copy) **precondition:** x $\in$ self **postcondition:** x_copy = x **and** $\qquad$ self = #self $-$ {x}	**op** Size (): int **precondition:** true **postcondition:** Size = |self|

Fig. 6. Specification of type Set<Item> and its methods

The representation invariant and the abstraction function for this component are presented in Figure 7. The representation invariant places two constraints on self.tree. The predicate Is_BST expresses that the binary tree denoted by self.tree is actually a binary *search* tree; that is, if x is the root node of any subtree of

Representation Invariant:	Is_BST (self.tree) **and**
	Items_Are_Unique (self.tree)
Abstraction Function:	**AF** (self) = Keys (self.tree)

Fig. 7. Representation Invariant and Abstraction Function for Set

self.tree, then every node y in the left subtree of x satisfies $y \leq x$, and every node z in the right subtree of x satisfies $x < z$. This property is required for the correctness of local tree operations. The predicate Items_Are_Unique requires that self.tree contain no duplicate key values. This property enforces the uniqueness of elements in a mathematical set, which is the model of the Set type. Given the strength of the representation invariant, the abstraction function is almost trivial: the abstract value of a Set is simply the set of all key values contained in the binary tree denoted by self.tree.

We now present an Early-Reply implementation of Set using the representation described above. The method bodies in Figure 8 make use of local operations on the BST representation. We describe the behavior of each local operation informally below. To ensure efficient implementations of the Set methods, each of the local tree operations Insert, Delete, and Delete_Root is assumed to re-balance the tree after altering it. Various mechanisms for maintaining balanced binary trees guarantee a worst-case time complexity of $O(log\ n)$ for each tree operation below, where n is the number of nodes in the tree [3].

Find (bst, x): Node
    Searches bst, returning the node with value x, or null if no such node exists.
Insert (bst, x)
    Traverses bst and inserts a node with value x at the appropriate location.
Delete (bst, n)
    Deletes node n and restores bst to a binary search tree.
Delete_Root (bst)
    Deletes the root node of bst and restores bst to a binary search tree.

The Add operation simply creates a local variable y of type Item, and swaps it with the formal parameter x. At this point, the postcondition is satisfied with respect to x – that is, Initial (x) holds – and so Add can Early-Reply, which completes its material computation in constant time. The residual computation of Add performs the actual insertion of the original value of x (which is now in the local variable y). By contrast, a blocking implementation would physically insert x before returning control to the client. For an idle Set component, deferring this task to the residual computation enables an Early-Reply implementation to reduce the worst-case response time of an Add invocation from $O(log\ n)$ to $O(1)$.

A blocking implementation of Remove would proceed roughly as follows: find the node with value x (by searching the tree), swap its value into x_copy, delete the old node, re-balance the tree, and then return control to the client. In an Early-Reply implementation of Remove, the work of deleting and re-balancing can

```
op Add (Item x)                          op Remove_Any (Item x)
begin                                    begin
      var Item y;                              x :=: self.tree.root;
      x :=: y;                                 Early-Reply;
      Early-Reply;                             Delete_Root ();
      Insert (self.tree, y);             end
end
                                         op Is_Member (Item x): boolean
op Remove (Item x, Item x_copy)          begin
begin                                          return (Find (self.tree, x) ≠ null)
      var Node y;                        end
      y := Find (self.tree, x);
      x_copy :=: y.data;                 op Size (): int
      Early-Reply;                       begin
      Delete (self.tree, y);                   return self.tree.size;
end                                      end
```

Fig. 8. An Early-Reply implementation of Set

be offloaded to the residual computation. The response time of both implementations is $O(log\ n)$, but the constant factor for the Early-Reply implementation is a fraction of the blocking implementation.

The Remove_Any operation is included for completeness, so that a client can manipulate a Set without knowing the key values of its elements. Since Remove_Any extracts an arbitrary element from the Set, a valid implementation is simply to remove the root node. For all but trivially small trees, this requires replacing the root in order to reëstablish the representation invariant that self.tree is a binary search tree. Blocking implementations of Remove_Any must establish the invariant before returning control to the client. With Early-Reply, however, an implementation can simply swap self.tree.root with the formal parameter x, and Early-Reply to the client, thereby offloading tree restoration and re-balancing to the residual computation. As with Add, the worst-case response time of Remove_Any on an idle component can be reduced by an order of magnitude. Figure 9 summarizes the foregoing results.

Operation	Blocking	Early-Reply
Set Add	$O(log\ n)$	$O(1)$
Set Remove	$O(log\ n)$	$O(log\ n)$
Set Remove_Any	$O(log\ n)$	$O(1)$

Fig. 9. Worst-case response time for idle Set components

5   Performance Analysis of **Early-Reply** Components

The *ideal* speedup of **Early-Reply** components is bounded by the amount of residual computation that can potentially execute in parallel with subsequent client computation. The *actual* speedup, however, depends on at least three factors, including synchronization overhead, hardware support for physical concurrency, and runtime component usage. We discuss these factors below, each in turn.

The first factor is the brute cost of synchronization. If an **Early-Reply** implementation replaces local invocations by remote procedure calls, this cost can be a significant bottleneck. Synchronization overhead can be masked, however, for applications that already require a distributed infrastructure such as CORBA, Java RMI, or COM+. For local environments, invocations can be replaced by lightweight threading constructs. Assuming a constant upper bound on synchronization costs, this overhead can be absorbed by **Early-Reply** components yielding order-of-magnitude performance improvements on suitably large data sets.

A second factor is run-time support for *physical* concurrency in hardware, as in multiprocessing or networked environments. When support is available, **Early-Reply** components automatically scale to exploit physical concurrency at run-time. This scaling is transparent, because client applications can reap the performance benefits without being re-engineered. Even for uniprocessor environments, **Early-Reply** is not without benefits, since multitasking increases resource utilization. For example, I/O-bound applications can increase resource utilization by overlapping residual computations with blocking I/O system calls.

A final factor is how intensively an **Early-Reply** component is used. During a bursty period of method calling, a client may block temporarily while the residual computation of a previous call completes. Overcoming this performance bottleneck involves reducing the lockout duration of residual computations. One approach is to use multi-invariant data structures to define *safe points* at which methods can *early exit* to service incoming calls [7]. For example, the re-balancing code for a BST can be abandoned at points where the representation invariant holds. In this paper, we propose a reuse-oriented alternative to new constructs like **Early-Exit** which minimizes residual computations by layering new **Early-Reply** components on an efficient substrate of existing **Early-Reply** components.

6   Minimizing Residual Computations

Early-Reply improvements in response time are a big win if a component is frequently idle, but long residual computations can negate the potential payoff. Recall the **Early-Reply** implementation of **Set** in Figure 8. An idle instance of this **Set** can **Early-Reply** to an **Add(x)** invocation in constant time, but will remain locked during its $O(log\ n)$ residual computation for inserting x into the BST. This is great if the client does not invoke another method on the **Set** during this time. The response time of invocations during the lockout period, however, can degrade to that of ordinary blocking components. This performance pattern is illustrated by an intensive calling sequence in Figure 10.

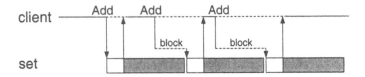

Fig. 10. Early-Reply Set with long residual computations

The key insight of this section is that the residual computation of a method can be reduced by offloading work to one or more subordinate Early-Reply components. When the internals of a component exhibit a high degree of independence, this goal can be accomplished without introducing novel stratagems. Sets, symbol tables, and databases are exemplary case studies in this respect. This section illustrates how *hashing* can be used as as a standard technique for reducing the residual computations for such components.

Consider a hashing implementation of Set represented using an array of subordinate Set instances. For clarity, we refer to this implementation as Hash-Set to distinguish it from the BST-Set implementation presented in Section 4. Hash-Set has two parameters: Item (which is the type of entry in the Set), and Base-Set (which is an arbitrary implementation of Set). A representation for this implementation contains a single member variable, denoted by self.table, which is of type Array of Base-Set. The hash table self.table represents the abstract Set as a string of subordinate Base-Set instances. This is a key feature to reducing the residual computations of the client-level Set methods. The Base-Set instances in each hash bucket are independent, so residual computations in multiple buckets can execute concurrently in addition to overlapping with subsequent invocations to the client-level Set. The representation invariant and abstraction function for Hash-Set are shown in Figure 11.

Hash-Set is also an Early-Reply implementation of the abstract component Set. The material computation of Add in Figure 12 simply creates a local variable y of type Item, swaps it with the formal parameter x, and then returns control to the client using Early-Reply. This can be accomplished in constant time. The Hash operation in the residual computation applies the hash function to its argument, and returns an integer-valued index into self.table corresponding to the appropriate bucket. Good hash functions are independent of the number of elements in the Set, and can often be computed in constant time. Thus, the primary determinant of the length of the residual computation of Add depends

---

Representation Invariant: The Base-Set instances in each bucket of the hash table are pairwise disjoint.

Abstraction Function: The abstract model of the Set is the union over all Base-Set instances in the hash table.

Fig. 11. Representation Invariant and Abstraction Function for Hash-Set

```
op Add (Item x)
begin
        var Item y;
        y :=: x;
        Early-Reply;
        var int i := Hash(y);
        self.table.i.Add(y);
end
```

Fig. 12. Implementation of Add in Hash-Set

on the duration of the lower-level invocation to Add on the Base-Set instance in the appropriate hash bucket.

At this point, it should be clear that we can reduce the lockout time associated with the *residual computation* of Add on the client-level component by reducing the *response time* of Add on the lower-level Base-Set component. Recall that Hash-Set is parameterized by Base-Set, which is an arbitrary implementation of Set to be selected at component-integration time. The only requirement on a component selected for Base-Set is that it implements the Set component specification. Now suppose we select the Early-Reply component BST-Set as our implementation, and use it to instantiate Hash-Set to get a new implementation ER-Set = Hash-Set<BST-Set>. In the material computation of the client-level ER-Set, the Add operation simply swaps the input parameter into a local variable, say y, and then returns control to the client via Early-Reply. During the residual computation, y is hashed to the correct bucket, and Add (y) is called on the corresponding BST-Set. Since the material computation of this secondary Add is also constant-time for an idle BST-Set (see Section 4), the residual computation of the client-level ER-Set is effectively minimized.

Figure 13 illustrates a possible trace of intensive client-calling on an ER-Set component. Given the nature of good hashing functions, the odds of having consecutive Add operations hash to the same bucket are statistically low. Thus, an idle ER-Set can Early-Reply in constant time, and – with high probability – complete its residual computation in constant time as well. By layering Early-Reply components using hashing, we have optimized the common case that enables an

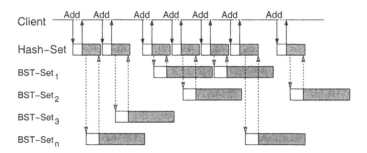

Fig. 13. Execution of ER-Set = Hash-Set<BST-Set>

ER-Set to minimize its residual computation, thereby decreasing the likelihood that subsequent client invocations will block.

The implementation of ER-Set is similar in mechanism to explicitly multi-threaded implementations that delegate client invocations to forking bucket updates. The primary advantage of our approach is that Early-Reply components encapsulate design choices about component concurrency and synchronization. In particular, the Set instances in each bucket support a synchronous *view* of component interaction. This insulates the hashing layer from having to reason about aspects of concurrency control or explicit thread management. A wider observation is that Early-Reply components are responsible for managing their own synchronization via local locking. This allows individual Early-Reply components to be incrementally deployed and integrated into existing or developing software projects without the need for system-wide synchronization support.

7 Lightweight Early-Reply Wrappers

In the previous section, we showed how the response time of an Early-Reply component could be improved by layering it on other Early-Reply components. In the absence of such components, however, what can one do? We address this question by presenting a lightweight, non-invasive technique for transforming some off-the-shelf, blocking components into Early-Reply components.

Consider an off-the-shelf blocking implementation of Set called Blocking-Set. One can transform this component into an Early-Reply component by using it to instantiate the parameterized Hash-Set wrapper presented in Section 6. Note that the resulting component Light-Set = Hash-Set<Blocking-Set> is now an Early-Reply implementation of Set with respect to the Add operation. When an Add(x) operation is invoked, the Hash-Set wrapper swaps the formal parameter with a local variable and then returns control to the caller with Early-Reply. Thereafter, the actual update can be delegated to the encapsulated Blocking-Set instance in the appropriate hash bucket.

The response time of the Add operation is now $O(1)$ for an idle Light-Set component, but it still suffers from the same problem that we identified with the BST-Set in Section 4; namely, the response time is $O(1)$ only under the condition that the client does not invoke subsequent operations on the Light-Set instance during its residual computation. Since the problem with Light-Set and BST-Set is the same, we can reuse the Hash-Set wrapper to minimize residual computations as we did in Section 6. Using Light-Set as the parameter to Hash-Set yields a new implementation Reuse-Set = Hash-Set<Light-Set> that is an Early-Reply component with minimized residual computations like the ER-Set from Section 6!

The foregoing wrapper technique is a reuse-oriented approach to transforming off-the-shelf blocking components into Early-Reply components. But when can this technique be applied? Methods that either *consume* or *preserve* their formal parameters can be directly recast as Early-Reply implementations using the wrapper approach. Since a layered-wrapper implementation uses the underlying implementation to service its clients, blocking implementations of methods that *produce* results are more difficult to transform into Early-Reply implementations. For some methods that produce their final parameter values, however, Early-Reply can be exploited to *prefetch* results that are not functionally dependent on input parameter values. This is accomplished by executing the material computation of a future invocation as part of the residual computation of the current invocation. For further applications and illustrations of Early-Reply, we refer the interested reader to our technical report [10].

8   Related Work

Our work relates to research in the area of active objects, where each object in the system has its own thread of control. The post-processing section of methods in the language POOL [1] bears closest resemblance to our notion of residual computations. In POOL, all objects are active, and therefore execute on their own thread. An object executes its *body* upon creation until it receives a method invocation in the form of a message from another object. The method computes the results (if any), returns them to the caller, and then proceeds with its post-processing section while the caller continues execution.

Several people have worked on introducing concurrency into object-oriented systems. Most of this work is in the form of active object extensions to current OO languages [11, 2]. These languages allow a method to return control to the client before the method actually completes execution. When the client later tries to access any of the formal parameters that were passed to the method, it is forced to block at that time. This is called *wait-by-necessity* [2] and the only synchronization used is *data-driven synchronization*.

Early-Reply is also related to amortized algorithms. Recall the implementation of the Length operation for Stack in Section 2. A naïve implementation of Length would count the number of items in the Stack upon each invocation. Instead, Push and Pop can be implemented to increment or decrement a local data member self.len to record the current length. This amortizes the net cost of Length over other Stack operations, so the response time of Length can be constant-time. The spirit of Early-Reply is similar, except that it amortizes the cost of an operation over calls to *different* components, rather than over calls to the *same* component.

Our research also relates to work on prefetching or precomputing results in anticipation of future method invocations [9]. One example of this would be a pseudo-random number generator. When a client requests the next number, the method can return a number, and then precompute the next number, so that it is available on demand for the next invocation. With Early-Reply, prefetching can be incorporated into the residual computation of previous invocations, thereby minimizing the material computation of future invocations. Another application of prefetching is in the tokenization phase of a compiler. The residual computation of a Get_Token method could prefetch and buffer subsequent tokens until the next invocation arrives. In general, prefetching can be applied to any method that produces a result that can be computed deterministically, independent of the input parameters and the method calling sequence.

Finally, a related approach to improving the efficiency of component operations is by incremental computation. The underlying idea is to transform programs so that an operation uses information from a previous run to compute future results [5]. When called repeatedly, such an operation performs better than a regular implementation since the entire operation is not executed every time; instead, results from a previous invocation are reused.

sectionConclusion

Component-based development is a cornerstone of scalable systems. Despite the benefits of componentry (both realized and promised), generic software suffers from a reputation for being inefficient. Among the cited benefits we include modular reasoning about components, abstractions, and their composition mechanisms. An acknowledged drawback, however, is the calling overhead associated with crossing the encapsulation barrier to interact with systems of components in layered or hierarchical compositions. Although procedure-calling overhead is rightfully a cost of information hiding, we believe that it may best be viewed as an *opportunity cost* for exploiting abstractions.

This paper has presented research directed at improving the performance of component-based software by exploiting the abstraction of a synchronous calling model. We have presented Early-Reply as a construct for introducing concurrency into synchronously-viewed systems by decoupling the flow of data to the caller from the flow of control within a component method. When components are designed to encapsulate design decisions about their data and implementation, Early-Reply can offload residual method computations to execute in parallel with subsequent client activities. In addition to reducing the response time of idle components, Early-Reply can be used in layered component implementations to increase resource utilization and reduce overall time complexity. We have also shown how lightweight, parameterized wrappers can be used to transform some off-the-shelf blocking components into efficient Early-Reply components.

Early-Reply leverages the performance benefits of encapsulated concurrency without compromising the sequential reasoning benefits of synchronous calls. To support this view, Early-Reply components lock themselves during their residual computations; this defers invocations that could otherwise compromise design-by-contract. In contrast to data-driven synchronization schemes which require system-wide support for deployment, Early-Reply components also encapsulate responsibility for their own synchronization via local locking. This aspect is critical to knowledge-transfer and reuse, because Early-Reply components can be incrementally deployed into both existing and developing systems.

Early-Reply presents many exciting avenues for future research including:

- Formal semantics and proof rules for Early-Reply.
- Formal characterization of material and residual computations.
- Performance analysis of actual speedup using Early-Reply components.
- Applications of Early-Reply to problems in distributed computing.
- Using Early-Reply to encapsulate intrinsically concurrent problems.
- Generalizing Early-Reply in the context of caller-callee synchronization.

Acknowledgments

We wish to thank the anonymous reviewers whose insightful comments greatly improved this paper. Also, we gratefully acknowledge financial support from the National Science Foundation under grant CCR-0081596, and from Lucent Technologies. Any opinions, findings, and conclusions or recommendations expressed in this paper are those of the authors and do not necessarily reflect the views of the National Science Foundation or Lucent.

References

1. P. America. POOL–T: A parallel object–oriented language. In A. Yonezawa and M. Tokoro, editors, *Object Oriented Concurrent Programming*, pages 199 – 220. MIT Press, 1987.
2. D. Caromel. Toward a method of object-oriented concurrent programming. *Communications of the ACM*, 36(9):90–102, 1993.
3. T. H. Cormen, C. E. Leiserson, and R. L. Rivest. *Introduction to Algorithms*. M.I.T. Press, Cambridge, Massachusetts, U.S.A., 1990.
4. D. E. Harms and B. W. Weide. Copying and swapping: Influences on the design of reusable software components. *IEEE Trans. Soft. Eng.*, 17(5):424–435, May 1991.
5. Y. A. Liu. *Incremental Computation: A SemanticsBased Systematic Transformation Approach*. PhD thesis, Dept. of Computer Science, Cornell University, 1996.
6. B. Meyer. Applying design by contract. *IEEE Computer (Special Issue on Inheritance and Classification)*, 25(10):40–52, 1992.
7. A. Moitra, S. Iyengar, F. Bastani, and I. Yen. Multilevel data structures: models and performance. *IEEE Trans. Soft. Eng.*, 18(6):858–867, June 1988.
8. D. L. Parnas and D. P. Siewiorek. Use of the concept of transparency in the design of hierarchically structured systems. *Comm. of the ACM*, 18(7):401–408, 1975.
9. H. A. Partsch. *Specification and Transformation of Programs: A Formal Approach to Software Development*. Springer-Verlag, 1990.
10. S. M. Pike and N. Sridhar. Early Reply: A basis for pipebranching parallelism with sequential reasoning. Technical Report OSU-CISRC-10/01-TR13, Dept. of Computer and Inf. Science, Ohio State University, October 2001.
11. G. Roberts, M. Wei, and R. Winder. Harnessing parallelism with UC++. Technical Report RN/91/72, Dept. of Computer Science, University College, London, 1991.

Concepts and Guidelines of Feature Modeling for Product Line Software Engineering

Kwanwoo Lee, Kyo C. Kang, and Jaejoon Lee

Department of Computer Science and Engineering,
Pohang University of Science and Technology,
San 31 Hyoja-Dong, Pohang, 790-784, Korea
{kwlee, kck, gibman}@postech.ac.kr
http://selab.postech.ac.kr/index.html

Abstract. Product line software engineering (PLSE) is an emerging software engineering paradigm, which guides organizations toward the development of products from core assets rather than the development of products one by one from scratch. In order to develop highly reusable core assets, PLSE must have the ability to exploit commonality and manage variability among products from a domain perspective. Feature modeling is one of the most popular domain analysis techniques, which analyzes commonality and variability in a domain to develop highly reusable core assets for a product line. Various attempts have been made to extend and apply it to the development of software product lines. However, feature modeling can be difficult and time-consuming without a precise understanding of the goals of feature modeling and the aid of practical guidelines. In this paper, we clarify the concept of features and the goals of feature modeling, and provide practical guidelines for successful product line software engineering. The authors have extensively used feature modeling in several industrial product line projects and the guidelines described in this paper are based on these experiences.

1 Introduction

Product line software engineering (PLSE) is an emerging software engineering paradigm, which guides organizations toward the development of products from core assets rather than the development of products one by one from scratch. Two major activities of PLSE are core asset development (i.e., product line engineering) and product development (i.e., product engineering) using the core assets. (Details of the product line software engineering framework can be found at [1].)

The paradigm of developing core assets for application development has been called domain engineering (DE), in which emphasis is given to the identification and development of reusable assets from an application "domain" perspective. Product line software engineering is similar to domain engineering in that they both attempt to exploit commonalities to build reusable core assets. However, PLSE differs from DE in that PLSE is founded on marketing. In PLSE, a product plan that specifies target products and their features from a market analysis is the primary input. Fielding

C. Gacek (Ed.): ICSR-7, LNCS 2319, pp. 62–77, 2002.

products with features that the market demands in a timely manner and then evolving those products as the market evolves is the major driving force in the asset development in PLSE. Therefore, the scope of analysis and development in PLSE can be narrower and more focused than in DE. However, most engineering techniques used in DE can be applied in PLSE as both paradigms attempt to build flexibility and reusability into core assets.

In order to develop reusable core assets, PLSE must have an ability to exploit commonality and manage variability. Although we build core assets for a product line, we must construct them with an understanding of the domain, which provides a wider engineering perspective for reusability and adaptability than a product line. Suppose, for example, a company manufactures freight elevators which aim at the factory market segment. Even if the immediate goal of product line engineering is to develop core assets for a set of freight elevators in the marketing plan, an understanding of the elevator domain, which may include passenger elevators, can improve the flexibility of core assets for future evolution. Therefore, domain analysis, which identifies commonality and variability from a domain perspective, is a key requirement for reusable core asset development for product lines.

Since Draco [2] was developed by Neighbors twenty yeas ago, various domain analysis techniques [2], [3], [4], [5], [6], [7], [8] have been proposed and developed. Neighbors coined the term "domain analysis" and defined it as the activity of identifying objects and operations of a class of similar systems in a particular problem domain. Many have attempted to develop domain analysis techniques, including Prieto-Diaz et al. at the Software Productivity Consortium and Kang et al. at the Software Engineering Institute. The work by Prieto-Diaz et al. is characterized as "faceted classification" [4], which originated from library science and was extended to implement a reusable software library. The primary focus of the work by Kang et al. was to establish feature oriented domain analysis (FODA) [3], which identifies and classifies commonalities and differences in a domain in terms of "product features." Feature analysis results are then used to develop reusable assets for the development of multiple products in the domain. Since the idea of feature analysis was first introduced in 1990, FODA has been used extensively for DE and PLSE both in industry (e.g., Italia Telecom [19], Northern Telecom [9], Hewlett Packard Company [11], [22], Robert Bosch GmbH [21], etc.) and academia (e.g., Software Engineering Institute [17], [18], Technical University of Ilmenau [16], Pohang University of Science and Technology [13], [14], [15], etc.).

Several attempts have also been made to extend FODA. For example, ODM (Organization Domain Modeling) [10] builds on both the faceted classification approach and FODA, generalizes the notion of "feature", and provides comprehensive guidelines for domain modeling. The main focus of ODM lies in defining a core domain modeling process that is independent of a specific modeling representation. FeatuRSEB [11] extended RSEB (Reuse-Driven Software Engineering Business) [12], which is a reuse and object-oriented software engineering method based on the UML notations, with the feature model of FODA. The feature model of FeatuRSEB is used as a catalogue of or index to the commonality and variability captured in the RSEB models (e.g., use case and object models). The authors have also extended the original FODA to address the issues of reference architecture development [13], object-oriented component engineering [14], and product line software engineering [15]. Recently, Czarnecki et al. developed DEMRAL [16], which is a domain engineering method for developing algorithmic libraries. A fundamental aspect of DEMRAL is feature modeling, which is used to derive implementation components for a product line and configure components in a product line.

All such feature-oriented methods are still evolving and being applied to various application domains. Some examples are listed below:

- The Army Movement Control Domain [17]
- The Automated Prompt Response System Domain [18]
- The Electronic Bulletin Board Systems Domain [13]
- The Telephony Domain [19]
- The Private Branch Exchange Systems Domain [20]
- The Car Periphery Supervision Domain [21]
- The Elevator Control Software Domain [14, 15]
- The E-Commerce Agents Systems Domain [22]
- The Algorithmic Library Domain [16]

There are several reasons why feature-oriented domain analysis has been used extensively compared to other domain analysis techniques. The first reason is that feature is an effective communication "medium" among different stakeholders. It is often the case that customers and engineers speak of product characteristics in terms of "features the product has and/or delivers." They communicate requirements or functions in terms of features, and such features are distinctively identifiable functional abstractions to be implemented, tested, delivered, and maintained. We believe that features are essential abstractions that both customers and developers understand, and should be first class objects in software development. The second reason is that feature-oriented domain analysis is an effective way to identify variability (and commonality) among different products in a domain. It is natural and intuitive to express variability in terms of features. When we say "the features of a specific product," we use the term "features" as distinctive characteristics or properties of a product that differ from others or from earlier versions (i.e. new features). The last reason is that the feature model can provide a basis for developing, parameterizing, and configuring various reusable assets (e.g., domain requirement models, reference architectural models, and reusable code components). In other words, the model plays a central role, not only in the development of the reusable assets, but also in the management and configuration of multiple products in a domain.

Feature modeling is considered a prerequisite for PLSE, and it is gaining popularity among practitioners and researchers. However, most users of feature modeling have difficulty in applying it to product line engineering. This difficulty comes from the imprecise understanding of feature models and the lack of practical guidelines for modeling. Thus, in this paper, we strive to clarify what feature model is and how it is used, and provide practical guidelines for the successful PLSE. The authors have extensively used feature modeling in several industrial problems and the guidelines in this paper are based on these experiences.

2   What Is Feature?

Informally, features are key distinctive characteristics of a product. We see different domain analysis methods use the term "feature" with slightly different meanings. FODA defines a feature as a prominent and distinctive user visible characteristic of a system. Several methods [11, 13] have been developed and extended based on this definition. ODM generalized the definition in FODA and defined it as a distinguishable characteristic of a "concept" (e.g., artifact, area of knowledge, etc.) that is relevant to some stakeholders (e.g., analysts, designers, and developers) [10]. Unlike FODA, ODM focuses on modeling key concepts that represent semantics of a domain. Based on the concepts, features are modeled as differentiators of concepts or multiple instances of a concept in the domain. DEMRAL [16] and Capture [5] follow the notion of feature in ODM.

Our notion of feature follows the FODA definition. Features are any prominent and distinctive concepts or characteristics that are visible to various stakeholders. Unlike ODM, we do not explicitly distinguish a concept from a feature. This is because the distinction between a concept and a feature is often unclear in certain situations. Consider a simple example of an elevator domain. Indicating the position of an elevator cage is a key operational concept in an elevator domain. Most elevators indicate their positions through lanterns while others use voice indication systems. In this example, it seems natural to model *lantern* and *voice* as presentation features of the operational concept (i.e., indicating a cage's position). However, if we become interested in lighting devices, the lantern can be modeled as a concept. Therefore, too much emphasis on the distinction between a concept and a feature may impose a burden on domain analysts. It is important to note that the focus of feature modeling should be laid in identifying commonality and variability in a domain rather than differentiating concepts from features. On the other hand, the fuzzy nature of feature makes it difficult to formalize its precise semantic, validate results, and provide automated support [23].

What are the differences between a feature and other conceptual abstractions (i.e., function, object, and aspect)? Functions, objects, and aspects have been mainly used to specify the internal details of a system. Structured methods specify internal details of a system in terms of functions, which represent procedural abstractions; object-oriented methods specify the structure and behavior of a system in terms of objects, which are uniquely identifiable key abstractions or entities. Recently, Aspect-Oriented Programming (AOP) postulates other abstractions crosscutting the boundary of modular units (e.g., functions and objects). AOP defines these crosscutting abstractions as *aspects* and specifies them separately from other modular units (e.g., objects). In other words, functions, objects, and aspects are conceptual abstractions that are identifiable from internal viewpoints. On the other hand, features are externally visible characteristics that can differentiate one product from the others.

Therefore, feature modeling must focus on identifying external visible characteristics of products in terms of commonality and variability, rather than describing all details of products such as other modeling techniques (e.g., functional modeling, object-oriented modeling, etc.). From the understanding of commonality and variability of products, we can derive functions, objects, aspects, etc. in a reusable form.

3   Feature Modeling Overview

Feature modeling is the activity of identifying externally visible characteristics of products in a domain and organizing them into a model called a feature model. The feature modeling described in this section is based on that of FORM [13].

Product features are identified and classified in terms of capabilities, domain technologies, implementation techniques, and operating environments. Capabilities are user visible characteristics that can be identified as distinct services (e.g., call forwarding in the telephony domain), operations (e.g., dialing in the telephony domain), and non-functional characteristics (e.g., performance). Domain technologies (e.g., navigation methods in the avionics domain) represent the way of implementing services or operations. Implementation techniques (e.g., synchronization mechanisms) are generic functions or techniques that are used to implement services, operations, and domain functions. Operating environments (e.g., operating systems) represents environments in which applications are used.

Common features among different products are modeled as mandatory features, while different features among them may be optional or alternative. Optional features represent selectable features for products of a given domain and alternative features indicate that no more than one feature can be selected for a product.

A feature diagram, a graphical AND/OR hierarchy of features, captures structural or conceptual relationships among features. Three types of relationships are represented in this diagram. The *composed-of* relationship is used if there is a whole-part relationship between a feature and its sub-features. In cases where features are generalization of sub-features, they are organized using the *generalization/specialization* relationship. The *implemented-by* relationship is used when a feature (i.e., a feature of an implementation technique) is necessary to implement the other feature.

Composition rules supplement the feature model with mutual dependency and mutual exclusion relationships which are used to constrain the selection from optional or alternative features. That is, it is possible to specify which features should be selected along with a designated one and which features should not.

Consider the Private Branch Exchange (PBX) systems domain as an example of feature modeling. PBX is a telephone system that switches calls between users within a small area, such as a hotel, an office building, or a hospital. Such switching is the primary service of PBX. In addition, it provides many supplementary services such as 'call forwarding' and 'call back'.

Fig. 1 shows a simplified feature model of PBX. Capability features of PBX consist of service features (e.g., *Call Request*, *Call Forwarding*, and *Call Answer*), operation features (e.g., *Tone Operation*, *LCD Control*, *Dial*, etc.), and a non-functional feature (e.g., *BHCA*[1]). Operating environment features of PBX are *Single Line, Multifunction,* and *ISDN,* each of which represents a different type of telephone terminal.

Domain technology features represent the way of implementing services or operations. In the PBX domain, *Digit Analysis* [2]and *Switching Method* [3]are used to implement services of PBX. Compared to domain technology features, implementation technique features are more generic and might be applicable to other domains. In this example, the *Search Algorithm* feature is used to implement a domain method (i.e., Digit Analysis), but this can be used in other domains (e.g., a graph library domain).

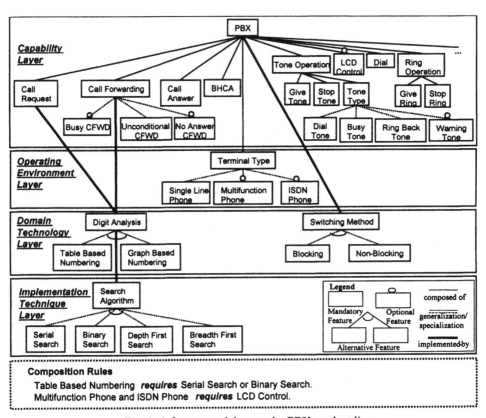

Fig. 1. A feature model example: PBX product line

All products in the PBX domain have common services such as *Call Request, Call Forwarding,* and *Call Answer,* which are modeled as mandatory features. On the other hand, services such as *Busy CFWD, No Answer CFWD,* and *Warning Tone* may not exist in a certain product, so they are modeled as optional features. Since only one of

---

[1] BHCA (Busy Hour Call Attempt) indicates the number of call attempts that PBX can handle for an hour.

[2] Digit Analysis is a method for analyzing digits of a requested call to determine its destination.

[3] Switching Method indicates the way of connecting a caller to a callee.

the two digit analysis methods (e.g., *Table Based Numbering* and *Graph Based Numbering*) can be used for a product, the features are modeled as alternative features.

The *PBX* feature consists of service, operation, and operating environment features, so they are organized with the *PBX* feature through the *composed-of* relationship. However, since *Digit Analysis* is used to implement *Call Request* and *Call Forwarding*, the *implemented-by* relationship is used among them. *Busy CFWD*, *Unconditional CFWD*, and *No Answer CFWD* are specializations of *Call Forwarding*, so they are organized according to the generalization/specialization relationship. The composition rules further constrain feature selection. For example, the lower portion of Fig. 1 shows that the *Table Based Numbering* feature must be selected along with the *Serial Search* or *Binary Search* feature, and *Multifunction Phone* and *ISDN Phone* must be selected with *LCD Control*.

4   Guidelines for Feature Modeling

Understanding commonality and variability from a domain perspective is essential for developing reusable core assets for a product line. Feature modeling is an effective and efficient method for identifying and organizing commonality and variability from a domain perspective.

At first glance, feature modeling seems to be intuitive. However, it is difficult to build a good feature model, which makes it easy to understand the problem domain in terms of commonality and variability and assists the development of reusable assets. We believe that the guidelines described in this paper will be helpful for those who are novices in domain analysis, especially feature analysis. We have applied feature modeling in several industrial cases and the following guidelines have been developed based on our work.

4.1   Domain Planning Guidelines

Domain planning is a preliminary phase to complete before starting feature modeling. This consists of activities for selecting a domain, clarifying the boundary of the selected domain, organizing a domain analysis team, and making a domain dictionary.

Domain Selection. The first step for domain planning is to determine the right domain (i.e., a set of products) that leads to successful product line engineering.

- *For organizations that do not have any domain engineering experience, we recommend that a domain be selected that is small and has a high level of commonality among the products.* Domain engineering, in general, requires a large initial investment and a long development time compared to single product development. Selecting a reasonable size for a domain with much commonality among products is the first step toward the economical and successful product line software engineering. After learning and exploring with the first domain, organizations should consider adding more and more product lines to the domain.

- *Exclude products with fixed delivery schedules from a domain.* In case a domain includes products with fixed delivery schedules, the manager will assign a higher priority to the development of the products instead of performing a detailed domain analysis as the time to deliver the products draws near. So products with fixed delivery schedules must be excluded from a target domain for successful feature modeling.

Domain Scoping. Once a right domain is selected, domain analysts should determine the boundary of a domain and relationships between the domain elements and other entities outside the domain, and should share information with each other. Without the consensus of the domain boundary, time-consuming discussions among domain modelers are unavoidable.

- *If there is a high degree of contextual differences, the domain may need to be re-scoped to a narrower domain.* Understanding of the extent of contextual differences (e.g., differences in underlying hardware) will help to re-scope the domain. For example, an elevator domain has *parking building* and *freight* elevator product lines. The variations in the underlying hardware (e.g., different types of devices) between them are high. This makes it very difficult to abstract out common hardware abstractions. In this case the domain must be re-scoped to a narrower domain, which includes only one of *parking building* and *freight* elevator product lines. Thus, the re-scoped domain is much easier to build common hardware interface components, which can handle different types of devices without major modification.

A Domain Analyst Team Organization. The purpose of domain modeling is to capture common and different concepts or characteristics in system development. Therefore, different stakeholders must be included in the domain analyst team. Different viewpoints from different stakeholders can be helpful for identifying important domain concepts or capabilities. For example, end-users help domain analysts identify services or functions provided by the products in a domain; domain experts might be helpful for identifying domain technologies (e.g., navigation methods in the avionics domain) that are commonly used in a domain; and developers provides generic implementation techniques.

- *Experts in different product lines of the same domain should be involved in a domain analysis activity.* No single individual has sufficient experience concerning all product-lines within the same domain. Domain experts from different product lines can provide a wider engineering perspective for reusability and adaptability. Therefore, in order to build highly reusable core assets, domain analysis must be performed with many domain experts from different product lines.

A Domain Dictionary. After organizing a domain analysis team, the last activity for domain planning is to prepare a domain dictionary for feature modeling.

- *In an immature or emerging domain, standardize domain terminology and build a domain dictionary.* In an immature or emerging domain, different terminologies with the same meaning may be used for different product lines. Standardizing domain terminologies is an essential activity in preparation for feature modeling.

If not done, different perceptions of domain concepts could cause confusion among participants in modeling activities and lead to time-consuming discussions. Domain planning is an important first step toward successful feature modeling. Without understanding the exact scope of the domain, the intended use of domain products, various external conditions, and common domain vocabularies, feature identification can be very difficult. Even the identified features may be useless. The next section describes the guidelines for feature identification.

4.2   Feature Identification Guidelines

Identification of features involves abstracting domain knowledge obtained from the domain experts and other documents such as books, user manuals, design documents, and source programs. The volume of documents to be analyzed, however, tends to be enormous in a domain of any reasonable size. In this context, the following guideline is useful.

–   *Analyze terminologies used in the product line to identify features*. We often see that domain experts in mature or stable domains use standard terms to communicate their idea, needs, and problems. For example, 'call-forwarding' and 'call-back' represent standard services in the telephony domain. Using standard terms for the feature identification can expedite communication between domain analysts and information providers (e.g., domain experts and end-users). Our experience has shown that analyzing standard terminologies is an efficient and effective way to identify features.

In our method, we provide feature categories, shown in Fig. 2, as a feature identification framework. The feature categories may be incomplete and not cover the entire domain knowledge space, but we are confident that these categories are the first applicable guidelines for identifying product features.

As discussed earlier, capability features are characterized as distinct services, operations, or non-functional aspects of products in a domain. Services are end-user visible functionality of products offered to their users in order to satisfy their requirements. They are often considered as marketable units or units of increment in a product line. Operations are internal functions of products that are needed to provide services. Non-functional features include end-user visible application characteristics that cannot be identified in terms of services or operations, such as presentation, capacity, quality attribute, usage, cost, etc.

There may be several ways to implement services or operations. Domain technology features are domain specific technologies that domain analysts or architects use to model specific problems in a domain or to "implement" service or operation features. Domain-specific theories and methods, analysis patterns, and standards and recommendations are examples. Note that these features are specific to a given domain and may not be useful in other domains.

Implementation technique features are more generic than domain technology features and may be used in different domains. They contain key design or implementation decisions that may be used to implement other features (i.e., capability and domain technology features). Communication methods, design patterns, architectural styles, ADTs, and synchronization methods are examples of implementation techniques.

Applications may run in different operating environments. They may run on different hardware or operating systems, or interface with different types of devices or external systems. Operating environment features include product line contexts, such as computing environments and interfaces with different types of devices and external systems. Protocols used to communicate with external systems are also classified as environment features.

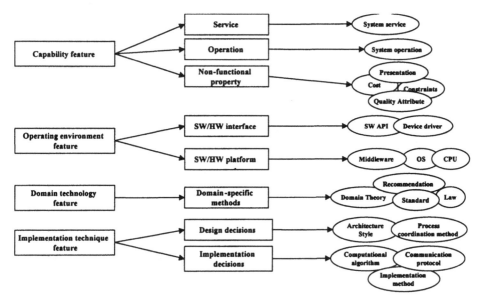

Fig. 2. Feature categories

Although the above feature categories are useful guidelines for identifying features, many people often make common mistakes in identifying features. The following guidelines must always be kept in mind during feature identification activity.

- *Try to first find differences among products envisioned for a product line and then, with this understanding, identify commonalities.* Products in the same product line share a high level of commonality. Hence, the "commonality space" would be larger to work with than the "difference space." It is our experience that finding differences is much easier than finding commonalities. We recommend, first, to identify product categories (e.g., freight and passenger elevators in an elevator product line), within each of which products should have a higher level of commonality and lower variability than those in other categories. Next, list features that characterize each category, i.e., differences between categories. Then, for each category, list products and do the same thing. With this understanding, we experienced that identification of commonalities became easier and we could proceed to listing common features and modeling them effectively and efficiently.

- *Do not identify all implementation details that do not distinguish between products in a domain.* A skillful developer tends to enumerate all the implementation details and identify them as features, even though there are no variations among them. It is important to note that a feature model is not a requirement model, which expresses the details of internal functions. The modeling focus should be on identifying properties, factors, assumptions that can differentiate one product from others in the same domain, not on finding all implementation details that are necessary to implement the products in a domain.

Once candidate features are identified based on the above guidelines, these features should be organized into a feature model. The following guidelines show how to organize a set of features into a feature model that is easy to understand and helpful for the development of reusable assets.

4.3 Feature Organization Guidelines

As noted earlier, features are organized into a feature diagram in terms of *composed-of*, *generalization/specialization*, and *implemented-by* relationships. Further, composition rules are used to specify mutual inclusive and exclusive relationships between variant features (i.e., optional and alternative features) that do not have an explicit relationship in a feature diagram.

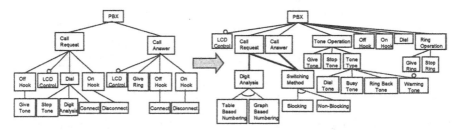

Fig. 3. A feature diagram like a functional call hierarchy

- Do not organize features to represent functional dependencies, like a function call hierarchy, but organize features to capture and represent commonalities and differences. Developers who are familiar with a structured development method often confuse a feature diagram with a functional call hierarchy. Thus they tend to identify all functions of products as features and organize them similar to a functional call hierarchy. However, features should be organized so that commonalities and variabilities can be recognized easily rather than representing interactions among features, like a function call hierarchy. For example, the left feature diagram of Fig. 3 merely enumerates all operations related to Call Request and Call Answer and organizes them like a functional call hierarchy. However, the right feature diagram of Fig. 3 shows common services (e.g., Call Request), operations (e.g., Tone Operation), and domain technologies (e.g., Switching Method) and explains how they are differentiated among products in a domain. For instance, Connect and Disconnect in the left feature diagram are grouped into a common domain method, i.e., Switching Method, which is further refined into Blocking and Non-Blocking to express variability in a domain.

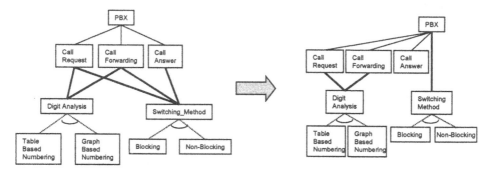

Fig. 4. An example of reducing complexity of a feature model

- *If many upper-level features are associated with a lower-level feature through the implemented-by relationship, reduce complexity of the feature model by associating the lower-level feature with the nearest common parent of its related upper-level features.* When upper-level features in a feature diagram are associated with several lower-level features through the implementation-by relationship, their implementation relationships between those features may be very complex. For example, the left feature diagram in Fig. 4 shows complex relationships between three service features (i.e., *Call Request, Call Forwarding,* and *Call Answer*) and two domain technology features (i.e., *Digit Analysis* and *Switching Method*). Since the primary concern of feature modeling is to represent commonality and variability in a domain rather than to model implementation relationships between features, complex relationships can be reduced by associating the lower-level feature with the nearest common parent of its related upper-level features. In this example, complexity is reduced by associating the *Switching Method* with *PBX*, which is the nearest common parent of its related service features (i.e., *Call Request, Call Forwarding,* and *Call Answer*). (See the right feature model in Fig. 4.)

4.4   Feature Refinement Guidelines

The feature model should be reviewed with domain experts who did not participate in the feature identification activity and with domain products, such as manual, programs, design documents, systems, etc. During the reviewing process, if necessary, a set of feature may be added, deleted, or refined.

- *Refine the feature model so that the logical boundary created by a feature model can correspond to the physical boundary created by its architecture models.* Product-line software should be adaptable for a set of features selected for a specific application. By designing each selectable feature as a separate component, applications can be derived easily from product-line software. If there is difficulty in establishing this relation, the feature must be refined into specific features so that features can be easily mapped into architectural components. This will enhance the traceability between architectural components and features. For example, the *Motor Control* feature was originally allocated to a single subsystem, *MotorControlSubsystem*. However, a certain type of elevator products (e.g., high-speed passenger elevators) requires a precise position control within its timing requirement. Thus we had to allocate sub-functions (i.e., position control) of the *Motor Control* feature into the different subsystem to satisfy the timing requirement. To enhance the traceability between architectural components and their features, we refined the *Motor Control* feature into *Position Control* and *Moving Control* features, as shown in Fig. 5.

- *Refine an abstract feature until no variations are exposed among products in a domain.* A feature need not be further refined into sub features if there are no variations among different products. However, although no variation exists in a feature among different products of a domain, if its refined sub features are associated with other features in the upper level, they may be refined further. For example, in the elevator control software domain [14], [15], the *Weight Detection Method* is an abstract domain method that is necessary to implement various operations (e.g., *Motor Control, Call Handling*, etc.). However, this feature is used somewhat differently according to different high-level features, for example, *Motor Control* mainly uses *Automatic Weight Detection* and *Call Handling* uses *Predefined Weight Setting*, the *Weight Detection Method* can be further refined, as shown in Fig. 6.

During the refinement of features, can any differences among products in a domain be a feature? For example, if two different developers implement the same algorithm with different programming styles, can the programming styles be identified as features? If the window size of a product is somewhat different from others, can the

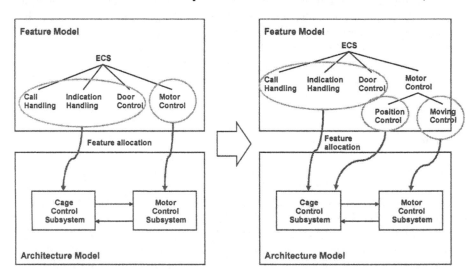

Fig. 5. An example of refinement of a feature whose sub-features are allocated into different architectural components

window size be a feature? In our view, features should be essential characteristics or properties in a domain. Therefore, if the differences are not essential in a domain, those differences can be eliminated through a standardization process. However, if they have special meanings – one programming style supports for understandability of a program and the other style for efficiency, they can be identified as features.

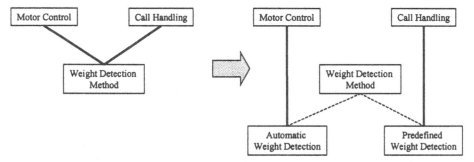

Fig. 6. An example of refinement of a common feature (e.g., Weight Detection Method)

Conclusion

We have applied our extensive experience with feature modeling to four domains, which include the electronic bulletin board systems (EBBS) [13], a private branch exchange (PBX) [20], elevator control software (ECS) [14], [15], and slab yard inventory systems domains [25]. We have found that feature modeling is intuitive, efficient, and effective for identifying commonality and variability of applications in a domain. The feature model is a good communication media among those who have different concerns in application development.

The following are lessons learned from our experience.

- An organization with a standard infrastructure (e.g., physical communication media) for its product line is usually unwilling to analyze the anticipated changes of the external environments or the implementation techniques. Engineers in such an organization tend to believe that there are few variations in terms of operating environments or implementation techniques as the products have been built on the standard of the organization. Therefore, we convinced them to analyze future changes as well as current variations, since the standard could also be changed.

- In an unstable domain, standardizing domain terminology and using the standard terms during analysis could expedite the feature identification process. Without standard terms, the team suffered greatly from time-consuming discussions on minor semantic differences between features. Therefore, analyzing the standard terminology is an effective and efficient way to identify features for the domainIn an emerging domain (e.g., a cellular phone domain), capability features, such as services or operations, change more frequently than domain technology and implementation technique features. On the other hand, in a stable domain (e.g., an elevator domain), services are nearly changed but operating environments and implementation techniques are changed more often than services.

Tool support for feature modeling is indispensable to handle hundreds of product features in a product line. We have developed a feature modeling tool, which can handle many product features (e.g., more than five hundred product features) efficiently through sub-tree expansion and hiding capabilities and check the consistency of composition rules in the feature model. It runs on any PC or workstation on which the Java development kit (JDK) software is installed for its run-time environment. The tool is available upon request via kck@postech.ac.kr.

References

1. Clements, P., Northrop, L.: Software Product Lines: Practices and Patterns, Addison-Wesley, Upper Saddle River, NJ (2002)
2. Neighbors, J.: The Draco Approach to Construction Software from Reusable Components, *IEEE Transactions on Software Engineering* SE-10, 5 (1984) 564-573
3. Kang, K., Cohen, S., Hess, J., Nowak, W., Peterson, S.: Feature-Oriented Domain Analysis (FODA) Feasibility Study, *Technical Report CMU/SEI-90-TR-21*, Pittsburgh, PA, Software Engineering Institute, Carnegie Mellon University (1990)
4. Prieto-Diaz, R.: Implementing Faceted Classification for Software Reuse, *Communications of the ACM* 34, 5 (1991) 88-97
5. Bailin, S.: Domain Analysis with KAPTUR, *Tutorials of TRI-Ada'93*, New York, NY (1993)
6. Frakes, W., Prieto-Diaz, R., Fox, C.: DARE: Domain Analysis and Reuse Environment, Annals of Software Engineering 5 (1998) 125-151
7. Coplien, J., Hoffman, D., Weiss, D.: Commonality and Variability in Software Engineering, *IEEE Software* 15, 6 (1998) 37-45
8. Weiss, D. M., Lai, C. T. R.: Software Product-Line Engineering: A Family Based Software Development Process, Addison-Wesley, Reading, MA (1999)
9. Zalman, N. S.: Making the Method Fit: An Industrial Experience in Adopting FODA, *Proc. Fourth International Conference on Software Reuse*, Los Alamitos, CA (1996) 233-235
10. Simos, M. et al, Software Technology for Adaptable Reliable Systems (STARS) Organization Domain Modeling (ODM) Guidebook Version 2.0, *STARS-VC-A025/001/00*, Manassas, VA, Lockheed Martin Tactical Defense Systems (1996)
11. Griss, M. L., Favaro, J., d'Alessandro, M.: Integrating Feature Modeling with the RSEB, *Proc. Fifth International Conference on Software Reuse*, Victoria, BC, Canada (1998) 76-85
12. Jacobson, I., Griss, M., Jonsson, P.: *Software Reuse: Architecture, Process and Organization for Business Success*, Addison-Wesley, New York (1997)
13. Kang, K., Kim, S., Lee, J., Kim, K., Shin E., Huh, M.: FORM: A Feature-Oriented Reuse Method with Domain-Specific Reference Architectures, *Annals of Software Engineering*, 5 (1998) 143-168
14. Lee, K., Kang, K., Chae, W., Choi, B.: Feature-Based Approach to Object-Oriented Engineering of Applications for Reuse, *Software-Practice and Experience* 30, 9 (2000) 1025-1046
15. Lee, K., Kang, K., Koh, E., Chae, W., Kim, B., Choi, B.: Domain-Oriented Engineering of Elevator Control Software: A Product Line Practice, In Proceedings of the First Software Product Line Conference (SPLC), August 28-31, 2000, Denver, Colorado, USA, Donohoe, P. (Eds.), *Software Product Lines: Experience and Research Directions*, Kluwer Academic Publishers, Norwell, Massachusetts (2000) 3-22

16. Czarnecki, K., Eisenecker, U., *Generative Programming: Methods, Tools, and Applications*, Addison-Wesley, New York (2000)
17. Cohen, S. G., Stanley Jr., J. L., Peterson, A. S., Krut Jr., R. W.: Application of Feature-Oriented Domain Analysis to the Army Movement Control Domain, *Technical Report, CMU/SEI-91-TR-28*, ADA 256590, Pittsburgh, PA, Software Engineering Institute, Carnegie Mellon University (1991)
18. Krut, R., Zalman, N.: Domain Analysis Workshop Report for the Automated Prompt Response System Domain, *Special Report, CMU/SEI-96-SR-001*, Pittsburgh, PA, Software Engineering Institute, Carnegie Mellon University (1996)
19. Vici, A. D., Argentieri, N.: FODAcom: An Experience with Domain Analysis in the Italian Telecom Industry, *Proc. Fifth International Conference on Software Reuse*, Victoria, BC, Canada (1998) 166-175
20. Kang, K., Kim, S., Lee, J., Lee, K.: Feature-Oriented Engineering of PBX Software for Adaptability and Reusability, *Software-Practice and Experience* 29, 10 (1999) 875-896
21. Hein, A., Schlick, M., Vinga-Martins, R.: Applying Feature Models in Industrial Settings, In Proceedings of the First Software Product Line Conference (SPLC), August 28-31, 2000, Denver, Colorado, USA, Donohoe, P. (Eds.), *Software Product Lines: Experience and Research Directions*, Kluwer Academic Publishers, Norwell, Massachusetts (2000) 47-70
22. Griss, M.: Implementing Product-Line Features by Composing Aspects, In Proceedings of the First Software Product Line Conference (SPLC), August 28-31, 2000, Denver, Colorado, USA, Patrick Donohoe (Eds.), *Software Product Lines: Experience and Research Directions*, Kluwer Academic Publishers, Norwell, Massachusetts (2000) 47-70
23. Simos, M., Anthony, J.: Weaving the Model Web: A Multi-Modeling Approach to Concepts and Features in Domain Engineering, *Proc. Fifth International Conference on Software Reuse*, Victoria, BC, Canada (1998) 166-175
24. Kiczales, G., Lamping, J., Mendheker, A., Maeda, C., Lopes, C., Loingtier, J., Irwin, J.: Aspect-Oriented Programming, In Proceedings of ECOOP'97 – Object-Oriented Programming, 11th European Conference, Jyvaskyla, Finland, June 1997, Aksit, M., Matsuoka, S. (Eds.), LNCS 1241, Springer-Verlag, Berlin and Heidelberg, Germany (1997)
25. Kang, K., Lee, K., Lee, J., Kim, S.: Feature Oriented Product Line Software Engineering: Principles and Guidelines, to appear as a chapter in *Domain Oriented Systems Development – Practices and Perspectives*, UK, Gordon Breach Science Publishers (2002)

Domain Modeling for World Wide Web Based Software Product Lines with UML

Hassan Gomaa[1] and Mark Gianturco[2]

[1] Department of Information and Software Engineering,
George Mason University, Fairfax, VA 22030-4444, U.S.A.
hgomaa@gmu.edu

[2] Strategic Information Solutions, Inc
11130 Main Street, Suite 301, Fairfax, VA 22030, U.S.A.
mdg@strategicinfo.com

Abstract. This paper describes a domain modeling approach using the Unified Modeling Language (UML) for modeling software product lines of World Wide Web (WWW) based applications, thereby permitting reuse of domain requirements and analysis models. The paper describes how the various views of the UML, in particular the use case modeling view and the static modeling view, may be used for modeling such product lines and illustrates this with a domain modeling exercise. It also describes how the feature model can be integrated with the UML for modeling product lines.

1. Introduction

The Unified Modeling Language (UML) has emerged as the standard approach for modeling object-oriented applications [2,6,14]. There has been considerable interest in applying UML and object-oriented approaches to modeling software product lines [4] as described by [1, 3, 7, 8, 9, 10] and others. This paper describes a domain modeling approach using (UML) for modeling software product lines (also referred to as software product families and families of systems) of World Wide Web (WWW) based applications. The paper describes how the various views of the UML, in particular the use case modeling view and the static modeling view, may be used for modeling such software product lines and illustrates this with a detailed domain modeling exercise. It also describes how the feature model [11], which has been used for modeling the common and variable requirements in software product lines, can be integrated with the UML.

2. Domain Modeling for Software Product Lines with UML

A Domain Model is a multiple view object-oriented analysis model for the application domain that reflects the common aspects and variations among the members of the software product line that constitute the domain. The domain modeling method [7] is

C. Gacek (Ed.): ICSR-7, LNCS 2319, pp. 78–92, 2002.

similar to other object-oriented methods when used for analyzing and modeling a single system [6]. Its novelty is the way it extends object-oriented methods to model software product lines. The method allows the explicit modeling of the similarities and variations in a software product line, and hence encourages reuse over the members of the software product line. The method uses the UML notation and is used to model software product lines as follows:

1. Requirements Modeling
   - Develop use case model for software product line
   - Develop feature model for software product line
2. Analysis Modeling
   - Develop static model for software product line
   - Develop dynamic model for software product line
   - Develop feature/class dependencies for software product line

There are two approaches for developing the domain model of the software product line [5, 7], the Kernel First Approach and the View Integration Approach. With the Kernel First Approach, the kernel of the application domain is determined first, i.e., the common aspects of the domain before the variability. With the View Integration Approach, which is most applicable when there are existing systems that can be analyzed, each system is considered a view of the application domain and the different views are integrated. This paper describes how the View Integration Approach was used to develop a domain model for a Web based software product line using the steps outlined above.

2.1 Domain Modeling for Web-Based Extended Product Lines with UML

The domain modeling exercise describes how a software development corporation, Strategic INFO, moved from a custom software development environment for building web products to a Web based software product line through systematic domain requirements and analysis modeling. The company originally sold a line of products referred to as PhysicianX, which consisted of many types of custom websites used by doctors and physician groups. The products all contain password protected administration areas to allow doctors and staff to modify website content and appearance by entering plain text and selecting from dropdown lists and buttons, as well as public or password protected web modules with encapsulated functionality. As each new product was sold, project requirements specifications were used to build it from scratch. Although there was some code reuse on new products within the PhysicianX product line, there was no systematic method for reuse. The company realized that significant reuse could be achieved by modeling the domain. The view integration approach was used to perform the domain analysis and modeling. The domain model was built by generating different views of the products in the PhysicianX product line, recognizing common elements such as features or classes, and representing those commonalities and variabilities in the domain model. As other markets were entered and new product lines emerged also based on custom website development, the company realized that these new product lines could also be integrated into the domain model for PhysicianX. These new product lines included

VetX, a custom web presence product for Veterinarians, and Health Web, containing website functionality for local health departments. The company called the new extended product line, or family of families, WebWizard. The final analysis and modeling effort performed in this exercise involved extending the WebWizard domain to support a family of families, and included the integration of the Club Central product line. The Club Central product line allows clubs to easily establish a presence on the web by automating several information and user interface functions.

3. Requirements Modeling

3.1 Use Case Model for Software Product Lines

The functional requirements of the product line are defined in terms of use cases and actors [2,10]. For a single system, all use cases are required. When modeling a software product line, only a subset of the use cases is required by any member of the product line. These use cases are referred to as kernel use cases. Optional use cases are those use cases required by some but not all members of the product line. Some use cases may be alternatives, that is different versions of the use case are required by different members of the product line. The alternative use cases are usually mutually exclusive. The UML stereotypes [2, 14] <<kernel>>, <<optional>>, and <<alternative>> are introduced to distinguish among the use cases from a product line perspective.

Using the View Integration Approach [5, 7] the use cases for each member of the product line are specified. If the use cases do not exist, then it is necessary to develop them; in effect this is a reverse engineering exercise. After developing the use cases for each member of the product line, the use cases from the different systems are compared. Common use cases to all members of the product line constitute the kernel of the application domain. Use cases that are only used by an individual system or a subset of the systems constitute the optional use cases. Situations where alternative versions of a use case are used by different members of the product line are also determined. A kernel, optional, or alternative use case may also be parameterized using variation points [10].

3.1.1 Use Case Model for Web-Based Extended Product Lines
To develop the use case model for the software product line, the PhysicianX product line was first examined. As there were already many family members produced for the PhysicianX product line, the View Integration approach was well suited to model it. An example of a functional requirement in the PhysicianX product line is the user interacting with the website to request an appointment online with a medical doctor. As this function is only required by some members of the product line, an optional use case for "Request Appointment" is added to the PhysicianX use case model. Briefly, in this use case the user fills out and submits a form to request an appointment with the health care provider.

In addition to use cases that only appear in some of the PhysicianX products, there are kernel use cases that appear in all of the PhysicianX members of the product line. An example of a kernel use case is the user interacting with the website to retrieve the list FAQs for the doctor or health group. This Show FAQs use case is a kernel use case for the PhysicianX product line.   Examples of use cases for the PhysicianX product line, including the Request Appointment and Show FAQs use cases, are shown in Fig. 1.

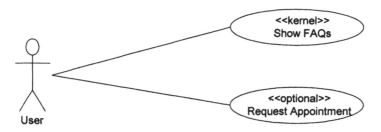

Fig. 1. Examples of PhysicianX Use Cases

3.1.2 Extending the Use Case Model to Web-Based Extended Product Lines

The next step is to integrate every other product line that already exists to create an extended product line use case model, which is called the WebWizard domain use case model. To do this, a use case model is built for every other product line using the view integration approach as described above. These use case models must then be further integrated to create the extended product line use case model. Use cases that are kernel in one product line may become optional as they become integrated into the domain use case model for the extended product line. Additionally, kernel or optional use cases may become alternative (1 and only 1 of) use cases as the domain use case model is extended. At the domain level, commonality is represented by kernel use cases that represent use cases that are present in every product for every product line in the domain. Variability can be represented in three ways: by representing optional use cases unique to a product or single product line, by parameterizing similar use cases in multiple products and/or multiple product lines, and by representing use case alternatives. As an example of this, consider the addition of the Club Central use case model to the Web Wizard model. As the analysis of the family use case model for Club Central progressed, it became apparent that there was a significant set of alternative use cases that should be developed based on whether a Club Central product was being developed versus a "health based" product (a PhysicianX, VetX or DentistryX product).   The set of "health based" product lines are referred to collectively as Health products. To model this variability with use cases, some use cases that had been previously categorized as kernel use cases are now categorized as alternative kernel use cases, based on whether the "Health" or "Club" member was being configured. A similar analysis was made concerning Club Central optional use cases, and to model the set of options that did not overlap between Club Central and the rest of the product families in the domain. These optional use cases were categorized as either "Health Options" or "Club Options" optional alternative use cases.

3.2 Feature Model for Software Product Lines

Feature analysis is an important aspect of domain analysis [3, 5, 7, 9, 11]. In domain analysis, features are analyzed and categorized as kernel features (must be supported in all target systems), optional features (only required in some target systems), and prerequisite features (dependent upon other features). There may also be dependencies among features, such as mutually exclusive features. The emphasis in feature analysis is on the optional features, since the optional features differentiate one member of the product line from the others. In modeling software product lines, features may be functional features, non-functional features, or parametric features.

Griss [9] has pointed out that the goal of the use case analysis is to get a good understanding of the functional requirements whereas the goal of feature analysis is to enable reuse. Use cases and features may be used to complement each other. In particular, use cases can be mapped to features based on their reuse properties. Functional requirements that are required by all members of the product line are packaged into a kernel feature. From a use case perspective, this means that the kernel use cases, which are required by all members of the product line, constitute the kernel feature. Optional use cases, which are always used together, may also be packaged into an optional feature.

3.2.1 Feature Model for Web-Based Extended Product Lines

For the Webwizard domain, matching a User actor initiated use case with a corresponding Administrator actor initiated use case was usually necessary to model a feature, because of the underlying functionality in every product line within the domain. For every page that is displayed to the users of the website, there is a corresponding page to manage this page, which is accessed by the site administrator. The UML package notation is used to depict use cases that are grouped into the same feature. For example, the "FAQs" feature (Fig.2) is created from the "Show FAQs" use case (involving the User actor) combined with the "Manage FAQs" use case (involving the Administrator actor). The user actor interacts with the "public" side of PhysicianX, and corresponds to patients of the doctor who visit the website to retrieve information or make requests of the doctor. The administrator actor internally maintains the website, by creating, updating and deleting relevant information for the patients to access.

After building the feature model, related features should be categorized and packaged, including packages for the kernel use cases and any optional use cases that may be appropriate. Packages may also be built to include prerequisite relationships, and 1 and only 1 of (alternative) requirements. As an example of this, the PhysicianX product line has a PhysicianX kernel use case package that includes 1 package for each of the kernel features in the PhysicianX product line (including the FAQs feature shown in Fig.2).

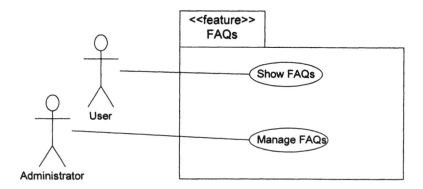

Fig. 2. FAQs feature as a Use Case Package

At this point, we have a feature model for each product line within the domain, which must be combined to produce the domain feature model (also called the extended product line feature model). The feature models that have been built for the domain may each be thought of as a separate view into the domain. We integrate the views using the view integration approach. To add the view for each family into the domain feature model, all of the common features in the view being integrated should already be represented as kernel features in the domain feature model. The product lines that are a part of the HealthBased group of product lines (PhysicianX, DentistryX, VetX, and Health Web), share most features, but have some features that are variants (as an example of this, we examine the Dr. Profile feature later in this paper).   In addition to a core set of kernel features, there are also 2 sets of kernel alternative features, which are "1 and only 1 of" selections, the "Health Kernel" feature set and the "Club Kernel" feature set. The core set of features is included in every product in every product line in WebWizard. Either the entire contents of the "Health Kernel" feature set or the entire contents of the "Club Kernel" feature set must be included in a given product of the WebWizard product line. The same feature breakout with Health or Club alternatives also occurs with feature options in the Webwizard domain, which are shown as packages in Fig.3. This figure also shows prerequisites and alternatives relationships.   Selection of the "Health Kernel" alternative package implies the exclusion of the "Club Kernel" alternative package and potential selection of one or more use cases from the "Health Options" package. It also implies exclusion of the "Club Options" alternative package.   In the case of an optional alternative feature package, any one of the optional features in the package is available for inclusion in the family member, once the corresponding kernel alternative feature package has been selected.

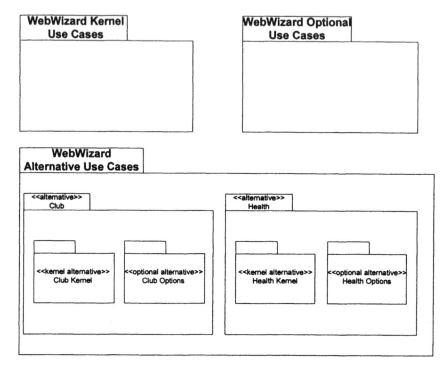

Fig. 3. Feature Package for the Extended Software Product Line

4 Develop Static Model for Software Product Lines

Static modeling for the domain involves modeling classes and their relationships on class diagrams. In addition to modeling associations between classes, this involves modeling the Aggregation Hierarchy and the Generalization / Specialization hierarchies [5, 7] used in domain models for software product lines. A static model for an application domain has kernel classes, which are used by all members of the product line, and optional classes that are used by some but not all members of the product line. Variants of a class, which are used by different members of the product line, can be modeled using a generalization / specialization hierarchy. The UML stereotypes [2, 14] <<kernel>>, <<optional>>, and <<variant>> are used to distinguish between kernel, optional, and variant classes.   Additionally, the <<alternative>> stereotype is used to represent "1 and only 1 of" choices for classes in the static model.

The way the static model for the product line is developed depends on the strategy used for developing the domain model. With the View Integration Approach, a separate static model is developed for each member of the product line. Each static model is considered a separate view of the application domain. The static model for the application domain is produced by integrating the individual views. When static models for the different members (views) of the product line are integrated, classes that are common to all members of the product line become kernel classes of the integrated static model, which is referred to as the domain static model. Classes that are in one view but not others become optional classes of the domain static model. Classes that have some common aspects but also some differences are generalized. The common attributes and operations are captured in the superclass while the differences are captured in the variant subclasses of the superclass.

4.1. Static Model for Web-Based Extended Product Lines

The first step in the static modeling is to determine the classes in the product line. There are several types of classes to be identified and categorized. To generate the class model, the architect must determine the classes that must be utilized to support each feature in the domain.

Product line classes are categorized using the structuring criteria described in [6] into interface classes, entity classes, control classes, application logic classes, and external classes. The class categories used to model the Web Wizard domain and their descriptions are:

User Interface Class – Provides an interface to an application domain user. An example is the "Web Browser Interface" class, which provides the interface to the browser being used to access the domain.

System Interface Classes – Provides an interface between the system and external systems. Examples of these classes include the Database Interface class.

Coordinator Class – Coordinates other classes. An example is the Design Coordinator class, which loads design elements based on stored user selections, while the Email Generation class generates and routes email based on input parameters.

State-dependent control class – Receives events that cause state transitions and generates state dependent output events. As an example, the Logon Validator class handles system security and user access control.

Algorithm Class - Contains computational algorithms used by the domain. The Image Manipulation class, which is used to handle file system image creation and deletion, is an example of this type of class.

Web Page Generator Class - Contains logic necessary to generate Web pages based on domain-specific information. An example is the Compute Appointment class, which builds and outputs a web page containing a form with user input fields for an appointment request based on several parameters.

Entity Classes – These classes contain information maintained in the domain, and include database wrapper objects, data abstraction classes, database tables, or other classes that encapsulate data. The EmailFormsInfo class and ContactInfo class are entity classes that support the appointment request feature.

4.2. Aggregation Hierarchy for Web-Based Extended Product Lines

To develop the aggregation hierarchy for the WebWizard domain, a hierarchy must be developed for each product line or group of product lines in the domain, and then the hierarchies must be integrated. As previously explained, the two main product lines in the WebWizard domain are health product lines and club product lines. Therefore, an aggregation hierarchy is built for each of these product lines. This is done in stages using the view integration approach, by first building an aggregation hierarchy for representative products within the individual product lines, then aggregating them into a hierarchy for the Health Web product line and a hierarchy for the Club Central product line, and then integrating these two product lines into an extended product line. Fig. 4 shows the aggregation hierarchy for the Health Web product line.

It should be pointed out that the Aggregation Hierarchy (AH) is an orthogonal product line view to the feature view and relates to the architectural design of the application. The AH is organized based on the class structuring criteria described in the previous section and on grouping related classes into aggregate classes. Thus, an aggregate class might contain all the classes required for one Web page. However, a user interface page and an administration page are functionally distinct and therefore appear in different branches of the hierarchy. Different administration pages, which share some common functionality, are grouped into a separate Admin aggregate class. However, as pointed out in Section 3.2.1, a feature is likely to contain both the user interface page and the admin page to manage it. Thus from a feature viewpoint, classes that support using the page and classes that support administering the page are likely to be in the same feature, although in different branches of the AH.

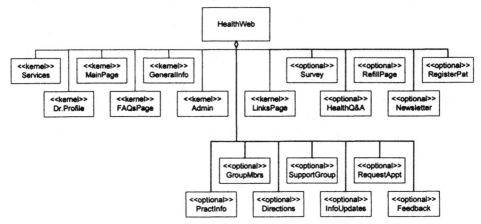

Fig. 4: Aggregation Hierarchy for Health Web Product Line

After the aggregation hierarchies have been developed for Health Web and Club Central product lines, they must be integrated into the aggregation hierarchy for the WebWizard extended product line. All kernel classes present in both product line AH are included in the extended product line AH as kernel classes. In Fig. 5, the Base Features kernel class is an aggregate class that contains the Main Page, General Info, and Links Page (from Fig.4), which are common to all members of the extended product line. All optional classes present in both product line AH are included as optional classes in the extended product line AH. Thus the Survey, Newsletter, and

Feedback optional classes from Fig. 4 are aggregated into the Product Opts optional aggregate class in Fig. 5. All remaining kernel classes in Health Web are aggregated as a kernel alternative class called Health Kernel, and all remaining kernel classes in Club Central are aggregated as a kernel alternative class called Club Kernel. Thus, the Services and Dr. Profile kernel classes in Fig. 4 are aggregated into the Health Kernel

The high-level aggregation for WebWizard shows classes that are aggregations of lower-level classes. At the lowest level of the hierarchy, the classes identified in the domain static modeling phase are depicted. There are two main alternatives that can be selected when using the aggregation hierarchy, corresponding to the Health Web versus the Club Central products. These alternatives are depicted by the <<kernel alternative>> and <<option alternative>> stereotypes, as well as the inclusion of the letter "A" or "B" at the bottom of the class box. If the aggregation being examined is Health Web, then all alternatives with "A" are selected. To examine a Club Central hierarchy, the "B" alternative is included.

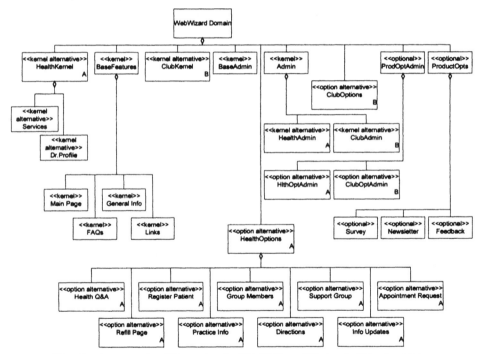

Fig. 5: Aggregation Hierarchy for WebWizard Extended Product Line

The generalization/specialization hierarchy is used to capture variations in class specifications that result from variations within the domain [6]. Consider the "Dr. Profile" class in the WebWizard domain. This class supports entering a detailed profile of a doctor in PhysicianX, a profile of a veterinarian in VetX, a profile of a health department in Health Web, and a profile of a dentist in dentistryX. Although the overall functionality is similar, there are differences that require use of the GSH, as shown in Fig. 6.

4.3 Feature/Class Dependencies Mapping for Software Product Lines

For each feature determined during feature modeling, the classes required to support it are determined during dynamic modeling [6] by considering the objects that interact with each other to support a given use case (and hence feature). The classes required to support a feature are depicted in a feature package. The Feature/Class dependency model for the domain is shown in Fig. 7. The features are organized as shown in Fig. 3 and described in Section 3.2.1. A feature set contains other features. Each feature is modeled in terms of the classes that provide the functionality defined by the feature. For many of the features, there are at least three classes required, a menu class, an administration class, and a webpage generator class. There may also be other classes required, such as entity classes. For example, Fig. 7 shows that the Newsletter feature is supported by five classes: an entity class, which encapsulates the Newsletter Info, two web generator classes, one for the newsletter page and one for the administration of the page, one coordinator class for Newsletter Generation, and one algorithm class for Image Manipulation

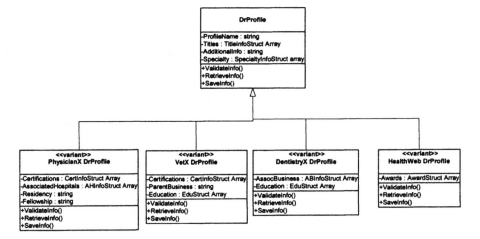

Fig. 6. Class GSH to support Dr. Profile Class

5. Target System Configuration

The analysis model for the target system (a member of the product line) is configured from the domain model of the product line by selecting the desired optional and alternative features subject to the feature/feature constraints [5, 7]. Kernel features are automatically included. The following sequence of steps should be followed to use the domain model to configure a new product line member in the WebWizard domain. First, the kernel of the target system is configured by including all classes defined in the kernel feature set. Then, for each optional feature desired in the target system, the classes supporting that feature are selected. For a WebWizard target system, the first decision is whether to select the newsletter and/or survey optional features. After that, the engineer selects either the Health or Club alternative. Selection of the alternative, e.g., Health, results in the kernel features of that alternative being automatically selected, e.g., the Health Kernel feature set, and provides the option for selecting features from the Health Optional feature set. All features in the Health Kernel as well as their corresponding classes, are automatically selected. The engineer may then select any of the Health Optional features, e.g., Appointment and Questions, which results in the supporting classes also being selected.

6. Discussion

This section summarizes the lessons learned through this domain modeling exercise:

a) The UML notation is a rich notation for capturing the different aspects of a product line through use case modeling, static and dynamic modeling. Space constraints have precluded the description of the latter in this paper.

b) The UML based domain modeling approach provides the capability for modeling and integrating product lines. The view integration approach worked effectively for this domain by successively integrating health related product lines into the Health Web product line and then integrating Health Web with Club Central.

c) Modeling the WWW based product line provided new insights into the domain modeling method. As originally conceived [5], the view integration approach results in kernel features, optional features, and alternative features. This turned out to be the case with the Health Web product line. However, when the Health Web and Club Central product lines were integrated into the Web Wizard extended product line, further categorization was required. As before, kernel features were required for all members of the product line and optional features could be selected by any member. However, there are also features which are always needed if a given alternative (health or club) is selected, while other features are optional within that alternative. To categorize these classes, the new categories of "kernel alternative" and "optional alternative" were coined.

d) The feature view, which is reuse oriented, should be kept separate from the Aggregation Hierarchy view, which is design oriented. As this exercise showed, the reuse perspective as to what is kernel and what is optional can change, whereas the architecture should be impervious to these changes.

e) For this domain, functional feature modeling was used extensively. Non-functional features were not modeled and parametric features were of limited use. Parameterization is widely used in the Web generation pages, where the pages are customized by information entered by the user, e.g., name and address of health care practice. However, this is handled as part of the design of the Web page and not

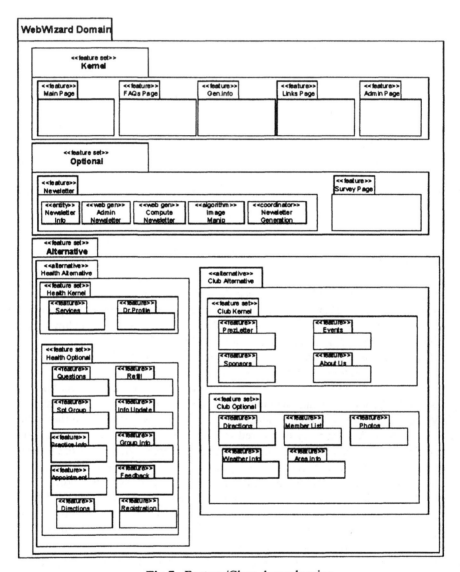

Fig.7. Feature/Class dependencies

explicitly as a feature to be selected. The FAQ feature is an example of an optional feature. However, the explicit information to be placed on the FAQ page is considered outside the scope of feature modeling.

f) The WWW domain turned out to be very amenable to domain modeling and it is instructive to understand why. The reason is that this domain is a very modular and scaleable domain. After developing certain essential classes (which are of course kernel classes), each product line has certain kernel features (and classes) and optional features, most of which relate to the functionality provided by different WWW pages.

The optional features mainly relate to WWW pages that are independent of each other, although they may need information entered on WWW pages supported by kernel features. Differentiating between different members of the product line is handled by alternative features (and classes as in the Dr Profile of Fig.6), only one of which must be selected. Modeling this type of domain is extensible from the viewpoint of adding extra optional features (WWW pages) or alternative features.

g) Some researchers have used the Aggregation Hierarchy as the primary representation of the domain model, which is then tailored to configure an individual member of the product line by deciding whether each individual optional class is required and selecting among alternative classes [13].   This approach works well when the engineers configuring the target system have an intimate knowledge of the Aggregation Hierarchy, i.e., the software architecture. Other researchers have used a decision model to guide the tailoring process, explicitly stating the tailoring decisions that need to be taken and in what sequence [1]. This approach works well when the engineers configuring the target system have detailed knowledge of the application domain but not necessarily of the architecture. The feature/class dependency modeling [12, 15] is a combination of the two approaches with the feature dependencies performing the role of the decision model and the feature/class dependencies defining how the Domain Aggregation Hierarchy should be tailored. Thus the approach is feature driven but results in configuring the Aggregation Hierarchy of the target system. The main advantage of this approach is that the tailoring process can be automated [15]. This approach works well for tailoring a domain model based on functional features, which is the case for the product lines described in this paper. Defining the values of parameterized features needs to be handled separately.

7. Conclusions

This paper has described a domain modeling approach using (UML) for modeling software product lines of Web-based applications. The paper has described how the various views of the UML, in particular the use case modeling view and the static modeling view, may be used for modeling such software product lines and illustrates this with a detailed domain modeling exercise. It also explained how the feature model, which has been used for modeling the common and variable requirements in software product lines, can be integrated with the UML. This project has shown that there can be a substantial benefit from domain analysis and modeling, through reuse of both architectural elements and code.   Future enhancements planned for the Webwizard domain include extensions to the domain to include new features and support for new product lines.   Other planned enhancements include eliminating redundancy in generated products through the use of a single centralized data store for resources such as images, and the ability to make WebWizard entirely data driven, thus eliminating the need for multiple copies of html, scripting and code in multiple directories.

Acknowledgements

The authors thank Maurizio Morisio and the anonymous reviewers for their insightful comments on an earlier draft.

References

1. Atkinson, C., Bayer, J., Muthig, D., *Component-Based Product Line Development: The KobrA Approach*, Proceedings, 1st International Software Product Line Conference, 2000.
2. Booch, G. et al., The Unified Modeling Language User Guide, Addison-Wesley Object Technology Series, ISBN:0-201-57168-4, 1998.
3. Cohen, S. and Northrop, L., "Object-Oriented Technology and Domain Analysis", Proc. IEEE International Conference on Software Reuse, Victoria, Canada, June 1998.
4. DeBaud, J.M. and Schmid, K., "A Systematic Approach to Derive the Scope of Software Product Lines", *Proc. IEEE International Conference on Software Engineering*, IEEE Computer Society Press, 1999.
5. Gomaa, H., "Reusable Software Requirements and Architectures for Families of Systems", Journal of Systems and Software, May 1995.
6. Gomaa, H., Designing Concurrent, Distributed, and Real-Time Applications with UML, Addison-Wesley Object Technology Series, ISBN:0-201-65793-7, July 2000.
7. Gomaa, H., "Object Oriented Analysis and Modeling For Families of Systems with the UML", Proc. IEEE International Conference on Software Reuse, Vienna, Austria, June 2000.
8. Gomaa, H., "Modeling Software Product Lines with UML", Proc. Workshop on Software Product Lines, ICSE, Toronto, May 2001.
9. Griss, M., Favaro, J., D'Alessandro, M., "Integrating Feature Modeling with the RSEB", Proc. International Conference on Software Reuse, Victoria, June 1998.
10. Jacobson, I., Griss, M., Jonsson, P., Software Reuse - Architecture, Process and Organization for Business Success, Addison Wesley, 1997.
11. Kang, K.C. et al., "Feature Oriented Domain Analysis", Technical Report No. CMU/SEI-90-TR-21, Software Engineering Institute, November 1990
12. B. Keepence, M. Mannion, "Using Patterns to Model Variability in Product Families", IEEE Software, July 1999.
13. Morisio M., Travassos G.H, Stark M., "Extending UML to Support Domain Analysis", 15th IEEE Automated Software Engineering Conference, September 2000.
14. Rumbaugh, J. et al., The Unified Modeling Language Reference Manual ,Addison-Wesley Object Technology Series, ISBN:0-201-30998-X, 1999.
15. H. Gomaa, L. Kerschberg, V. Sugumaran, C. Bosch, I Tavakoli, "A Knowledge-Based Software Engineering Environment for Reusable Software Requirements and Architectures", Journal of Automated Software Engineering, Vol. 3, 285-307, 1996.

Enhancing Component Reusability
through Product Line Technology

Colin Atkinson and Dirk Muthig

Fraunhofer Institute for Experimental Software Engineering (IESE)
Sauerwiesen 6, D-67661 Kaiserslautern, Germany
{atkinson, muthig}@iese.fhg.de

Abstract. The idea of building software systems from semi-autonomous components that can be reused in numerous applications is intuitively appealing. However, simply organizing software systems in terms of components does not by itself ensure that the components will be reusable, or that significant levels of reuse will actually occur. In practice, to achieve meaningful levels of reuse the scope and generality of components must be carefully analyzed and optimized. In this paper we make the case that one of the most effective and systematic ways of achieving this is to complement component-based development with product line engineering techniques. Product line engineering not only provides concrete criteria for maximizing the reusability of components, but also provides enhanced mechanisms for reusing them within new applications. After first outlining the pertinent features of component-based development and product line engineering, the paper explains how they can be integrated under the umbrella of a model-driven architecture (MDA) approach to software development.

1   Introduction

Software reuse is one of the main motivations for component-based development. Decomposing large software systems into smaller, semi-autonomous parts opens up the possibility of reusing these parts again within other applications. Reusing a prefabricated component in another application not only saves the associated development costs but also the effort involved in ensuring the quality and integrity of the component. Component reuse therefore promises significantly enhanced returns on investment in development activities.

Component-based development differs from traditional approaches by splitting software development into two distinct activities.

Development for Reuse - creating the primitive building blocks which hopefully will be of use in multiple applications

Development with Reuse -   creating new applications (or possible larger components) by assembling prefabricated components.

The ultimate goal is to separate these activities to the extent that they may be performed by completely different organizations. Component vendors, *developing for*

C. Gacek (Ed.): ICSR-7, LNCS 2319, pp. 93–108, 2002.
© Springer-Verlag Berlin Heidelberg 2002

reuse, will focus on constructing and marketing high-quality, specialized components, which concentrate on doing a specific job well. Component Assemblers, *developing with reuse*, will select, purchase and assemble a variety of such Commercial-Off-The-Shelf (COTS) components to create systems for their own customers (possible larger grained components).

While this model is fine in principle, traditional component-based development methods give very little consideration to the factors and properties that actually go into creating truly reusable artifacts. Moreover, when reuse factors are taken into account, it is typically in an ad hoc way. Most methods that address component-based development provide only "rule of thumb" heuristics for optimizing their reusability [1][2]. The assumption is that simply implementing a software artifact as a component will naturally make it reusable, but this is rarely the case.

We believe one of the most effective ways of addressing this problem is to augment component-based development with product-line-engineering techniques. Product line engineering not only offers concrete criteria for optimizing the reusability of components, but also provides enhanced mechanisms for reusing them within new applications. Thus, the principles of product line engineering provide a natural complement to the concepts of component-based development. Combining the two in practice is not as straightforward as it might at first appear, however. This is because traditionally, product line engineering and component-based development have focused on different parts of the software life-cycle. The leading product line engineering methods tend to focus on very early life-cycle phases, such as domain analysis and scoping, while traditional component technologies, in contrast, are very much focused on the implementation and deployment phases. Indeed, components are generally viewed as simply a convenient way of packaging the results of the analysis and design phases.

Effectively using the two paradigms together, therefore, requires this gap to be bridged. From the perspective of component-based development, this means that the concept of components must play a much more important role in the earlier phases of development, such as analysis and design, in which graphical modeling is an important activity. In short, the concept of components needs to be manifest much more strongly in the models that characterize the architecture of the system. Today, the explicit modeling of software architectures in this way is often associated with the one model-driven architecture (MDA) initiative of the OMG. Bridging the gap from the perspective of product-line engineering implies that product line concepts be explicitly supported in later phases of development. Again, this comes down to the need to explicitly capture product line issues, such as common and variable features, within the models that capture the architecture (or reference architecture). Enhancing component-based development with product-line-engineering concepts therefore requires the two paradigms to be applied in the context of a MDA approach. In practice, this usually implies the use of the UML.

The central goal of this paper is to illustrate how the strengths of component-based development can be enhanced by means of product line techniques. As a preparation, in the following section we first describe the main principles involved in leveraging the concepts of components in a model-driven way. We use the KobrA method [3] to illustrate the principles involved since this has a comprehensive approach for modeling component using the UML. However, the basic ideas presented are not restricted to KobrA. Section 3 then briefly introduces the important ideas of product line engineering and integrates the product line paradigm with the component paradigm in order to support a more powerful approach to reuse than offered by either separately. Finally, in section 4 we provide some concluding remarks.

2   Model-Driven, Component-Based Development

As its name implies, a component is any independent part of a product or system that has the potential to be used elsewhere independently. In the context of software development, the concept has mainly been limited to the implementation and deployment phases of the software life-cycle, largely due to the influence of the "big three" contemporary component technologies (CORBA, .NET and EJB). However, in order to gain the full reuse benefits of the component concept, it is necessary to exploit components in the early analysis and design phases of development as well the later implementation phases. Several methods offer approaches for component modeling [2][4]. We base our approach in this paper on the KobrA approach [3] since this has one of the most general approaches to the modeling of components and also supports product line engineering concepts.

Supporting the modeling of components involves more than just using component diagrams to document the static interfaces and interconnections of component instances in the form of a UML component diagram. In general, components can be complex behavioral abstractions offering multiple services and possessing complex dependencies. A component-based, model-driven architecture thus involves the modeling of all the complex and subtle properties of components and how they are interconnected at both run-time and development time. Component-based MDA thus involves many UML diagrams providing multiple, interconnected views of a system and its components.

The basic rule that governs the use of the UML in a component-based architecture

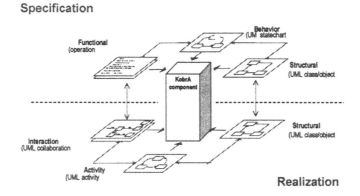

Fig. 1 KobrA component model suite

is that individual diagrams should focus on the description of the properties of individual components. In KobrA, this is known as the *principle of locality*. The use of a suite of UML diagrams to model a single complex component according to the principle of locality is depicted in Fig. 1.

The specification diagrams collectively define the externally visible properties of the component, and thus in a general sense can be viewed as representing its interface. The structural diagram describes the types that the component manipulates, the roles with which it interacts, and the list of services and attributes that it exports. The functional model provides a declarative description of each of the services or operations supported by the component in terms of pre and post conditions. Finally, the behavioral model describes the externally visible (i.e. logical) states exhibited by the component.

The realization diagrams collectively define how the component realizes its specification by describing the architecture and/or design of the component. The realization's structural diagram is a refinement of the specification structural diagram that includes the additional types and roles needed, such as externally acquired server components, or subcomponents that the component creates and manages itself. The interaction diagrams document how each operation of the component is realized in terms of interactions with other components and objects. Finally, the activity diagrams documents the algorithm by which each operation is realized.

A complete model-driven architecture of a system is, in KobrA, created by hierarchically organizing the models of its individual components. The hierarchy of components is organized according to the logical containment structure as illustrated in Fig. 2. The system is regarded as the root of the containment tree whose services

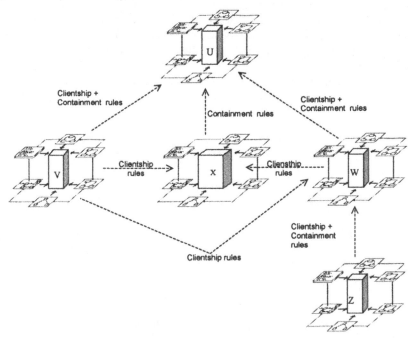

Fig. 2 KobrA component containment tree

are utilized by the users. Subcomponents that form part of its realization are documented in the same way as children in the containment hierarchy.

2.1   Development for Reuse

The development of a component for reuse must take into account the fact that simply developing software in terms of components is not, on its own, likely to lead to significant increases in reuse levels. Experience indicates that reusing a component usually involves more than simply plugging it into a new context. Reuse almost always requires the adaptation of existing components to the reuse context and, thus, information on intended usage contexts, assumptions made with respect to the component's environment, and a documentation of its internals are essential. Consequently, components tend to be difficult to reuse beyond the application for which they were written unless they are carefully written to maximize their reusability.

Development activities for reuse must therefore ensure that the produced components, which are developed for reuse in different contexts, differ in two ways from components that represent only a subsystem of a particular single system. First, a reusable component must be defined more generally with respect to potential future usages. Second, the component and its generality must be documented in a more precise and detailed way.

The definition of a component encompasses two logical steps: component identification and component specification. The identification step initially establishes a component as a logical unit at a coarse-grained level. Typical component candidates are subsystems representing inherent blocks of a particular system's functionality. Fig. 3 shows the component hierarchy of a simple bank system, which we will use to illustrate our approach throughout the paper. The decomposition of *Bank* is shown in form of a KobrA containment tree. At the top level, the simple international bank consists of two subsystems; *Teller* is one of them providing the services related to the management of accounts. *Teller* is developed for reuse and thus it is defined in a more general way than is needed for any one particular system. *Teller*'s static structure at the specification level is shown in Fig. 4. It encompasses functionality that is not supported by every bank such as support for multiple currencies or a limit specifying

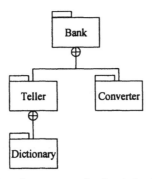

Fig. 3 Containment tree of a simple bank system

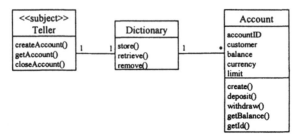

Fig. 4 Realization class diagram of *Teller*

to what extent a customer is allowed to overdraw his/her account. In the KobrA approach, each of the *Teller*'s services is specified in the form of an operation specification. **Table 1.**, for example, contains the specification of the *createtAccount()* operation.

Table 1. Operation specification - *Teller.createAccount()*

Name	Teller.createAccount()
Informal Description	A new account is opened in a particular currency for a customer, and the Account ID is returned
Receives	customer currency
Returns	id:AccountID
Changes	teller new AccountID id new Account account
Result	A new Account account with a unique AccountID id in the currency has been created. Its balance and limit has been set to 0. Its owner, customer, has been stored in account. The AccountID id has been returned

At the realization level, the services of a component are defined in more detail. Problems may therefore arise due to insufficient definition of the component's scope. Additional concepts that have not yet been assigned to any specific component may be used or manipulated by services provided by the component under development. For example, an account managed by *Teller* is related to a customer who owns the account. When *Teller* was initially identified, it was not explicitly decided whether customer-related data is managed together with accounts. This would not have been the case if a component for managing customer data has been identified independently of *Teller* and its services.

In general, there is a lack of detailed guidelines or heuristics for identifying good components (i.e. components that can be reused in several future contexts) particularly their detailed boundaries. Only at abstraction levels close to the implementation may the analysis of the data flow within a system support decisions related to components' boundaries objectively. There, component boundaries may be determined by minimizing the frequency and amount of data transfers across components. In the example, *Teller*'s services do not use customer-related data and thus *Teller* only stores references to *Customer* objects, which are owned by another component that provides services to manipulate customer data. Note that as a consequence, in any of its future reuse contexts *Teller* must acquire a component that manages customer data.

In general, however, the identification of components, as well as the quality of their reusability, relies on the expertise and the experience of individuals rather than on objective criteria. This is because developing a component for reuse often means starting with a component specification, which is taken from a particular system context, and then generalizing or parameterizing this specification in a way that the involved experts believe optimizes the component's reusability.

The dependency on individuals is even stronger in practice because components are often not documented in a way that supports their reuse sufficiently. Existing documentation schemes especially fail to provide ways of capturing information on expected reuse contexts and intended ways for customizing a component. The documentation of *Teller* as presented so far does not, for example, capture that fact that the features 'multiple currencies' and 'overdraw limit' are optional, as well as how these optional features can be removed in cases when they are not needed.

Development with Reuse

When an application is developed by recursively decomposing the problem to be solved and then developing solutions for its sub-problems, development with reuse means that existing solutions are used and adapted to the particular problem at hand instead of developing a solution completely from scratch. Thus, it involves repeated decisions about whether a reusable component exists whose adaptation would be cheaper than the development of a new component from scratch. This decision in the overall reuse process is visualized in Fig. 5.

Experience has shown that reuse happens only if the left path in Fig. 5 is more efficient than the right path - that is,

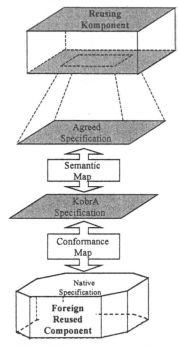

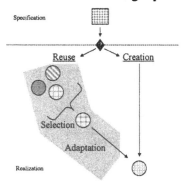

Fig. 5 Realizing a component with reuse or from scratch

Fig. 6 KobrA's process for reusing foreign components

only if the reusing developer immediately experiences the reuse benefits. Organizational benefits, like reduced maintenance effort in the future are only of minor importance. Unfortunately, this decision is not well supported today because the typical techniques used to specify generalized components do not allow good estimates of required adaptation effort to be derived. In practice, consequently, only two types of component reuse happen.

In the first type, a developer adapts the overall system structure to enable the use of a big and complex component because s/he prefers not to touch a component's internals and fears redeveloping (parts of) its functionality due to the component's size and/or complexity. Here, the used components are typically foreign components, such as COTS or legacy components. A process for this type of reuse, as it is defined by the KobrA method, is schematically depicted in Fig. 6.

While realizing the component at the top of the diagram, the need for a subcomponent is identified. This is captured in the form of the desired specification. The foreign component at the bottom is a reuse candidate. In order to validate the foreign component, a specification of the foreign component comparable with the desired specification needs to created. Therefore, a conformance map is used to translate the foreign specification into a KobrA form. Table 2 presents a conformance map that supports the translation of javadoc information into a KobrA specification. Obviously, javadoc does not provide all the desired information but allows structural and functional KobrA models to be derived with manual intervention. Behavioral information is not captured by the javadoc format.

Table 2: Conformance mapping from javadoc to KobrA specification models

Structural Model	
Model Element	**JavaDoc Element**
Class with stereotype <<subject>>	<classname>
Implements relationship	implements <interface1>, ...
Inheritance relationship	extends <superclassname> or inheritance hierarchy
Class	parameter types in constructor summary and return types and parameter types in method summary
Attributes of <<subject>> or Classes	field summary
Functional Model	
Schema Clause	**JavaDoc Element**
Name	<classname>.<methodname> (create an operation schemata for each method in method summary)
Informal Description	text below method signature in method detail section.
Receives	<parameter.name>:<parameter.type> (for every <parameter> in <method.signature>
Returns	<return type>, <returns> clause of method details
Result	<returns> clause of method details
Behavioral Model	
Model Element	**JavaDoc Element**

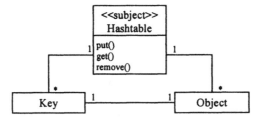

Fig. 7 Specification Class Diagram of *Hashtable*

<no state information in javadoc available>

To illustrate this type of reuse, the java class *Hashtable* is reused to realize the *Dictionary* of the *Teller* component. The above conformance map is applied to the javadoc description of *Hashtable*[1] to produce KobrA specification models. The structural specification diagram is shown in Fig. 7, and a part of the functional model, the operation schema of the *get()* operation, is presented in Table 3. The grayed text has been manually reworked or added.

Table 3: Operation specification - *Hashtable.get()*

Name	Hashtable.get()
Informal Description	Returns the value to which the specified key is mapped in this hashtable
Receives	key:Object
Returns	null or value:Object
Changes	-
Result	if the key is mapped in this hashtable to a value, value has been retrieved and returned. Otherwise, null has been returned.

When the native specification offered by the foreign component has been mapped to a KobrA specification, the desired and the offered specification can be systematically compared. Discrepancies between these two specifications must be resolved in a negotiation process. That is, it must be decided whether the realization of the reusing component or the foreign component is changed. In the case of different terminology, a semantic map is created to identify related concepts. Table 4 maps model elements used in *Teller*'s realization structural diagram (Fig. 4) to elements used in *Hashtable*'s specification structural diagram (Fig. 7).

Table 4: Semantic map mapping *Dictionary* to *Hashtable*

Dictionary	java.util.Hashtable
retrieve()	Object get(key:Object)
store()	Object put(key:Object, value:Object)
remove()	Object remove(key:Object)
accountID	key:Object
Account	value:Object

---

[1]see http://java.sun.com/j2se/1.4/docs/api/java/util/Hashtable.html

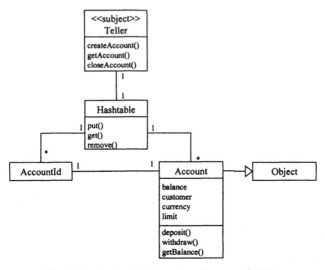

Fig. 8 Revised realization class diagram of *Teller*

At the end of the negotiation process, both components agreed on a specification - the contract between the reusing component and the reused component. The assembly of the two components is then the integration of the agreed specification into the realization of the reusing component. Optionally, the semantic map is also applied. *Teller*'s realization structural diagram after the reuse of *Hashtable* is shown in Fig. 8. In the collaboration diagrams *Hashtable* is directly used, for example, while creating a new account as shown in Fig. 9.

In the second type of component reuse, which is what typically happens in practice, a developer reuses a component by adapting it to a reuse context. First, the adaptation is usually done in straightforward way without an explicit evaluation and negotiation between reuse context and offered services. Second, the adaptation is often done in an unsystematic way without recording and documenting the made changes. Both will lead to an increased maintenance effort for the overall organization.

When Teller is reused in the development of a bank system that does not allow accounts to be overdrawn by customers, the developer must understand *Teller* first as a whole and is then able to adapt it. There are two possible alternative adaptations: the developer either removes the attribute *limit* of *Account* and all of its usages or s/he simply sets *limit* always to zero. In both cases, the resulting system fulfills its requirements. However, the particularly chosen solution depends on the individual developer and thus may be different for bank systems without overdraw limit shipped by the same organization. As a result, maintenance becomes more complex and must be performed for every system separately. For example, a bug fix in a general, reused component must be manually propagated to every system that has reused the

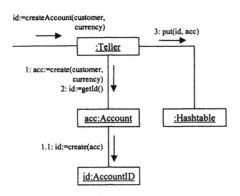

Fig. 9 Collaboration diagram of Teller.*createAccount()*

changed component, and even worse, the necessary changes will vary from system to system.

In this section, component-based development has been presented as it corresponds to today's state-of-the practice. As explained, reuse still depends on individuals and thus is not an inherent and systematic part of component-based development. In short, although the component paradigm is a powerful means to identify and integrate parts of a larger software system, to be successful in enabling large-scale reuse, additional support is needed to enhance the reusability of components and to systematize component assembly.

3   Product-Line-Oriented, Component-Based Development

Product-line engineering is based on the principle of creating generic software artifacts that can be instantiated multiple times to create specific versions tailored to the needs of specific systems or customers. From the perspective of reuse, product line engineering differs from traditional approaches by splitting software development into the following two distinct activities.

Development for Reuse - creating generic artifacts that are sufficiently general to span a domain or family of applications

Development for Use - creating specific artifacts tailored to the needs of a specific application or user.

Both, component-based development and product line technology are two distinct paradigms for developing software and for enabling reuse. In this section, they are combined to show that product line technology can complement component-based development to enhance the reusability of components. Fig. 10 shows the space span by the two dimensions: the component dimension that separates development for reuse from the development with reuse, and the product line dimension that separates development for reuse from the development for use. In this section, we show how KobrA realizes the four quadrants. As a result, the product line dimension – in contrast to section 2 - dominates the structure. To illustrate

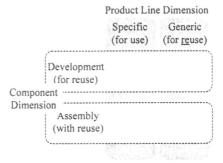

Fig. 10 Component versus Product Line Dimension

the approach, we enrich the *Teller* component with product line concepts following the KobrA approach. The modeling of product line concepts in KobrA is described in detail in [9]. Basically, all KobrA models may contain variant model elements that represent variation points. The relationships among these variation points are captured in a decision model. Both, a component's specification and realization have their own but interrelated decision models.

3.1   Development for Reuse

Development for reuse is also called domain, family, framework, or platform engineering in a product line context. In all cases, the output is a reuse infrastructure that is supposed to support the development of product line members, particular applications.

Development for reuse (component dimension)
From a component-oriented point-of-view, product line concepts support both the identification and the specification of components. The identification of components is no longer based only on the experience and expertise of individuals but is also motivated and justified by domain knowledge. Each component has a semantic meaning and is cohesive about "something". This "something" is typically a domain concept that is owned by, and is a commonality of, the component. This means that if the commonality is not needed in a software system, the whole component is obsolete.

In our example, *Teller* owns, and is responsible for the management of, accounts. Domain knowledge indicates that every bank needs accounts and thus it is clear that *Teller* will be part of any bank system. The *Converter,* as the second subsystem of bank, is an optional component because support for different currencies is only an optional feature as mentioned before. Often a concept is realized as a separate component only because its functionality is optional; otherwise it could also be realized as an inherent part of a related component.

Components whose domain concept is a commonality of the product form the skeleton of the systems in the domain. For variant components, the skeleton must define variation points where they can be integrated if required.

For the specification of components, product line concepts provided three

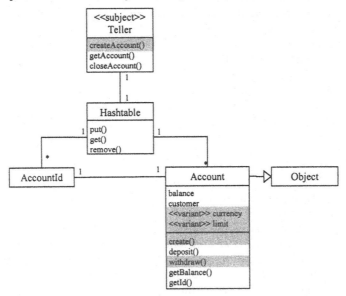

Fig. 11 Generic realization diagram of Teller

improvements. First, the boundaries of components can be systematically determined based on the analysis of commonalities and variabilities in the application domain. Second, the generalization and parameterization of components is based on the analysis of future usage scenarios rather than on the personal judgments of experts. On the one hand, this avoids unnecessary generalizations that only lead to too complex components, and on the other hand, it limits unnecessary rework due to the integration of variability that could have been known before. Third, introduced generalizations and parameters based on variability are systematically and explicitly documented.

Fig. 11 shows the realization diagram of *Teller* with explicitly modeled variability. The attributes *currency* and *limit* are marked as variant; the realization of the grayed operations is also affected by these variabilities, which is visible in the corresponding collaboration diagrams.

An additional decision model captures the relationships between variabilities and documents the relationships between variant model elements and domain variability. Table 5 shows the decision model for *Teller*. It shows that the two variabilities are independent of each other. It also documents how *Teller* must be modified if optional functionality is not needed.

Table 5: Decision model of *Teller*

Question		Diagram	Effect
1. Is a customer allowed to overdraw his/her account up to a certain limit?	Y	...	...
	N	Class Diagram	Remove attribute Account.limit
		...	...
2. Is it an international bank that handles different currencies?	Y	...	...
	N	Class Diagram	Remove attribute Account.currency
		...	...

In general, taking product line concepts into account by explicitly basing the definition of components on an analysis of commonality and variability ultimately leads to more reusable components.

Development with Reuse (Component Dimension)
Development with reuse while developing for reuse in the product line dimension simply means that already generic components are assembled to realize bigger components, which are by definition again generic. The process is similar to the reuse process described in section 2 (see Fig. 6) except that the negotiation process must additionally consider also desired and offered variability. That is, the reuse process becomes more complex.

3.2   Development for Use

Development for use is typically called application engineering in a product line context. Application engineering constructs particular applications (i.e. product line members) mainly by reusing assets from the reuse infrastructure. The output of development for use are non-generic artifacts which are supposed to be used for a particular system and thus do not consider any product line concepts anymore.

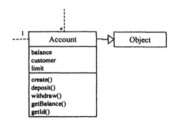

Fig. 12 Instantiated realization class diagram of *Teller*

Development for Reuse (Component Dimension)

The development of non-generic components in a product line context means one of three things: either the development of a common infrastructure component without any variability, the instantiation of generic components, or the development of application-specific functionality.

In the first case, components are developed that always appear in the same form in every product line member. Note that although these components do not contain any variability they can represent functionality that is variant as a whole. For example, a product line infrastructure may contain several mouse drivers that do not contain any variability. In the context of a particular PC, only one of them is needed, the driver for the connected mouse.

In the second case, the variabilities in a generic component are resolved by answering the questions in the decision model. Table 6 shows an example resolution of the decisions for *Teller*: the overdraw limit is supported but not multiple currencies. A part of the instantiated class diagram, which has been modified according to the effects described in the decision model, is shown in Fig. 12.

Table 6: An example resolution model for *Teller*

Question	Resolution
1. Is a customer allowed to overdraw his/her account up to a certain limit?	Y
2. Is it an international bank that handles different currencies?	N

The decision model clearly guides the instantiation process and thus the reuse of a generic component. The decision model and the resolution model both abstract from the realization of a variability, which becomes important when *Teller* is changed in response to a reported bug. In contrast to pure component-based development, the explicit product line concepts allow *Teller* to be systematically re-instantiated and thus to share maintenance effort among all product line members. Additionally, optional features are always removed in an identical way as described in the decision model.

In the third case, components are developed for a particular system only, or instantiated components are modified. In both cases, it is not intended to integrate the developed functionality into the product line infrastructure. This decision is part of the evolution and management activities associated with a reuse infrastructure. It is based on the evaluation of the required functionality: either it is needed for further application or it is a special case that does not fit into the product line strategy or the existing infrastructure.

Development with Reuse (Component Dimension)
The reuse of specific components is similar to development with reuse in the component dimension except that the reused components are created for the particular reuse context. Hence, reuse of components is here much closer to the ideal straightforward assembly of components. If functionality is needed that is not already supported, development for reuse activities are triggered.

4   Conclusions

Although component-based development provides a powerful basis for reuse, blindly creating components will not guarantee that significant levels of reuse will actually occur. Components must not only be carefully identified and selected, but must also be scoped to provide an optimal balance of generic and concrete features. Components that are too generic will be inefficient and bloated, while components that are too specific will have only a minimal range of reuses. One of the most effective ways of improving the reusability of components is to complement component-based development ideas with product-line engineering techniques. By analyzing the family of systems that a company wishes to build, and the similarities and differences between these systems, components can be chosen which best match the company's future reuse requirements. Some components can be defined for the prime reason of encapsulating variabilities, while others can be provided with the optimal balance of generic/specific features based on the variation points in the family architecture.

Applying product-line concepts in the context of component-based development is not as straightforward as it might at first appear, however. As explained in the paper, the most effective synergy between the approaches is achieved when the two paradigms are applied in tandem with the model-driven architecture approach - that is, when the full richness of components and product lines can be modeled at an abstract level using a language such as the UML.

In the paper we illustrated how this can be achieved using the new component-based development method, KobrA [3]. Although the ideas are not restricted to KobrA, this is one of the few existing methods that combines component-based development and product line concerns with UML-based modeling. Using a small example, the paper first illustrated how specific components and component assemblies can be modeled using a suite of interrelated diagrams, and how the concerns for development "for reuse" and "with reuse" can be separated at the model level. In particular, a concrete mechanism for integrating existing components into a new system (development with reuse) was demonstrated. Then, the reuse ideas from the product line approach are integrated that make the usually kept private by developers public and explicit, which ultimately leads to systematic reuse [10]. We believe that the observations made in this paper represent a step towards a more systematic and rigorous approach to reuse in all areas of software engineering, which we already experienced while applying KobrA in projects and case studies [11].

References

[1] Kruchten, P. B., The Rational Unified Process. An Introduction, Addison-Wesley, 2000.
[2] D'Souza, D. F. and Wills A. C., Objects, Components and Frameworks with UML: The Catalysis Approach, Addison-Wesley, 1998
[3] C. Atkinson, J. Bayer, C. Bunse, O. Laitenberger, R. Laqua, E. Kamsties, D. Muthig, B. Paech, J. Wüst, and J. Zettel. Component-based Product Line Engineering with UML, Component Series, Addison-Wesley, 2001
[4] J. Cheesman and J. Daniels. UML Components: A Simple Process for Specifying Component-Based Software, Addison-Wesley, 2000
[5] Cooks, S., and Daniels, J., Designing Object Systems, Prentice Hall, England 1992
[6] Forsell, M., Halttunen, V., and Ahonen, J. Use and Identification of Components in Component-Based Software Development Methods. In Software Reuse. Advances in Software Reusability. 6th International Conference, ICSR-6. Lecture Notes in Computer Science, 1844, Springer-Verlag, 2000.
[7] W. C. Lim. Managing Software Reuse - A Comprehensive Guide to Strategically Reengineering the Organization for Reusable Components, Upper Saddle River: Prentice Hall PTR, 1998
[8] Bayer, J., Flege, O., Knauber, P., Laqua, R., Muthig, D., Schmid. K., Widen, T, and Debaud, J.-M., PuLSE: A Methodology to develop Software Product Lines, Proceedings of the Symposium on Software Reuse(SSR'99), May 1999
[9] C.Atkinson, J. Bayer, and D. Muthig. Component-Based Product Line Development: The KobrA Approach, in [12]
[10] S. Bailin, M. Simos, L. Levin, and D. Creps. Learning and Inquiry Based Reuse Adoption (LIBRA) - A Field Guide to Reuse Adoption through Organizational Learning, Version 1.1, Software Technology for Adaptable, Reliable Systems (STARS), Informal Technical Report STARS-PA33-AG01/001/02, February1996
[11] J. Bayer, D. Muthig, and B. Göpfert. The Library System Product Line – A KobrA Case Study, Technical Report, Fraunhofer IESE-Report No. 024.01/E, IESE, 2001
[12] P. Donohoe. Software Product Lines - Experience and Research Directions, Kluwer Academic Publi/subjectshers, 2000

Modeling Variability with the Variation Point Model

Diana L Webber[1] and Hassan Gomaa[2]

[1] Booz - Allen – Hamilton,
8283 Greensboro Drive, McLean, VA 22102, 703-633-3118
webber_diana@bah.com

[2] Department of Information and Software Systems Engineering,
George Mason University, Fairfax, VA 22030
hgomaa@gmu.edu

Abstract. A major challenge for software reuse is developing components that can be reused in several applications. This paper describes a systematic method for providing components that can be extended through variation points, as initially specified in the software requirements. Allowing the reuser or application engineer to extend components at pre-specified variation points creates a more flexible set of components. The existing variation point methods do not provide enough design detail for the reuser. This paper introduces a method called the Variation Point Model (VPM), which models variation points at the design level, beginning with the common requirements.

1. Introduction

Modeling variation points is accomplished with two major approaches in the context of software product lines. The first approach is to model the variation points [1] so that the developer of the core assets can manage the variability of the core assets or core components. The second approach models the variation points so that the reuser of the core assets can build unique variants from the variation points. Jacobson defines a variation point as follows: "A variation point identifies one or more locations at which the variation will occur" [1]. The Variation Point Model (VPM) adds the mechanism of variability to this definition. The Software Engineering Institute defines a core asset as follows: "Core assets are those assets that form the basis for the software product line. Core assets often include, but are not limited to, the architecture, reusable software components, domain models, requirement statements, documentation and specifications, performance models, schedules, budgets, test plans test cases, work plans, and process descriptions" [2].

In the first approach, the design of the variation points is only understood and used by the core asset developer. The core asset developer builds and maintains the variants used in the applications. The reuser chooses between a set of variants for each variation point and creates an application. When the reuser needs a variant that is not

C. Gacek (Ed.): ICSR-7, LNCS 2319, pp. 109–122, 2002.

available in the core assets, the core asset developer adds that variant to the core assets and makes it available to all reusers. Modeling the variation points, helps the core assets developer to manage and build new variants.

The objective of the second approach is to make the core assets more reusable by allowing the reuser to build variants from variation points. This approach gives the reuser the flexibility of tailoring the core assets to his/her needs. However, a variation point must be modeled such that the reuser has enough knowledge to build a variant. This approach keeps the core asset developer from the task of maintaining every possible variant. This is very useful when a variant is unique to a reuser and not needed by other reusers. In either approach, variation points must be adequately modeled so that they can be maintained and managed. Core assets that include variation points are referred to as the common core in this paper.

2. Survey of Variability Methods

The following survey is a summary of the most relevant pieces of related work. Jacobson described six variability mechanisms for providing variation points in a software product line: inheritance, uses, extensions, parameterization, configuration, and generation [1]. Bosch describes five variability mechanisms: inheritance, extensions, configuration, template instantiation, and generation [3].

Alcatel/Thomson-CSF Common Research Laboratory (LCAT) are leading an ongoing PRAISE project that focuses on the design and representation of a product-line architecture with UML [4]. They use a UML package to represent a variation point or hot spot with the stereotype <<hot spot>>. They also tag any collaboration with a variant with "variation point". Hot Spots are a method to model variation points [5]. Hot spots show a reuser where the variation point is located and when a reuser must extend a component's functionality.

In addition to PRAISE, LCAT also has a project entitled Software Product Line Integrated Technology (SPLIT) [6]. SPLIT is an experimental method that helps LCAT define and build product lines. SPLIT considers variation points to have attributes and therefore uses the UML classifier, class, to depict a variation point. The attributes SPLIT gives a variation point are attributes used to help provide information needed to choose a variant. A subsequent paper on SPLIT discusses the three variability mechanisms: insert, extend, and parameterize [7].

Looking at some product-line case studies clearly shows the need for VPM. CelciusTech uses parameterization as a variability mechanism [11]. They are in need of a way to manage the parameters and understand the dependencies between them. NASA Goddard Space Flight Center Flight Software Branch (FSB) has come to the same conclusion and created a technique to represent variability [12,13]. FSB created a new symbol to identify the variable elements. However, the reuser must define, for each specialized class, if a tagged operation is kept or not. Software Technology for Adaptable Reliable Systems (STARS) [14, 15] and Boeing's avionics software [16, 17] both use the same logic as FODA and EDLC by providing the reuser with a list of variants to choose from rather than the ability to create a unique variant of their own.

Product Line Software Engineering (PuLSE) [18], KobrA [19, 20], Wheels [6], Bosch's Product-Line Design Process [3], and Family-Oriented Abstraction, Specification, and Translation (FAST) [21] are all processes specifically for building product lines. Although Bosch and FAST discuss variability mechanisms, they do not include a method to model variation points. A more detailed survey is given in reference [26].

In summary, the related work discussed in this section lays the foundation for variation point modeling. VPM builds on the concepts presented in the different methods and processes described in this section. VPM builds on the idea of commonalities and variabilities from domain analysis to concentrate on the point of variation. VPM extends the definition of a variation point to include its variability mechanism in addition to its location. VPM builds on Jacobson's and Bosch's variability mechanisms by creating variation point types that are directly related to their modeling technique. At this time, three variation point types have been modeled: parameterization, inheritance, and callback. The survey showed that parameterization followed by inheritance are the two most widely used types today. Callback was modeled due to its appealing flexibility and the availability of a product line that used the callback type. VPM builds on the related work to create a method to model variation points so a reuser can build a unique variant.

3. Introduction to VPM

The Variation Point Model (VPM) is designed to model variation points, which are contained in reusable software components. VPM can be used with any reusable software development process that contain variation points. VPM is most compatible with the Product Line Architecture or a family of systems. VPM has the following qualities:
1. VPM visualizes the variation points.
2. VPM adds the variation point view to the requirements.
3. VPM adds the variation points to the reference architecture.
4. VPM uses the well-known and accepted Unified Modeling Language (UML) [23,]24, 25]. Using UML to model software product lines is also described in [1, 4, 13, 19, 20, 22].
5. VPM categorizes the variation points into three types of variation points, Parameterization, Inheritance, and Callback.
6. VPM gives the reuser an understanding of how to build a variant from a variation point.

The structure of a variation point includes looking at the variation point from at least four different views. The structure of a variation point includes describing the variation point function in the requirements. The structure of a variation point includes showing all the components that are created to realize the variation point. Lastly, the structure of a variation point includes showing all its static and dynamic aspects. Each type of variation point has a different static and dynamic structure.

The following four views are necessary to adequately communicate the variation points to the reuser.

1. Requirements View
2. Component Variation Point View
3. Static Variation Point View
4. Dynamic Variation Point View

The *requirements variation point view* shows the variation point in terms of the requirements of the common core. This view is created during the analysis phase of developing the common core. This allows the variation points to be captured at the same time the requirements are captured.

The *component variation point view* is a composite view that shows all the variation points that belong to a particular component. This view also shows if a variation point belongs to more than one component and if several variation points belong to one component.

The *static variation point view* shows the static parts of the variation point and their relationships. This view shows which classes and methods are involved in the variation point. Since it is necessary to understand the variation point type to create this view, this is the stage at when the variation point type is determined. When a variant is created for a variation point, the component needs to know this variant now exists and the *dynamic variation point view* shows how to make the variant known to the rest of the components. For example, if a variation point is to create a new class that contains a new method, this new class and method must now be registered with the component so the component knows to use this new method.

The static variation point view and the dynamic variation point view are created during the design phase of the common core development. This is where the design of the component needs to be understood so the common core developer can also design the variation point. Together the static and dynamic variation point views give the reuser an understanding of how to build a variant from a variation point.

The Common Core Process (CCP) is a software process to create a product line using variation points. In summary, CCP has four phases. The first phase includes the domain analysis effort to create the requirements and the variation points. This requirements variation point view is created during this phase. This phase determines the different reuser needs for variations. However, since variation points are used, this phase does not need to determine all the different variants. Phase 2 included the architecture work to determine the different components of the common core. The component variation point view is created during this phase. The variation points in the requirements variation point view are traced to a component in the component variation point view. Phase 2 also determines if a variation point involves one or more components. Phase 3 includes the design of the common core. The static and dynamic variation point views are created in phase 3. The developer of the common core designs the variation point in this phase. Phase 4 includes the reuser building variants from the common core created in the first three phases. Reference [26] contains a comprehensive discussion of CCP.

This paper introduces the VPM model with an example of an Automated Teller Machine (ATM). The design used is from the Banking System Case Study [25]. The Banking System Case Study was modified to include six variation points to create a common core that can be used on several different banking solutions. The BSCS common core solves a problem for a bank that has several automated teller machines (ATMs). Each ATM is geographically distributed and connected via a wide area network to a central server. Each ATM has a card reader, a cash dispenser, a keyboard display, and a receipt printer. The six variation points that concentrate on the startup and validate PIN use cases. These use cases along with the six variation points were implemented in Java. The implementation as a proof of concept exercise is briefly discussed in Section 8.

4. Requirements Variation Point View

The requirements variation point view shows the variation point in terms of the requirements of the core assets. This view is created during the analysis phase of developing the common core. Figure 1 shows a generic depiction of the requirements variation point view in both the enumerated shall statement form and the use case form.

Enumerated Shall Statements

A requirement in the Common Core Specification:

The Common Core shall perform a function
Variations:

1. vp ⟨mvo⟩ ⟨VariationPointName⟩: *The Common Core shall provide a mechanism where the reusers can specialize the function.*

Use Cases

vp ⟨mvo⟩ ⟨VariationPointName⟩: *A mechanism will be provided which allows the reuser to specify an alternate action.*

Fig. 1. Requirements Variation Point View

A variation point is labeled with the first two characters "vp" followed by an "m" for mandatory or an "o" for optional. A mandatory variation point does not supply a default variant. The reuser must supply one, and it is essential for the reuser to understand where the mandatory variation points exist.

In order to demonstrate the usage of the four variation point views, an example for a stolen ATM card is used throughout this paper and given below.

vpoStolenCard. A mechanism will be provided which allows the reuser to add any action as a result of a stolen card. The default action is to confiscate the card.

The purpose of the vpoStolenCard variation point is to allow the bank to take a unique action to a stolen card based on unique rules or logic. A reuser may wish to call the police or call the local bank if a stolen card is presented to the ATM machine.

5. Component Variation Point View

The component variation point view is a composite view that shows all the variation points that belong to a particular component. Figure 2 shows a generic model of a component variation point view. This view shows the relationship from a component to its variation points. It shows that the variation point is allocated to the component. VPM models a component using the UML package. Since VPM looks at a component as a collection of classes, the UML package symbol is chosen to represent the collection. The UML stereotype <<Component>> is used to designate the package as a component. The variation points are designated by a • symbol. Although not included in the UML User's Guide [23], Jacobson introduced the • symbol for variation points [1].

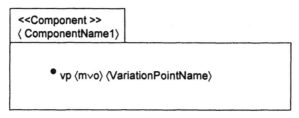

Fig. 2. Component Variation Point View

The component variation point view also shows if a variation point belongs to more than one component and if several variation points belong to one component. This view is created during the phase that also creates the architecture of the core assets. As requirements are allocated to components, so are the variation points. Figure 3 shows an example of a component variation point view for the Banking System Case Study. The system was designed using the COMET/UML method as described in [25] and then modified to support VPM. The classes are structured using the COMET class structuring criteria, which are depicted using stereotypes such as <<user interface>>.

This example shows six variation points and how they are allocated to the core assets. This figure gives a high-level view of where the variation points are and what components or classes are affected. If the reuser wants to exercise a variation point, they now know which class to extend. Notice that the class PIN Validation Transaction Manager contains two variation points. Also notice that the vpoExpiredCard variation point belongs to two classes, ATM Control and Language Prompt. This means that both classes must be examined to build a variant from this variation point. For the stolen card example, vpoStolenCard is allocated to the class Debit Card.

6. Static Variation Point View

The static variation point view shows the static aspects of the variation point. This view shows which classes and methods are involved in the variation point. This view only shows what the reuser needs to know. There may be other classes affected by the variation point view, but only the classes the reuser needs to be aware of are shown in this view.

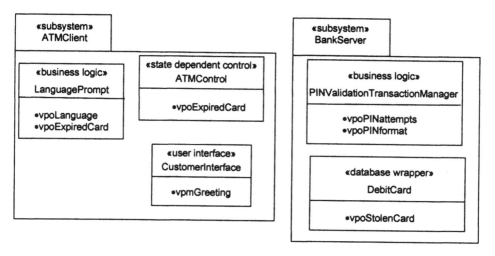

Fig. 3. Component Variation Point View Example

The static variation point view uses the UML class diagram. The class diagram shows the set of classes, interfaces, and collaborations and their relationships. The static variation point view includes the classes that are involved in the variation point.

The static variation point view uses two UML extensibility mechanisms: tagged values and constraints. The most critical part of the static variation point view is tagging the variation point. In other words, tagging the methods or attributes of the class that are involved in the variation point. A UML tagged value {variation point = vp ⟨mvo⟩ ⟨VariationPointName⟩} is placed after the element it affects. Not only does this show the reuser the parts of a variation point, but it also shows which classes the variation point impacts that the reuser must understand in order to build a variant. The UML extension mechanism, constraint, is used to show that the relationships in the static variation point view are for reuse purposes only. In other words, these are the relationships the reuser uses to build a variant. Three types of variation points have been modeled thus far: inheritance, parameterization, and callback.

6.1 Inheritance Variation Point Type

Figure 4 shows the static variation point view for the inheritance type. Anything within the symbols ⟨⟩ are for the builder of the variation point model to supply. In this view the variation point model developer will supply the name of the common core component, the name of the class contained in the common core component, and the name of any attributes and methods which make up the class. The variation point tag is contained within brackets {} and is placed after any method or attribute that is to be overwritten in the common core class. This is the actual location of the variation point in the common core component. The symbols [ ] are used to designate information supplied by the reuser. In the inheritance case, the derived class name is to be supplied by the reuser. The inheritance relationship is constrained with "reuse only" to explicitly say that the common core component does not supply this variant, only the variation point. If the variant were to include other classes derived from other components, this would also be shown in this view and all methods or attributes would have the same variation point tag with the same variation point name to show all the parts of the variation point.

The common core component contains class factory. The class factory contains a registry of all parent child variant relationships. When a common core method is executing which may use a variant, this method will ask the class factory for the variant object. The common core components know about variants because the reuser registers the variants with the common core via a class factory.

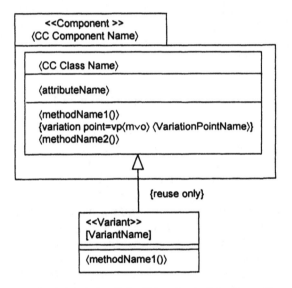

Fig. 4. Static Variation Point View for the Inheritance Type

6.2 Parameterization Variation Point Type

Parameterization allows the common core developer to build a component with the specific values of the parameters to be supplied by the reuser. The parameters are supplied to the common core component via an interface. The parameters are defined during the design stage and modeled in this view.

A generic parameterization static variation point view is shown in figure 5. The method used to supply these parameters is tagged with the variation point name in the common core component. This shows where the variation within the common core component is taking place without changing the common core component itself.

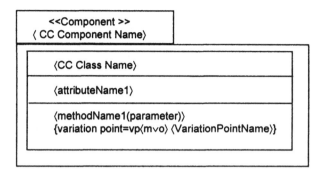

Fig. 5. Static Variation Point for Parameterization Type

6.3 Callback Variation Point Type

Callback allows the common core developer to build a component that contains a callback to the reuser's code. This allows control to be passed to the reuser's code. The common core component contains a registry of callbacks. A callback is a pointer to a reuser provided function. When a common core method is executing which may have a callback, this method will check to see if a callback is registered and then call that method in the variant class. The common core components know about callbacks because the reuser registers the callback with the common core. Therefore, the reuser can perform whatever function is needed and return control to the common core.

Figure 6 shows a generic static variation point view for the callback type. The variation point tags show the parts of the variation point the reuser needs to know about. The reuser does not need to know which method is using the variant. The reuser needs to know how to build the variant and how to register it. Figure 6 shows that the common core has a set of methods that may have a need to call a variant. It is not important which method calls the variant. The reuser builds the variant class. This variant class is a class that contains a member function. The callback is a pointer to that member function. The reuser then registers this callback with the common core component. This registration is done by a common core developer supplied interface. In this case, the interface or method is registerCB(*VariantMethodPointer). During registration, the reuser's code sends the common core component a callback that is a pointer to the variant's method. The method to register the callback is tagged. This is the method the reuser uses to register the callback that in turn extends the functionality of the common core component.

Since a callback is done with a callback to the reuser's variant class, the common core component is dependent on the variant. This is shown in UML by a dotted arrow. Another part of the reuser's code registers the variant.

6.4 Example of Static Variation Point View for Callback Type

Figure 7 shows the static variation point view for vpoStolenCard. The reuser supplies the information contained between the angle brackets [ ].

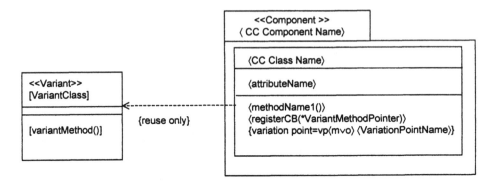

Fig. 6. Static Variation Point View for Callback Type

The vpoStolenCard example is a callback variation point type.The unique behavior is captured in the variant and control is passed to this variant. This shows that the reactToStolenCard (in CardID) method is the required method for executing the variant.

In order to model this behavior, the UML tag is used. This example shows that below the method registerStolenCardCB (in StolenCardI) is the tag {variation point = vpoStolenCard}. This tag informs the reuser that this is the method used to register the variant. This is what the reuser needs to know in order to execute the variant. The reuser does not know which part of Debit Card actually uses the Stolen Card Variant.

Once the variant is registered, the IStolenCard interface specifies the operation reactToStolenCard (in cardID), which the reuser has to implement. The DebitCard class belongs to the core assets and uses the method reactToStolenCard (in cardID), which is built by the reuser. The reuser implements this method to execute the reuser-defined functionality, such as calling the local police and/or confiscating the customer's card.

The difference between figure 6 and 7 shows the dependency on the language used. Figure 6 uses a pointer to a method. Java does not support method pointers. Therefore, a Java interface was used in figure 7. This demonstrates that VPM can be used to represent variation points in any language.

7. Dynamic Variation Point View

When a variant is created for a variation point, the component needs to know this variant now exists and the dynamic variation point view shows how to make the variant known to the component. For example, if a variation point is to create a new class that contains a new method, this new class and method must now be registered with the component so the component is aware that it must use this new method

Figure 8 shows the vpoStolenCard example of a dynamic variation point view. This shows that the object StolenCardVariant() is registered with the Customer Interface and which method in the Customer Interface to use to register this callback.

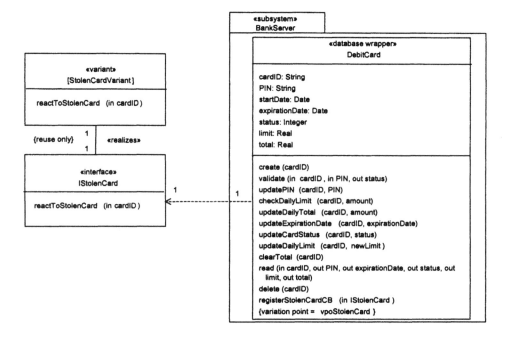

Fig. 7. Static Variation Point View for vpoStolenCard

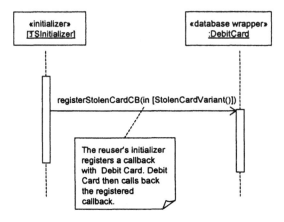

Fig. 8. Dynamic Variation Point View for vpoStolenCard

The static variation point view and the dynamic variation point view are created during the design phase of the common core development. This is where the design of the component needs to be understood so the core asset developer can also design the variation point. These views represent the inner workings of the core component become part of the reference architecture provided to the reuser. Together the static and dynamic variation point views give the reuser an understanding of how to build a variant from a variation point.

8. Proof of Concept Exercise

A proof of concept exercise was done to demonstrate that variation points modeled using VPM could be implemented. The proof of concept exercise was performed to create a system given the variation points modeled using VPM as part of the software architecture. This exercise implemented the ATM problem using the Java programming language. Six variation points were implemented as illustrated in Figure 3. A common core was developed first and tested in an application engineering environment. Once the common core was completed, four target systems were created. This exercise achieved its objective, which was to demonstrate that the variation points could be implemented using the variation points modeled using VPM. The implementation as a proof of concept exercise is discussed in more detail in [26].

9. Conclusions

VPM is a method for modeling variation points, thereby allowing a reuser to build variants. Modeling the variation points is crucial to communicating to the reuser how the core assets can be extended. This allows the reuser to know where the variation points exist in the core assets, how to build a variant from a variation point, and if a variation point is mandatory where a variant must be provided.

This paper has described how VPM has modeled the parameterization, inheritance, and callback variation point types. A detailed step-by-step method exists for each VPM view. In future, other variation point types could also be modeled with VPM.

Acknowledgements

The authors thank Dave Rine for his valuable advice and Vinesh Vonteru for his implementation of the proof of concept prototype. Acknowledgements are also due to Addison Wesley Publishing Company for permission to use material from the Banking System Case Study in Chapter 19 of "Designing Concurrent, Distributed, and Real-Time Applications with UML", by Hassan Gomaa, Addison Wesley Object Technology Series, 2000.

References

[1] Jacobson, I., Griss, M., Jonsson, P., Software Reuse-Architecture, Process and Organization for Business Success. ACM Press, New York, NY, 1997.
[2] Clements, P., Northrop, L., *A Framework for Software Product Line Practice, Version 3.0*, Software Engineering Institute, Carnegie Mellon University, Pittsburgh, PA, September 2000. Available online, http://www.sei.cmu.edu/plp/framework.html.

[3] Bosch, J., Design & Use of Software Architectures: Adopting and Evolving a Product-Line Approach, Addison-Wesley, Harlow, England, 2000.

[4] El Kaim, W., Cherki, S., Josset, P., Paris, F., *Domain Analysis and Product-Line Scoping: a Thomson-SCF Product-Line Case Study*, Proceedings, Software Product Lines: Economics, Architectures, and Implications, June 2000.

[5] Pree, W., Design Patterns for Object-Oriented Software Development, Addison-Wesley, 1995

[6] Coriat, M., Jourdan, J., Fabien, B., *The SPLIT Method*, Alcatel/Thomson-CSF Common Research Laboratory, France, 2000.

[7] El Kaim, W., *Managing Variability in the LCAT SPLIT/Daisy Model*, Proceedings, Product Line Architecture Workshop SPLC1, August 2000.

[8] Kang, K., *Feature-Oriented Domain Analysis*, Technical Report No. CMU/SEI-90-TR-21, Software Engineering Institute, Carnegie Mellon University, Pittsburgh, PA, 1990.

[9] H. Gomaa, L. Kerschberg, V. Sugumaran, C. Bosch, I Tavakoli, *A Knowledge-Based Software Engineering Environment for Reusable Software Requirements and Architectures*, J. Auto. Softw. Eng., Vol. 3, Nos. 3/4, Aug. 1996.

[10] H. Gomaa and G.A. Farrukh, "Methods and Tools for the Automated Configuration of Distributed Applications from Reusable Software Architectures and Components", IEEE Proceedings – Software, Vol. 146, No. 6, December 1999.

[11] Brownsword, L., Clements, P., *A Case Study in Successful Product Line Development*, Software Engineering Institute, Carnegie Mellon University, Pittsburgh, PA, October 1996. Available online,
http://www.sei.cmu.edu/publications/documents/96.reports/96tr016.html

[12] McComas, D., Leake, S., Stark, M., Morisio, M., Travassos, G., White, M., *Addressing Variability in a Guidance, Navigation, and Control Flight Software Product Line*, Proceedings SPLC1, Product Line Architecture Workshop, August 2000.

[13] Morisio, M., Travassos, G., Stark, M., *Extending UML to Support Domain Analysis*, Proceedings, 1st International Software Product Line Conference, Pittsburgh, PA, 2000.

[14] STARS. *Software Technology for Adaptable Reliable Systems, The Product-Line Approach*. Available online, www.asset.com/stars/afdemo/prodline.htm.

[15] STARS. *Software Technology for Adaptable Reliable Systems, Product-Line Concept*. Available online, www.asset.com/stars/darpa/prodline.htm.

[16] Sharp, D., *Reducing Avionics Software Cost Through Component Based Product Line Development*, Product Line Issues Action Team (PLIAT) Workshop, 1998.

[17] Bergey, J., Campbell, G., Clements, P., Cohen, S., Jones, L., Krut, B., Northrop, L., Smith, D., *Second DoD Product Line Practice Workshop Report*, Software Engineering Institute, Carnegie Mellon University, Pittsburgh, PA, October 1999. Available online,

http://www.sei.cmu.edu/publications/documents/99.reports/99tr015.html

[18] Bayer, J., Flege, O., Knauber, P., Laqua, R., Muthig, D., Schmid, K., Widen, T., DeBaud, J., *PuLSE: A Methodology to Develop Software Product Lines*, Proceedings of the Fifth Symposium on Software Reusability, 1999.

[19] Atkinson, C., Bayer, J., Laitenberger, O., Zettel, J., *Component-Based Software Engineering: The KobrA Approach*, Proceedings, 3rd International Workshop on Component-based Software Engineering, 2000.

[20] Atkinson, C., Bayer, J., Muthig, D., *Component-Based Product Line Development: The KobrA Approach*, Proceedings, 1st International Software Product Line Conference, 2000.

[21] Weiss, D., Lai, C., Software Product-Line Engineering: A Family-Based Software Development Process, Addison-Wesley, Reading, MA, 1999.

[22] H. Gomaa, "Object Oriented Analysis and Modeling for Families of Systems with the UML", Proc. IEEE International Conference on Software Reuse, Vienna, Austria, June 2000.

[23] Booch, G., Rumbaugh, J., Jacobson, I., The Unified Modeling Language User Guide, Addison-Wesley, Reading MA, 1999.

[24] Rumbaugh, J., Jacobson, I., Booch, G., The Unified Modeling Language Reference Manual, Addison-Wesley, Reading MA, 1999.

[25] Gomaa, H., Designing Concurrent, Distributed, and Real-Time Applications with UML, Addison-Wesley, 2000.

[26] Webber, D., *The Variation Point Model for Software Product Lines*, Ph.D. Dissertation, George Mason University, 2001.

Reusing Open-Source Software and Practices: The Impact of Open-Source on Commercial Vendors

Alan W. Brown and Grady Booch

Rational Software,
8383 158th Avenue NE, Redmond WA 98052
abrown@rational.com, egb@rational.com

Abstract. One of the most intriguing ways that commercial developers of software can become more efficient is to reuse not only software but also best practices from the open-source movement. The open-source movement encompasses a wide collection of ideas, knowledge, techniques, and solutions. Commercial software vendors have an opportunity to both learn from the open-source community, as well as leverage that knowledge for the benefit of its commercial clients. This paper looks at a number of the characteristics of the open-source movement, offers a categorization of open-source dimensions, and provides an analysis of the opportunities available to commercial software vendors when applying the lessons from the open-source movement.

Introduction

Open-source represents one of the most interesting and influential trends in the software industry over the past decade. Today, many organizations are looking toward open-source as a way to provide greater flexibility in their development practices, jump-start their development efforts by reusing existing code, and provide access to a much broader market of users [1].

However, what is widely referred to as the "open-source movement" is in reality a plethora of relative independent initiatives representing a variety of technology innovations and approaches. Elements of the movement's best practices include broadening the notion of a project team, frequent release of new software builds, greater collaboration across geographically dispersed teams enabled by the Internet, and creation of publicly available source code for adaptation and reuse. While a few common threads and community voices have emerged (e.g., Richard Stallman, Eric Raymond, Linus Torvalds, and Tim O'Reilly), the "community" remains essentially a collection of different activities galvanized by a recognition of the benefits of broader, more open access to the software development process, and to the results of that process.

A number of these innovations and approaches have a direct impact on commercial software vendors. There are some aspects on which these vendors can build, others that are in direct competition, and some that offer partnering opportunities in the spirit of "coopetition".

C. Gacek (Ed.): ICSR-7, LNCS 2319, pp. 123–136, 2002.

In this paper we examine the relationship between commercial software vendors and open-source. While there is a great deal that could be said, here we concentrate on a few of the major threads with an eye toward the business and economic aspects of this relationship. Many more aspects of the technical and legal relationships require further exploration. Additionally, this paper assumes that the reader does not require too much background or motivation for commercial software vendors' interest in open-source.

Many commercial software perspectives could be adopted in this analysis of open-source, each with its own peculiarities and concerns. However, in this paper the authors assume the perspective of one particular class of commercial software vendor – vendors of software development methods and tools. This is the community with which the authors are most familiar, and in many respects this view is representative of the broader set of perspectives. Hence, the term "commercial software vendor" can be interpreted to refer to this narrow definition, although with obvious application in most cases to the broader commercial software vendor community.

Reuse and Open-Source

It can be argued that the open-source approach is the software industry's most successful form of large-scale software reuse. Open-source software offers the most astounding range of reusable assets for any software project. Open-source software is available for virtually all activities, runs on every platform, and can be used in almost every business domain for which software is written. The open-source movement is predicated on reuse, in many cases with licensing that insists that derived products are themselves released into the public domain.

Two kinds of open-source software reuse can be observed. In the first case, the reuse of open-source software is a planned strategy to augment a popular free product, taking advantage of the wide informal network of open-source developers and users and thus minimizing internal development resources. Often these efforts focus around highly popular open-source products such as Linux, Apache, or StarOffice. Similarly, efforts may be specifically designed in this way through industry consortia. An interesting example of this is the group of commercial software development organizations who have committed to using the Eclipse platform as the basis for software development tools.[1] Eclipse provides an open-source tools framework with an extensible plug-in architecture. As a result, commercial tool vendors do not have to re-implement common functions for managing menus and toolbars, file explorers, and drawing surface manipulation. Rather, they can concentrate on extending this framework with their own value-added domain-specific behavior.

In the second case, reuse of open source is more ad hoc. Particularly in terms of the infrastructure of software development, there are many open-source software products that are so pervasive that they have become part of the fabric of most development organizations. Examples of such products include EMACS, the GNU compilers, build tools such as Ant, and scripting languages such as Perl, PHP, and TCL.

---

[1] The Eclipse consortium includes IBM, WebGain, Borland, TogetherSoft, Merant and Rational Software. See www.eclipse.org for details.

We observe that the reuse of open-source software is just as prevalent in the commercial world as it is in the academic world. Many commercial software organizations would simply not be able to function without some open-source software.

What Is Open-Source?

There are many different views on open-source. A great deal of confusion and misunderstanding often results because discussions on open-source and its impact are frequently not grounded in some common context.

However, as with many topics, describing a laundry list of different definitions of open-source and then positing a new one is not particularly fruitful. Rather than attempt that here, in this section we simply characterize some of the main elements of an open-source approach, and identify some of the issues that arise from those characteristics.

In particular, we focus here on two aspects of open-source that are of special interest to commercial software vendors: the open-source business model, and the open-source development process. The first - the open-source business model - is relevant because it allows us to discuss why mainstream software engineers[2] are looking toward open-source and what they hope to achieve from it.[3] The second - the open-source development process - is equally important because any development environment offering tools for a software engineering community must be well-matched to the development process being followed. With the growing influence of open-source initiatives on all aspects of software engineering it is important to understand open-source development as it offers insight into the requirements for any set of services aimed at the software development community.

Definition and Reality

There does exist a common definition for open-source used by the open-source community (see http://www.opensource.org/osd.html) that is succinct and well crafted. However, it is rather narrow in scope, referring most particularly to the kind of licensing used in a released product, and the rights of third parties to be able to extend, customize, and reuse that product.

However, in reality most individuals and organizations claiming some affinity or use of open-source see it far more broadly than a licensing issue. They frequently see it in terms of:

- Releasing (part of) the source code for a product to broaden its usage base, and encouraging a 3rd party developer community around that product. This is the essential tenet of the Open Software Foundation (OSF).

---

[2] We hesitate to talk about "mainstream" in this context as too pejorative a term. But alternatives such as "traditional" or "commercial" do not seem any better!

[3] This really refers to project managers and decision makers, rather that practitioners per se.

- A way to break the stranglehold on software development held by a few large software vendors – or more likely a way to "keep them honest" through the presence of competition
- A philosophy that aims at leveraging the skills of a wider base of talented software engineers over the Internet.
- Not building new systems from scratch, or with only proprietary code.
- An approach to releasing systems more frequently in line with users expectations for greater responsiveness and shorter cycle times associated with doing business at "Internet speed".

For many commercial organizations interested in open-source the issue of licensing and public release of source code is a secondary consideration. In some cases it is considered a necessary evil to achieve the other goals. At best it is considered a means to an end, not an end in itself. This is confirmed, in fact, in a recent survey of Linux developers [2] in which half of the people developing Linux application said that less than 25% of the Linux based applications they developed were being released and licensed as open-source.

This begs the question: what is open-source? Because of this diversity of opinion, it may be useful to consider the following categories in place of the general term "open-source"[4]:

- **Open-software** – release of source code with a product, and use of an open-source license to encourage or ensure further source distribution, licensing, and redistribution.
- **Open-collaboration** – Internet-based communication and synchronization involving discussion groups, virtual meeting rooms, shared access to development assets, and so on.
- **Open-process** – external visibility of development and release processes, including external auctioning of some aspects of a project, with coordination of multiple resources from within and outside the organization.
- **Open-releases** – use of frequent product releases (at least weekly, if not more often) that gives access for developers to the latest enhancements, and allows early testing and hardening of fixes and enhancements.
- **Open-deployment** – targeting new product releases to a platform that consists (mostly) of open-source products (such as Linux, Apache, Samba, Postfix, etc.).
- **Open-environment** – development of systems using tools and utilities that consist (mostly) of open-source products (such as emacs, GCC, CVS, GNATS, etc.).

Of course, many of these ideas are not unique to the open-source movement. For example, the ideas of open-process are fundamental to approaches such as extreme programming (XP), and open-deployment is arguably the key motivation for Sun's Java initiative (which is not currently open-software according to the definition above).

Note also that these categories are frequently seen in some combination. For example, it seems that the Printer Group at HP are primarily motivated by a move toward open-releases and an open-process, but not open-source or open-software as defined above. The development may use proprietary tools and services, and the results of these efforts will still be included in proprietary product releases.

The Open-Source Business Model

If the open-source approach – actually, if *any* approach - is to be considered a viable way to develop commercial software, it is important to understand the business model

---

[4] We are not proposing all these new terms to be used formally. Rather, in discussions and readings we find it valuable to keep this set of "virtual categories" in our head to gain a deeper understanding of priorities and expectations.

that allows this to occur. The basic premise of an open-source approach is that by "giving away" part of the company's intellectual property, you receive the benefits of access to a much larger market. These users then become the source of additions and enhancements to the product to increase its value, and become the target for a range of revenue-generating products and services associated with the product.

The key, then, is in deciding which projects and products make good candidates for an open-source approach. In [3], Brian Behlendorf[5] suggests that open-source can be a successful business model for commercial projects only within a limited scope. In any such project the following consideration must be taken into account:

- *Characteristics as a software platform.* As a base for developing other applications, a platform fulfils a key role. Because a platform performs a strategic role in those solutions, it is frequently undesirable to have the platform controlled by a single organization. Hence, an open-source approach is particularly appropriate for software that can become a key platform for others to build upon. It makes the platform widely available, encourages its use across the widest possible user community, and fosters a rich set of 3rd party solutions using the platform.

- *Impact on your revenue model.* The financial impact of giving away core parts of an existing product as open-source must be carefully considered. The financial argument typically made is that by doing this it makes the software much more widely available, offering a much larger base of users for additional products, courses, training, and consulting. Such economic forecasts must be validated before a company should be willing to bet its business on an open-source model.

- *Identified market need.* Making (part of) a product open source is only effective if the product is found to be useful. Providing source code is not in itself sufficient to displace a well-entrenched commercial product, or a rival open-source product. Before an open-source decision is made a full analysis of its value to others must be made.

- *Emphasis on server-focused services.* Successful open-source software has tended to implement infrastructure or server-side services. That is because server-side solutions tend to be more pervasive and stable than desktop solutions, incremental additions to functionality are more easily managed, and the developers using open-source solutions tend to be more knowledgeable in these domains (due to their engineering backgrounds). Another factor is the dominance of Microsoft technology on the desktop – something Microsoft is trying to repeat on the server-side.

- *Choosing the right open-source license.* Many kinds of open-source license exist. These vary based on who and how extensions to the software can be made, and whether those extensions also become public domain. Care needs to be taken choosing the appropriate license, and selecting the open-source software on which you build.

- *Making sure you gain momentum.* Early momentum is needed to form a vibrant community of developers and users. Open-source does not mean that no resources are needed to make the software successful. Typical tasks to be managed include active use of discussion groups, provision of management and

---

[5] Brian Behlendorf is a leader of the Apache web server project, and founder of Collab.net.

infrastructure of open-source tools and software, frequent communication through a web site, responding to many enquiries and suggestions, and so on. An open-source project splits into different factions, or falls into disrepute, if the original developers fail to respond to suggestions, do not interact with the user community, or fail to incorporate submitted fixes and updates.

- *Using appropriate tools.* A suitable environment for sharing, synchronizing, and managing the open-source is required. Typically, many different issues and requests will be made, and new fixes and updates will occur from people all over the globe. In addition, users will expect to be able to have visibility into the tracking and management process. In open-source projects these are often managed using tools such as CVS and GNATS.

In summary, we see that a successful, economically-viable open-source approach requires a number of rather stringent requirements be met. Candidate projects for an open-source approach must be very carefully examined based on these requirements. An interesting illustration of this business decision being made in practice is found in [5]. Here, the authors reached the decision that making key parts of their web authoring toolkit open-source increased the value of their company many-fold due to the much wider market access it provided. It allowed them to build their product's position as a widely used platform for web development from which they can gain revenue in add-on products and services.

The Open-Source Development Model

The common, public image of an open-source project is that of a chaotic series of development "accidents" that by some miracle of nature results in a software that compiles and executes. The reality, of course, is very different. The open-source movement has evolved toward a well-defined development process geared to the unique requirements placed upon it – coordination of large numbers of people across the Internet bound together by common interests and goals. The main characteristics of this process include:

- *Encouraging a wide community of users, testers, and developers.* Much of the power of an open-source approach arises from the fact that a large community of people are available to use and exercise the software. This contributes to early diagnosis of problems, consolidation on which new features provide value, and helps to encourage development of patches, updates, and enhancements to the software.
- *Communicating with developers frequently and vigorously.* Open-source projects are renowned for their open forums containing lively technical exchanges. Requirements, designs, and work arounds are widely discussed. New ideas must be proposed and vigorously defended to ensure that they are accepted and introduced into the code base. In addition, e-mail exchanges are frequently the basis for much of the project's history and design documentation.
- *Releasing new software often.* Due to the large developer base, fixes and updates are submitted daily, if not even more frequently. In many open-source projects this new code is typically baselined into the released software on a daily basis.

For example, it is not unusual in some open-source projects to have multiple releases of a code base each week. Often, this is controlled by also maintaining a stable build on a longer time cycle (say, monthly). This quick release of updates ensures that users who choose to can immediately take advantage fixes and new functionality. With this approach any bad fixes or ill-conceived additions are quickly found and removed.

- *Applying strong coordination.* To support frequent releases there must be a strong coordination model. Often this is due to tight control exerted by the open-source coordinator. Their responsibility is to maintain design authority over the code, make decisions on the appropriateness of each addition, and to apply proper configuration control to the builds. This is the most important role in the open-source development process. It can be argued that every interesting open-source product has a strong intellectual leader and hard-core developer behind it. Each wields a strong hand in the content of that product, making these development projects more like a benign dictatorship than a true bazaar.

- *Being responsive.* The developers involved in an open-source project are not generally motivated by salary, or career enhancement. They tend to get involved due to their need to solve problems, work with their peers in a collaborative environment, and demonstrate their development prowess.[6] It is important that their ideas are examined, analyzed, and considered for inclusion. This requires those in charge of an open-source project to be intelligent, diligent, and responsive. It is the least that the development community expects.

- *Ensuring visibility into the process.* One of the expectations about an open-source project is that there is some measure of openness in the process that is used for development. That requires a set of tools and services that allow developers to submit requests and changes, view their status, and interact with the open-source coordinators to ensure appropriate decisions have been made. This is most often carried out using mailing lists, discussion forums and Internet-based developer portals. Additionally, for larger projects there are meetings, workshops, and developer conferences.

Each of these characteristics contributes to the open-source development process to create a highly interactive approach. In many ways these projects represent the antithesis of the large, "waterfall"-style projects that in the past dominated mainstream software engineering.

When (and When Not) to Reuse Open-Source Software

The discussion above is useful for highlighting the diversity of perspectives on open-source. However, it does little to illustrate the practical considerations faced by many organizations in the most prevalent form of reuse involving open-source – when reusing open-source software as part of a non-open-source software development project. In such situations there are many important considerations.

---

[6] The motivation and ethics of open-source development is complex topic in its own right, and discussed in detail in [3].

Typically, during the project's conception or early analysis phases there are some aspects of the proposed solution that appear to be candidates for reuse of open-source software. At this point all the traditional reuse techniques for evaluating, adapting, and including the open-source software into the new system are applicable. However, due to the open-source nature of the reused software, there are a number of special considerations that must be taken into account. While the functionality and accessibility of the open-course software may be ideally suited for reuse in this new context, these additional considerations are frequently dominant in the decision process concerning whether the open-source software can be reused.

Based on the authors' practical experiences, we have found two issues to be the most difficult and complex to consider: licensing and security. It can rightly be argued that both of these must be considered in any reuse situation. However, practical experience leads us to conclude that they take on disproportionately more significance when open-source software is involved.

It is interesting to note that these concerns are in-line with other commercial software vendors. The most prominent warnings about the problems of reusing open-source software in a commercial context have come from Microsoft. In a recent speech[7] Craig Mundie, a Microsoft Senior Vice President, stated that:

> "The [open-source software] development model ... has inherent security risks and can force intellectual property into the public domain."

This concern has led to Microsoft labeling open-source software as "viral" software, and to warnings that open-source software licensing approach such as the GNU Public License (GPL) has a viral nature that poses a threat to the intellectual property of any organization that derives its products from GPL source. We explore these concerns in more detail below.

Licensing

Open-source software licenses are typically rather straightforward, but their implications on any systems reusing that software can be rather profound. The main concern often hinges on the notion of whether the system reusing the open-source software is considered to be a "derived work". If so, according to many open-source licenses the system reusing the software must also be considered open-source software and subject to the same licensing agreements. This is a basic tenet, for example, in the GNU Public License (GPL).

Commercial software development efforts are at most risk from license violations, and of course large commercial organizations are the most attractive targets for being sued for infringements of any licensing agreements. Even the remote possibility that a large-scale commercial product could be claimed to be risking its commercial viability by reusing open-source software frequently results in most commercial organizations insisting on an "open-source review" before the release of any new commercial product. Indeed, most large commercial software organizations have legal

---

[7] See "Prepared Text of Remarks by Craig Mundie, Microsoft Senior Vice President, The Commercial Software Model, The New York University Stern School of Business, May 3, 2001" - http://www.microsoft.com/presspass/exec/craig/05-03sharedsource.asp.

experts on call who specialize in ensuring the legal ramifications of reuse of open-source software are well understood.

From a legal perspective there seem to be four possible strategies to consider when reusing open-source software:

1. Don't reuse open-source software;
2. Clearly separate (architecturally) the pieces of the system that rely on open-source software from independent layers that leverage them – the independent layers can then be considered proprietary;
3. Hire a good open-source software lawyer;
4. Place all the resulting software in the public domain too!

Security

Recent publicity has highlighted the inherent insecurity of many of the software-based systems that we all rely on everyday. These concerns have increased the scrutiny on how software is developed, and in particular the origins of much of this software. Reuse of open-source software has raised the most concern. The media makes a great deal of the fact there can often be many individual contributors to a single open-source software system. As a result, they ask "if you don't know who developed your software, how do you know what it will do?"

Clearly, there is some substance to this argument. Large software systems involve millions of lines of code developed over an extended period of time by literally hundreds of developers. Verifying that there are no hidden security flaws (whether intended or otherwise) is practically impossible. When part of the system is a piece of reused open-source software, the risk of security problems increases.

Of course everyone does not hold this view. As open-source advocates point out, open-source software such as Linux and Apache is probably the most widely known and used code base in existence. The wide availability of the source code has meant that many thousands of programmers around the world have at some stage looked at and examined parts of the software. In contrast, large commercial systems are rarely released as source code. Therefore, as a consumer you have no ability to find out what that system really does.

Regardless of many company's positions on this debate, the possibility of security issues by reusing open-source software has itself been sufficient to ensure that many companies do not reuse open-source software in their systems. Instead, they rely on the support provided by commercial systems.

From a security perspective there seem to be three strategies you can take when reusing open-source software:

1. Don't reuse open source software;
2. Only reuse open-source software that has been through extensive internal code reviews typical of all software you develop;
3. Foster a strong relationship and understanding of the open-source software community, closely follow the newsgroups for open-source software that you reuse, and get involved in the development of that open-source software!

Taking Advantage of Open-Source in a Commercial Setting

Commercial software is rarely released as open-source, simply because there is no sustainable economic business case for such a practice. Typically in commercial settings there is no intention to release the developed software into the public domain using one of the open-source licenses. In fact, in many cases it would be impossible to do so given that at its core many such solutions aggregate, integrate, and extend commercially acquired tools and services.

However, commercial software vendors have been significantly influenced by open-source initiatives, and leverage open-source products in a number of areas. This can be seen through inclusion of open-source software, in the targeting of open-source technologies for deployment, in support for the creation and management of interactive open communities, and in the move to supporting open styles of collaborative software engineering.

Here we review how commercial software organizations can best take advantage of the open-source movement. In the discussion below we focus on a specific class of commercial software vendors – the commercial software tools vendors, as represented by companies such as Rational Software.

Targeting an Open-Source Deployment Platform

Almost all organizations have standardized on (some flavor of) Microsoft Windows as the platform for the desktop, running client applications such as Microsoft Office Suite. However, many commercial organizations are now looking to deploy server-side solutions to a target platform containing a number of open-source products. Typically, this refers to the Linux operating system and Apache web server. Much of the demand for server-side open-source deployment is due to the perceived lack of reliability and speed offered by Microsoft, and the failure to offer low priced commercial server-side solutions by Microsoft's main rivals. As a consequence, commercial organizations are attracted by the low cost of setting up powerful server farms of Intel-based machines running open-source software.

However, there are many elements required to achieve success in the deployment of solutions to an open-source platform. Currently there appear to be three major barriers to success:

- *Few development tools.* While the open-source community provides a number of code-centric development tools, in general there are few robust, team-based tools supporting the broader software life-cycle. A wider range of tools for deploying applications to open-source platform is required.
- *Lack of practical advice on open-source deployment in a commercial setting.* There is little available knowledge on how to design, implement, and manage server farms constructed from groups of open-source products. In this context commercial organizations require a great deal of guidance and advice on many aspects of the software development process, models and "how-to" guides defining common architectural solutions, and heuristics and metrics on performance.

- *Scarcity of available skills.* There are few people currently with the skills to develop robust open-source deployment platforms for use in a commercial setting. To be successful requires not only greater training and education, it also requires access to a broader community of open-source expertise, and the opportunity to share knowledge and experiences with other organizations following a similar approach.

Commercial software vendors are in an excellent position to provide solutions to each of these three barriers.

First, commercial software vendors offer a range of best-of-breed development services covering the complete life-cycle. The tools offered by commercial software vendors are far in advance of anything currently available in the open-source community.

Second, the commercial software vendors approach to content management is to allow practical advice and information to be made available to the right people at the appropriate time in the development process. It would be an excellent basis on which to create a body of knowledge on deployment to an open-source platform in a commercial setting.

Third, the commercial software vendors' community activities and infrastructure support communication, and asset sharing among organizations using the commercial software vendors services. Many of these mechanisms could be focused on providing access to a range of expertise to commercial organizations targeting open-source deployment.

However, to support these communities effectively requires commercial software vendors to take a number of initiatives directly aimed at making progress in this area.

Measuring Up to the Open-Source Bar

There are already a number of organizations offering hosted development and collaboration services to the open-source community. The three main contenders here are Collab.net, OpenAvenue (which includes SourceXchange), and SourceForge.[8] Other sites not directly targeting the open-source community also offer free hosted services frequently used by open-source projects (e.g., egroups). Their primary services are in the areas of collaboration and discussion forums, code-centric tools, and project hosting.

To a large extent it can be said that these organizations have already "set the bar" with respect to a minimum set of services expected by organizations today as collaborative tool support for distributed teams of developers. The sites offer the standard against which other commercial software vendors will be measured. As a result, it is essential that commercial software vendors understand the services they offer, and can articulate their offering in relation to them. In this sense, the open-

---

[8] There are also many sites focused on information exchange (e.g., slashdot as well as platform-specific portals such as MSDN and developerWorks).

source offerings already available provide an important "touchstone" that the commercial software vendors can use to measure their services and capabilities.

Leveraging the Open-Source Community

One of the most intriguing questions concerns how commercial software vendors should leverage the open-source community. In particular, the open-source community represents a large body of software developers who are themselves potential clients for the commercial software vendors' offerings. Furthermore, they represent a significant set of influencers, trendsetters, and thought leaders in the software engineering community. There appear to be at least 3 possible opportunities for commercial software vendors to leverage the open-source community:

- *Target the open-source community as clients of commercial software products.* It is possible to consider integrating open-source artifacts to provide access to commercial software vendors services, and to encourage interaction between the open-source community and the commercial community. This has many attractions for both commercial software vendors and its clients. However, it must be balanced with the knowledge that there is little chance of direct revenue from this strategy because commercial software vendors will be in direct competition with the freely available open-source solutions. This may do more to expose commercial software vendors' weaknesses and gaps, rather than highlight its strengths.
- *Actively attract the open-source community to visit, take part in discussions, and share expertise.* While not integrating open-source projects, it is still desirable to attract the open-source community to commercial software vendor communities. They offer a perspective on software development that is essential to today's commercial organizations. Additionally, they may provide a marketplace for commercial organizations to obtain consulting and development resources. Commercial software vendors could position themselves as the place where "open-source meets the commercial market" for the benefit of both parties.
- *Provide a synthesis of open-source knowledge, technology, and techniques for use in a commercial setting.* A valuable service that commercial software vendors could offer would be to offer a synthesis of the open-source community for commercial software developers. There is so much knowledge and assets available for use, the commercial world has a great deal of trouble deciding what may be useful. Commercial software vendors could be sufficiently "plugged-in" to the open-source community to offer the best advice, knowledge, techniques, and solutions. This would be of tremendous value to the commercial community. It gives commercial software vendors a clear role, and does not directly compete with other open-source offerings.

Summary

As a result of the open-source movement there is now a great deal of reusable software available in the public domain. This offers significant functionality that commercial software vendors can use in their software projects. Open-source approaches to software development have illustrated that complex, mission critical software can be developed by distributed teams of developers sharing a common goal.

Commercial software vendors have an opportunity to both learn from the open-source community as well as leverage that knowledge for the benefit of its commercial clients. Nonetheless, the open-source movement is a diverse collection of ideas, knowledge, techniques, and solutions. As a result, it is far from clear how these approaches should be applied to commercial software engineering. This paper has looked at many of the dimensions of the open-source movement, and provided an analysis of the different opportunities available to commercial software vendors.

References and Notes

1. It can be argued that the open-source community has produced really only two essential products[9] -- Apache (undeniably the most popular web server) and Linux – although both are essentially reincarnations of prior systems. Both are also somewhat products of their times: Apache filled a hole in the then emerging Web, at a time no platform vendor really knew how to step in, and Linux filled a hole in the fragmented Unix market, colored by the community's general anger against Microsoft.
2. Evans Marketing Services, "Linux Developers Survey", Volume 1, March 2000. This provides a number of interesting statistics on the current practices of open-source developers.
3. Eric Raymond, "The Cathedral and the Bazaar: Musings on Linux and Open Source by an Accidental Revolutionary", O'Reilly Press, 2000.
   Raymond positions open-source as a logical evolution of previous development practices. In particular, argues that there is a strong sense of control, ownership, and process that is common to open-source projects.
4. Chris DiBona et al. (eds.), "Open Sources: Voices from The Open Source Revolution", O' Reilly Press, 1999.
   A selection of papers from the most prominent people in the open-source movement.
5. Paul Everitt, "How We Reached the Open Source Business Decision", Zope, http://www.zope.com/Members/paul/BusinessDecision, 1999.
   An enlightening case study on the business decision to go open-source, driven by the need to create a platform for web development.
6. David Brauer, "Toyota to save $3M a year with the help of Linux", Enterprise Linux Today, http://eltoday.com, October 24, 2000.
   The reason that Toyota chose Linux and Apache to connect their 1200 dealerships. Focuses

---

[9] Of course, there is Emacs, sendmail and all sorts of related products, but most of these are the products of a single person with contributions from various Darwinian-selected contributors. There are also products such as Sun's open source office product, but those did not rise organically from the primordial seas of the open source community, but rather were seeded by their patrons to serve some larger business goal.

on the small footprint, connectivity, and the deal between Redhat and Gateway to produce Linux boxes.

7. David Brauer, "Stocktalklive.com – A Business Case for Linux", Enterprise Linux Today, http://eltoday.com, July 17, 2000.
    A case study of stocktalklive.com and their use of Linux.

8. Alan MacCormack and M. Iansiti, "Developing Products on Internet Time", *Harvard Business Review*, 75th Anniversary Edition, Sep-Oct 1997.
    A look at the changing business practices in the software community due to the need to create systems more quickly and with greater flexibility. An extract from McCormack's Ph.D. thesis on this topic.

9. George Lawton, "Opening the Gates to a New Era", ADT Magazine, October 2000.
    A general discussion of the move to open-source. It contains a couple of interesting short case studies, and some industry opinions.

10. Ming-Wei Wu and Ying-Dar Lin, "Open Source Software Development: An Introduction", IEEE Computer, Vol. 34 No. 6, June 2001.
    A useful overview of open source initiatives, concentrating on the various kinds of licenses.

11. Haiqing Wang and Chen Wang, "Open Source Software Adoption: A Status Report", IEEE Computer, Vol. 18 No. 2, March/April 2001.
    A review of various open source software available, and a framework for evaluating the appropriateness of various open source software systems.s

Integrating Reference Architecture Definition and Reuse Investment Planning*

Klaus Schmid

Fraunhofer Institute for Experimental Software Engineering (IESE),
Sauerwiesen 6, D-67661 Kaiserslautern, Germany,
Klaus.Schmid@iese.fhg.de

Abstract. When developing a product line, the definition of an appropriate reference architecture that supports the required variabilities is of crucial importance to the success of the product line. In this paper we present an approach to the identification of the key variabilities and to determining the economic benefit of packaging these variabilities in terms of reusable components. This approach provides reusability requirements that can then be taken as an input to product line development. The analysis is based on the economics of the product line. Thus, the approach ensures the optimization of the economic benefit of a product line that is based on a reference architecture that takes these reusability requirements into account.
In this paper, we will describe our approach for deriving the reusability requirements, discuss its relationship to different possible investment scenarios, and study the results of the application of our approach in some case studies.

1 Introduction

In this paper, we provide an approach for linking two key concepts of product line reuse: architectures and investments. We will describe some case studies we performed in an industrial environment to study the benefits and applicability of our approach. Product line reuse is a systematic reuse approach, which has recently been getting significant attention as numerous industrial organizations embark on this approach and derive respectable benefits from its use.

Product line reuse can be defined as vertical reuse (i.e., in an application domain) within an organization, aiming at a specific line of products. The key to this specific reuse approach is the presence of a *reference architecture*. The reference architecture provides a common *structural framework*, which allows to build all systems according to a certain scheme and thus makes it possible to reuse significant components across the different products.

Independent of the specific approach to reuse, the key driver for reuse is always the desire to achieve significant economical benefits. The benefits can be of various types such as quality improvements, effort reduction, and so on. A more detailed account of

---
* This work has been partially funded by the ESAPS project (Eureka Σ! 2023 Programme, ITEA project 99005

the potential benefits and their relationship to reuse can be found in [19]. These benefits always derived from a previous investment that aimed at introducing reuse. Thus, throughout reuse efforts, one key question is always where to focus reuse investments.

In the classical notion of reuse (e.g., [23]), the reuse benefits are used to determine which components need to be developed in a reusable manner. However, in the specific case of product line reuse, this information must already be taken into account while developing the reference architecture, as the functionality where we are willing to invest in reuse must be packaged into exchangeable components in architecture definition. Thus, we regard the decision of reusability, similar to other requirements, as an input to the architecture definition process. We therefore call these constraints *reusability requirements*. These requirements are, however, soft requirements. They can conflict with each other, and these conflicts need to be resolved during architecting. Ideally, for this conflict resolution the required investment and the expected benefits are used as parameters to determine the requirements that should take precedence.

In this paper, we describe a specific technology that aims at identifying reusability requirements on the basis of an investment analysis and also provides us with the necessary quantitative information that allows us to perform the relevant trade-offs. The approach we describe here is actually only one part of the overall PuLSE-Eco V2.0 approach [16] to product line scoping. PuLSE-Eco V2.0 is, in turn, a major extension of the PuLSE-Eco approach as described in [6]. Here, we focus on the specific technology for performing quantitative analysis in PuLSE-Eco V2.0. We also analyze our approach using case studies that were performed in an industrial environment. This aims both at analyzing the benefits of our approach as well as the necessary conditions for its application.

In the following section, we will discuss some work related to architecture definition and to identifying and evaluating related trade-offs. In Section 3, we will describe the approach we are using for deriving the reusability requirements on the software architecture. In Section 4, we will discuss how our approach addresses the notion of investment models and how it integrates them in the derivation of the reusability requirements. In Section 5, we will focus on the transformation of the basic evaluation results into the final reusability requirements. Our approach has been thoroughly validated in the context of some case studies. We will discuss an excerpt of these validation results in Section 6. Finally, in Section 7 we will conclude.

2 Related Work

Software architecture is a concept that has received considerable attention over the last few years. Consequently, a bulk of work exists in this area. However, this work mostly concentrated on single system architectures. Only recently the interest in reference or product line architectures has increased strongly [3, 9], but in these approaches the aspect of product lines is introduced mostly in a qualitative manner and trade-offs are usually performed implicitly.

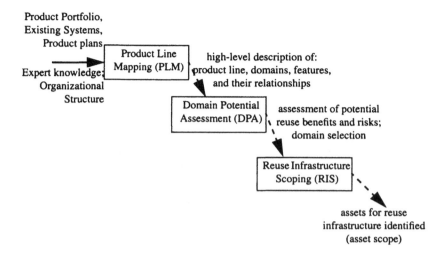

Fig. 1. PuLSE-Eco V2.0 Components

Only few approaches explicitly address reusability requirements in a quantitative manner [14]. Also in the context of architectural trade-offs the trade-offs are usually performed only in a qualitative manner. A notable exception is [10]. To our knowledge, this approach is the only approach so far that supports quantitative architectural trade-offs focusing particularly on reusability requirements across a product line.

3 The Approach

The approach we describe here is a major extension and formalization of a predecessor approach, which was described as PuLSE-Eco in [6]. Meanwhile this approach was also extended by further components like a qualitative assessment component, which has been described in [18]. An overview of the current version of the PuLSE-Eco V2.0 approach is given in Figure 1.

Here, we will only discuss the details of the reuse infrastructure scoping component (Figure 1). This component maps in its key concepts to the former PuLSE-Eco approach. Thus, we will only give a short description of the approach in this section, highlighting the extensions to the previous approach. Based on this overview we will then discuss the key aspects of this paper in the following sections.

The key idea of the PuLSE-Eco approach is to identify the products that shall be part of the product line along with their key functionality early in the planning phase. Then a quantitative analysis is performed to determine which features should be developed for reuse across the different products. This analysis relies on estimation models that aim at quantifying the specific goals that drive product line reuse in the organization (e.g., effort reduction, time-to-market reduction).

An overview of the process used to perform the analysis is given in Figure 2. This approach relies on the following preconditions that are established by the components product line mapping (PLM) and domain potential analysis (DPA):

- A disciplined description of the relevant products and their functionality has been developed.
- This functionality is adequately decomposed (in terms of technical sub-domains) so as to allow individual estimations (e.g., of effort) based on them to be combined.
- Risks that are inherent to product line development in the context of the specific products are identified and adequate counter-measures are devised.

One key aspect that is important to the overall success of the approach — in particular, in terms of the expected architecture information — is the way how the functionality is decomposed. Thus, we briefly describe our approach here, although this is part of the *product line mapping (PLM)* component. This component works in two stages. The first one aims at identifying the relevant products and their key functionality from an end-user perspective. However, these features are obviously not adequate as a basis to express reusability requirements. (Actually, they are not adequate as a basis for performing the quantitative analysis, either.)

Therefore we introduced a second step, which is actually a key difference to the approach described in [6]: this step aims at identifying internal features, i.e., functionality that is relevant to bring about the features visible to the end-user that were previously identified. This functionality is also organized in terms of technical domains, i.e., areas of functionality. As these domains are described (among other things) in terms of the functionality they bring about, as well as the data they store and interchange with other domains, together they can be regarded as a form of conceptual

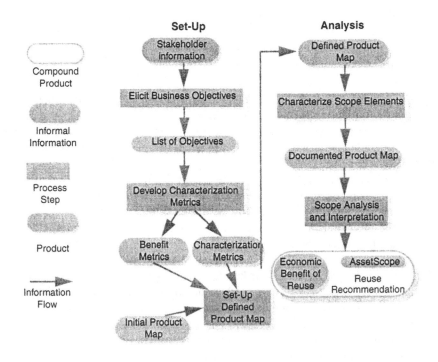

Fig. 2. Reuse Infrastructure Scorping Process

architecture. They are obviously not the final architecture, as this will only be developed at a later stage during architecture development. However, the conceptual architecture already aims at a decomposition of the functionality that *could be used* to bring about the intended functionality. This decomposition of functionality is typically performed using input from experts as well as any existing architectural information on similar systems. This information basis ensures that the features can later be mapped in a meaningful manner to the architecture. However, from our experience [12] we also found that even in cases where this information is not available, our approach ensures that an adequate structuring is found, although it may lack in such a situation in terms of completeness of the identified functionality.

We will now discuss the reuse infrastructure scoping component of our scoping process. A brief overview of the various steps is given in Figure 2. At this point in the overall scoping process, the other two components established the feature structure and analyzed the benefits and risks associated with the various domains. The first step in the process is to elicit the business objectives that are relevant to the organization for product line reuse. Here, we found that the following criteria are the standard criteria that re-occur over and over: reduction of time-to-market (for the first product, across the initial products in all market segments, on the average of the product line), development effort reduction, maintenance effort reduction, risk reduction (for first project, on average of product line), quality improvement, and expert load reduction.

However, while these criteria are quite standard, detailed interpretation needs to be elicited on an organization-specific basis, like, for example, what exactly should be regarded as maintenance costs depends on the environment.

When the goals have been defined, they are operationalized in terms of base metrics (*characterization metrics*) that are on a level so that actual data can be gathered from experts. This refinement process is similar to the GQM approach [26] as will be described in more detail in Section 4. In parallel to this refinement, a formalization of the goal is performed, so that it can be mathematically expressed in terms of the characterization metrics. Also in combination with this effort, the trade-offs among the different goals are captured (e.g., x days of development effort reduction is worth as much as y days of maintenance effort reduction). All information that was captured up to this point was captured by a small group of people: typically, product line management, marketing, project personnel, and a method expert. This can easily be done in a one-day workshop.

At this point in the process, the necessary information infrastructure has been developed to start the evaluation. To this end a table is set up, which is structured as shown in Figure 3. On the vertical axis, this table contains, the list of the features that have been developed as described above. On the horizontal axis, the table contains the list of products that are envisioned for the product line and the various characterization metrics (the values for the characterization metrics may differ for the various products, thus they need to be captured on a per-product basis). Now the various driver values can be captured from the different relevant experts (marketing, project leaders, product managers, technology experts, etc.). This will usually require a bit longer (typically, less than one person-day, but distributed over several days) as more people must be contacted.

On the basis of this information, the benefit metrics can be computed, characterizing the different goals, as these are expressed in terms of the characterization metrics. In practice, these benefit metrics describe the specific savings (corresponding to the underlying goal) that can be accrued by making the specific feature they are relating to reusable (e.g., development effort saved by a reusable implementation of the corresponding feature).

The individual benefits are then combined using the trade-offs that were captured together with the goals. This leads to a resulting score for the feature. In order to perform a semantically meaningful integration of the various benefits, the benefits need to be expressed in a common unit of measurement. This is usually a monetary unit. This overall score can then be interpreted as the benefits that can be accrued if the feature is made reusable and consequently reused across the product line as opposed to developing individual, specific implementations for the various products. (Likewise, a negative score needs to be interpreted as a reusable implementation that will actually cost more than benefits that can be expected.) A key role in determining the overall score is played by the benefit models, which will be discussed in further detail in Section 4. The final scores are then interpreted in terms of the specific reusability requirements on the architecture. We will describe this in Section 5.

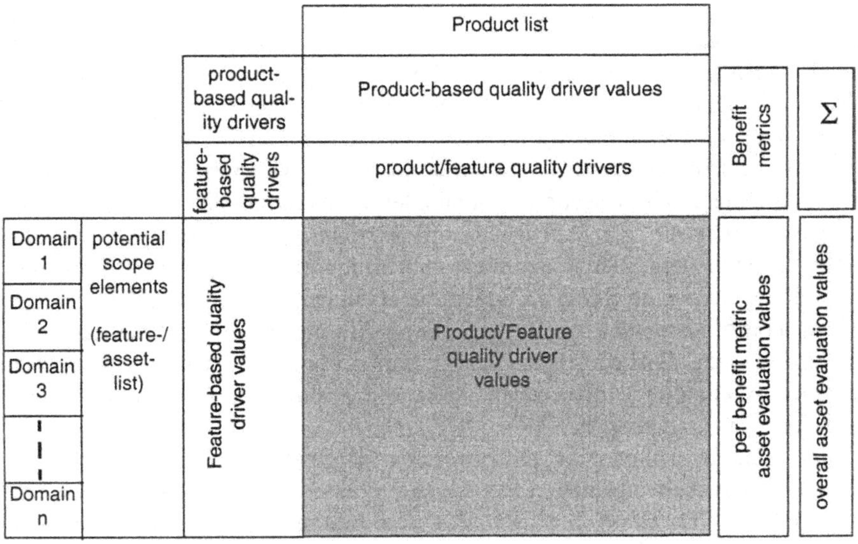

Fig. 3. Reuse Infrastructure Scorping Process

4   The Benefit Models

The key in determining what functionality should be reused and thus, the key to the reusability requirements are the benefit models. In this section, we will first discuss some key distinctions that need to be taken into account when analyzing the economics of product line reuse, then we will discuss the specific approach we used for deriving our models in the case studies (cf. Section 6). Finally, we will address the influence the specific development context has on the formulation of the model.

4.1 Dimensions of Investment Models

The key difficulty in addressing product line benefits is that they may take on many different forms such as effort reduction, time-to-market or quality improvement. This makes it hard to combine them to arrive at a final valuation. In order to solve this problem, we described the core of an appropriate product line economics model elsewhere (cf. [19]). Here, we will only give a high-level overview of the model. The specific model we propose consists of three main levels:
- The first level addresses the basics of costs and revenues without taking into account any adaptations due to financial theory.
- The second takes into account the aspect of discounted cash-flows.
- And the third level introduces the notion of uncertainty and consequently, of decision alternatives and options.

The model is further sub-divided in an orthogonal manner in terms of software development issues and market issues. While this distinction holds in principal across all three levels, it is the key on the first level and can then be propagated in a straight-forward manner to the other two levels. We make this distinction as we need to arrive at a common basis in order to integrate the different kinds of benefits.

Obviously, one common unit is money. The mapping to this unit is rather clear for goals like development effort reduction. However, some goals can only be indirectly mapped to money, like time-to-market. The relationship here is in terms of the revenues that can be accrued, which in turn depends on the specific market situation and the specific time of market entry, and it may actually vary strongly among the different products in the product line. This led us to introduce market revenues into the model. Fortunately, for specific situations this model can often be approximated without going back to the market level (e.g., if no time-to-market aspects are present or the time-dependency of revenues is weak).

The aspects that may influence a benefit model for a certain product line situation are numerous and organization-dependent. The specific approach we use for deriving specific benefit models is described in the next section.

4.2 Developing Investment Models

For standard goals like effort and schedule, there exist generic models like CoCoMo [3] or reuse models as described in [23]. While in principle those can be used, we use an approach that leads to specifically adapted models. This has many reasons: first, developing context-specific models usually leads to more adequate models [13]; second, our approach is open to integrate other aspects like quality for which no standardized models exist. The problem of deriving specialized investment models (i.e., models of the benefit- and cost situation) is very similar to the problem of developing a measurement plan in order to characterize a certain situation. A well-known approach to this is the GQM approach [26]. Thus, we modeled our approach to the development of benefit models based on GQM.

The approach works in a top-down fashion. The high-level goal is operationalized by transforming it into a benefit metric. As in GQM, this operationalization is performed using focusing questions to determine what exactly should be expressed by this metric. However, the benefit metric itself is not yet fully operational. Rather, it needs to be operationalized using characterization metrics, for which values can be easily determined by experts. Let us illustrate this with a simple example. The top-level goal *development effort reduction* can be operationalized into a benefit metric $E(f)$ that gives the saved development effort by making a certain feature reusable. However, in order to effectively determine the values of $E(f)$ we need to express it in the form of characterization metrics like $req(f,p)$, $eff_r(f,p)$, $eff(f,p)$:

req(f,p): is feature f required for product p? (1=yes; 0=no)
eff(f,p): effort of implementing f for product p [in hours]
eff_r(f,p): effort of reusing f in product p [in hours]
Using these characterization metrics we can describe $E(f)$:

$$E(f) = \sum_p req(f, p) \cdot eff(f, p) - \left(eff(f_{gen}) + \sum_p req(f, p) \cdot eff_r(f, p) \right)$$

Here, $eff_r(f_{gen})$ denotes the effort required for developing feature f for reuse. Using this approach we can define a (simplistic) model to express the desired business objective as the result of properties of the features and products in a way that can be determined by the experts. While this example is very simplistic, real benefit metrics take a similar form. However, we need to include certain aspects like: what kind of efforts are regarded as being relevant, what aspects are important to determining the effort. Thus, we can express *eff(f,p)* itself in terms of characterization metrics (e.g., the COCOMO factors [3]).

The level on which we will actually define the characterization metrics may vary considerably in practice. It strongly depends on the information available and the level of abstraction the experts feel most comfortable with. In our case studies we had a measurement program in place that allowed us to estimate the various efforts based on influential factors (e.g., quality of available documentation, new feature) and the expected size of the implementation. This allowed very detailed estimations and enabled us to include a considerable number of characterization metrics. However, a measurement program is not a prerequisite for our approach.

4.3   Influence of the Development Situation on the Investment

Determining the specific operationalization of the benefit metrics is clearly a non-trivial task, as it is influenced by a multitude of different aspects of the development situation. We can distinguish three main types of influences:
1. Process- and organization-related aspects
2. The existing assets
3. The product-line introduction scheme

The process- and organization-related aspects influence the relevant costs. This is known well for any form of software development (cf. COCOMO, [3]). Thus, we need to determine these aspects as would commonly do. However, we need to determine them particularly for *development with reuse, for reuse*, and *without reuse*; and in case we also need to address quality goals, we similarly need a quality estimation model like COQUALMO [7].

The existing assets influence the benefits that can be accrued from product line development insofar as with existing assets (e.g., from already existing systems) the required investments for reusable assets will be reduced. The investments precisely required in turn depend on whether we can simply adapt assets from existing systems or whether we need to reengineer them.

Finally, *the product-line introduction scheme* needs to be reflected by the benefit models. Here, many different approaches can be imagined. However, the key distinction is between an incremental introduction and a complete introduction. In a complete introduction, all foreseeable assets are engineered (if this is beneficial) so that they can be reused across all foreseeable products. In an incremental introduction, we can differentiate between the step-wise transformation to a reuse scheme for the different components vs. incrementally adding additional products. This obviously has severe consequences on the specific benefits that can be accrued. Even more complex schemes can be devised. For example, for time-to-market reasons, the following approach is not uncommon: first develop a system-specific version for the first product, then extend these assets into generic assets and reintroduce these assets into the products for future versions.

Actually, the specific scheme may vary both for the different products and for the different components. While this complicates the construction of benefit models, it also has the advantage that the different introduction scenarios can be compared and a specific scenario can be chosen so as to improve the overall benefit.

4.4   The Investment Perspective

While so far we focused on the optimization of the overall benefit, a more detailed analysis would take on a more investment-oriented focus.

Maximizing the benefit is not the only criterion. Rather, we want to optimize the return on investment [14] and we also want to minimize the risks. For this reason we need to take into account the necessary investments, the time when they will be required, and the benefits that can be accrued. Fortunately, when we have developed benefit models like the ones discussed above, this information is available as well: We can regard the additional cost of development for reuse plus the cost of reusing once versus the cost of single-system development as the investment in reuse and can contrast this with the specific benefits. Furthermore, from the specific introduction scheme we use as a basis for the analysis we know the specific timing to expect.

Developing all these models with very high scrutiny requires a considerable effort. Fortunately, we found that even simple models already provide a very appropriate basis for deriving reusability requirements (cf. Section 6).

5 Reusability Requirements

Once the basic benefit analysis has been performed, it is essential to transfer this information (i.e., the expected benefits) into reusability requirements, so that the reference architecture can be adequately developed. As it is very hard to use something like two person-months of effort saving expected according to effort model for reuse development directly as architecting input, we transfer the quantitative benefits into the final recommendations (reusability requirements). To this end we differentiate six different levels of recommendation:

1. A generic implementation of *<feature>* should be made available
2. A generic implementation of *<feature>* should be considered
3. In case of further products using *<feature>* a generic implementation should be developed
4. A generic interface to *<feature>* is strongly needed
5. A generic interface to *<feature>* is needed
6. Generic support for *<feature>* is currently not useful

These levels are then assigned to a certain functionality based on the achieved benefit score. The specific assignment scheme depends on the overall situation, e.g., what is the overall effort required for developing a feature, what kind of estimation models are available, what is their uncertainty? The specific rules used in the case study are described in Section 6.

The reuse requirements thus identified are then treated as soft constraints in the context of developing the reference architecture. In particular, the PuLSE-DSSA approach to developing software architectures takes advantage of such a prioritization [1]. These requirements basically inform the architecting process to localize functionality appropriately and to define adequate interfaces to it so that adequate, reusable components are built.

Obviously, during architecting these recommendations can be found to conflict. Then the different recommendation levels (together with the known benefits) can be used for conflict resolution. Here, again, the known information about the benefits relating to reusability can be used to determine the specific benefits that will be foregone if a certain functionality can not be made reusable. This helps to perform trade-offs among different design alternatives.

A key aspect in the usage of the reusability requirements is that the requirements are connected with an architecturally meaningful feature. This is ensured by the product line mapping component. We found this even to be the case for situations where no domain experts where available [12]. However, in this case some features could not be identified upfront and thus an extension might be required as part of architecting.

We studied the quality of the results and the preconditions that needed to be in place in order to apply this approach successfully. This is described in Section 6.

6 Case Studies

In this section, we will discuss certain case studies we performed in order to analyze the quality and adequacy of our approach.

6.1 Architectural Relevancy of Features

One key aspect of our approach is that the features identified by the *Product Line Mapping (PLM) component* are architecturally relevant. In order to validate this assumption, we performed a case study. This case study was based on the following setting: On the Internet there exists a simulation of radio models that describe a product line (at http://www.blaupunkt.de). A student worker was given the task to perform a product line mapping of this product line in order to identify the basic features. To perform this task he had the following information sources available: the description of the product line mapping approach [17], the online simulations, as well as some brief descriptions of the product line that did not contain architectural information. From these information sources, a product line mapping was developed. After finishing the task, the implementation description [8] also became available. This was now used to compare the structure derived using the product line mapping and the documented software architecture.

The two analyses led to two hierarchical clusterings. The product line mapping clustering consists of three levels (including the feature level). The architecture description consists of four levels (including feature level). Based on the provided architecture description, we also identified features that were missing in the original product line mapping.

During the comparison we established a mapping between the two types of leaf nodes. At this point we found that all features identified in product line mapping were also present in the architecture. The mapping was used for analyzing the closeness of the match between the two structures. This was done in the following manner: for each feature from the product line mapping we identified an optimal position in the architecture (i.e., the position with which it is associated according to its meaning). We then used the number of levels over which it needed to be moved to fall into the most appropriate category. We did not penalize if the product line mapping was more fine-grained than the software architecture description. Using this approach, we got a value of 0.23. Thus, the average distance of a feature from its optimal position was 0.23, and this distance was mostly due to cases where a single PLM feature matched several architectural features. This problem could be easily resolved, by having the product line mapping more fine grained. Thus, we found the structural match between software architecture and product line mapping result to be very good and the identified features as well as the structuring to be an adequate basis for the identification of reusability requirements for architecting.

6.2 Identification of Reusability Requirements

While the above case study only dealt with adequate identification of the features that are the basis for the reusability requirements, we will now deal with the identification of the reusability requirements themselves. For this, different case studies were performed. The first case study we performed was done using only very informal benefit models. Despite the very rough nature of the underlying models, we already achieved very good results. This case study was described in [11], thus we will here focus on more detailed case studies we could perform recently, which allowed us to perform more sophisticated analysis.

These case studies were performed in the context of a small company. The specific product line focuses on stock-market information systems on the Windows platform. In this environment we could apply our approach to two different sub-domains to which the software was extended. For the first sub-domain, no software existed yet, while for the second one a system-specific implementation already existed, which was supposed to be extended across the product line. In this context we had set up an effort measurement program, which allowed to develop specifically adapted estimation models. Actually, we developed several models:

(A) Purely data-based model (without cost drivers)

(B) Cobra model [5] based on input by the responsible domain expert

(C) Cobra model [5] based on input by two other participating experts from the product line

For determining the recommended reuse level, the first matching category was selected from the following list.

1. *A generic implementation of <feature> should be made available* — All three models proposed an overall positive benefit.

2. *A generic implementation of <feature> should be considered* — Models (A) and (B) propose an overall benefit of at least two person-hours and a benefit ratio (benefit / effort for generic implementation) of at least 0.5 is expected.

3. *In case of further products using <feature> a generic implementation should be developed* — Twice as many required implementations would lead to a categorization as scoping level 1.

4. *A generic interface to <feature> is strongly needed* —
At least two implementations are required and twice as many implementations would result in scoping level 2.

5. *A generic interface to <feature> is needed* — At least two implementations are required.

6. *Generic support for <feature> is currently not useful* — No specific preconditions.

While these rules are somewhat ad-hoc, we had good experiences with them in our case studies. However, the specific numbers need to be adapted in a context dependent manner. For example, the number of two person-hours was related to the fact that the typical feature size was about ten working hours, while the ratio of 0.5 was related to the overall impreciseness of the estimation models. The small value of effort was related to the fact that for the validation case study, we had to use a rather small part of the software. In more realistic situations we would use person-months instead.

In order to perform the validation of our approach, we performed a detailed validation scheme in this case study: we elicited the expected reuse level before and after and applied our approach on the data available before implementation. When

Table 1. Expert Opinions vs RIS Results

Domain 1		Domain 2	
Difference	Count	Difference	Count
+/- 0	5	+/- 0	8
+/- 1	10	+/- 1	1
+/- 2	9	+/- 2	1
+/- 3	2	+/- 3	1
Total	26	Total	11

comparing expert judgment before implementation and RIS result, we get an average difference of the two values (absolute error) of 1.31 for the first domain and 0.55 for the second. This difference is actually rather small, given a range from 1 to 6 of possible values corresponding to a 25% average deviation for the first and 11% for the second domain.

We also analyzed the drift of the architects' opinion during development and compared it to the RIS result. (Only a subset of the features were actually developed during the case study.) Actually, for nine out of ten cases where the original expert evaluation and the evaluation provided by RIS differ in domain 1, the RIS evaluation was closer to the expert opinion after implementation than the original expert estimate! Only for one feature, the estimate before and after was 1, while RIS provided a value of 2.

For domain 2, eight of the features were implemented after the scoping was performed. In this case, implementation of some features also existed prior to the whole scoping effort. There was only one feature where the pre-evaluation by the expert differed from the evaluation given by the RIS. However, this difference was marginal (one level) and the evaluation after implementation corresponded to the evaluation prior to the scoping. For all other implemented features, all three evaluations were identical. Thus, our approach (while purely relying on objective information like LoC or expected effort) did arrive at the same results as a highly experienced expert without taking architectural knowledge into account. Thus, the results of our case studies strongly support our hypothesis that the quality of our results in determining reusability requirements are actually rather high. In some cases, it is rated even more adequate than the proposals given by experienced product line experts.

6.3 Architectural Relevancy

Besides the basic question of whether the reusability requirements are adequate, the second important aspect is whether they are architecturally relevant. In our case studies we addressed this issue by directly capturing feedback on the architectural relevancy of the given recommendations from product line experts. We got a 88% agreement to this for the first domain (26 features) and ~67% for the second domain (nine features). The lower relevancy for the second domain can probably be explained by the fact that in this domain, certain architectural decisions were already fixed, since independent implementation did exist.

After implementation was performed, we also asked for the experienced architectural relevancy of the reuse decision. For domain 1, this was stated as 100% of the implemented features, thus supporting the high relevancy of the reuse decision for the architecture definition. For domain 2, this was only rated as 38%. This was also due to the fact that here, implementation already existed for a single system, which was (mostly) easily extendable to the generic case.

6.4 Dependency on Benefit Model Quality

In the preceding sections, we established the architectural relevancy and quality of the reusability requirements given by our approach. However, one important aspect is that the results are not too strongly dependent on the quality of the estimation models, as sometimes adequate models may not be easily available. Thus, small perturbations of the model should not be reflected in different reusability requirements.

An early insight into this was given by a case study that was performed without having measurement data available [11]. In addition, using the models that were available in the context of the case studies described above, we could perform some sensitivity analyses.

In the context of the case studies we introduced additional parameters into the benefit models. These simulated some sort of learning effect in the sense that the development effort would be reduced for development without reuse for subsequential products. Similarly, we introduced a parameter to reflect the amount of effort that was required for reusing a feature. On the other hand, we had developed three different effort estimation models using both the Cobra approach [5] and basic data analysis (i.e., average effort without influential factors).

While we found that the overall benefit is clearly not independent from the specific parameters, we also found that for reasonable parameter values (e.g., changing both values by 0.2), the influence of the parameter is no larger than the influence of the choice of specific estimation models and hardly has an impact on the final result. Thus, we can see that developing very detailed benefit models is not appropriate, given the inherent uncertainty of the available estimation models. Therefore we see that rather coarse models are fully appropriate as a basis for the benefit models.

7 Conclusions

In this paper we presented an approach that aims at deriving reusability requirements as input to software architecture development from models of reuse investment. We did not discuss the aspect of domain potential assessments, thus, the presented approach is actually only part of a full-fledged product line scoping approach called PuLSE-Eco V2.0 [16].

Besides describing the general approach that is used for deriving the reusability requirements, we focused on the development of the investment (benefit) models, as they establish the relationship between the product line situation and the necessary reusability requirements. A particular advantage of this approach is that the reusability requirements are derived from objective values for making the specific features reusable. This allows to perform trade-offs in an objective manner during architecting. Another important characteristic of the approach is that it can already be applied during the product line planning stage.

In the presentation of the approach we focused, in particular, on how to derive adequate benefit models, and on the specific influence certain characteristics of the product line development situation (e.g., existing assets, specific introduction approach) will have on the derived models.

We validated our approach in case studies that can be regarded as very successful. In particular, the results we achieved were very good, even when compared to evaluations given by experts that were very experienced in development in their product line.

Future work on our approach will include more detailed development and analysis of investment models. We are also strongly interested in applying our approach to further case studies to achieve a more detailed validation.

Acknowledgements

Thomas Willger and Timo Jakob from MARKET MAKER Software AG strongly contributed to this work. Thanks also go to Raul Maldonado for performing the product line mapping case study and Steffen Thiel from Bosch GmbH for providing the necessary information.

References

1. Michalis Anastasopoulos, Joachim Bayer, Oliver Flege, and Cristina Gacek. *A process for product line architecture creation and evaluation — PuLSE-DSSA - Version 2.0.* Technical Report 038.00/E, Fraunhofer IESE, 2000.
2. Barry Boehm, Bradford Clark, Ellis Horowitz, Chris Westland, Ray Madachy, and Richard Selby. Cost models for future software life cycle processes: COCOMO 2.0. *Annals of Software Engineering*, 1995.
3. Jan Bosch. *Design and Use of Software Architectures.* Addison–Wesley, 2000.
4. Lionel C. Briand, Khaled El Emam, and Frank Bomarius. COBRA: A hybrid method for software cost estimation, benchmarking, and risk assessment. In *Proceedings of the Twentieth International Conference on Software Engineering*, pages 390–399, April 1998.
5. Sunita Chulani. COQUALMO (COnstructive QUALity MOdel) — a software defect density prediction model. In *Proceedings of the ESCOM — SCOPE'99*, pages 297–306, 1999.

6. Jean-Marc DeBaud and Klaus Schmid. A systematic approach to derive the scope of software product lines. In *Proceedings of the 21st International Conference on Software Engineering*, pages 34–43, 1999.

7. John M. Favaro. A comparison of approaches to reuse investment analysis. In *Proceedings of the Fourth International Conference on Software Reuse*, pages 136–145, 1996.

8. Georg Gawol. Produktsimulationen mit Java im Internet. Master's thesis, Fachhochschule Frankfurt am Main, Fachbereich MND, Allgemeine Informatik, 1999.

9. Mehdi Jazayeri, Alexander Ran, and Frank van der Linden. *Software Architecture for Product Families*. Addison–Wesley, 2000.

10. Rick Kazman, Jai Asundi, and Mark Klein. Quantifying the costs and benefits of architectural decisions. In *Proceedings of the 23rd International Conference on Software Engineering*, pages 297–306, 2001.

11. Peter Knauber and Klaus Schmid. Using a quantitative approach for defining generic components: A case study. In *Proceedings of the Fourth International Software Architecture Workshop (ISAW'4)*, pages 131–135, 2000.

12. Raul Maldonado and Klaus Schmid. *Applying the product line mapping approach to a family of web-radios*. Technical Report 095.01/E, Fraunhofer IESE, 2001.

13. Shary Pfleeger. Measuring reuse: A cautionary tale. *IEEE Software*, 13:118–127, 1996.

14. Jeffrey S. Poulin. *Measuring Software Reuse*. Addison–Wesley, 1997.

15. David M. Raffo, Stuart Faulk, and Robert R. Harmon. A customer value-driven approach to product-line engineering. In Peter Knauber and Giancarlo Succi, editors, *First Workshop on Software Product Lines: Economics, Architectures, and Implications, Limerick*, pages 3–7, 2000.

16. Klaus Schmid. An economic perspective on product line software development. In *First Workshop on Economics-Driven Software Engineering Research, Los Angeles (EDSER-1)*, May 1999.

17. Klaus Schmid. Multi-staged scoping for software product lines. In Peter Knauber and Giancarlo Succi, editors, *First Workshop on Software Product Lines: Economics, Architectures, and Implications*, pages 8–11, 2000. The proceedings appeared as IESE-Report 070.00/E.

18. Klaus Schmid. *The product line mapping method*. Technical Report 028.00/E, Fraunhofer IESE, 2000.

19. Klaus Schmid. An assessment approach to analyzing benefits and risks of product lines. In *The Twenty-Fifth Annual International Computer Software and Applications Conference (Compsac'01)*, pages 525–530, 2001.

20. Klaus Schmid. An initial model of product line economics. In *Proceedings of the International Workshop on Product Family Engineering (PFE-4), 2001*, 2001.

Control Localization in Domain Specific Translation

Ted J. Biggerstaff

tbiggerstaff@austin.rr.com

Abstract. Domain specific languages (DSLs) excel at programming productivity because they provide large-grain composite data structures (e.g., a graphics image) and large-grain operators for composition (e.g., image addition or convolution). As a result, extensive computations can be written as APL-like one-liners that are equivalent to tens or hundreds of lines of code (LOC) when written in a conventional language like Java. The problem with DSL specifications is that they de-localize the code components making un-optimized machine translations significantly slower than for the human optimized equivalent. Specifically, operations on DSL composites imply multiple control structures (e.g., loops) that process the individual elements of large-grain composites and those multiple, implicit control structures are distributed (i.e., de-localized) across the expression of operators and operands. Human programmers recognize the relation among these distributed control structures and merge them to minimize the redundancy of control. For example, merged control structures may perform several operations on several large-grain data structures in a single pass. This merging is the process of *control localization*. This paper discusses strategies for automating localization without large search spaces and outlines a domain specific example of transformation rules for localizing control. The example is based on the localization method in the *Anticipatory Optimization Generator* (AOG) system [3-8].

1 Introduction

1.1 The General Problem

DSLs significantly improve program productivity because they deal with large-grain data structures and large-grain operators and thereby allow a programmer to say a lot (i.e., express a lengthy computation) with a few symbols. Large-grain data structures (e.g., images, matrices, arrays, structs, strings, sets, etc.) can be decomposed into finer and finer grain data structures until one reaches data structures that are atomic (e.g., field, integer, real, character, etc.) with respect to some conventional programming language. Thus, operators on such large-grain data structures imply some kind of extended control structure such as a loop, a sequence of statements, a recursive function, or other. As one composes large-grain operators and operands together into longer expressions, each subexpression implies not only some atomic computations (e.g., pixel addition) that will eventually be expressed in terms of atomic operators (e.g., +) and data (e.g., integers), but it also implies some control structure to sequence

C. Gacek (Ed.): ICSR-7, LNCS 2319, pp. 153–165, 2002.
© Springer-Verlag Berlin Heidelberg 2002

through those atomic computations. Those implied control structures are typically distributed (i.e., de-localized) across the whole expression.

For example, if one defines an addition operator[1] for images in some graphics domain and if A and B are defined to be graphic images, the expression (A + B) will perform a pixel-by-pixel addition of the images. To keep the example simple, suppose that the pixels are integers (i.e., A and B are grayscale images). Then the expression (A + B) implies a two dimensional (2D) loop over A and B. Subsequent squaring of each pixel in (A + B) implies a second 2D loop. Human programmers easily identify this case and merge the two loops into a single 2D loop.

This kind of transformation seems simple enough but the real world is much more complex and when all of the cases and combinations are dealt with, it may require design tricks to avoid the generator's search space from becoming intractably large. More complex operators hint at some of this complexity. For example, consider a *convolution operator*[2] ⊕, which performs a sum of products of pixels and weights. The pixels come from image neighborhoods, each of which is centered on one of the image's pixels, and the weights come from the neighborhood definition, which associates a weight value with each relative pixel position in the neighborhood. The weights are defined separately from ⊕. Suppose the weights are defined in a domain object S, which is called a *neighborhood* of a pixel, where the actual pixel position defining the center of the neighborhood will be a parameter of S. Then (A ⊕ S) would define a sum of products operation for each neighborhood around each pixel in A where the details of the neighborhood would come from S. Thus, S will provide, among other data, the neighborhood size and the definition of the method for computing the weights. The ⊕ operator definition will contribute the control loop and the specification of the centering pixel that is to be the parameter of S. The translation rules not only have to introduce and merge the control structures, they have to weave together, in a consistent manner, the implied connections among the loop control, the definition of ⊕ and the definition of S.

Thus, localization can be fairly complex because it is coordinating the multi-way integration of specific information from several large-grain components. The greater the factorization of the operators and operands (i.e., the separation of parts that must be integrated), the more numerous and complex are the rules required to perform localization. In fact, localization is a subproblem of the more general problem of *constraint propagation* in domain specific translation, which is NP Complete [15]. As a consequence, localization has the potential to explode the solution search space. To thwart this explosion, AOG groups localization rules in special ways and makes use of domain specific knowledge to limit the explosion of choices during the localization process. Both of these strategies reduce the search space dramatically. The downside of using domain specific knowledge in localization is that localization in different domains may have different rules. But that is a small price to pay because the strategy

---

[1] The meta-language definitions used are: 1) `courier for code`, 2) `courier italics for meta-code`, and 3) `courier italics underlined for comments`.

[2] A more formal definition of the convolution operator is given in the next section.

transforms a general problem that has the potential of an exploding solution space into a specialized problem that does not.

While this paper will focus on the Image Algebra (IA) domain [22], the localization problem is universal over most complex domains. Localization is required when the domain's language separates and compartmentalizes partial definitions of large-grain operators and data structures and then allows compositional expressions over those same operators and data structures. Other domains that exhibit DSL-induced de-localization are: 1) the user interface domain, 2) the network protocol domain, 3) various middleware domains (e.g., transaction monitors), 4) data aggregations (e.g., fields aggregated into records) and others. AOG implements localization rules for two control domains: 1) loops over images and similar large grain data structures and 2) iterations induced by fields within records.

2 The Technology

2.1 An Example Mini-domain

To provide a concrete context for discussing the issues of localization, this section will define a subset of the Image Algebra [22] as a mini-DSL for writing program specifications.

Domain Entity[3]	Description	Definition	Comments
Image	A composite data structure in the form of a matrix with pixels as elements	$A = \{a_{i,j} : a_{i,j} \text{ is a pixel}\}$ where A is a matrix of size $[(imax - imin +1)$ by $(jmax - jmin +1)]$ s.t. $imin \le i \le imax$ and $jmin \le j \le jmax$	Subclasses include images with grayscale or color pixels. To simplify the discussion, assume all images have the same size.
Neighborhood	A matrix overlaying a region of an image centered on an image pixel such that the matrix associates a numerical weight with each overlay	$W(S) = \{ w_{p,q} : w_{p,q}$ is a numerical weight$\}$ where S is a neighborhood of size $[(pmax - pmin + 1)$ by $(qmax - qmin + 1)]$ s.t. $pmin \le p \le pmax$	Neighborhoods are objects with methods. The methods define the weights computation, neighborhood size, special case behaviors, and methods to compute

---

[3] See 22 for a more complete and more formal definition of this domain.

	position	and $qmin \le q \le qmax$	a neighborhood position in terms of image coordinates.
Convolution	The convolution $(A \oplus S)$ applies the neighborhood S to each pixel in A to produce a new image $B = (A \oplus s)$	$(A \oplus S) = \{\forall_{i,j} (b_{i,j} :$ $b_{i,j} = (\Sigma_{p,q} (w_{p,q} *$ $a_{i+p,j+q}))\}$ where $w_{p,q} \in W(S)$, p and q range over the neighborhood S; i and j range over the images A and B	Variants of the convolution operator are produced by replacing the $\Sigma_{p,q}$ operation with $\Pi_{p,q}$, $Min_{p,q}$, $Max_{p,q}$, & others and the * operation with +, max, min & others.
Matrix Operators	$(A+B)$, $(A-B)$, $(k*A)$, A^n, $\sqrt{A}$ where A & B are images, k & n are numbers	These operations on matrices have the conventional definitions, e.g., $(A+B) = \{\forall_{i,j} (a_{i,j} + b_{i,j})\}$	

Define the weights for concrete neighborhoods S and SP to be 0 if the neighborhood is hanging off the edge of the image, or to be

$$w(s) = P \left\{ \begin{array}{c} \\ 0 \\ 1 \end{array} \overbrace{\begin{bmatrix} -1 & -2 & -1 \\ \phi & \phi & \phi \\ 1 & 2 & 1 \end{bmatrix}}^{Q} \begin{array}{l} -1 \\ \\ \end{array} \right. \qquad w(sp) = P \left\{ \begin{array}{c} \\ 0 \\ 1 \end{array} \overbrace{\begin{bmatrix} -1 & \phi & 1 \\ -2 & \phi & 2 \\ -1 & \phi & 1 \end{bmatrix}}^{Q} \begin{array}{l} -1 \\ \\ \end{array} \right.$$

if it is not. Given these definitions, one can write an expression for the Sobel edge detection method [22] that has the following form:

$$B = [(A \oplus S)^2 + (A \oplus SP)^2]^{1/2}$$

This expression de-localizes loop controls and spreads them over the expression in the sense that each individual operator introduces a loop over some image(s), e.g., over the image A or the intermediate image $(A \oplus S)$. What technology will be employed to specify localization? AOG uses a pattern-directed transformation regime.

2.2 Pattern-Directed Control Regimes

In the simplest form, generic pattern-directed transformation systems store knowledge as a single global soup of transformations rules[4] represented as rewrite rules of the form

> Pattern ⇒ RewrittenExpression

The left hand side of the rule (*Pattern*) matches a subtree of the Abstract Syntax Tree (AST) specification of the target program and binds matching elements to transformation variables (e.g., ?operator) in Pattern. If that is successful, then the right hand side of the rule (*RewrittenExpression*) is instantiated with the variable bindings and replaces the matched portion of the AST. Operationally, rules are chosen (i.e., triggered) based largely on the syntactic pattern of the left hand side thereby motivating the moniker "Pattern-Directed" for such systems.   Beyond syntactic forms, *Pattern*-s may also include 1) semantic constraints (e.g., type restrictions), and 2) other constraints (often called *enabling conditions*) that must be true before the rule can be fully executed. In addition, algorithmic checks on enabling conditions and bookkeeping chores (e.g., inventing translator variables and objects) are often handled by a separate procedure associated with the rule.

One of the key questions with transformation systems is what is the control regime underlying the system. That is, what is the storage organization of rules and how are the transformations chosen or triggered? We will consider the question of storage organization in a minute but first we will look at triggering strategies. In general, control regimes are some mixture of two kinds of triggering strategies: pattern-directed (PD) triggering and metaprogram controlled triggering. PD triggering produces a control regime that looks like a search process directed mostly by syntactic or semantic information local to AST subtrees. PD searches are bias toward programming syntax and semantics mainly because the tools used are biased toward such information.

The problem with pure PD control strategies is that rule choice is largely local to an AST subtree and therefore, often leads to a strategically blind search in a huge search space. In contrast, the triggering choices may be made by a goal-driven metaprogram. Metaprograms are algorithms that operate on programs and therefore, save state information, which allows them to make design choices based on earlier successes or failures. This purposefulness and use of state information tends to reduce the search space over that of PD control. However, case combinations can still explode the search space. This paper will look at the techniques that are used to overcome these problems.

---

[4] Most non-toy transformation systems use various control machinery to attempt to overcome the inefficiencies of the "global soup" model of transformations while retaining the convenience of viewing the set of transformations more or less as a set of separate transformations.

3 Localization Technology

3.1 Defusing Search Space Explosions

Since program generation is NP Complete, it will often produce large and intractable search spaces. How does AOG overcome this? AOG uses several techniques, one of which is localization. More narrowly, AOG localization reduces the search space by: 1) defining localization as a specialized optimization process with a narrow specific goal, 2) grouping the localization rules in ways that make irrelevant rules invisible, and 3) using domain knowledge (e.g., knowledge about the general design of the code to be generated) to further prune the search space.

One way to reduce the search space is by grouping transformations so that at each decision point only a small number of relevant transformations need to be tried. AOG implements this idea by grouping the rules in two dimensions: 1) first under a relevant object (e.g., a type object) and 2) then under a *phase* name. The meta-program goal being pursued at a given moment determines which objects and which phases are in scope at that moment. The phase name captures the strategic goal or job that those rules as a group are intended to accomplish (e.g., the LoopLocalize phase is the localization phase for the IA domain). In addition, the object under which the rules are stored provides some key domain knowledge that further prunes the search space. For example, in order for loop localization to move loops around, it needs to know the data flow design for the various operators. The general design of the operator's data flow is deducible from the resulting type of the expression plus the details of the expression. In AOG, an expression type combined with the result of a specific rule's pattern match provides the needed data flow knowledge. Thus, the localization process for a specific expression of type X is a matter of trying all rules in the LoopLocalize group of the type X object and of types that X inherits from. AOG rules provide this organizational information by the following rule format:

```
(⇒ XformName PhaseName ObjName
     Pattern RewrittenExpression Pre Post)
```

The transform's name is *XformName* and it is stored as part of the *ObjName* object structure, which in the case of localization will be a "type" object, e.g., the image type. *XformName* is enabled only during the *PhaseName* phase (e.g., LoopLocalize). *Pattern* is used to match an AST subtree and upon success, the subtree is replaced by *RewrittenExpression* instantiated with the bindings returned by the pattern match. *Pre* is the name of a routine that checks enabling conditions and performs bookkeeping chores (e.g., creating translator variables and computing equivalence classes for localization). *Post* performs various computational chores after the rewrite. *Pre* and *Post* are optional.

For example, a trivial but concrete example of a PD rule would be

```
(⇒ FoldZeroXform SomePhaseName dsnumber `(+ ?x 0) `?x)
```

This rule is named FoldZeroXform, is stored in the dsnumber type structure, is enabled only in phase *SomePhaseName*, and rewrites an expression like (+ 27

0) to 27. In the pattern, the pattern variable ?x will match anything in the first position of expressions of the form (+ ____ 0). Now, let's examine an example localization rule.

3.2 RefineComposite Rule

The IA mini-DSL will need a refinement rule (RefineComposite) to refine a composite image like a to a unique black and white pixel object, say bwp27, and simultaneously, introduce the elements of a loop control structure to iteratively generate all values of bwp27. These will include some target program loop index variables (e.g., idx28 and idx29), some shorthand for the putative target program loop control to be generated (e.g., an expression (forall (idx28 idx29) ...)), a record of the correspondence relationship between the large-grain composite a and the component bwp27 (e.g., the expression (mappings (bwp27) (a)), and the details of the refinement relationship (e.g., some rule bwp27 => a[idx28, idx29]). How would one formulate RefineComposite in AOG?

Given a routine (e.g., gensym) to generate symbols (e.g., bwp27), an overly simple form of this rule might look like:

```
(=> RefineComposite LoopLocalize Image `?op
    (gensym `bwp))
```

where ?op matches any expression of type Image and rewrites it as some gensymed black and white pixel bwp27. But this form of the rule does not do quite enough. An image instance may be represented in the AST in an alternative form – e.g., (leaf a ...). The leaf structure provides a place to hang an AST node property list, which in AOG is called a *tags* list. Thus, the rule will have to deal with a structure like (leaf a (tags Prop1 Prop2 ...)). To accommodate this case, the rule pattern will have to be extended using AOG's "*or*" pattern operator, $(por pat1 pat2 ...), which allows alternative sub-patterns (e.g., pat1 pat2...) to be matched.

```
(=> RefineComposite LoopLocalize Image
    `$(por (leaf ?op) ?op) (gensym `bwp))
```

Now, (leaf a ...) will get translated to some pixel symbol bwp27 with ?op bound[5] to a (i.e., {{a/?op}}). However, the rule does not record the relationship among the image a, the pixel bwp27, and some yet-to-be-generated index variables (e.g., idx28 and idx29) that will be needed to loop over a to compute the various values of bwp27. So, the next iteration of the rule adds the name of a pre-routine (say

---

[5] A binding list is defined as a set of {value/variable} pairs and is written as {(val1/vbl1) (val2/vbl2) ...}. Instantiation of an expression with a binding list rewrites the expression substituting each valn for the corresponding vbln in the expression.

RCChores) that will do the translator chores of gensym-ing the pixel object (bwp27), binding it to a new pattern variable (say ?bwp), and while it is at it, gensym-ing a couple of index objects and binding them to ?idx1 and ?idx2. The next iteration of the rule looks like:

```
(=> RefineComposite LoopLocalize Image
    `$(por (leaf ?op) ?op) `(leaf ?bwp) `RCChores)
```

Executing this rule on the AST structure (leaf a ...) will create the binding list {{a/?op} {bwp27/?bwp} {idx28/?idx1} {idx29/?idx2}} and rewrite (leaf a ...) to (leaf bwp27). However, it does not yet record the relationship among a, bwp27, idx28, and idx29. Other instances of images in the expressions will create analogous sets of image, pixel, and index objects, some of which will end up being redundant. In particular, new loop index variables will get generated at each image reference in the AST. Most of these will be redundant. Other rules will be added that merge away these redundancies by discarding redundant pixels and indexes. To supply the data for these merging rules, the next version of the rule will need to create a shorthand form expressing the relationship among these items and add it to the tags list. The shorthand will have the form

```
(_forall (idx28 idx29)
         (_suchthat
             (_member idx28 (_range minrow maxrow))
             (_member idx29 (_range mincol maxcol))
             (mappings (bwp27) (a))))
```

The idx variable names will become loop control variables that will be used to iterate over the image a, generating pixels like bwp27. bwp27 will eventually be refined into some array reference such as (aref[6] a idx28 idx29). The _member clauses define the ranges of these control variables. The lists in the mappings clause establish the correspondences between elements (e.g., bwp27, bwp41, etc.) and the composites from which they are derived (e.g., a, b, etc.) thereby enabling the finding and elimination of redundant elements and loop indexes.

The final form of the RefineComposite rule (annotated with *explanatory comments*) is:

```
(=> RefineComposite LoopLocalize Image
      `$(por (leaf ?op)   Pattern to match an image leaf
             ?op)         or image atom. Bind image to ?op.

      `(leaf ?bwp         Rewrite image as ?bwp pixel.
            (tags         Add a property list to pixel.

              (_forall    Loop shorthand introducing
                (?idx1 ?idx2) loop indexes and
                (_suchthat    loop ranges & relations.
                  (_member ?idx1 (_range minrow maxrow))
                  (_member ?idx2 (_range mincol maxcol))
```

---

[6] (aref a idx28 idx29) is the AST representation of the code a[idx28,idx29].

```
(mappings (?bwp) (?op))))

(itype bwpixel)))
```
Add new type expression.

`RCChores)`   *Name the pre-routine that*
                         creates pixel & indexes.

3.3 Combining Loop Shorthands

After `RefineComposite` has executed, the loop shorthand information will be residing on the tags list of the `bwp27` leaf in the AST. But this loop shorthand is only one of a set of incipient loops that are dispersed over the expression. These incipient loops must be moved up the expression tree and combined in order to reduce redundant looping. AOG will require a set of rules to do this job. For example, one rule (`ConvolutionOnLeaves`[7]) will move the loop shorthand up to the convolution operator and another (`FunctionalOpsOnComposites`[8]) will move it up to the mathematical square function. These two rules rewrite the AST subtree[9] from

```
(** (⊕ (leaf bwp27
             (tags (forall (idx28 idx29) ...)... )) s)
     2)
```

to

```
(** (⊕ (leaf bwp27 ...) s
       (tags (forall (idx28 idx29) ...)))) 2)
```

and then to

```
(** (⊕ (leaf bwp27 ...) s) 2
       (tags (forall (idx28 idx29) ...)... )).
```

Eventually, the process will get to a level in the expression tree where two of these incipient loops will have to be combined to share some portions of the loop. In this case, it will share the index variables, preserving one set and throwing the other set away. For example, the rule `FunctionalOpsOnParallelComposites` will perform such a combination by rewriting[10] the AST subtree

```
(+  (**(⊕ bwp27 s) 2
       (tags (forall (idx28 idx29) ...)... ))
```

---

[7] Definition not shown due to space limitations.

[8] Definition not shown.

[9] These examples omit much of the actual complexity and enabling condition checking but capture the essence of the rewrites.

[10] These examples omit details (e.g., leaf structures) when they are not essential to understanding the example.

```
(**(⊕ bwp31 s) 2
   (tags (forall (idx32 idx33) ...)... )))
```

to

```
(+ (**  (⊕  bwp27 s) 2)
   (**  (⊕  bwp31 s) 2)
   (tags (forall (idx32 idx33) ...)...)))
```

throwing away idx28 and idx29 and retaining idx32 and idx33.

This movement and combination process continues until the dispersed, incipient loop structures are localized to minimize the number of passes over images. Follow-on phases (CodeGen and SpecRefine respectively) will cast the resulting shorthand(s) into more conventional loop forms and refine intermediate symbols like bwp27 and bwp31 into a computation expressed in terms of the source data, e.g., a[idx32,idx33]. But this refinement presents a coordination problem to be solved. How will SpecRefine know to refine bwp27 into a[idx32,idx33] instead of its original refinement into a[idx27,idx28]? Just replacing bwp27 with bwp31 in the AST during the combination rule (FunctionalOpsOnParallelComposites) does not work because bwp27 may occur in multiple places in the expression due to previously executed rules. Worst yet, there may be instances of bwp27 that are yet to appear in the expression due to deferred rules that are pending. Other complexities arise when only the indexes are shared (e.g., for different images such as a and b). Finally, since the replacement of bwp27 is, in theory, recursive to an indefinite depth, there may be several related abstractions undergoing localization combination and coordination. For example, an RGB color pixel abstraction, say cp27, may represent a call to the red method of the pixel class – say (red pixel26) – and the pixel26 abstraction may represent an access to the image – say a[idx64, idx65]. Each of these abstractions can potentially change through combination during the localization process. So, how does AOG assure that all of these generated symbols get mapped into a set of correctly coordinated target code symbols?

3.4 Speculative Refinements

Speculative refinement is a process of dynamically generating and modifying rules to create the correct final mapping. When executed in a follow-on phase called SpecRefine, these generated rules map away discarded symbols and map the surviving symbols to the properly coordinated target code symbols (e.g., array names and loop indexes).

As an example, consider the RefineComposite rule shown earlier. Its pre-routine, RCChores, will create several speculative refinement rules at various times while processing various sub-expressions. Among them are:

```
(=> SpecRule89 SpecRefine bwp27[11] `bwp27
```

---

[11] Notice that these rules are stored on the gensym-ed objects.

```
`(aref a idx27 idx28))
(=> SpecRule90 SpecRefine bwp31 `bwp31
  `(aref a idx32 idx33))
```

Later, the pre-routine of the `FunctionalOpsOnParallelComposites` rule chose bwp31 to replace the equivalent bwp27. It recorded this decision by replacing the right hand side of rule `SpecRule89` with bwp31. `SpecRule89` will now map all bwp27 references to bwp31 which `SpecRule90` will then map to (`aref a idx32 idx33`).

Thus, at the end of the loop localization phase all speculative refinement rules are coordinated to reflect the current state of localization combinations. The follow-on speculative refinement phase recursively applies any rules (e.g., `SpecRule89`) that are attached to AST abstractions (e.g., bwp27). The result is a consistent and coordinated expression of references to common indexes, images, field names (e.g., red), etc.

4   Other Explosion Control Strategies

AOG uses other control regimes and strategies that are beyond the scope of this paper. These include an event driven triggering of transformations called *Tag-Directed (TD) transformation control*[12] that allows cross-component and cross-domain optimizations (code reweavings) to occur in the programming language domain while retaining and using domain specific knowledge to reduce the search space. TD rules perform architectural reshaping of the code to accommodate external, global constraints such as interaction protocols or parallel CPU architectures. See 3 and 5-9.

5   Related Research

Central sources for many of the topics in this paper are found in [4, 11, 21, 23, 26].

This work bears the strongest relation to Neighbor's work [18-19]. The main differences are: 1) the AOG PD rules are distributed over the two dimensional space of objects and phases, 2) the use of the specialized control regimes (including TD control) for specialized program optimization strategies, and 3) the inclusion of cross-domain optimization machinery.

The work bears a strong relationship to Kiczales' Aspect Oriented Programming [12, 16] at least in terms of its objectives, but the optimization machinery appears to be quite different.

This work is largely orthogonal but complementary to the work of Batory [1,4, 11] with Batory focusing on generating class and method definitions and AOG focusing on optimizing expressions of calls to such methods.

---

[12] Patent number 6,314,562.

AOG and Doug Smith's work are similar in that they make heavy use of domain specific information [24, 11]. However, Smith relies more on generalized inference and AOG relies more on partial evaluation [11, 26].

The organization of the transformations into goal driven stages is similar to Boyle's TAMPR [9]. However, Boyle's stages are implicit and they do not perform localization in the AOG sense.

The pattern language [6] is most similar to the work of Wile [28,29], Visser [25] and Crew [10]. Wile and Visser lean toward an architecture driven by compiling and parsing notions, though Visser's pattern matching notation parallels much of the AOG pattern notation. Both Wile and Visser are influenced less by logic programming than AOG. On the other hand, logic programming influences both ASTLOG and the AOG pattern language. However, ASTLOG's architecture is driven by program analysis objectives and is not really designed for dynamic change and manipulation of the AST. In addition, AOG's pattern language is distinguished from both ASTLOG and classic Prolog in that it does *mostly local reasoning* with a distributed rule base.

There are a variety of other connections that are beyond the space limitations of this paper. For example, there are relations to Intentional Programming [11], metaprogramming and reflection [11, 23], logic programming based generation, formal synthesis systems (e.g., Specware) [11], deforestation [27], transformation replay [2], other generator designs [13, 14] and procedural transformation systems [17]. The differences are greater or lesser across this group and broad generalization is hard. However, the most obvious general difference between AOG and most of these systems is AOG's use of specialized control regimes to limit the search space.

References

1. Batory, Don, Singhal, Vivek, Sirkin, Marty, and Thomas, Jeff: Scalable Software Libraries. Symposium on the Foundations of Software Engineering. Los Angeles, California (1993)
2. Baxter, I. D.: Design Maintenance Systems. Communications of the ACM, Vol. 55, No. 4 (1992) 73-89
3. Biggerstaff, Ted J.: Anticipatory Optimization in Domain Specific Translation. International Conference on Software Reuse Victoria, B. C., Canada (1998a) 124-133
4. Biggerstaff, Ted J.: A Perspective of Generative Reuse. Annals of Software Engineering, Baltzer Science Publishers, AE Bussum, The Netherlands (1998b)
5. Biggerstaff, Ted J.: Composite Folding in Anticipatory Optimization. Microsoft Research Technical Report, MSR-TR-98-22 (1998c)
6. Biggerstaff, Ted J.: Pattern Matching for Program Generation: A User Manual. Microsoft Research Technical Report MSR-TR-98-55 (1998d)
7. Biggerstaff, Ted J.: Fixing Some Transformation Problems. Automated Software Engineering Conference, Cocoa Beach, Florida (1999)
8. Biggerstaff, Ted J.: A New Control Structure for Transformation-Based Generators. In: Frakes, William B. (ed.): Software Reuse: Advances in Software Reusability, Vienna, Austria, Springer (June, 2000)
9. Boyle, James M.: Abstract Programming and Program Transformation—An Approach to Reusing Programs. In: Biggerstaff, Ted and Perlis, Alan (eds.): Software Reusability, Addison-Wesley/ACM Press (1989) 361-413

10. Crew, R. F.: ASTLOG: A Language for Examining Abstract Syntax Trees. Proceedings of the USENIX Conference on Domain-Specific Languages, Santa Barbara, California (1997)
11. Czarnecki, Krzysztof and Eisenecker, Ulrich W.: Generative Programming: Methods, Tools, and Applications. Addison-Wesley (2000)
12. Elrad, Tzilla, Filman, Robert E., Bader, Atef (Eds.): Special Issue on Aspect-Oriented Programming. Communications of the ACM, Vol. 44, No. 10 (2001) 28-97
13. Fickas, Stephen F.: Automating the Transformational Development of Software. IEEE Transactions on Software Engineering, SE-11 (11), (Nov. 1985) 1286-1277
14. Kant, Elaine: Synthesis of Mathematical Modeling Software. IEEE Software, (May, 1993)
15. Katz, M. D. and Volper, D.: Constraint Propagation in Software Libraries of Transformation Systems. International Journal of Software Engineering and Knowledge Engineering, 2, 3 (1992)
16. Kiczales, Gregor, Lamping, John, Mendhekar, Anurag, Maede, Chris, Lopes, Cristina, Loingtier, Jean-Marc and Irwin, John: Aspect Oriented Programming. Tech. Report SPL97-08 P9710042, Xerox PARC (1997)
17. Kotik, Gordon B., Rockmore, A. Joseph, and Smith, Douglas R.: Use of Refine for Knowledge-Based Software Development. Western Conference on Knowledge-Based Engineering and Expert Systems (1986)
18. Neighbors, James M.: Software Construction Using Components. PhD Thesis, University of California at Irvine, (1980)
19. Neighbors, James M.: The Draco Approach to Constructing Software From Reusable Components. IEEE Transactions on Software Engineering, SE-10 (5), (Sept. 1984) 564-573
20. Neighbors, James M.: Draco: A Method for Engineering Reusable Software Systems. In: Biggerstaff, Ted and Perlis, Alan (eds.): Software Reusability, Addison-Wesley/ACM Press (1989) 295-319
21. Partsch, Helmut A.: Specification and Transformation of Programs. Springer-Verlag (1990)
22. Ritter, Gerhard X. and Wilson, Joseph N.: Handbook of Computer Vision Algorithms in the Image Algebra. CRC Press, (1996)
23. Sheard, Tim: Accomplishments and Research Challenges in Meta-Programming. SAIG 2001 Workshop, Florence, Italy (Sept., 2001)
24. Smith, Douglas R.: KIDS-A Knowledge-Based Software Development System. In: Lowry, M. & McCartney, R., (eds.): Automating Software Design, AAAI/MIT Press (1991) 483-514
25. Visser, Eclo: Strategic Pattern Matching. In: Rewriting Techniques and Applications (RTA '99), Trento, Italy. Springer-Verlag (July, 1999)
26. Visser, Eclo: A Survey of Strategies in Program Transformation Systems. In: Gramlich, B. and Alba, S. L. (eds.): Workshop on Reduction Strategies in Rewriting and Programming (WRS '01), Utrecht, The Netherlands (May 2001)
27. Wadler, Philip: Deforestation: Transforming Programs to Eliminate Trees. Journal of Theoretical Computer Science, Vol. 73 (1990) 231-248
28. Wile, David S.: Popart: Producer of Parsers and Related Tools. USC/Information Sciences Institute Technical Report, Marina del Rey, California (1994) (http://www.isi.edu/software-sciences/wile/Popart/ popart.html)
29. Wile, David S.: Toward a Calculus for Abstract Syntax Trees. In: Bird, R. and Meertens, L. (eds.): Proceedings of a Workshop on Algorithmic Languages and Calculii. Alsac FR. Chapman and Hill (1997) 324-352

Model Reuse with Metamodel-Based Transformations

Tihamer Levendovszky[1], Gabor Karsai[1], Miklos Maroti[1],
Akos Ledeczi[1], Hassan Charaf[2]

[1] Institute for Software Integrated Systems, Vanderbilt University
P.O. Box 36, Peabody, Nashville, TN 37203
{tihamer.levendovszky,gabor.karsai,miklos.maroti,akos.ledeczi}
@vanderbilt.edu
http://www.isis.vanderbilt.edu/

[2] Budapest University of Technology and Economics
Goldmann György tér. 1. V2 458, Budapest, XI., Hungary
hassan@avalon.aut.bme.hu

Abstract. Metamodel-based transformations permit descriptions of mappings between models created using different concepts from possibly overlapping domains. This paper describes the basic algorithms used in matching metamodel constructs, and how this match is to be applied. The transformation process facilitates the reuse of models specified in one domain-specific modeling language in another context: another domain-specific modeling language. UML class diagrams are used as the language of the metamodels. The focus of the paper is on the matching and firing of transformation rules, and on finding efficient and generic algorithms. An illustrative case study is provided.

1 Introduction

Modeling has become fundamental in developing complex software systems where controlling and understanding every detail is beyond the capability of human comprehension using a general-purpose programming language. Presently, modeling can be considered as programming in a very high-level language that allows the designers to manage the complexity of the system. This approach has resulted in a number of different, yet related, modeling concepts that attempt to solve very similar representation problems.

Without the ability to perform model transformations, every existing model must be developed and understood separately, and/or has to be converted manually between the various modeling formalisms. This often requires as much effort as re-creating the models from scratch, in another modeling language. However, when automatic model transformations are used, the mapping between the different concepts has to be developed only once for a pair of meta-models, not for each model instance.

To map models that have different metamodels is vital in software reuse, even for those software systems that are automatically generated directly from their models. This problem (and its solution) is the main concern of this paper.

C. Gacek (Ed.): ICSR-7, LNCS 2319, pp. 166–178, 2002.
© Springer-Verlag Berlin Heidelberg 2002

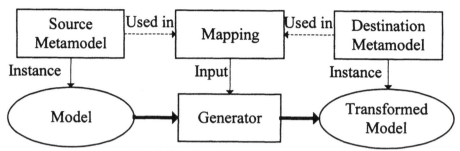

Fig. 1. Transformation process overview.

The overview of the concepts is depicted in Figure 1. The source and target models of the transformation are compliant with their corresponding metamodels. We create a representation of the mapping in terms of the metamodels. A generator, which is based on the mapping, is used to produce an output. The output from the generator is a transformation of the input model. The motivation for the automatic translation is that we wish to reuse the input model in an environment that supports the concepts of the output model.

To define the mapping between two conceptually different models requires a common basis that describes both the source and target domains of the transformation, and the transformation vocabulary. This common basis in our case is the metamodel [1]. We consider the metamodel as a set of metamodel elements, and we will use the widely adopted UML class diagram terminology [2] to describe the metamodel. Choosing the UML class diagram as a metamodel formalism implies that the two domains must share their meta-metamodel - namely, the UML class diagram metamodel (which is satisfied for a wide range of the practical applications). We regard a model as a set of model elements that are in correspondence with a metamodel element via the instantiation relationship. Metamodel-based transformations use only the elements of the metamodels, thus the transformation description is expressed in terms of the two metamodels.

Graph rewriting [3][5] is a powerful tool for graph transformations. The graph transformation is defined in the form of rewriting rules, where each such rule is a pair of graphs, called the LHS (left hand side) and RHS (right hand side). The rewriting rule operates as follows: the LHS of a rule is matched against the input graph, and the matching portion of that graph is replaced with the RHS of the rule. The replacement process is referred to as firing of the rewriting rule. In this work, we will use the context elements [5] to describe the rewriting rules that change the edges between objects.

When we consider a match, we cannot match one model element in the input graph to two elements in the rewriting rule (identity condition) [5]. In our case, the complication we address is caused by the "schematic" nature of the metamodel. In a simple case, all models consist of objects with (typed) links between them. In the source graph we have to find exact matches to the left hand side of the rewriting rule, and replace it with precisely the right hand side of the rewriting rule. In the metamodel-based approach, the situation is more complex. The source and the destination model each consist of objects and their links. However, the left and right hand side of the rewriting rules are described in terms of the metamodel (i.e., classes, not instances). Under these circumstances the match is a subgraph of the source model that can be instantiated from the left hand side of the rewriting rules. If we have found a match, we can tell which model element (for instance a specific link) was instantiated from which metamodel element (in case of a link, which specific association). Then the right hand side of the rewriting rule is transformed into objects and links using these instantiation assignments. If an association names an instantiated link "l" during the matching phase, any occurrences on the right hand side of the rewriting rule will be replaced with "l." Afterwards, we will replace the match with these objects and the links based on the instantiation of the right hand side. Naturally, this may be a time-consuming, iterative process.

One of our basic objectives is to introduce a metamodel-based model transformation that is open to extension mechanisms that specialize the core algorithms. The reason why we need this extensibility is the algorithmic complexity of the matching and firing algorithms. There are practical reuse cases when a special property of the input graph can simplify the searching, and there are specific rules, where the firing algorithm can be simplified significantly by introducing new facilities in firing. Here, our main focus is on the core constructs and the related searching and firing algorithms. However, in our case study we present a sample extension to the firing rules. We have discovered in the literature many proven efficiency-increasing heuristics (e.g., [7]) that can be applied to extend the core concepts presented here.

2 A Case Study

Our example models contain processes and pipes. Suppose we have a modeling language that allows processes (P), containers (C) and connections between them. Containers may contain processes and other containers. Both containers and processes have ports (O), which can be connected to each other. For simplicity, processes must belong to a container. A sample model is depicted in Figure 6. This hierarchy is a very useful technique for organizing the models of complex systems, because higher-level containers hide the lower level details. Thus, the composite components can be regarded as a "black box" without the need to pay attention to the internal structure. Suppose that the modeling language and tool of the target domain supports only processes and their connecting pipes. However, we want to reuse the hierarchical models in the target environment.

The input and output domain of the transformation can be seen on Figure 2ab. The textual description of the transformation is as follows:

> *We need to remove the containers. If an O_l port in a C_l container is connected to other O_l ports that are contained in other containers, the O_c ports of the elements in C_l that are connected to O_l, should be connected to those O_t ports, and the port O_l should be removed together with all its connections.*

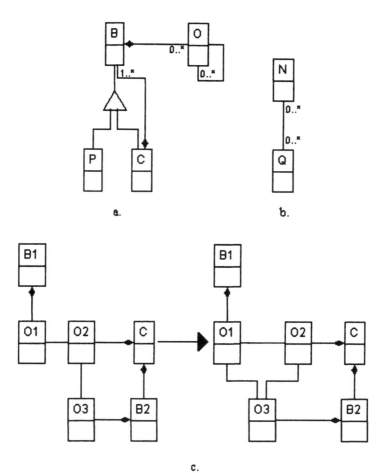

Fig. 2a. Metamodel of the source modeling language (uses containers). Containers are denoted by **C**, processes by **P** and ports by **O**. **2b.** Metamodel of the target modeling language (without containers). **N** denotes processes, **Q**s are pipes. **2c.** Transformation steps.

First we can give a solution that is close to the textual transformation description. It can be seen in Figure 2c.

But, if we examine how this solution works, we can observe that rule 1 makes a fully connected graph between all the ports that are connected to a path in the input model. So this solution works and can be easily applied, but produces overhead.

Hence, the main problem in the solution proposed above is that, in this structure, it is hard to find a rule that "shortcuts" at least one port of a specific **C**, and deletes it in one step. If we try to shortcut a **C**-port in more than one step, we do not know if there is another match that will make another shortcut, and if the given port can be deleted. In order to accomplish this, we need an operation, which includes *all* the other connections of the port to each port.

We can identify a tradeoff that can be summarized as follows: On one hand, we use simple constructs to specify the LHS, but, as it was experienced in the example above, we cannot express complex patterns like *"all* the connections." In this case it is easy to match and fire the rewriting rule, but produce significant overhead (creating a fully connected graph in the example). This will be referred to as the basic case in the sequel. On the other hand, we apply more complex constructs to express the LHS, but these constructs require more complex matching and firing algorithms to support them.

In the next section we propose a set of complex constructs and their supporting algorithms.

3 Matching Algorithms

One of the most crucial points of a graph rewriting-based transformation is the strategy for finding a match. As we introduced in Section 1, this is a particular problem in the case of a metamodel-based transformation, because there is an indirection in applying the left hand side of the rewriting rule: we want to find a match that can be generated from the left hand side of that rule. By allowing the multiplicity of objects to be different from the one in the metamodel, an increasing number of the model elements can be instantiated. To deal with this question, we consider the basic metamodel structures and how the multiplicity defined in the metamodel is related to the models.

3.1 The Basic Case

If we assume the multiplicity of the roles in an association to be one-to-one, we have an easy task because each of the metamodel elements can be instantiated to only one model element (except if the model uses inheritance). Without inheritance, we can generate only one link for every association, and only one object for every class, in order to avoid the aforementioned indirection.

Because of this one-to-one mapping, the match can be considered as a form of type checking: if an object type is a specific class, then that object matches this class. The situation is exactly the same in the case of links ("instances") and associations (their "class"). If we have an inheritance relationship, we suggest a simple procedure: for every class that has a base class, a list should be maintained containing the type of all base classes. An object of any type in the list is regarded as a match. We assumed this basic case in Figure 2c.

Algorithm 1. Matching association of multiplicity one-to-one (basic case)
1. Form a type list for every derived class containing all of its base types and the derived class.
2. Assume there is an association **L** between classes **A** and **B**. Then, to match an object **a** having type **A** on the type list of its class, scan the neighbors of **a** to find an object **b** having **B** on its type list via a link of type **L**.

For the sake of simplicity, we use the term "type **A**" object instead of the precise description "having **A** on the type list of its class" in the sequel.

3.2 One-to-Many Case

The one-to-many case is depicted in Figure 3a. If we consider the example model in Figure 3b, we can see that the A class can only have one instance, which allows us to find it with the aforementioned type checking method.

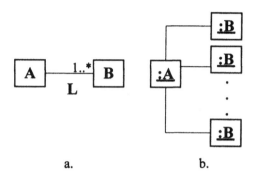

a.   b.

Fig. 3. One-to-many association: 3a. metamodel, 3b. example model.

After finding an object of type A, we can access all of its neighbors via links of type L. We also must check the multiplicity on the B-side of the association. The x denotes the number of found links. If this value (x) is in the multiplicity range, then there is a match and the rule can be fired.

Algorithm 2. Matching one-to-many associations.
1. Find an object of type A.
2. Find all of the B type neighbors of A type object via links type of L.
3. N denotes the set of integers containing the legal values for multiplicity. There is a match if and only if the number of links of type L from A to B is equal to n, and n∈ N.

Effectively, Algorithm 2 is a breadth-first-search considering the type mechanism of the metamodel.

3.3 One-to-One Case

The difference between the basic case and the one-to-one case is that the basic case considers one link of the several links of a many-to-many association as a match, and the one-to-many case does not. So the one-to-one is a specific case of the one-to-many.

Algorithm 3. Matching one-to-one associations.
1. Find an object of type A.
2. Find all of the B type neighbors of A type object via links type of L.
3. There is a match if and only if the number of links from A to B is precisely one.

3.4 Many-to-Many Case

The many-to-many case is the most complex construct. Matching many-to-many associations could be approached as follows:

1. Apply *Algorithm 2* to an arbitrary chosen **A** type object
2. Apply it again to the **B** type objects found in the previous steps.

This construction, however, could be substituted with multiple one-to-many relationships.

One may propose a definition as follows: the instantiated N-to-M association is a connected graph with vertices of type **A** and **B**, and links of type **L** (connecting only different object types). The degree n of an arbitrary **A** type vertex, and degree m of an arbitrary **B** type vertex must satisfy that $n \in N$, and $m \in M$.

The problem is that it can be hard to find a match for the many-to-many case (this is actually an arbitrary object net with type constraints), and even harder to apply the rule (see Section 4), so by default we do not use this construct to describe a transformation.

3.5 Iterative Cases

In Figure 2c we can find a model element (in this specific case class **C**), which can be instantiated only once. We refer to these classes as *single classes* in the sequel. We can identify the single class easily: if there is no association end with multiplicity greater than 1 connected to a class, then it is a single class.

If a rule has a single class, we can find an object of the single class, and apply the basic search algorithms following the metamodel structure of the LHS of the rule. But, if we do not have single class, we have to iterate.

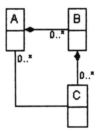

Fig. 4. Metamodel with no single classes

To trace the instantiation we use a set denoted by **OA** that contains the model elements matched by **A**. This notation is refined in Section 4.

Algorithm 4. Iteration from the "many" (> 1) multiplicity side.
1. Take a non-single class **A** as if it were single class.
2. Find all associated classes with **A** on the "many" side of the association. (On Figure 4. the result is **C**).

3. Find the **A** objects reachable via links from these **C** objects. Add these objects to the basic **OA** set, and iterate until there is no **A** object to add. (This can take significant time, so creating rules containing single classes is recommended.)

Another situation arises when we have to use iteration in the matching process and we reach a point where there is no unprocessed LHS association having multiplicity 1 at the processed object. In that case, the iteration scheme will be the same: we choose a link to go to the object on 1 side of the association, and search the other links.

3.6 The General Search Algorithm

We now outline the search algorithm needed to match the left sides of the rules using the concepts we described above.

Algorithm 5. Matching.
1. Find a single class. If we cannot find such a class, apply *Algorithm 4* for a class that participates in an association with the smallest (>1) multiplicity.
2. Following the left hand side of the transformations, match the associations using *Algorithm 2* or *Algorithm 3* based on the multiplicity values. When possible, follow the associations from the side with multiplicity 1 to the side with multiplicity >1 (many). When this is not possible, apply *Algorithm 4*.

Remarks. If the instantiation sets for the same class are different, we should consider only the intersection of the sets removing the connecting links.

After we successfully matched a class to an object, we mark it with the class name. To satisfy the identity condition, an already marked object can only instantiate the class it is marked with and nothing else.

3.7 Another Solution to the Case Study

Using the concepts described in Section 3, we present another solution for our case study. One can see a more complex pattern in Figure 5. The lower case labels on the associations are for identification purposes only. The symbol **d+e** means the following: where there was a path via links of type **d** and **e** on the LHS, there must be a link along the association marked **d+e** on the RHS. This will be elaborated in Section 4. We concluded in Section 2 that there is a trade-off between the complexity of the rules and the efficiency of the application. Metamodel elements with the same name, but different numbers at the end of the name, refer to the same class, but to different instances of the class, because the identity condition has to be enforced. The matching algorithm checks all these classes regarding the multiplicity.

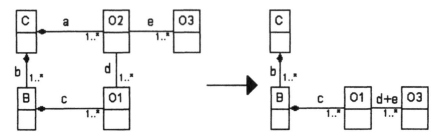

Fig. 5. A more efficient solution with more complicated search. This rule replaces the first rule in Figure 2c.

4 Applying Rules

After finding a match to the left hand side of a rewriting rule, we have to fire it. But, in case of the metamodel-based transformation, the right hand side of the rule also contains an indirection that we have to resolve.

A notation suitable for handling the instantiation assignment is described below. This also facilitates the basic applicability checking on the right side of the rules.

An instantiation set, written as **OX**, means a collection of objects that are instances of class X of the LHS. An instantiation set LY denotes a collection of links, which are instances of the association Y of the LHS. For the rule on Figure 5, and the model on Figure 6b, the notation can be used as follows:

OC: $\{C_1\}$
La: $\{C_1/OC_{11}, C_1/OC_{12}\}$
OO$_2$: $\{OC_{11}, OC_{12}\}$
Ld: $\{\{OC_{11}/OP_{11}\}, \{OC_{12}/OP_{12}, OC_{12}/OP_{21}\}\}$
OO$_1$: $\{\{OP_{11}\}, \{OP_{12}, OP_{21}\}\}$

Lb: $\{C_1/P_1, C_1/P_2\}$
OB: $\{P_1, P_2\}$
Lc: $\{\{P_1/OP_{11}, P_1/OP_{12}\}, \{P_2/OP_{21}\}, \{P_1/OP_{13}\}\}$
OO$_1$': $\{\{OP_{11}, OP_{12}\}, \{OP_{21}\}, \{OP_{13}\}\}$

Le: $\{\{OC_{11}/OC_{21}, OC_{11}/OC_{22}\}, \{OC_{12}/OC_{23}\}\}$
OO$_3$: $\{\{OC_{21}, OC_{22}\}, \{OC_{23}\}\}$

We denoted the links using the object names they connect. As it has been mentioned in Section 3.6, to conform with the identity condition we mark all the objects and links assigned to a metamodel element on the right side of the rule as an instance, but we can assign the same right side metamodel element to a specific model element more than once, approaching from different directions (**OO$_1$**, and **OO$_1$'** in our example). This means that a metamodel element can have many different instantiation sets. In this case, we consider the intersection of the sets, but we keep all these sets around, because their structure can be different. In the example, this means removing OP_{13} from OO_1'. To easily trace the structure, we use nested sets to represent the tree structure of the instantiation sets. This redundancy facilitates checking mechanisms based on sets, without considering the topology.

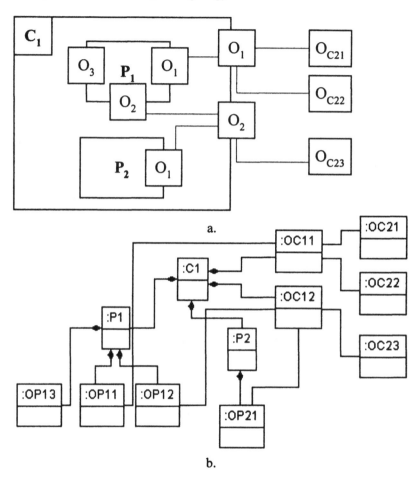

Fig. 6. A specific example. **6a.** Layout. **6b.** Model.

Having completed the matching algorithm, we then build the instantiation set for the match. The instantiation set must be put together based on the right hand side of the rule. During the firing process we consider every right hand side metamodel element as a collection of model elements specified by the instantiation sets. First, we delete all the links and objects of right hand side classes and associations that do not appear on the left hand side of the rule. The notation **d+e** has the following semantics: *where there was a path via links of type **d** and **e** on the LHS, there must be a link along the association marked **d+e** on the RHS.* We define the extensions using the instantiation sets. The "+" operation defined below (for the sake of simplicity, we give the definition for only the case depth 1 here, but it can be easily generalized).

Algorithm 6. Computing the "+" operation between two subsequent associations.
1. Take the first operand, **d**. Replace every nested set with the Cartesian product of this set and the corresponding nested set in the second operand **e**.
2. The result will be in the first operand.

In our case the application of Algorithm 6 yields:

Ld+e: $\{\{OC_{11}/OP_{11}+ \ OC_{11}/OC_{21}, \ OC_{11}/OP_{11}+ \ OC_{11}/OC_{22}\}, \ \{OC_{12}/OP_{12}+$
$OC_{12}/OC_{23}, OC_{12}/OP_{21}+ OC_{12}/OC_{23}\}\}$
Simplifying:
Ld+e: $\{\{OP_{11}/OC_{21}, OP_{11}/OC_{22}\}, \{OP_{12}/OC_{23}, OP_{21}/OC_{23}\}\}$

After putting together the sets, the solution can be checked on Figure 6b. This case study illustrates the matching and firing mechanism, as well as the proposed notation and algorithms that support them in an extensible manner.

5   Related Work

With respect to metamodel-based transformation, an approach has been proposed that uses semantic nets (sNets) for metamodel descriptions [4]. This approach, however, does not deal with algorithmic, matching, and multiplicity issues. It uses mainly a textual representation for transformation rules.

The PROGRES graph rewriting system [6] also uses graph rewriting to transform, generate, and parse visual languages. The heuristic approaches to find a match in PROGRES reduces the algorithmic complexity using principles from database query systems. These heuristics can be easily integrated with those that are described in this paper.

Triple graph grammars [8] maintain a correspondence graph to specify the homomorphic mapping between the source and the target graph. This approach does not use object-oriented concepts.

An approach, similar to triple graph grammars is contributed by Akehurst [9], which is object-oriented and UML/OCL-based. This technique uses OCL and UML constructs to define the mapping between class diagrams, but it does not use graph replacement rules. Both the triple graph grammars and the UML/OCL techniques are bi-directional.

However, in several practical cases, the specification of a bi-directional mapping is hard or impossible, because information loss is inherent in the transformation. In our experience, the transformations need more than one pass to complete, thus more than one different, sequential transformation step is required. Direct mapping is not always possible in model reuse applications, because direct correspondence cannot be found between the different metamodeling concepts, but it can be specified between model constructs as it has been presented in our case study.

6 Conclusion

This paper presents an approach for reusing models based on different concepts that overlap somewhere in the domain. We require that these models have a common meta-metamodel: specifically a metamodel represented as UML class diagrams. We proposed a common language (the metamodel), defined transformations using the elements of the metamodel, and offered algorithms to apply these transformations as graph rewriting rules. We intend this to serve as an algorithmic background for a forthcoming implementation where additional mechanisms will be added to control the application of the transformation rules.

A working case study has been presented showing the basic algorithms, formalisms and tradeoffs between the complex search algorithm and the size of the graph created during the intermediate transformation steps.

There are unsolved issues, however. We presented an extension in Section 4, but future work is needed to specify a general transformation system with the fewest number of extensions.

In this paper mainly the topological reuse issues have been covered. One can easily extend this transformation approach with simple constraints on the model elements (for instance, an attribute value must be greater than a specific value), but checking complex constraints, even those which are applied in the target domain, is the subject of ongoing research.

Acknowledgements

The DARPA/ITO MOBIES program (F30602-00-1-0580) has supported, in part, the activities described in this paper.

References

[1] Sztipanovits J., Karsai G., "Model-Integrated Computing," *IEEE Computer*, pp. 110-112, April, 1997.

[2] Rumbaugh, J., Booch, G., and Jacobson, I., "The Unified Modeling Language Reference Manual", Addison-Wesley, Reading, MA, 1999.

[3] D. Blostein, H. Fahmy, A. Grbavec, "Practical Use of Graph Rewriting", *Technical Report No. 95-373*, Department of Computing and Information Science, Queen's University, Kingston, Ontario, Canada, January, 1995.

[4] R. Lemesle, "Transformation Rules Based on Meta-Modeling", *EDOC '98*, La Jolla, California, 3-5 November 1998, pp.113-122.

[5] G. Rozenberg (ed.), "Handbook on Graph Grammars and Computing by Graph Transformation: Foundations", Vol.1-2. *World Scientific*, Singapore, 1997.

[6] The PROGRES system can be downloaded from http://www-i3.informatik.rwth-aachen.de

[7] A. Zündorf, "Graph Pattern Matching in PROGRES", In: "Graph Grammars and Their Applications in Computer Science", LNCS 1073, J. Cuny et al. (eds), Springer-Verlag, 1996, pp. 454-468.

[8] Schürr, A., "Specification of Graph Translators with Triple Graph Grammars", *Proceedings of the 20th International Workshop on Graph-Theoretic Concepts in Computer Science*, LNCS 903, Berlin: Springer-Verlag; June 1994; 151-163.
[9] Akehurst, D H, "Model Translation: A UML-based specification technique and active implementation approach", PhD Thesis, University of Kent at Canterbury, 2000.

Generation of Text Search Applications for Databases. An Exercise on Domain Engineering[1]

Omar Alonso

Oracle Corp.,
500 Oracle Parkway, Redwood Shores, CA 94065 - USA
oalonso@us.oracle.com

Abstract. In this paper we present an example of a software infrastructure to support domain engineering activities. An important piece of the infrastructure is the ability to connect the outputs of the domain analysis to the inputs of the domain implementation. The combination of XML and Java provides a very interesting alternative to classical parser generation tools. XML can be used as a specification language to describe programs. In this paper we will describe how to connect the output of a domain analysis tool to a program generator. We will also describe how to use Java and XML tools to write program generators in Oracle9*i*. We will show how we can specify a search engine application in XML and how the generator can produce code for three different languages: Java Server Pages, PL/SQL, and PL/SQL Server Pages.

1 Introduction

The process of creating an infrastructure to support systematic reuse is called domain engineering. Domain engineering has two main phases: domain analysis and domain implementation. Domain analysis is the activity of identifying and documenting the commonalities and variabilities in related software systems in a domain. Domain implementation is the use of knowledge acquired in domain analysis to develop reusable assets for the domain and the creation of a production process for systematically reusing assets to generate new products. Some authors distinguish between domain analysis, design, and implementation.

Traditionally there has been work on underlying technologies for domain analysis like analysis and design tools, and domain implementation like program generators tools. To achieve domain based reuse the outputs of the domain analysis phase must be linked to the inputs of the domain implementation phase.

Recently the introduction of generative programming reinforces the importance of an automatic process that, given a requirements specification, can produce an end-product that is built from reusable components [6].

---

[1] The statements and opinions presented here do not necessarily represents those of Oracle Corp.

C. Gacek (Ed.): ICSR-7, LNCS 2319, pp. 179–193, 2002.

The combination of XML and Java provides a very interesting alternative to classical parser generation tools for implementing program generators. XML can be used as a specification language to describe programs and configurations.

In this paper we describe how to connect (and implement) the output of a domain analysis tool to a program generator. We show how to implement the generator in Java using a XML as a specification language. We also present a real case application for the text searching domain.

2 Domain Analysis and Domain Implementation

The main goal of the domain analysis phase is to define and scope a domain, collect the relevant information, and to produce assets that describe commonalities and variabilities in related software systems.

The minimal domain analysis must result in a domain model that includes:

- Domain scope or domain boundaries
- Domain vocabulary
- Commonalities and variabilities

There are several domain analysis methods like DARE [9], FAST [16], and FODA [11] among others. We will follow DARE (Domain Analysis and Reuse Environment) as the domain analysis tool.

DARE supports the capture of domain information from experts, documents, and code in a domain. Captured domain information is stored in a domain book that will typically contain a generic architecture for the domain and domain-specific reusable components.

The domain book helps to capture domain information from domain experts, domain documents, and code from systems in the domain. The domain book also supports recording analyses and design decisions, and a generic architecture for the domain. It is also a repository of reusable assets. DARE arranges content in three main parts:

1. Domain Sources. This part contains the source documents, code, system descriptions, architectures, feature tables, and other notes.
2. Vocabulary Analysis. This part contains the basic vocabulary, facets, synonyms, templates, thesaurus, and other notes.
3. Architecture Analysis. This part contains the generic architecture of the analysis along with the generic features, code structure and other notes.

DARE Web is a database backed web version of the original DARE [1]. It includes features like searching and security that were not available on the previous prototypes. It also leverages several features of the Oracle database along with the XML tools available in the Oracle platform [13]. DARE Web could be viewed as a content management system for software engineering environments.

Domain implementation is the use of knowledge acquired in the domain analysis phase to develop and implement reusable assets for that particular domain. It is also the creation of a production process for reusing assets to generate new products.

We present the domain analysis for the text searching domain in section three and its domain implementation in section four.

3 Text Searching Analysis

Text search applications like a search engine are a sub-area of information retrieval. In a generic way the user of a text search application has to translate his information need into a query in the language provided by the system. This normally implies specifying a set of words in a particular syntax. The retrieval system processes the query and then returns a set of documents along with other metadata information. At this point the user can reformulate the query if the answer was not satisfactory. Otherwise the user selects a document and performs some operations on it.

At a high level the architecture of a text search application consists of five main components or modules: index creation and maintenance, query parser, search, user interface, and document services.

The index creation and maintenance module provides mechanisms to create text indexes and the ability to synchronize them. Usually the text indexes are implemented as an inverted file.

The query parser module checks the correctness of the query in a particular syntax and semantics. At the very basic level a query parser supports, for example, a Web-like syntax (AND, OR, NOT, and phrase).

The search module actually implements the query specification. For some systems like Oracle, it is an extension to the SQL language. In others is a function of a C search library for example.

The document services component provides several "views" of a given document. A view could be the most relevant paragraph given the query or an HTML version of a binary format.

As part of the domain analysis, in our case we will scope the text searching domain to every Oracle database so we can leverage the Text search API [14]. A taxonomy and in-depth description of information retrieval systems can be found in [2] and [7]. A collection of papers from industry with an emphasis on integration of databases and information retrieval can be found in [10].

3.1 Commonalities and Variabilities

The analysis presented in this section is a short version of the actual study. A significant number of details like database versions, APIs differences, internationalization features, and language constructions were omitted for presentation purposes.

We identify the following commonalities and variabilities for our domain analysis. We scope the analysis to Oracle databases[2].

Commonalities:

- Text index. Every text search application uses a text search index (usually an inverted text index or some variation of it).
- User interface. Every application has a user interface where the user can enter the query and visualize the result set. We will scope the user interface to Web browsers only.
- Query parser. The user must enter the search query using an existing set of available operators.
- Search. The actual specification of a full-text search query for a particular product.
- Document services. The user must be able to perform some operations on the returned documents.

Variabilities:

- Schema. Using Oracle Text a user can define where the documents are located: tables, file system, websites, or program generated. Documents can be in several formats (e.g. PDF, MS Office, HTML, XML, etc.) and filters need to be used to extract content. All this information needs to be part of the actual index creation script. In Oracle the text index is stored like any regular table.
- User Interface. There are several interface design choices for text search applications. In our case we will use two: a traditional search engine interface based on a table model and a more advanced one based on a two-view model. A more detailed presentation of information visualization interfaces can be found in [2].
- Query parser. We have the following options: AltaVista-like syntax, Web query, or a full Oracle Text syntax. A Web query parser includes only the following operators: AND, OR, NOT, and phrase. Note that there are other possibilities for parsers like natural language or visual ones but we decided not to include them.
- Search. The actual search predicate depends on the underlying product API. In our case is a SQL statement that includes a `contains` extension[3].
- Document services. The basic service is to show the contents of the document. Other services are: display an HTML version of a document for binary formats, display a document with highlighted query terms, show the summary of a document, and to display the main themes of a document (based on a linguistic analysis of the text).

---

[2] The inclusion of other vendors in the same area is out of the scope of this paper.
[3] The `contains` extension to SQL is also supported by other vendors.

- Language. We plan to generate code for three languages: PL/SQL, JSP (Java Server Pages), and PSP (PL/SQL Server Pages). The reason behind this decision is requirements from the field.

In DARE the facets table stores information that can be used for creating a generic architecture of the system. Table 1 shows a facets table for the analysis of text search applications.

Table 1. Facetes table.

Schema	Query	Search	User interface	Document services	Language
Table/column	AltaVista-like	SQL contains	Table	Markup	PSP
File system	Web-like		Two-view	Highlighting	PL/SQL
Websites	Oracle Text			Summary	JSP
				Themes	

3.2 Implementation

With DARE Web we captured and stored all the assets from the domain analysis phase. The assets are stored in tables using the CLOB data type. Some of those assets are in XML form and some not. With the XML tools available it is possible to produce XML from SQL queries.

Figure 1 shows a DARE Web screenshot. The left frame contains the domain book outline. The structure of the components is based on the 3Cs model (concept, content, and context).

4 The Generator

The generator takes a specification of a system or component and returns the finished system or component in a specified language. The specification describes the task performed or the product to be produced by the generator. This specification can be textual or interactive [3]. Once the generator is done a compiler (e.g. Oracle JSP implementation) will translate the output (e.g. .jsp file) to an executable (e.g. .class file). Figure 2 shows an overview of a program generator.

The work in the area of application generators has always been very active. We use XML and Java technology to build a stand alone generator. We don't claim that is the best implementation. We think that implementing application generators with this kind of tools are easy for software engineers who want to automate part of their development efforts. Smaragdakis and Batory provide an excellent description of different methods and techniques for building generators in [15]. Other approaches like template programming with C++ are presented in [5].

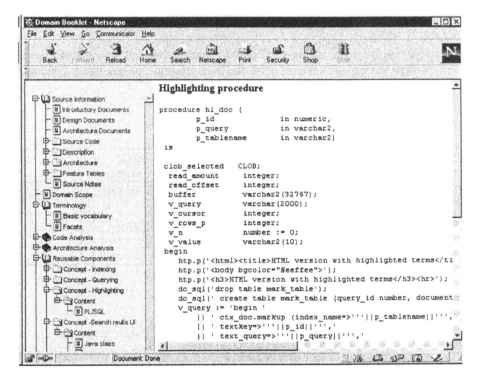

Fig. 1. The source code for a PL/SQL highlighting procedure in DARE Web .

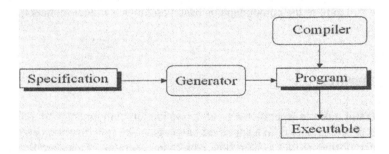

Fig 2. An application generator.

4.1 Using XML and DOM to Generate Programs

We followed some of the ideas introduced by Cleaveland [4] for building program generators with XML and Java. The main reason behind our decision is the availability of all the tools in the Oracle platform at no extra cost. Also XML and Java are widely available from different vendors and as open source.

The Document Object Model (DOM) is a platform and language neutral interface that will allow programs and scripts to dynamically access and update the content, structure, and style of documents. A program generator using XML input requires an XML parser to convert an XML file to a DOM object.

There are three general approaches for parsing and storing the specification [4]:

1. Pure DOM. Uses a standard XML parser to create the DOM data structures. The transformation and analysis are applied directly on the DOM data structures. The code generator also works on the DOM data structures.
2. DOM to Custom. Uses a standard XML parser to create the DOM data structures. There are extra data structures created for the transformation and analysis phase. The code generator works on the new data structures instead of the original DOM data structures.
3. SAX to Custom. Uses a SAX (Simple API for XML) to create a custom XML parser. The SAX API provides an event-based interface. SAX is more efficient that DOM.

We choose the DOM to Custom model because it offers flexibility during code generation. Figure 3 shows the main phases of the DOM to Custom model.

4.2 XML as a Specification Language

XML is the universal format for structured documents and data on the Web. XML is a human readable, machine-understandable, general syntax for describing hierarchical data; applicable to a wide range of applications. XML has been adopted by several companies as a standard for exchanging data between different networked systems among other applications.

Cleaveland presented XML as a way of describing computer programs not just record-level data. We use XML for specifying our application. The specification of a text search application for an Oracle database looks like the following:

```
<?xml version="1.0"?>
<features>
        <query>text</query>
        <table>mydocs</table>
        <column>id</column>
        <column>url</column>
        <column>title</column>
        <textcol>content</textcol>
        <documentservice>highlight</documentservice>
        <ui>table</ui>
        <source>psp</source>
</features>
```

The tags represents:

- query: the query syntax. In the example, Oracle Text

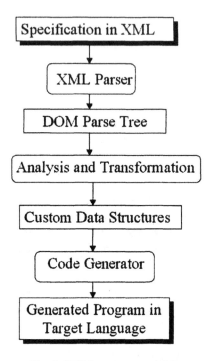

Fig. 3. DOM to custom model.

- `table`, `column`, and `textcol`: the schema information. There is also a distinction between the regular columns of the table and the searchable column (`textcol`).
- `documentservice`: the document service(s). In the example, display the document with highlighted query terms.
- `ui`: the user interface. In the example, a simple table model very similar to web search engines.
- `source`: the target language.

Note that we did not include "search" because we are producing a product for an Oracle database only.

The generator will take the XML specification and using DOM will generate the application source code.

4.3 Generator Architecture

There are two general approaches for generating code: code driven and table (or template driven) [3], [4]. In the code driven approach the generator generates code with embedded data. In the table approach, the generator uses a special data structure to generate code.

An earlier version of YASEC (the generator) was implemented using the table driven approach. The templates were stored in a database schema and it was very useful for generating PL/SQL code. Since PL/SQL is Oracle's procedural language it was very practical to store tables in the schema and manipulate the compilation process. However this was not very portable if you wanted to run the generator as a stand-alone application.

The current implementation of YASEC uses a code driven approach. It is possible to use YASEC from a user interface (the interface generates the XML) or to provide an XML file specification from the command line.

The following Java snippet shows the overall code structure of the generator. Basically the main structure manipulates the DOM tree and generates the main search module. While generating the search module and depending on the specification, scripts and components are also generated.

```java
import java.io.*;
import org.w3c.dom.*;

public class YasecGen extends DOM {

    public static void main(String args[]) {

        // generation of index script

        YasecIndexGenerator mySqlscript = new YasecIndexGenerator();
        mySqlscript.IndexCreation(d.table,d.table, d.textcol);

        if (compareTo(d.source, "psp") {
            // PSP (PS/SQL Server Pages) code generation

            // generation of the package for the document services.
            // the package contains a header section, the procedures,
            // and the trail section.

            YasecServicesP myServices = new YasecServicesP();
            myServices.serviceHeader(d.name,currentServices);

            // procedures generation for document services

            myServices.serviceTrail();

            // main structure of a PSP search

            out.println("<%@ plsql procedure=\""+d.name+"\" %>");

            // rest of the PSP generation

            // generation of scripts and documentation.

            out.close();
        }
        if (compareTo(d.source, "jsp") {
            // JSP generation
        }

        if (compareTo(d.source, "plsql") {
            // PL/SQL generation
        }
```

```
    // other sql scripts and installation.

  }
}
```

The following Java snippet also shows the overall structure of the services components for PL/SQL. The service class has a method for each document service plus a package header and trailer.

```java
import java.io.*;

public class YasecServicesPL {

    public void serviceHeader (String values[]) {

      // generates the package header.

    }

    public void showHTMLdoc (String values[]) {

      // generates the procedure that displays a an HTML version
      // of a binary document.

    }

    public void showHighlightDoc (String indexName) {

      // generates the procedure that displays a document
      // with highlighted terms.

    }

    public void showThemes (String indexName) {

      // generates the procedure that display the main themes of a
      // document.

    }

    public void showSummary (String indexName) {

      // generates the procedure that display a summary of a document.

    }

    public void serviceTrail () {

      // generates the trail of the package.

    }
}
```

5 Connecting DARE Web Output to the Generator

As we mentioned earlier, to achieve domain based reuse the outputs of the domain analysis phase must be linked to the inputs of the domain implementation phase.

Frakes summarized the DARE to Metatool mapping in [8]. In this section we provide a way of connecting the DARE output to a YASEC using XML.

We already mentioned the importance of identifying commonalities and variabilities in the analysis phase. Commonalities are decisions made during the text search analysis about what is common across a family of search applications. Variabilities are decisions made during the generation of the application.

As we mentioned before DARE Web's implementation takes advantages of numerous database features including native XML support in the database.

Given the facets implementation in a database, we can query using XSU, the facets table and return the content in XML. For example for a text search application that uses an AltaVista query syntax, with regular table user interface, with only one document service (highlighting) and the target language is JSP:

```
<?xml version="1.0"?>
<features>
        <query>AV</query>
        <table>mydocs</table>
        <column>id</column>
        <column>url</column>
        <column>title</column>
        <textcol>content</textcol>
        <documentservice>highlight</documentservice>
        <ui>table</ui>
        <source>jsp</source>
</features>
```

The above XML code is not enough for generating a "product". We need more data for generating the product like the name of the application and information about the specific configurations (e.g. database version, drivers, security, etc.). The configuration data is also useful for compatibility with certain environments.

YASEC will work with the product specification only. Figure 4 shows how to derive the specification for the generator.

The product specification looks like:

```
<?xml version="1.0"?>
<product name="SearchApp">
    <configuration>searchapp</configuration>
    <query>text</query>
    <table>mydocs</table>
    <column>id</column>
    <column>url</column>
    <column>title</column>
    <textcol>content</textcol>
    <documentservice>highlight</documentservice>
    <ui>table</ui>
    <source>jsp</source>
</product>
```

The configuration data is also in XML and contains in this example, the name and location of the driver, the database version, user name, password, port numbers, etc.

Note that the configuration can also contain information about the Web server, directories for the source code and so on.

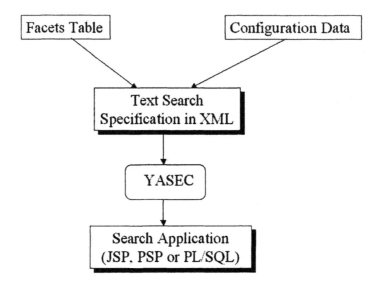

Fig. 4. Deriving the specification for the generator.

```
<configuration>searchapp
<username>demo</username>
<password>demo_p</password>
<dburl>jdbc:oracle:thin:@localhost:1521:betadev</dburl>
<version>8.1.7.2</version>
</configuration>
```

Figure 5 shows how to connect the output of the domain analysis tool (in our case DARE-Web) to an application generator (YASEC) using XML tools. With the XML SQL Utility (XSU) we can query the facets table and return XML. Then with the configuration data (also in XML) we have the full specification for the text application. With the specification as input, YASEC generates the search application.

In the case of this type of database applications YASEC also generates the installer script, plus all the specific database scripts (e.g. index creation, set preferences, etc.). These are the sub-products that YASEC generates:

- Search Application in target language including components.
- SQL scripts (e.g., index creation, synchronization, etc.)
- Documentation

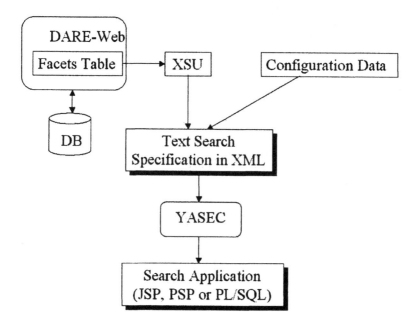

Fig. 5. Using XML tools to connect the output of a domain analysis tool to an application generator.

6 Experience Summary

The project described in this paper is still an ongoing effort. In this section we summarize the overall experience.

The domain analysis tool (DARE Web) and the application generator (YASEC) were implemented on top of the Oracle database (versions 8*i*/9*i*) using the XML toolkit available with the platform [9], [10]. The Java compiler is the standard JDK from Sun Microsystems.

The generator was designed to be a stand-alone component. It can work with the DARE Web implementation, with a user interface, or from the command line. We are currently working on a servlet flavor and a Web service version of YASEC.

The infrastructure is in use and it produced several products:

- Sample code for external websites and customers.
- A number of mini Applications for customers and software events.
- Source code for reference manuals.

We also reused all the domain analysis and domain implementation experience to design a wizard-like text search application generator that will be part of a commercial product.

Large software systems like databases, operating systems, and programming environments evolve over time. A product like the Oracle database is shipping a new release every year (average) without counting patches. So there is number of information about new features, deprecated features, drivers, and so on that we need to keep as part of knowledge of the generator. We choose to separate the high-level product information from the configuration data.

We tried using XSLT for building the application generator but we found it was difficult to develop compared to XML with DOM.

We didn't explore the specification of a user interface using XML. Instead we used pre-defined styles (e.g. table, two-view). We are considering using XML to define simple user interfaces for future versions of the application generator.

We found that the literature about measuring the reuse level in program generators is weak. A known metric is to measure the ratio of the size of the specification to the size of the generated code. We believe there should be a set of metrics that we can apply for domain engineering projects.

7 Conclusions and Future Directions

We showed that is possible to use the Oracle platform for building infrastructure that supports domain engineering at a low cost of ownership. The domain analysis and implementation was built on one platform with no additional cost.

We also demonstrated that DARE Web can be effectively hooked to a code generation process thus achieving systematic reuse at the requirements level. The linking of a domain analysis tool like DARE to a code generator was implemented using XML tools. We believe that XML as a specification language has it disadvantages over other techniques but for database application we think is the right tool. We plan to continue working on using Oracle as infrastructure for building this type of environments.

Acknowledgments

We want to thank Rubén Prieto-Díaz for all the feedback on an earlier version of the paper. Craig Cleaveland and Bill Frakes answered several questions on different aspects of domain engineering. We also like to thank the anonymous reviewers for they helpful comments.

References

1. Omar Alonso and William Frakes. "DARE-Web. Domain Analysis in a Web Environment". *Americas Conference on Information System*, Long Beach, CA (2000).
2. Ricardo Baeza-Yates and Berthier Ribeiro-Neto. *Modern Information Retrieval*. Addison-Wesley, Longman, UK (1999).

3. J. Craig Cleaveland. "Building Application Generators", *IEEE Software*, Vol. 5, No. 4, July (1988).
4. J. Craig Cleaveland. *Program Generators with XML and Java*, Prentice-Hall, Upper Saddle River, NJ (2000).
5. Krzysztof Czarnecki and Ulrich Eisenecker. "Components and Generative Programming". *Proceedings of the 7th European Software Engineering Conference*, Toulouse, France (1999).
6. Krzysztof Czarnecki and Ulrich Eisenecker. *Generative Programming. Methods, Tools, and Applications*. Addison-Wesley, Reading, MA (2000).
7. William Frakes and Ricardo Baeza-Yates. *Information Retrieval: Data Structures and Algorithms*. Prentice-Hall, Upper Saddle River, NJ (1992).
8. William Frakes. "Linking Domain Analysis and Domain Implementation", *Fifth International Conference on Software Reuse*, British Columbia, Canada (1998).
9. William Frakes, Ruben Prieto-Diaz, and Edward Fox. "DARE: Domain Analysis and Reuse Environment", *Annals of Software Engineering*, Vol. 5 (1998).
10. Luis Gravano (Editor). "Special Issue on Text and Databases", *IEEE Data Engineering*, Vol. 24, No. 4, December (2001).
11. Kyo Kang *et al.* "Feature-Oriented Domain Analysis (FODA) Feasibility Study" (CMU/SEI-90-TR-21), Software Engineering Institute, CMU (1990).
12. Oracle XML Page (http://otn.oracle.com/tech/xml/content.html).
13. Oracle Corp. *XML Applications Development Reference*, Redwood Shores, CA (2001).
14. Oracle Corp. *Text Reference Manual*, Redwood Shores, CA (2001).
15. Yannis Smaragdakis and Don Batory, "Application Generators", Dept. of Computer Sciences, The University of Texas at Austin (1999).
16. David Weiss and Robert Lai. *Software Product Line Engineering*. Addison-Wesley, Reading, MA (1999).

Domain Networks
in the Software Development Process

Ulf Bergmann[1] and Julio Cesar Sampaio do Prado Leite[2]

[1] Departamento de Engenharia de Sistemas, Instituto Militar de Engenharia,
Praça General Tibúrcio 80, Rio de Janeiro, RJ, 22290-270, Brasil
ulf@ime.eb.br

[2] Departamento de Informática, Pontifícia Universidade Católica do Rio de Janeiro
Rua Marquês de São Vicente, 225 Rio de Janeiro, 22453-900, Brasil
www.inf.puc-rio.br/~julio

Abstract. Domain Network (DN) is a set of domains interconnected by transformations. A previous implementation of this concept has been done by using the Draco-Puc machine, a software system that provides a very powerful transformation engine. In order to obtain the integration of this DN with approaches that use XML related technologies, we present a new DN implementation that allows an XML application to become a Draco-Puc domain. We believe that in this way we can use the power of Draco-Puc and gain a broadly use of DN by enabling the use of XML applications.

1 Introduction

Domain Network (DN) is a set of domains interconnected by transformations. Each domain is defined by its Domain Specific language (DSL) and by transformations to other domains. In a previous work[1] the concept has been defined and used in the generation of reverse engineering tools.

Using DN in software generation has two main advantages. First, while a usual software generator uses a single refinement step, a DN based generator provides more effective reuse by using several refinement steps. Second, we don't need to implement a new DSL from scratch because we create the transformations to other domains that are represented as DSLs.

An impediment to a broader use of DN is that their actual implementation uses an academic restrict software system - the Draco-Puc machine. The Draco-Puc has a very powerful transformation engine and it is a good choice to implement DN but we need to connect our DN implementation to an industrial standard.

The Extensible Markup Language (XML) and related technologies are broadly used and there are several applications in use today which have been developed using

C. Gacek (Ed.): ICSR-7, LNCS 2319, pp. 194–209, 2002.

this technology. In particular, the XML Metadata Interchange Format[1] (XMI) is used by many tools (like Rational Rose) to express the content of OO models in a format that allows the interchange with other tools.

In this work we will propose a more powerful implementation of DN by combining the Draco-Puc with the XML related technologies, allowing that an XML application can be a Draco-Puc domain. We believe that in this way we can use the power of Draco-Puc and at the same time, make possible that XML based applications be treated by a powerful transformation system.

In Session 2, three implementations of the DN concept will be presented: the Draco-Puc approach (Session 2.1); an XSL-Based approach (Session 2.3); and the combined approach (Session 2.3). In Session 3, examples of the DN use in the software development process will be shown. Finally, Session 4 brings the conclusions where this work's contributions and future work are pointed out.

2   Domain Network

A Domain Network[1][2] is a set of domains interconnected by transformations. Each domain encapsulates the knowledge of a specific area and is described by a domain specific language (DSL). We divide the domains in the network as: application domains, which express the semantics of real world domains or problem classes; modeling domains, which are domains built to help the implementation of application domains; and executable domains, which are domains to which a generally accepted translator exists, as it is the case of well-known programming languages.

Programs written in an application domain language need a refinement process to, across modeling domains, reach an executable language. This refinement process is made by applying transformations from a source to a target domain through a DN.

The use of DN in software generation has two main advantages. First, while a usual software generator uses a single refinement step, a DN based generator provides a more effective reuse by using several refinement steps. Second, we don't need to implement a new DSL from scratch because we create the transformations to other domains that are represented as DSLs.

In the next Sub-Sessions three ways which can be used to implement the Domain Network concept will be presented: the Draco-Puc approach; an XSL-Based approach; and a combination of both.

2.1   The Draco View of Domain Network

The Draco-Puc machine is a software system based on the construction of domains. A Draco-Puc domain must contain syntax, described by their specific grammar, and semantics, expressed by inter domains (vertical) transformations. Draco-Puc is

---

[1] XMI specifies an open interchange model defined by the Object Management Group (OMG) that is intended to give developers working with object technology the ability to exchange programming data over the Internet in a standardized way.

composed of: a powerful general parser generator, a prettyprinter generator and a transformation engine. The executable domains (like C) do not need semantics reduction since there is already an available compiler/interpreter.

Figure 1 shows an example of the domain construction in Draco-Puc. To create the lexical and syntactic specifications we use an internal Draco domain called *GRM* (grammar domain). This domain uses an extended BNF. Embedding commands from the Draco domain *PPD* (prettyprinter domain) in the syntactic specification provides the prettyprinter specification. The file *cobol.grm* in Figure 1 shows a partial implementation for the Cobol domain. The semantics for the domain are specified by transformations to other domains. These transformations are described using the Draco domain *TFM* (transformation domain). Basically, a transformation has a recognition pattern (the *lhs*) and a replacement pattern (the *rhs*): when the *lhs* matches any part of the original program it is replaced by the *rhs*. The file *cobol2c.tfm* shows an example of the Cobol to C transformation.

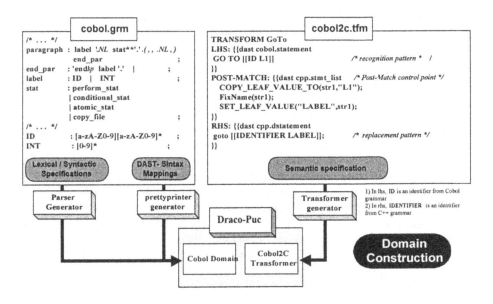

Fig. 1. Domain Construction in Draco-Puc

What makes Draco-Puc transformations more powerful is their very flexible structure. Figure 2 shows the entire transformation structure. Before and after the usual matching sides of a production rule we have 5 possible control points. *Pre-Match* is activated each time the *lhs* is tested against the program. *Match-Constraint* is activated when there is a bind between a variable in *lhs* and a part of the program. *Post-Match* is activated after a successful match between the program and the *lhs*. *Pre-Apply* is activated immediately before the matched program section is substituted by the *rhs*. *Post-Apply* is activated after the program has been modified.

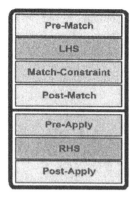

Fig. 2. Transformation Structure

Figure 3 shows an operational description of Draco-Puc main components. The parser for the original program is used by Draco-Puc to convert the program into the internal form used in Draco-Puc (DAST – Draco Abstract Syntax Tree). Transformations are applied to modify the DAST and, at any time, we can use the pretty-printer to unparse the DAST.

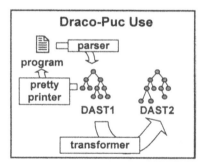

Fig. 3. Draco-Puc main components

Figure 4 shows the actual domain network available in Draco-Puc Machine. The main domains are briefly described in Table 1. This DN has been successfully used in previous work to generate reverse engineering tools[1].

2.2   The XSL Approach towards Domain Network

This approach uses several W3C technical recommendations[2] to implement a DN. Each domain is defined using a Document Type Definition (DTD) or a XML Schema

---

[2] The W3C (World Wide Web Consortium) technical recommendations used here are: the XML - Extensible Markup Language; the DTD - Document Type Definition; the XML

to specify the syntax. The syntax domain doesn't define a real DSL, but a structure of XML documents for this domain.

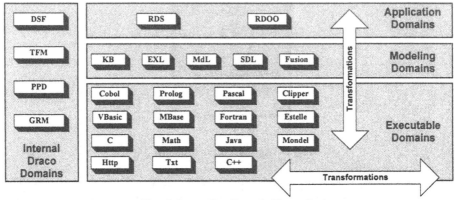

Fig. 4. Draco-Puc Domain Network

Table 1. Draco-Puc domains

Domain	Description
GRM	Describe the domain language syntax and its lexicon
TFM	Specify transformations
PPD	Specify the prettyprinter
RDOO	Recover Design from OO Systems
RDS	Recover Design from Structured Systems
KB	Manipulate a Knowledge Base
EXL	Specify source code extractions
MdL	Specify the visualization of information extracted from source code
SDL	Define a Graphics User Interface
C++, C, ..	Programming Languages

The semantic of the domain is expressed by a set of structural transformations defined in an XSL (Extensible Stylesheet Language). A stylesheet consists of a series of templates, together with instructions based on XPath expressions (the recognition pattern) which tell an XSL processor how to match the templates against nodes in a XML input document. When a node matches the recognition pattern, the instructions in the template are executed in an output XML file. Figure 5 shows an example of the CRC[3] (Class Responsibilities and Collaborations) domain constructed by using this approach. The file *crc.dtd* defines the structure of a XML used to specify a CRC card and the *crc2java.xsl* stylesheet has a set of templates which generate Java code for the class in the card.

Schema; the XSL - Extensible Stylesheet Language; and the XPath - XML Path Language, all available at http://www.w3c.org/TR

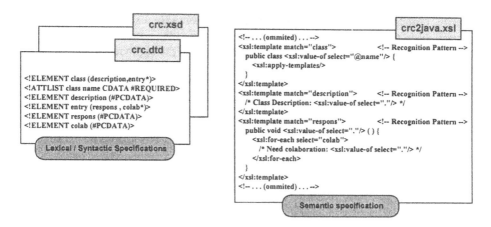

Fig. 5. An example domain in XSL-based approach

To put all these elements to work we need a DOM Parser[3] to read an XML file and construct the DOM Tree, and a XSL Engine to apply the stylesheets. Figure 6 shows an implementation of the XSL-Based approach. The file *sourceDef.dtd* defines the structure of the *source.xml*, which contains the program of the source domain. The DOMTree1 is build by applying the DOMParser on the source XML file. To obtain the correspondent tree in the target domain, the DOMTree2, a XSL Engine is used to apply the transformations in the stylesheet *transf.xsl*. Finally, the program in the target domain (*target.xml*) is obtained after applying another stylesheet (*view.xsl*) which formats the tree in the target domain.

The DN for this approach is showed in Figure 7 and enables the generation of Java code starting from an extended subset of the requirements baseline model proposed by Leite[6]. The domain Scenario is used to describe the situations in the user environment. Each scenario is a structure composed of goal, context, resources, actors and episodes for the scenario. The domain LEL (Language Extended Lexicon) is used in the elicitation of the user language in the macrosystem. The domain CRC (Class Responsibilities and Collaborations) shows the system classes and the distribution of functionality among these classes.

The program wrote in the domains Scenario and CRC can be transformed into the executable domain Java using the descriptions stored in the LEL domain. To make this transformation, we use the intermediate modeling domain XMI.

2.3 Integrating Draco-Puc and XML Based Technologies to Implement a Domain Network

The preceding approaches have some issues that limit the full application of DN in the software development process. The Draco-Puc approach has a very flexible and

---

[3] A DOM Parser uses the Document Object Model (DOM) view of an XML document. The DOM specification can be found at http://www.w3c.org/TR/REC-DOM-Level-1. The parser used here is the Xerces from the Apache XML Project, available at http://xml.apache.org

powerful transformation mechanism but it is not broadly used. The XSL-Based approach uses a set of technologies already used by the industry but is not very flexible. In Table 2 we show a more complete analysis of the approaches.

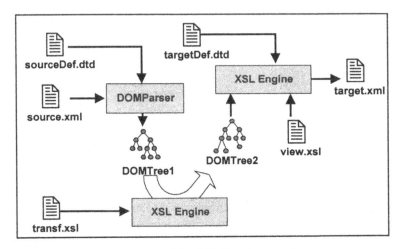

Fig. 6. Use of the XSL-Based approach

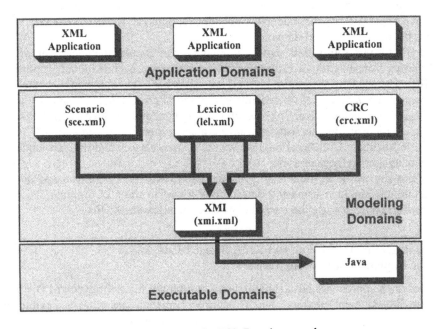

Fig. 7. DN for the XSL-Based approach

Table 2. Draco-Puc and XSL-Based approach comparison

	Draco-Puc	XSL-Based
Domain Language	- Uses the same words as the real world	- Uses XML which is not the user language, it is a markup language
Syntactic Specification	- Uses BNF-like syntax which is more flexible	- Can use DTD or XML Schema. Every document must be a tree
Semantic Specification	- Can use any other domain language within a transformation - Has many different control points to insert code: Pre-Match, Match-Constraint, Post-Match, Pre-Apply, the rhs rule and the Post-Apply	- Can use extensions to access Java code - Only one local to put code: de rhs rule
Use	- Restricted to a small set of researchers - Not used by the industry	- Large set of researchers - Used by many real applications

In order to avoid these problems we decide to design a DN which integrates these two approaches by providing a gateway between them. Figure 8 shows this gateway, implemented by a set of Draco-Puc transformations (see file *dtd2grm* in Fig. 8). This gateway permits every domain in the XSL-Based approach, the *DomainA*, to have an equivalent Draco-Puc domain, the *DomainA'*. The creation of the equivalent domain *DomainA'* is done by applying either the transformation *dtd2grm.tfm*, if *DomainA* syntax is defined by a document type descriptor (DTD), or the transformation *xsd2grm.tfm*, if the syntax is defined by an XML Schema file (XSD). The semantics of the *DomainA* (XSL transformations) is transformed into the equivalent Draco-Puc transformations (TFM) by applying the *xsl2tfm.tfm* transformations.

Figure 9 exemplifies the use of the gateway concept: the syntax for the domain CRC (Class Responsibilities and Collaborations) are originally described in the XSL-Based approach using the Document Type Description (file crc.dtd); and the correspondent syntax in Draco-Puc (file crc.grm) are obtained by applying the transformation *dtd2grm*. In the same way, the semantics specified as XSL are translated to Draco-Puc transformations. This combined approach to DN permits every XML application to be a Draco-Puc domain or, in others words, we can use the Draco-Puc Domain Network to manipulate XML applications as showed in figure 10 where a set of class described in CRC syntax are transformed to Java source code using either the XSL-Based approach or the Draco-Puc approach.

3. Examples of Domain Networks in the Software Development Process

Domain networks in the software development process has a very large range of applications. We highlight two cases of the DN use: identification of models regions where some predefined heuristic can be applied (the identify-and-apply application) and traceability. These cases will be presented and will be compared with other proposed approaches.

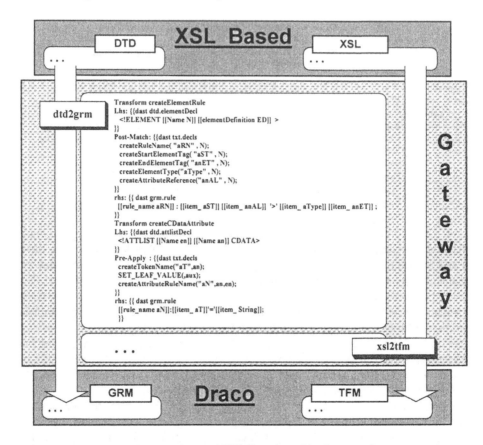

Fig. 8. Draco-Puc and XSL-Based combined approach

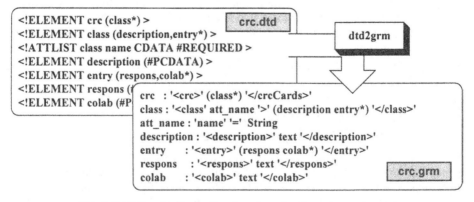

Fig. 9. Building the Draco-Puc domain using the gateway concept

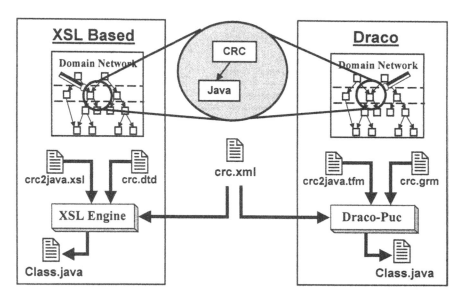

Fig. 10. Using the domain network combined approach

Another example shows the role of DN in software maintenance and can be characterized by extracting information from a legacy system by analyzing their source files and by making some transformations to solve a particular problem. This example has been presented previously by the authors in [1].

3.1   Identify-and-Apply Applications

In this kind of applications we group the work done by the developer when he identifies a particular situation an apply a correspondent rule, where the situation and the rules are previously specified by experts. Examples of these applications are heuristics, a guidance for making design decisions, Design Patterns[4], which provides solutions to a recurring problem, and Anti-Patterns[5], which describes a bad solution to a particular problem.

The example presented in Figure 11 shows how to use a DN to apply the heuristic *from the scenario model an actor can be derived in a class*[6]. The Draco-Puc apply a transformation which finds an actor in the scenarios, asks the developer if he wants to create a class for it and creates the correspondent class.

The source code transformation (using the Draco-Puc TFM domain, a domain to define transformations) which applies this heuristic is presented bellow. When the recognition pattern (lhs) matches some piece of code (an actor) the Post-Match control point is executed to ask the developer if he wants to create the correspondent class. Finally, the replacement pattern is inserted in the crc.xml file creating a new class. Figure 12 shows the DN used in the identify-and-apply example.

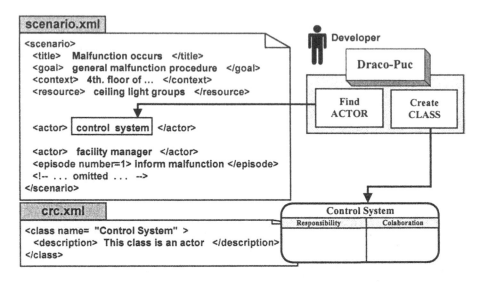

Fig. 11. Apply heuristic example

```
TRANSFORM createClassFromActor
LHS: {{dast scenario.actor
   [[ID name]]    /* recognition pattern */    }}
POST-MATCH: {{dast cpp.stmt_list /* control point */
   COPY_LEAF_VALUE_TO(str1,"name");
   if(askToUser("Create class for" + str1)) {
     FixName(str1);                    /* Normalize string */
     SET_LEAF_VALUE("CLASSNAME",str1);
   } else SKIP_APPLY;
}}
RHS: {{dast crc.class        /*  replacement pattern */
<class name= [[ID CLASSNAME]]>
   <description>This class is an actor</description>
</class>
}}
```

Related Work

OOPDTool[7] is a tool designed to support design expertise reuse by detecting good (Design Patterns) and bad (anti-patterns) OO design constructions and suggesting some hints for a better solution. This tool uses deductive databases to store Design Patterns, Heuristics and Anti-Patterns, as well the facts extracted from a design model recovered from OO source code. To identify where the recovered design model implements some (anti-)pattern or heuristic, it uses an inference machine and machine learning techniques. Our approach has a more powerful way to identify patterns and heuristic application points: first, we can use a Knowledge Base in Draco-Puc machine (it has an inference machine implemented); second, we can use our own transformation engine to recover the design models; and finally, our search engine has a more power to identify points in the design models where patterns and heuristics can be applied. Our approach also allows an automatic application of the patterns.

Some others proposed approaches[8][9], but don't provide an automatic way to identify and/or apply heuristics or (anti-)patterns.

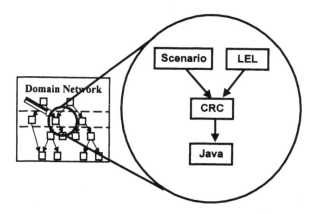

Fig. 12. Domain network used

3.2   Traceability

In their work about reference models for requirements traceability, Ramesh and Jarke[10] define a traceability system as a semantic network in which nodes represent objects among which traceability is established through links of different types and strengths, and classify these links as: <u>Satisfaction Links</u> used to ensure that the requirements are satisfied by the system; <u>Evolution Links</u> used to document the input-output relationships of actions leading from existing objects to new or modified objects; <u>Rationale Links</u> which represent the rationale behind objects or to document the reasons for evolutionary steps; and <u>Dependency Links</u> between objects.

Murphy et al. [11] put that despite the effort spent in generating and validating trace information, they are often mistrusted since they may have become obsolete due to separate evolution of models and systems. We believe that the only approach to avoid this issue is by automatically generating trace information. We will show how to use DN in the implementation of a traceability system which provides an automatic way to capture trace information about the evolutionary and rationale links.

Figure 13 shows this system. It stores trace information as transformations between models and has three main activities: Generate Trace Transformation, Create Plan and Refine.

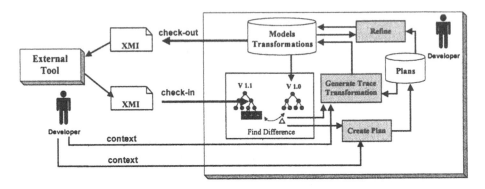

Fig. 13. DN applied to traceability

The Generate Trace Transformation is done by identifying the differences (the delta) between an artifact before it check-out from the system and after the check-in. The delta corresponds to the changes made by the developer. Next, the system applies a Plan Recognition[12] technique into the delta and the context information about the current work of the developer, to infer the intentions of the developer. Finally, it generates a new transformation which can be applied in the original artifact to create the modified artifact. This transformation is then stored in the transformations base. If any plan is selected during this activity, a new plan can be created by the developer and used in other interactions.

The Refine activity provides a way to reuse the stored plans to refine a model. The developer specifies the work context and the system selects the plans which can be applied. The developer selects a plan and the system applies it to the model.

Figure 14 shows the DN used in the traceability application.

Related Work

Egyed [13] presents a scenario driven approach which generates trace information by observing test scenarios that are executed on running software systems. This approach requires the design models and an executable version of the software system. The generated information is restricted to requirements traceability and shows which model elements implement each test scenario. Our approach can be used in any phase of the development and provides not only requirements traceability, but also design traceability which shows the relationship between the design models.

Pinheiro[14] uses a formal approach to maintain traceability information as relations between artifacts. This information must be manually entered by the developer. The DN approach provides an automatic way to capture these pieces of information.

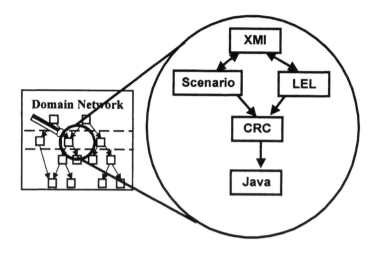

Fig. 14. Domain network for the traceability application

Haumer et. al.[15] propose the use of extended traceability to manually recording concrete system usage scenarios using rich media and interrelating the recorded observations with the conceptual models, in a manner which helps the reviews.

A very similar approach to ours is presented by Antoniol et. al. [16] which compute delta between versions to help the user to deal with inconsistencies by pointing out regions of code where differences are concentrated. They use an intermediate representation, the Abstract Object Language (AOL), and compute de delta by analyzing this code. This work differ from ours because we compute the delta directly by analyzing the abstract trees for each version and, consequently, we don't lose any information when translating to an intermediate representation. Also, the AOL used by Antoniol handle only aspects related to Class Diagrams and we can compute delta in any model. The use of the inferred information also differs because we want to use it to maintain the relationships between models and not only to show inconsistencies between versions to the user. Antoniol approach is only for OO systems and ours can be used by others development methods as well.

4.   Conclusion

Integrating XML related technologies into the concept of Domain Network opens a new opportunity to the use of transformation technology. Since XSL has limitations, we believe that using the Draco-Puc transformation engine on XML languages is a considerable gain in expressiveness power. By using the concept of Domain Network and of Domain Specific Languages we have shown that the integration can be performed in a seamless manner.

We have shown that the DN concept can be applied to different aspects of a software development process. In particular we have shown the capability of manipulating software architectures (design patterns) and software processes (traceability).

Our experiments so far are very positive, but we need to augment our transformation library and use this concept in other applications, mostly some large and complex to verify its applicability in the real world. Future work will continue to try to make the Draco-Puc transformation system more usable and available for a more widespread use. We understand that making possible to use Draco-Puc transformation engine on XML based descriptions will empower software developers in several ways.

References

1. Bergmann, U., Leite, J.C., From Applications Domains to Executable Domains: Achieving Reuse with a Domain Network, in Proceedings of the 6th International Conference on Soft-ware Reuse, 2000.
2. Neighbors, J., Software Construction Using Components, PhD thesis, University of California at Irvine, 1980. http://www.BayfrontTechnologies.com/thesis.htm
3. Wirfs-Brock, R., Wilkerson, B., Wiener, L., Designing Object-Oriented Software, Prentice Hall International, Englewood Cliffs, NJ, 1990.
4. Gamma, E., et. al., Design Patterns - Elements of Reusable Object-Oriented Software, Addison-Wesley Co., 1994.
5. Brown, K., et. al., Anti-patterns - Refactoring Software, Architectures and Projects in Crisis, Wiley Computer Publishing, 1998.
6. Leite, J.C., et. al., Enhancing a Requirements Baseline with Scenarios, in Proceedings of the Third International Symposium on Requirements Engineering, IEEE Computer Society, pp. 44--53. (1997).
7. Correa, A., Werner, C., Zaverucha, G., Object Oriented Design Expertise Reuse: An Approach Based on Heuristics, Design Patterns and Anti-patterns, in Proceedings of the 6th International Conference on Software Reuse, 2000.
8. Cinnéide, M., Nixon, P., Program Reestructuring to Introduce Design Patterns, in Proceedings of the Workshop on OO Software Evolution and Reengineering, ECOOP98.
9. Zimmer, W., Experiences using Design Patterns to Reorganize an Object Oriented Application, in Proceedings of the Workshop on OO Software Evolution and Reengineering, ECOOP98.
10. Ramesh, B., Jarke, M., Toward reference Models for Requirements Traceability, IEEE Transactions on Software Engineering, 27(1), 2000.
11. Murphy, G. C., Notkin, D., and Sullivan, K.: "Software Reflexion Models: Bridging the Gap Between Source and High-Level Models," in Proceedings of the 3th ACM SIGSOFT Symposium on the Foundations of Software Engineering, New York, NY, October 1995, pp.18-28.
12. Kautz, H.A., Allen, J.F., Generalized Plan Recognition, in Proceedings of the 5th Nat. Conf. AI, pp 32-37, 1986.
13. Egyed, A., A Scenario-Driven Approach to Traceability, in Proceedings of the International Conference on Software Engineering, 2001.
14. Pinheiro, F., Goguem, J., An Object Oriented Tool for Tracing Requirements, IEEE Software, 13(2), 1996.

15. Haumer, P., et al., Improving Reviews by Extended Traceability, in Proceedings of the 32nd Hawai International Conference on Systems Science, 1999.
16. Antoniol, G., Canfora, G., De Lucia, A., Maintaining Traceability During Object-Oriented Software Evolution: a Case Study, in Proceedings of the International Conference on Software Maintenance, 1999.

Supporting Reusable Use Cases

Robert Biddle, James Noble, and Ewan Tempero

School of Mathematical and Computing Sciences,
Victoria University of Wellington, New Zealand
{Robert.Biddle,James.Noble,Ewan.Tempero}@mcs.vuw.ac.nz

Abstract. Use cases are a part of common practice for capturing functional requirements for object-oriented software development. But, as with any artifact, there is a cost of producing them. Reusing use cases can reduce this cost. We discuss how use cases can be made reusable, in particular looking at the reusability of *essential use cases*. We also introduce Ukase, a web-based use case management tool that provides support for the reuse of use cases.

1 Introduction

Use cases [13] are a part of common practice for capturing functional requirements for object-oriented software development, and they are widely supported in modelling languages such as UML [21, 11], and in development processes such as the Rational Unified Process [12]. Given the investment organisations are making in use cases, it is reasonable to seek ways to reduce the cost of their development. One possibility is to *reuse* use cases, but in order for this to be effective, we need to understand what makes use cases *reusable*. In this paper, we examine the concept of supporting reusable use cases.

One issue that affects the likelihood that anything will be reused is the form in which it is described. We have been using a particular form of use cases, known as *essential use cases*. These were introduced by Constantine and Lockwood for their *Usage-Centered Design* [8]. Essential use cases are written specially to be abstract, lightweight, and technology-free. Our observation is that use cases written this way are applicable in more situations than the conventional forms of use cases, which suggests they are more reusable. In order to gain an objective understanding of their reusability, we apply a reusability support model [4]. This model suggests the kind of support for reuse that is appropriate. We use this to develop tool support in the form of Ukase, a web-based use case management tool (see figure 1). We are also working on content guidelines for reusable use cases by exploring *patterns*, following the approach taken in documenting object-oriented design patterns [10], and we discuss this work elsewhere [1].

This paper is organised as follows. In the next section, we discuss use cases and essential use cases, and summarise the reusability support model. Section 3 examines reusability of use cases by traversing the model. We then introduce Ukase and examine how reuse of use cases is supported in section 4. Section 5 discusses related work, and we present our conclusions in section 6.

C. Gacek (Ed.): ICSR-7, LNCS 2319, pp. 210–226, 2002.
© Springer-Verlag Berlin Heidelberg 2002

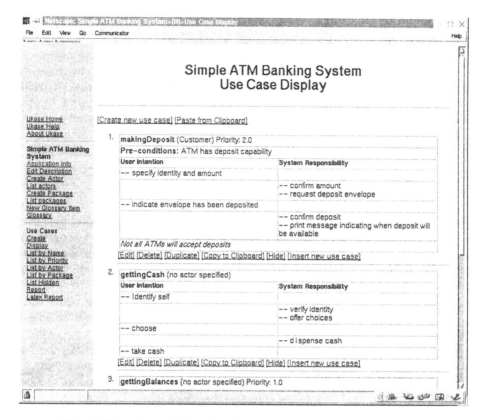

Fig. 1. Ukase is a web-based tool for managing essential use cases.

2   Background

2.1   Use Cases

Jacobson et al. define a use case in their 1992 book as "a behaviourally related sequence of transactions in a dialogue with the system" [13]. A more recent definition for the Rational Unified Process shows little real change, saying a use case is "a description of a set or sequence of actions, including variants, that a system performs that yields an observable result of value to a particular actor" [12].

The general idea of use cases is the representation of intended sequences of interaction between a system (even if not yet implemented) and the world outside that system. This idea is very powerful, for several reasons.

In the early stages of development, use cases help to focus on interactions as a way of eliciting desirable system behaviour, and so help capture requirements and determine specifications. The narrative or dialogue form typical of use cases is very easy for people to recall or imagine, and especially useful when involving end-users, background stake-holders, and others with no direct experience or role in actual system development. In the later stages of development, use cases help again because of the focus on interactions. The interactions can now be regarded as the embodiment of functional specifications that the system must meet.

Use cases also lead to a useful partitioning of requirements. This happens naturally, because use cases are based on sequences of interaction, and desirable interactions typically follow a structure of coherent progression, on a limited scale, toward a goal or sub-goal. This partitioning then allows organisation by grouping, filtering, prioritising, and so on, and is helpful in overall management throughout development.

2.2   Essential Use Cases

Essential use cases are part of Usage-Centered Design [8], developed by Larry Constantine and Lucy Lockwood, who see some difficulties with ordinary use cases: "In particular, conventional use cases typically contain too many built-in assumptions, often hidden or implicit, about the form of the user interface that is yet to be designed."

Essential use cases were designed to overcome these problems. The term "essential" refers to essential models that involve "technology-free, idealised, and abstract descriptions".

Essential use cases are documented in a format representing a dialogue between the user and the system. This resembles a two-column format used by Wirfs-Brock [25]. In Wirfs-Brock's format, the column labels refer to the *action* and the *response*. In contrast, essential use cases label the columns as *user intention* and *system responsibility*.

These new labels indicate how essential use cases support abstraction by allowing the interaction to be documented without describing the details of the user interface. Note that the abstraction does not really relate to the use case as a whole, but more to the steps of the use case. In this way an essential use case does specify a sequence of interaction, but a sequence with abstract steps. Constantine and Lockwood give the examples shown in figure 2. The steps of the essential use case are more abstract, and the whole use case is more brief.

Constantine and Lockwood introduced essential use cases for user interface design and development. We have, however, applied essential use cases in more general systems analysis and development. We found significant advantages from using essential use cases in providing better traceability between requirements and responsibility-driven design[2].

2.3   Modelling Reusability Support

In this section we briefly review a reusability support model for programming languages [4]. This model provides a set of structures and principles that explain how programming languages support code reusability.

The model addresses the kind of code arrangements where one unit of code *invokes* another unit of code. The invoking unit is called the *context* and the

gettingCash *(conventional)*

User Action	System Response
insert card	
	read magnetic stripe
	request PIN
enter PIN	
	verify PIN
	display transaction menu
press key	
	display account menu
press key	
	prompt for amount
enter amount	
	display amount
press key	
	return card
take card	
	dispense cash
take cash	

gettingCash *(essential)*

User Intention	System Responsibility
identify self	
	verify identity
	offer choices
choose	
	dispense cash
take cash	

Fig. 2. On the left, a conventional use case for getting cash from an automatic teller system. On the right, an essential use case for the same interaction. (From Constantine and Lockwood.)

invoked unit the *component*. An important aspect of this structure is that support for reusability works both ways, as shown in figure 3. The common case is *component reuse*, shown on the left of figure, where two contexts both use a component. This reflects reusability of classes in a library. The other case is *context reuse*, shown on the right of the figure, where one context may invoke

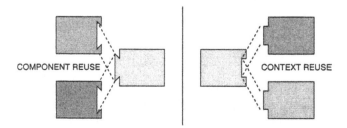

Fig. 3. The invoking unit is the *context* and the invoked unit is the *component*. Component reuse involves several different contexts invoking the same component. Context reuse involves one context invoking different components using the same interface.

different components. This addresses the possibility of multiple implementations for a single component specification, and also reflects the reusability of frameworks [15].

When a context invokes a component, it has expectations as to what the component does. Similarly, the component has expectations as to how it will be invoked. These expectations are called *dependencies*, and they are the fundamental low-level concept of the model:

> *A dependency between two units of code is a condition that one unit meets so that it can use the other unit, or so that the other unit can use it.*

Dependencies can adversely affect the reusability of a unit of code, because they limit the number of contexts that can invoke it, or the number of units it can invoke. The model identifies three techniques involved in addressing such dependencies: customisability, flexibility, and checkability.

Flexibility: Flexibility is a property of a language that makes it possible to write code that is not specific to only one situation. For example, in object-oriented languages, polymorphism supports flexibility.

Customisability: The customisability of a component is the amount of control a context has over how the context dependencies are met, and vice-versa. For example, parameters provide different ways for the context calling a component function to dictate how the function behaves to meet the context's requirements.

Checkability: Where there are dependencies, it is desirable if it can be checked that the dependencies have been met. For example, in procedure calls the parameters represent dependencies, and checkability can be supported by the requirement that values passed match the parameters in number and type. Other approaches range from simple run-time checks to formal static verification.

The model defines the reusability of a unit in terms of the amount of context or component reuse possible, affected by the dependencies of the unit, and strategies to address these dependencies.

3   Reusable Use Cases

In this section, we will discuss how the reusability support model above might apply to use cases. We will take each of the concepts in the model, and explore how they might be applied to make use cases more reusable. Whereas the model originally addressed the support for reusability in programming languages, the following discussion involves the "language" of use cases. We begin by discussing why essential use cases attracted our interest. In section 4 we will show how we applied all these ideas in providing tool support for reusable use cases.

3.1   Essential Use Cases and Reuse

The key characteristic of essential use cases (EUCs) is the abstraction of details about the technology involved in the interaction between user and system. The reason for this abstraction is to assist in capturing the requirements without making premature commitments to any particular details of the user interface. As we have become more familiar with EUCs, we have realised that they also facilitate reuse.

The abstract representation of interaction in EUCs is useful in analysis and when capturing requirements. In actual system development, however, the interaction will eventually be specified concretely as "enactments" of the EUCs. For example, the EUC on the right of figure 2 could lead to the concrete use case on the left. Concrete use cases can then be used to facilitate implementation. One set of EUCs can lead to several very different concrete enactments and implementations, depending on particular user interface requirements, such as software or hardware platforms. So, in this way, EUCs facilitate reuse because they allow many different concrete systems to be specified with one set of EUCs. One set can be used over and over to generate different concrete systems on different platforms. By the definition given in section 2.3, this means EUCs are more reusable than conventional use cases.

In fact, the abstraction sometimes means that some EUCs may apply not only to different concrete versions of the same system, but may also be useful in specifying completely different systems. Our experience is that there are some common kinds of use case that in the abstract form of an EUC do not mention any context of the system or domain at all. In particular, this is true for small units of simple interaction such as alarm notification, queries and confirmations, and so on. We have begun to identify these as *patterns* for EUCs [1].

3.2   Use Cases, Contexts, and Components

Recognising EUCs as offering the advantages of reusability, we decided to try and apply the reusability support model as a way of exploring ways to make use cases even more reusable.

Use cases themselves can be regarded as the units of reusability, and we can see that the main principles of context and component reuse also apply. When wishing to specify a new system, one might take a use case from elsewhere, and reuse it in a new system; this is component reuse because it reuses the use case as a component. Alternatively, one might start with a system already specified, and create new use cases as well as or instead of the ones already there; this is context reuse because it reuses the existing context.

As well as building system requirement models based on use cases, some approaches involve use cases invoking other use cases. For example, in UML [11, 21], use cases can *include* or *extend* other use cases. These two invocation mechanisms allow articulation so that use cases can be used to describe single sequences of interaction, but do not require excessive redundancy or over-emphasis of exceptional behaviour. These invocation structures also allow reuse, because several different use cases may include the same use case, and a use case may also extend several other use cases.

3.3 Dependencies

The reusability of a use case is affected significantly by dependencies within it. A use case will be of limited reusability if it contains references unique to the system, or even the application domain, for which it was created. The reusability support model suggests several ways to address such limitations.

As with program code, a primitive but sometimes useful way to reuse units while addressing dependencies is cut-and-paste, or more correctly *copy-and-edit*. That is to say, one can simply copy the text of a use case, and then edit the copy, reducing dependencies or modifying them to suit the new circumstances. This is crude, but does at least permit reuse, and allows great latitude in recognising and addressing dependencies.

But the disadvantages of copy-and-edit are strong. Some problems involve the edit step. Dependencies are not typically easy to identify, and so careful understanding and assessment of all the text is required. Also, because the edit power is unrestricted, it is easy to introduce problems where none previously existed.

Other problems with copy-and-edit involve the copy step. Some of the advantages of reuse concern the potential for sharing, rather than copying, the same unit. For example, much reuse of code is done by *calling* or *linking to* a code unit, rather than copying. If the unit is improved, by enhancement or debugging, all those sharing can easily benefit, and this in turn justifies increased investment in enhancement or debugging. This would be worthwhile when sharing use cases between systems or domains, but especially in the common case within a system where a use case may be reused by being included or extending other use cases within the same system. To share use cases, however, we need to address dependencies so that exactly the same use case can be used in different situations.

3.4 Flexibility and Customisation

The reusability support model identified two strategies for allowing dependencies in a single unit: flexibility and customisation.

Flexibility is the ability to work with a general category of things, rather than only one specifically. In programming languages this includes polymorphism, where program code refers to some class or procedure, but exactly which class or procedure is not absolutely determined until necessary.

Flexibility is the principle by which EUCs facilitate reuse. Dependencies are what Constantine and Lockwood are referring to in the passage quoted earlier: "conventional use cases typically contain too many built-in assumptions, often hidden or implicit" [8]. The abstraction in the steps of an EUC works in a similar way to polymorphism. The abstraction means that dependencies between the use case text and the implementation technology are reduced, and this means that the EUCs are themselves more reusable and may be used in specifying different systems. At the same time, the abstract terms allow EUCs to apply to various later use cases in concrete interaction specification.

The way in which EUCs incorporate abstraction involves use of abstract language in the steps. This kind of abstract language is typically a kind of well-constrained ambiguity, where an abstract word or expression is understood to allow multiple more precise alternatives. This facility of natural language is similar to polymorphism, and is familiar where specifications must accomodate some well-constrained variation, for example in laws written to concern "vehicles", meaning cars, trucks, and so on. A more general approach to harnessing this aspect of natural language is suggested by Jacobson et al. [14], who discuss how the text in use cases may involve "variation points" that can form the basis for a hierarchy of use cases from more abstract to more specific.

The reusability support model also identifies that dependencies can be reduced by allowing customisation. Customisation is the ability to change parts of a unit whenever it is invoked. In programming languages this includes parameter passing, where parameters are used as place-holders within a unit of code, and values for the parameters are passed when the unit is invoked.

One approach to customisation appropriate to use cases is simple textual parameterisation. This is the approach taken by text macro processors, which have been used for some time to support software reusability and especially portability [5]. These allow arbitrary text to be specified with embedded parameters, and later invocation with values specified for the parameters. The macro processor then generates a new unit of text, substituting the values for the parameters in the original text.

With a text macro processor, it would be possible to write use case text with embedded parameters for specific details, so eliminating dependencies. The use case could then be invoked for a particular system by specifying the values for the parameters, thus employing a reusable use case to yield a use case specific to the system.

Parameters in use cases are also suggested by Jaconson et al. [14] who discuss how they might be used in connection with an abstraction hierarchy of use cases, as well as in templates for macro processing.

3.5   Checkability

The reusability support model identifies dependencies as detrimental to reusability. We have discussed above how flexibility and customisability allow us to reduce dependencies. A supplementary strategy involved in addressing dependencies is checkability.

By checkability, we mean the ability to easily check whether dependencies are met when units are reused. In programming, we often reuse code that contains dependencies, such as global variables or parameters that refer to values set elsewhere. We can sometimes check that these dependencies are met by comparing names and types. Such checking is not strictly required, as can be shown with low level typeless programming languages, but checking does help reduce errors that are otherwise potentially difficult to detect and costly to correct.

If we are going to reuse use cases, there is similar potential for problems in accidentally combining use cases that do not work together. For example, if we allow customisation of use cases, as discussed above, there are problems that will arise should parameter values be inappropriately specified. We therefore suggest that, in any plan to reuse use cases, we should support checkability. Of course, the typical descriptions of use cases are not formal, and so checkability can not be provided with great rigour. The experience in programming languages indicates, however, that checkability can still be useful even if it simply uses visibility and redundancy to help avoid typographical errors and similar slips.

4   Ukase: Tool Support for Reusable Use Cases

In the previous section, we gave a theoretical discussion on how use cases could be made more reusable. In this section, we show how the theory has been translated to practice, by presenting Ukase[1], a tool we have developed that supports reuse in essential use case models. The original purpose of Ukase was just to make the recording of use case models easier, but we quickly found it was useful for the development of the models themselves, and that in order to do development, better support for reuse was desirable. Below, we give an overview of what the tool does and describe the forms of reuse it currently supports.

4.1   Tool Overview

Ukase is a *web-based* application. That is, one uses the tool by using a web browser to go to a URL. It is implemented as a Perl [23] CGI script [9], with the information stored in a MySQL database [17]. It is highly accessible (anywhere on the Internet), and may be used as group-ware (multiple people can access a model simultaneously). It is light-weight, that is, requires little effort to learn to use effectively, and imposes few restrictions on how it can be used.

As mentioned above, Ukase provides support for recording essential use cases. It provides a mechanism for entering the details of the essential use cases, and a mechanism for displaying the results. The input is done using a CGI form laid out the way that a use case would look in a report (figure 4). As well as the steps of the interaction, users may specify pre and post conditions, and there is also an area for notes and comments.

As well as the name of the use case and its interactions, Ukase also allows users to organise the use cases (by package, or by primary actor) and some basic support for incremental development (priority). We are also experimenting with other meta information to help with organisation (status and order).

Ukase provides a variety of ways to organise use cases. Developers will typically use the view shown in figure 1, and once development is complete, the

---

[1] *Ukase: Edict of Tsarist Russian government; any arbitrary order. (Concise Oxford Dictionary)*

resulting model is available as a report (figure 5). Use cases can also be listed in a variety of ways (figure 6, for example).

Any use case model typically uses many terms particular to the application domain, which can make the intent difficult to understand. Ukase provides a *glossary*, where such terms can be more fully explained. Some of these terms are often concepts that would show up in an *analysis model*, and so Ukase allows such terms to be tagged as "candidate" classes (figure 7). While the glossary is useful in its own right, it also turns out to be useful for supporting reuse, as we show below.

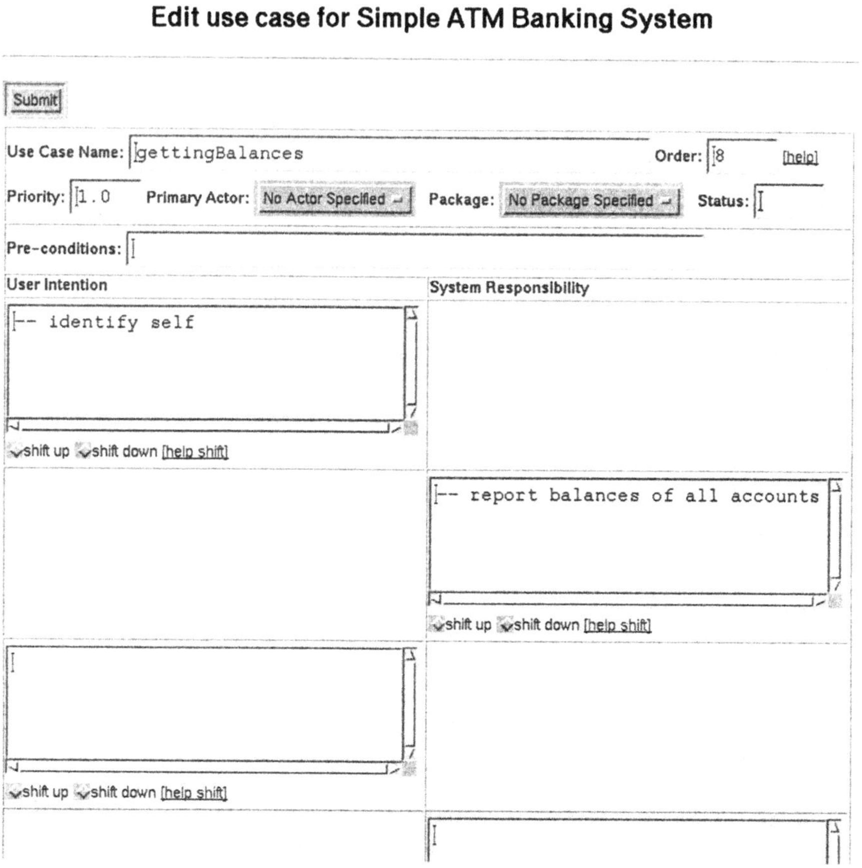

Edit use case for Simple ATM Banking System

Fig. 4. Entering the details of an essential use case in Ukase.

Use Cases

1.	**makingDeposit** (Customer) Priority: 2.0	
	Pre-conditions: ATM has deposit capability	
	User Intention	**System Responsibility**
	-- specify identity and amount	
		-- confirm amount -- request deposit envelope
	-- indicate envelope has been deposited	
		-- confirm deposit -- print message indicating when deposit will be available
	Not all ATMs will accept deposits	

2.	**gettingCash** (no actor specified)	
	User Intention	**System Responsibility**
	-- identify self	
		-- verify identity -- offer choices
	-- choose	
		-- d i spense cash
	-- take cash	

3.	**gettingBalances** (no actor specified) Priority: 1.0	
	User Intention	**System Responsibility**
	-- identify self	
		-- report balances of all accounts

4.	**listingAccounts** (Customer)	
	User Intention	**System Responsibility**
		-- List all Accounts in alphabetical order

5.	**performingSelfTest** (Servicer)	
	User Intention	**System Responsibility**
		-- report status of cashbox -- report status of keypad -- report status of network connection

Fig. 5. Showing all the details of the use case model.

4.2   Support for Reuse

As discussed in section 3, we see a number of ways to support reuse. Ukase provides some of this support. One form of support it provides is to act as a *repository* of use cases. By providing access to all the use case models, it allows easy browsing, which can provide inspiration for use cases in models being created. It also helps in finding *patterns* in use cases [1].

Interestingly, the most immediately useful form of support for reuse has been the use case equivalent of copy-and-edit. Any use case can be *copied* to a per-user clipboard, and then *pasted* into any use case model. The semantics of this

Simple ATM Banking System
Use Cases grouped by Actor

Actor Customer
      1. [Edit] – listingAccounts
      2. [Edit] – makingDeposit
Actor Servicer
      1. [Edit] – performingSelfTest
No Actor specified
      1. [Edit] – gettingBalances
      2. [Edit] – gettingCash

Fig. 6. Listing the use cases grouped by primary actor.

Glossary for Simple ATM Banking System

Account (Candidate Class)[edit] [delete]
    These are units of organisation of finance for Customers

Actual Balance (Glossary Entry)[edit] [delete]
    Due to delays in processing deposits, the amount available to be withdrawn from an Account via the ATM may not be what
    the real balance of the Account is.

Balance (Glossary Entry)[edit] [delete]
    The amount of money available from an Account via the ATM. (see Actual Balance)

Customer (Candidate Class)[edit] [delete]
    Customers operate on Accounts

Fig. 7. The glossary, showing some of the terms that might be useful in the domain model.

operation are similar to that of any text editor or word processor. In particular, no relationship between the original and the copy is maintained. The copy is treated exactly as if a new use case had been created and it just so happens that the text is identical to the original. The copy can then be edited independently of the original.

In fact, this is often exactly what is wanted. We often want to create use cases that are very similar to each other, for example, following particular conventions for describing details the bodies of the use case. Using the copy-and-edit operation makes this very convenient. However, as we've discussed earlier, sharing also has its advantages and we are working on providing such support.

Where the Ukase copy-and-edit differs from that of a text editor is that it operates on whole use cases, rather than on arbitrary pieces of text, as would be the case in any editor. This supports the fact that the unit of reuse is the use case. We believe that having the copy-and-edit operation recognise semantic boundaries in this way significantly improves support for reuse, because it

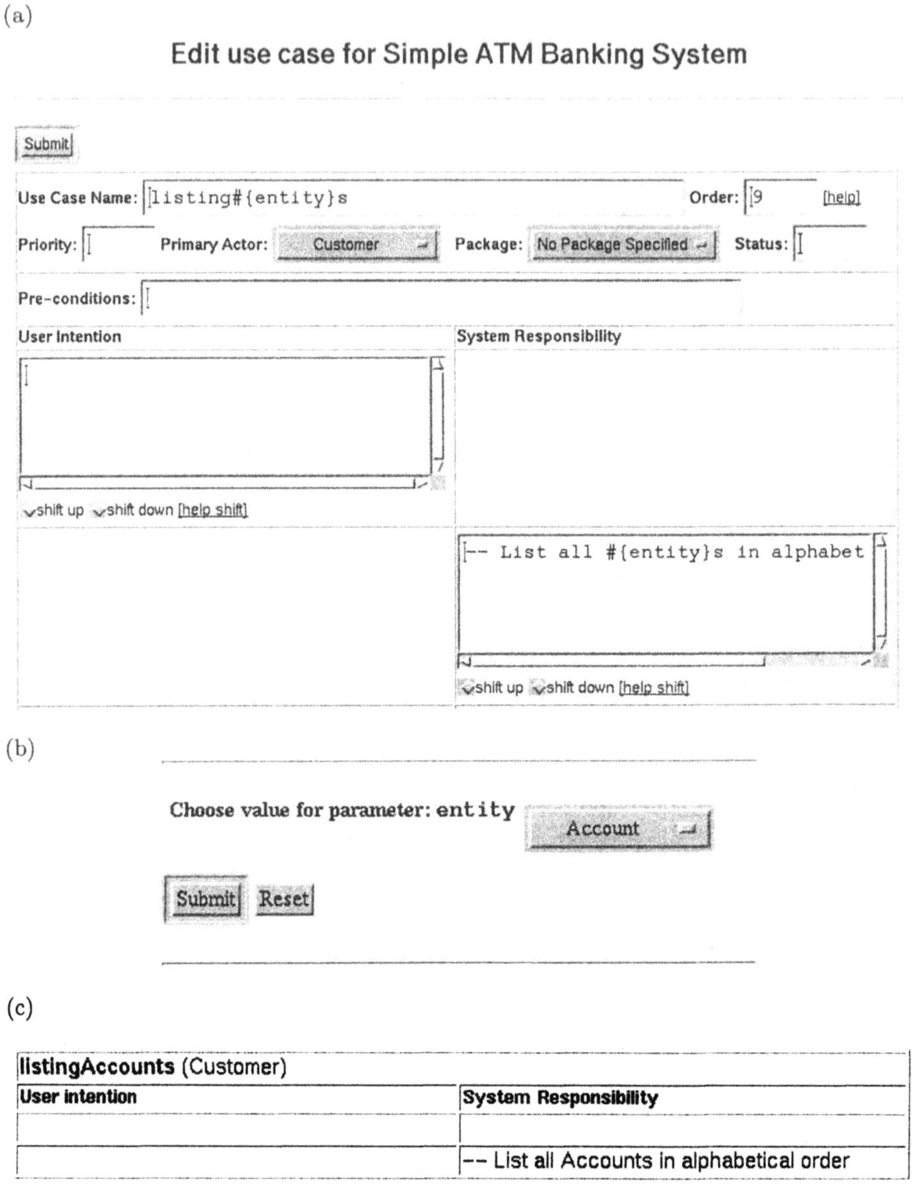

(a)

Edit use case for Simple ATM Banking System

| Submit |

Use Case Name: |listing#{entity}s   Order: |9   [help]

Priority: | Primary Actor: Customer ⌐   Package: No Package Specified ⌐   Status: |

Pre-conditions: |

| User Intention | System Responsibility |

⌄shift up ⌄shift down [help shift]

|-- List all #{entity}s in alphabet

⌄shift up ⌄shift down [help shift]

(b)

Choose value for parameter: entity   Account ⌐

Submit Reset

(c)

listingAccounts (Customer)	
User intention	System Responsibility
	-- List all Accounts in alphabetical order

Fig. 8. Part (a) shows how the user names the parameter entity. Whenever the set of parameters for a use case changes, the user is required to assign values to the parameters when the changed use case is submitted (b). Part (c) shows the resulting use case, with the glossary item Account substituted for entity.

maintains the integrity of what is being reused. We have also been exploring this idea in programming environments [24], and a more general exploration of related ideas for *conceptual editors* has been undertaken by Bucci [6].

Ukase also provides support for customisation of use cases through *parameterised* use cases as discussed in section 3.4. Users may specify parameters anywhere in the name or body of a use case using the convention: `#{parameter name}`, where `parameter name` identifies the parameter. The specification of values to use for a particular parameter is done as part of the editing of a use case. Parameters cannot be replaced by arbitrary strings. To provide some checkability, Ukase requires that only entries from the glossary may be used as values for parameters (see figure 8).

While this support for parameterisation of use cases is somewhat primitive, as with the support for copy-and-edit, it is surprisingly effective.

4.3 Experience

The first version of Ukase was first in use about August 2000, and since then it has been used in several research projects, a commercial case study, and in three courses (final year undergraduate and graduate).

Ukase has also undergone heuristic evaluations [18] for usability, and the students in the graduate course critiqued its usefulness it as part of a course report. These evaluations confirm its usefulness, in that it makes the development and management of use case models much easier than doing so manually, and its usability, in that it most of its functionality is easy to learn and use.

Ukase was initially created for our own use in recording and management of use cases in our own projects, as well as a project in its own right. This has meant that we have developed aspects of Ukase that we saw as priorities in supporting our other project work. In particular, we have emphasised essential use cases and reusability, and are working on support for decomposition of system responsibilities [2, 3]. We are still planning how to address other aspects of use case management, in particular support for use cases to *include* or *extend* other use cases.

5   Related Work

Reuse of requirements is not a new idea. Any artifact of the software development process is a candidate for reuse [16, 22]. What we have done is to examine how one might enable reuse of a particular form of requirements documement, namely use cases.

Use cases themselves were introduced as a key focus of Object-Oriented Software Engineering (OOSE) [13]. There are many forms for use cases, and we have been influenced especially by Wirfs-Brock discussing use cases as "conversations" [25, 26]. The particular kind of use case we adopt in practice is the "essential use case", developed originally for analysis in the development of user interfaces [8]. Cockburn presents a survey of issues and approaches involving use cases [7].

The closest work to ours is by Jacobson et al. [14], who provide a useful framework in which to discuss and develop reuse processes. In their discussion, they identify *components* as workproducts engineered for reuse, so what we call reusable use cases they call use case components. Our development of reusable use cases parallels theirs, which serves to validate our model.

There are some differences. Jacobson et al. divide components into *concrete* and *abstract* components. Concrete components are ones that can be reused as is, whereas abstract components are incomplete in some way and must be specialised before they can be reused. Essential use cases do not fit into either of these categories. Early in the requirements capture process, essential use cases may capture exactly what is needed, and so be used as is. However, later in the process they get refined into concrete enactments, and so the originals may also be regarded as "incomplete".

Jacobson et al. also discuss the use of parameters in use cases, however, their use of parameters is to provide generalisation, whereas our use provides customisation. In fact, the mechanisms are very similar, and can be used for both purposes. We also address the need for checkability when parameters values are specified.

The best tool support for management of use cases that we are aware of is Requisite Pro [20]. This tool manages conventional use cases as documents, and provides traceability between other related documents (such as a Vision document), and to object-oriented development models supported by Rational Rose [19]. While Requisite Pro does act as a repository for use case models, it provides no other direct support for reuse. Our tool also takes a more light-weight approach, and so is useful for the early stages of system analysis.

6   Conclusions

We have discussed what reusable use cases might mean, how use cases may be made more reusable, and what tool support would be appropriate for reusing use cases. We used the reusability support model to guide our discussion, and paid particular attention to essential use cases. We then presented Ukase, a tool that supports the reuse of use cases.

Our approach in this work has been quite pragmatic: we wanted to reuse use cases in the same way we might reuse code, and we wanted tool support to help us. We found that many of the principles that underlie code reusability also make sense for use cases. We also found that these principles helped us to understand how to develop tool support, and found that even straightforward tool support was clearly useful.

Our work in this area continues by further development of our tool support, along with our parallel work in identifying patterns for use cases.

References

1. Robert Biddle, James Noble, and Ewan Tempero. Patterns for essential use cases. In *Proceedings of KoalaPLoP 2001*, 2001. Available as Technical Report CS-TR-01-02 at http://www.mcs.vuw.ac.nz/comp/Publications.

2. Robert Biddle, James Noble, and Ewan Tempero. Essential use cases and responsibility in object-oriented development. In Michael Oudshoorn, editor, *Proceedings of the Twenty-Fifth Australasian Computer Science Conference (ACSC2002), Conferences in Research and Practice in Information Technology*, volume 4, Melbourne, Australia, January 2002.

3. Robert Biddle, James Noble, and Ewan Tempero. Sokoban: a system object case study. In James Noble and John Potter, editors, *Proceedings of the 40th International Conference on Technology of Object-Oriented Languages and Systems (TOOLS Pacific 2002), Conferences in Research and Practice in Information Technology*, volume 10, Sydney, Australia, 2002.

4. Robert Biddle and Ewan Tempero. Understanding the impact of language features on reusability. In Murali Sitaraman, editor, *Proceedings of the Fourth International Conference on Software Reuse*, pages 52–61. IEEE Computer Society, April 1996.

5. P. J. Brown. *Macro processors and techniques for portable software*. Wiley, 1974.

6. Paolo Bucci. *Conceptual Program Editors: Design and Formal Specification*. PhD thesis, The Ohio State University, Columbus, Ohio, United States of America, 1997.

7. Alistair Cockburn. *Writing effective use cases*. Addison-Wesley, 2001.

8. Larry L. Constantine and Lucy A. D. Lockwood. *Software for Use: A Practical Guide to the Models and Methods of Usage Centered Design*. Addison-Wesley, 1999.

9. National Center for Supercomputing Applications (NCSA). The common gateway interface. http://hoohoo.ncsa.uiuc.edu/cgi/.

10. Erich Gamma, Richard Helm, Ralph E. Johnson, and John Vlissides. *Design Patterns*. Addison-Wesley, 1994.

11. Object Management Group. Unified modeling language (UML) 1.3 specification, 2000.

12. Ivar Jacobson, Grady Booch, and James Rumbaugh. *The Unified Software Development Process*. Addison-Wesley, 1999.

13. Ivar Jacobson, Mahnus Christerson, Patrik Jonsson, and Gunnar Overgaard. *Object-Oriented Software Engineering*. Addison-Wesley, 1992.

14. Ivar Jacobson, Martin Griss, and Patrik Jonsson. *Software Reuse: Architecture, Process and Organization for Business Success*. Addison-Wesley, 1997.

15. Ralph E Johnson. Frameworks = (components + patterns). *Communications of the ACM*, 40(10):39–42, October 1997.

16. Hafedh Mili, Fatma Mili, and Ali Mili. Reusing software: Issues and research directions. *IEEE Transactions on Software Engineering*, 21(6):528–561, June 1995.

17. Mysql. http://www.mysql.com.

18. Jakob Nielsen. *Usability Engineering*. Academic Press, New York, 1992.

19. Rational Software. Rational Rose. http://www.rational.com/products/rose/.

20. Rational Software. Requisite Pro. http://www.rational.com/products/reqpro/.

21. James Rumbaugh, Ivar Jacobson, and Grady Booch. *The Unified Modeling Language Reference Manual*. Addison-Wesley, 1998.

22. Will Tracz. *Confessions of a Used Program Salesman: Institutionalizing Software Reuse*. Addison-Wesley, 1995.

23. Larry Wall, Tom Christiansen, and Jon Orwant. *Programming Perl*. O'Reilly, 3rd edition, July 2000.

24. Glen Wallace, Robert Biddle, and Ewan Tempero. Smarter cut-and-paste for programming text editors. In *The Austrialasian User Interface Conference*, pages 56–63, Gold Coast, Australia, January 2001. IEEE Computer Society.

25. Rebecca J. Wirfs-Brock. Designing scenarios: Making the case for a use case framework. *The Smalltalk Report*, 3(3), 1993.
26. Rebecca J. Wirfs-Brock. The art of meaningful conversations. *The Smalltalk Report*, 4(5), 1994.

Project Management Knowledge Reuse through Scenario Models

Márcio de O. Barros, Cláudia M.L. Werner, and Guilherme H. Travassos

COPPE / UFRJ – Computer Science Department
Caixa Postal: 68511 - CEP 21945-970 - Rio de Janeiro – RJ
Voice: 5521 562-8675 / Fax: 5521 562-8676
{marcio, werner, ght}@cos.ufrj.br

Abstract. Project management is a knowledge intensive activity. Managers use their skills and experience to make decisions during the execution of a software development process. Better results in terms of attending to schedule, budget, and functionality, are usually achieved due to managers' accumulated experiences and knowledge. In this paper we address the creation and reuse of software project management knowledge. We present a knowledge representation, namely *scenario models*, which allows a manager to verify the impact of theories, procedures, actions, and strategies that can be applied or imposed upon a software project. Scenario models compose a reusable knowledge base useful for project managers, who can reuse scenarios to assess the impact of their assumptions upon their projects. We present an application of the proposed approach within a risk management process and the results from a first experimental analysis of the techniques.

Keywords: Knowledge reuse, project management

1 Motivation

The last decades have been marked by a revolution that is affecting several economic sectors, such as telecommunications, health care, insurance, banking, and so on. Industries within these sectors are progressively looking beyond their physical commodities to increase the value of a less tangible asset: the knowledge possessed by their employees and used by them in their daily tasks [1].

Knowledge management aims the capturing and representing of organization's knowledge assets to facilitate knowledge access, share, and reuse [2]. Knowledge management technologies seem to be promising for knowledge intensive tasks, especially for those where knowledge comes from interaction and experience collected through years of practice in a field.

Within the software development industry, the recurring failures to produce large and complex systems have often been associated to management problems, like bad communication, malformed teams, and unreliable risk analysis [3]. Project management is a knowledge intensive activity. It is well accepted that experienced managers usually perform better than novice managers due to the experience they

C. Gacek (Ed.): ICSR-7, LNCS 2319, pp. 227–239, 2002.
© Springer-Verlag Berlin Heidelberg 2002

have accumulated by taking part in past projects and the knowledge acquired from this experience. As proposed by the "recognition-primed decision model" [4], managers tend to keep a collection of patterns in their minds and compare them to the current context when making decisions.

Since managing a software project strongly depends on manager's experience, knowledge management techniques and tools should be useful to support project management. It would be desirable to represent and store each senior manager's collection of patterns in a centralized repository, allowing these patterns to be reused by less experienced managers. Although project management heuristics are available for a long time [5] [3], only limited improvements were observed in project management [6]. The information – the heuristics – is available, but knowledge, that is, the inference about the expected effects of applying this information in a software project, is still missing.

By analyzing the knowledge management process from a reuse perspective, we observe the need for an activity to guide users on how to apply the retrieved information in their context. This activity is the ultimate responsible for knowledge transfer, the process that evaluates and presents expected effects of using just retrieved information in the user's context. Although several knowledge management approaches acknowledge the need for such activity, most of them fails to provide it, being limited to storing and retrieving information from a repository. As information is often represented in ambiguous formats, such as textual documents, images, video, and sound, the knowledge transfer process is left without much automated support. One could argue how effective these techniques are when the task of interpreting the retrieved information is not easy enough to be held by the user alone.

In this paper we address this limitation in the context of software project management knowledge. We propose the use of formal models to represent this type of knowledge. These models, namely *scenario models*, allow a manager to verify the effects provided by management theories, procedures, actions, and strategies (the retrieved information) that can be applied or imposed upon a software project. We present an application of the proposed techniques in a risk management process that explores both scenario and project model integration for risk evaluation. We also present an experimental study that analyzes the feasibility of applying the proposed techniques while managing a software project.

This paper is organized in six sections. The first section comprises this motivation. Section 2 presents the scenario models and the techniques that allow their impact evaluation upon a software project. Section 3 presents an application of these techniques within a risk management process. Section 4 presents the results of an experimental study regarding the proposed techniques. Section 5 compares the proposed approach to related works. Finally, section 6 presents some final considerations and future perspectives of this work.

2   Representing Project Management Knowledge as Scenarios

Highsmith [7] observed that successful software projects convey a blend of careful objective evaluation, adequate preparation, continuous observation and assessment of the environment and progress, and adjustment of tactics. Senior managers usually make this environmental assessment mentally. They construct a mental model of the project, create mental models for the problems and opportunities under investigation, and scan their pattern repository for adequate actions to be taken against the problems or to explore the opportunities. Since a mental model cannot be directly reused by less experienced managers, it suggests the need of an explicit representation for such tacit knowledge and the development of a technique to evaluate the impact of such problems and opportunities upon a software project behavior (that is, project cost, schedule, quality, and so on).

Figure 1 presents the architecture for the proposed solution. It is centered on two artifacts: the project model and scenario models. The project model, represented by the "PM" blocks in Figure 1, defines the user context, that is, the expected behavior for a software project. Scenario models represent specific problems and opportunities, conveying senior manager's tacit knowledge.

Scenario models are developed by experienced managers and stored in a repository, known as a *scenario base*. While planning a software project, a manager first builds a project model for the project. Next, the manager searches for the relevant scenarios in the current development context, retrieving them from the scenario base. Finally, the manager executes an iterative analysis, where combinations of the retrieved scenario models are integrated into the project model. The integration process occurs within the simulation environment, evaluating the impact provided by each scenario model combination upon the project model behavior. As development unfolds, the project model is continually updated with status information and new scenario analysis can be carried out to test project sensibility to uncertain events in the same fashion as in planning.

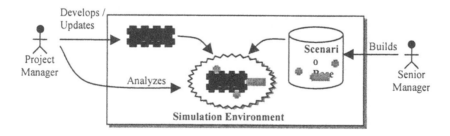

Fig. 1. The architecture of the proposed solution

Both project and scenario models are formal models, represented using system dynamics. System dynamics is a modeling language to describe complex systems, focusing on their structural aspects [8]. This technique identifies and models cause-effect relationships and feedback loops using flow diagrams, which are composed by four elements: stocks, rates, flows and processes. *Stocks* represent elements that can be accumulated or consumed over time. A stock is described by its level, that is, the number of elements in the stock at a given moment. *Rates* describe stock variations, formulating their raises and depletions in an equation. *Processes* and *flows* complement complex rate equations and calculate intermediate model variables.

System dynamics has been previously used in software engineering. Abdel-Hamid and Madnick [9] developed the first system dynamics software project model. This model formalizes the effects of management policies and actions taken during a software development project. Later, other models extended the original model or focused on different aspects of software projects [10] [11]. Our project model differs from previous system dynamics software project models due to its support to the development and integration of reusable scenario models. This feature required two major modifications in the former modeling approach: raising the abstraction level of the model and making clear the separation of facts from assumptions.

To raise the level of abstraction of project models is a strategy to allow the operational use of system dynamics in project management. Traditionally, system dynamics models are described through mathematical equations, which are very hard to understand and adapt, inhibiting the use of system dynamics to describe software projects in a practical manner. The proposed project model is described through a high-level modeling language, which can be translated to system dynamics in order to be simulated [12]. Such language helps the interaction between the user and the model, without losing representative capabilities.

The project model representation is based on four major project elements: activities, developers, artifacts, and resources. Activities represent work packages that must be accomplished to conclude the project. Developers represent people working in a project. They perform activities using resources. Resources represent physical or logical elements that are used throughout project development, such as computers, software packages, and reusable components, among others. Activities create or evolve software artifacts, eventually using other artifacts as income.

The project elements and their relationships are represented in a metamodel. Each project element is represented by a class, which contains equations to describe its behavior and properties to parameterize these equations. The project model declares its specific project elements as instances of the metamodel classes, specifying the values for their properties. The metamodel is defined only once, while each project defines its own project model. The metamodel simplifies the development of project models, since the later does not need any equation to describe its elements' behavior: each element inherits the behavior described for its class in the metamodel.

```
MODEL ProjectModel
{
    CLASS Developer
    {
        PROPERTY HourlyCost 0;
        PROC Cost HourlyCost * 8;
        PROC Productivity 1;
        PROC ErrorGenerationRate 1;
    };
...
```

Fig. 2. An extract from the metamodel for a software project

Figure 2 presents an extract from the metamodel, describing the behavior and properties for the class that describes a developer. The class provides a single property and three behavior equations. The *HourlyCost* property indicates the cost of a work hour for the developer. The *Cost* equation calculates the developer's daily cost. The *Productivity* and *ErrorGenerationRate* equations describe the base productivity and error generation rates for a developer. These values are expressed as baseline values (unity), assuming an average developer working in an average environment. Scenarios models can be developed to consider the implications of developer's experience, work environment, tools, application domain, and any other factor upon the productivity and error generation rates. The metamodel descriptions are forcefully simple: scenarios are responsible for their refinements. Figure 3 shows an extract of a project model, where two developers are described. Observe that property values are independently specified for each developer, allowing them to show different behavior.

```
DEFINE ControlPESC ProjectModel
{
    Johnny = NEW Developer
        SET HourlyCost = 30;

    Martha = NEW Developer
        SET HourlyCost = 25;
    ...
};
```

Fig. 3. An extract from a project model

The separation of facts from assumptions within a project model allows a manager to test project sensibility to different combinations of uncertain events and theories. Traditionally, system dynamics project models blend known facts about the real-world elements that compose a project with several assumptions upon their behavior and interaction. This framework allows a manager to analyze the implications of such assumptions upon project relevant variables, such as conclusion time and cost. However, it is generally difficult to test other assumptions than those provided with the model. By separating facts from assumptions, the project model supports the evaluation of several combinations of assumptions upon the provided facts. The project model represents known facts, while scenarios separately model assumptions.

Scenarios hold the representation of events, policies, management procedures, actions, and strategies that cannot be considered part of a project, but practices imposed or applied to the project and exceptional situations that may happen throughout its development. Since such practices are valid for several projects, scenarios convey potentially reusable project management knowledge. Figure 4 presents the equations that compose a simple scenario.

The scenario presented in Figure 4 represents productivity gains or losses regarding developer's expertise. Its equations and assumptions were adapted from [9]. A scenario is composed by connections linking the scenario to metamodel classes. Each connection contains property and behavior definitions, which are included in the behavior of an instance when the scenario is activated upon this instance in a model. Thus, scenario models are not limited to the equations and properties defined by the metamodel, but can extend the behavior contained in the metamodel or represent any new behavior that can be described in mathematical terms.

```
SCENARIO ProductivityDueExpertise ProjectModel
{
    CONNECTION TheDeveloper Developer
    {
        PROPERTY Experience 0.5;      # 0..1

        AFFECT Productivity (0.67 + Experience*0.66) * Productivity;
    };
};
```

Fig. 4. A scenario that captures variations in productivity due to developer's expertise

The connection also contains behavior redefinition clauses, namely AFFECT clauses. These clauses can overwrite the original behavior defined for a class in the particular instance upon which the scenario was enacted. For instance, the AFFECT clause in the scenario presented in Figure 4 indicates that the scenario modifies the *Productivity* equation defined for the *Developer* class. The equation that describes a developer's productivity rate in the metamodel is overridden by the scenario definition. The new *Productivity* equation refers to the original equation. Since several scenarios can adjust the same equation, scenario integration ordering is relevant.

Simulation is the technique that allows project model behavior evaluation. Since project models are described by mathematical formulations, their equations can be evaluated to reveal the underlying project behavior. The simulation of the isolated project model describes project expected behavior, without the influence of the events and theories selected by the project manager. The integration of scenarios to a project model may reveal changes in the project behavior. Simulating a project model with a specific scenario demonstrates the potential impact of the scenario occurrence in the project behavior. This kind of simulation allows the manager to test project sensitivity to the events, theories, and strategies described by the scenario model.

Senior project managers create scenario models based on their experience, allowing less experienced managers to share their knowledge by retrieving and reusing such scenarios. Even though the mathematical representation of scenario models allows the simulation environment to translate reused information to knowledge, this representation is not well suited for retrieval. Thus, scenario models must be embedded in other representation better suited for this purpose. Once retrieved, scenario models can be separated from the previous representation and integrated to project models as shown in this section. The next section presents a risk management process that uses scenario models encapsulated within an information pattern to describe software risks.

3   A Risk Management Process Based on Scenario Models

In this section we show an application of scenario models in a risk management process. The process is based on documenting risks through scenarios, reusing these scenarios along several projects, and simulating the impact of scenario combinations upon a project model for risk evaluation. These activities imply two different concerns in the risk management process. First, risks are identified and documented using scenarios. Next, risks are reused along several projects, allowing the simulation of their impact upon the project behavior.

These different concerns resemble a generic reuse process framework composed by two sub-processes: one to develop reusable artifacts (i.e., development *for* reuse), identifying and documenting these software assets, and the other for application development based on reusing previously crafted artifacts (i.e., development *with* reuse), selecting and adapting them from a reusable information base. Attending to this framework, the risk management process is divided into two sub-processes: one for risk identification, and the other for risk reuse during application development.

The main objective of the risk management process for risk identification is to describe common risks associated to a specific *project element*, such as an application domain, technologies, developer roles, software artifacts, and resources. For instance, applications developed for certain domains usually present higher requirement volatility, certain languages are subjected to low portability issues, the adoption of a software process may inflict some risks to a project, and so on. The risk management process for risk identification organizes such information about development risks and allows its reuse in several application development processes.

The main objective of the risk management process for application development is to identify and evaluate risks that can affect a project due to its specific project elements. This process reuses risks associated to the project elements, identified and documented by the former risk management process. It occurs in parallel with an application development cycle, tracking the evolution and resolving its risks. This process explores the project elements used by the application, tracing to potential problems associated to these elements. A project model, previously developed for the application, determines its project elements.

The reusable artifact connecting both risk management processes is the information describing a risk, represented as *risk archetypes*. A risk archetype is a description of a potential recurring problem, which can cause some kind of loss to a software product or development process. It includes a description of the context where the problem can occur and provides solution strategies that can be applied before and after the problem occurrence. Risk archetypes serve as an awareness mechanism to the project manager and as containers for scenarios that model risk impact, contention and contingency strategies. They are associated to project elements, helping the retrieval of relevant scenario models for an application based on the project elements defined in the application's project model.

Risk archetypes exemplify how scenario models can be embedded within an information structure to provide both formalism, used in knowledge evaluation, and readable representation, used in knowledge retrieval. Figure 5 presents an example of a risk archetype for the validation risk, that is, the risk of developing the wrong system. Although the figure does not directly present models, the "scenario models" statements convey the mathematical representation for scenario models, such as Figure 4. Five blocks, described in the following paragraphs, compose the risk archetype information structure:

- **Archetype Identification**: describes the potential problem represented by the risk archetype. This block contains a textual and a scenario model description for the impact of the potential problem upon a software project;

- **Identification Mechanisms**: describes the mechanisms used to identify the risk in a particular project. This block contains a textual description of the context in which the risk occurs, a checklist to identify the conditions that promote the risk in a project, and a list of known cases of its occurrences;

- **Contention Strategies**: describes resolution strategies to inhibit or eliminate the potential problem described by the risk archetype before the risk occurs in a project. It provides a textual and a scenario model of each contention strategy, associating these strategies with the conditions when they can be applied;

- **Contingency Strategies**: describes resolution strategies to reduce the impact of the potential problem described by the risk archetype after its occurrence in a project. As in the contention strategies block, this block provides a textual and a scenario model for each contingency strategy;

- **Related Archetypes**: describes risk archetypes that occur in similar situations or risk archetypes that can replace the current risk archetype in software projects.

4   Experimental Analysis of the Proposed Techniques

After establishing the basis for scenario and project model development, integration and simulation, we chose to execute an empirical feasibility analysis before spending effort to refine the proposed techniques. In this study, we focused on applying scenarios for project management, instead of building new scenarios, because we wanted some evidence of scenario models efficacy before investing in better scenario and project model development tools.

Subjects: The subjects were students from a graduate software engineering course (2 DSc and 7 MSc degree), students from a graduate software engineering program (1 DSc and 7 MSc degree) and one student from an undergraduate computer science department. Eight subjects had been project leaders in industrial projects, while 3 subjects had been leaders in academic projects, and 7 subjects had never been project leaders. From the later seven students, 6 have previous software development experience in industrial or academic settings.

Objective: To observe whether managers who applied the integration and simulation techniques to support their decision would perform better than managers who relied only on their experience and other techniques. The selected performance criterion was time to conclude a project: managers were asked to conclude their project in the less time as possible. Also, we intended to qualitatively evaluate the feasibility and usefulness of the proposed techniques.

Archetype Identification	Contention Strategies
1. Name: Validation risk 2. Alias: Incorrect requirements 3. Potential problem: developing a system whose functionality does not satisfy the client. 4. Effects: quality loss of the software product 5. Impact: *scenario model*	1. Plan: Development of prototypes 2. Condition: Low planned validation mechanisms 3. Effects: Schedule overrun (time for prototyping) 4. Impact: *system dynamics scenario model* 1. Plan: Application of JAD techniques 2. Condition: user involvement is low 3. Effects: Schedule overrun 4. Impact: *scenario model*

Identification Mechanisms	Contingency Strategies
1.　Context: projects with little users involvement, projects with several clients, innovative projects. 2.　Checklist: 　•Evaluate the ambiguity in requirements 　•Evaluate user involvement in the project 　•Were operational simulation or prototyping applied during the project? 3.　Known cases: 　•<u>Project 105</u>: polymer classification 　•<u>Project 112</u>: e-supermarket	1. Plan: schedule extension 2. Effects: allow prototyping and requirement refinement; 3. Impact: *scenario model*
	Related Archetypes
	1.　Induced Risks: 　• <u>Schedule overrun</u> 　• <u>Reputation</u> 2.　Similar Risks:

Fig. 5. Validation risk archetype

Procedure: The subjects were randomly assigned into two groups: one to apply the proposed techniques and one to serve as a control group, accomplishing the study without the aid provided by the techniques. Each subject was asked to manage a small software project, aiming to develop part of an academic control system and comprising about 67 function points. Subjects from the first group (2 DSc and 7 MSc students) were trained to use the proposed techniques and the simulation environment, while subjects from the second group (1 DSc, 7 MSc and 1 undergraduate student) only received a project debriefing. Since a real project could not be created for each subject, we have developed a project emulator to be used in the study. Decision points where subjects could act included: determining the developer to assign for each project activity, deciding how much time to spend in quality control activities, and defining the number of hours each developer should work per day. The subjects from the first group could test the project sensibility for their decisions in the simulation environment before applying them to the project emulator.

Materials: All subjects received the project emulator, conveying a process for the proposed project and the descriptions of a set of developers to take part on the project team. All subjects received a brief description of the project. Subjects applying the techniques under study also received the simulation environment, a project model, and a set of scenarios models, built from knowledge presented in the technical literature, mostly from [13] and [9].

Data Collection: Questionnaires were used to collect qualitative data that characterized each subject and addressed the questions of feasibility and usefulness. The project emulator gathered quantitative information about subject performance, that is, the time that each subject took to conclude the project, measured in days.

Analysis: The quantitative data was submitted to outlier elimination procedures that removed two subjects from the first group and three subjects from the second group. Next, the quantitative data was submitted to a 95% T-test. A T-test [14] is a statistical analysis procedure based on the T distribution that compares if the averages of two groups are the same (to a degree of certainty, such as 90% or 95%) in the lights of their variances. The T-test showed that the average time to conclude the project for subjects applying the proposed techniques is less than the average time taken by the ones who did not applied the techniques. A Mann-Whitney [14] rank-based statistical analysis asserted the T-test results. Table 1 summarizes the analysis results.

Result and Lessons Learned: The quantitative data from this study showed that subjects using the proposed techniques performed better than subjects not using them. Also, all subjects from the first group agreed that the techniques were helpful. Thus, the data and positive results drawn from it show some indications that the techniques can be feasible and that they can provide help for project managers. The qualitative data indicates that the research upon the techniques is not concluded. Also, we found some points where a future replication of the experimental study could be improved, including: allowing subjects from the first group to use the simulator in a "toy" project during the training session; providing training on how to use the project emulator for subjects from both groups; and perfecting the mechanisms that present simulation results to the user.

Table 1. Analysis results for the experimental study

Project Conclusion	Subjects applying the techniques	Subjects not applying the techniques
Average	28,1 days	34,3 days
Maximum	38,0 days	42,0 days
Minimum	25,0 days	28,0 days
Standard deviation	4,7 days	4,9 days

5   Related Works

The relationships among knowledge management and software reuse have been previously addressed. Henninger [15] proposes an evolutionary organizational learning approach where domain knowledge is built from cases that document project experiences and design artifacts. Recurrent cases are progressively refined and translated to domain knowledge as they appear in projects. Like risk archetypes, cases are documented by standard structures that resemble design patterns. Though Henninger's work is close to our proposal, it misses the knowledge transfer activity, since cases are described in natural language and there is no automated support for their interpretation.

Yglesias [16] describes two reuse programs running at IBM. The first reuse program attempts to capture the knowledge possessed by consultants, while the second is a traditional reuse effort, focusing on software artifacts, such as code, design and analysis models. Although the author is not clear about the selected knowledge representation, we can infer that it is not a formal one, since Lotus Notes is the major knowledge capture and distribution tool. So, IBM knowledge reuse effort also lacks knowledge transfer activities.

Althoff et al. [17] propose mechanisms to organize, retrieve, and reuse software development experience. Managers can use such experience to predict problems early in the software development life cycle. Finally, Williamson et al. [18] present a formal representation for engineer's knowledge and design rationale. The proposed representation is used to document software components assertions and constraints, being tied to the components stored on a reuse library. Although the representation is formal and unambiguous, the authors present no mechanisms to integrate it to an incomplete project design in order to evaluate component fitness to the project.

6   Final Considerations

This paper described an approach to develop, retrieve, and reuse project management knowledge and experience. Such knowledge is represented in scenario models, which are formal models of management actions and theories. Scenarios can be integrated to a project model, a model that describes the expected behavior for a project under development, to allow the evaluation of their impact upon the project. We presented an application of the proposed techniques within a risk management process that uses scenarios to model risk impact and resolution strategies efficacy.

The main contribution of this paper is to show how scenario models can represent reusable project management knowledge in a form that supports knowledge transfer. Empirical results about the usefulness and feasibility of the proposed techniques were shown to support this contribution. Next steps are related to the definition of more complex scenario models and applying them to concrete project management situations. As the results of the first experimental study had proposed, there is a need for improvements of the tools that currently support the integration and simulation techniques. Also, we intend to provide tools to help scenario and project model development. Finally, more experiments are planned to explore both scenario construction and application techniques.

Acknowledgements

The authors would like to thank CNPq, CAPES, and FINEP for their financial investment in this work, Dr. Shari Lawrence Pfleeger for her insights, and the subjects of the experimental study for their valuable contribution.

References

1. Lucca, J., Sharda, R., Weiser, M. (2000) "Coordinating Technologies for Knowledge Management in Virtual Organizations", in: Proceedings of the Academia/Industry Working Conference on Research Challenges (AIWORC'00), pp. 21 – 26
2. Dieng, R. (2000) "Knowledge Management and the Internet", IEEE Intelligent Systems, Vol. 15, No. 3, pp 14 – 17, (May/June)
3. Brown, N. (1996) "Industrial-Strength Management Strategies", IEEE Software, Vol. 13, No. 4, pp 94–103 (July)
4. Klein, G. (1998) *Sources of Power*, MIT Press, Cambridge, Massachusetts
5. deMarco, T. (1982) *Controlling Software Projects*. New York, NY: Yourdon Press, Inc.
6. Reel, J.S. (1999) "Critical Success Factors in Software Projects", *IEEE Software*, Vol. 16, No. 3, pp. 18 – 23, (May/June)
7. Highsmith, J. (1992) "Software Ascents", American Programmer Magazine (June)
8. Forrester, J.W. (1961) *Industrial Dynamics*, Cambridge, MA: The M.I.T. Press
9. Abdel-Hamid, T., Madnick, S.E. (1991) *Software Project Dynamics: an Integrated Approach*, Prentice-Hall Software Series, Englewood Cliffs, New Jersey
10. Tvedt, J.D. (1996) *An Extensible Model for Evaluating the Impact of Process Improvements on Software Development Cycle Time*, D.Sc. Thesis, Arizona State University, Tempe, AZ
11. Lin, C.Y., Abdel-Hamid, T., Sherif, J.S. (1997) "Software-Engineering Process Simulation Model (SEPS)", *Journal of Systems and Software*, Vol. 37, pp. 263-277
12. Barros, M.O., Werner, C.M.L., Travassos, G.H. (2001) "From Models to Metamodels: Organizing and Reusing Domain Knowledge in System Dynamics Model Development", *Proceedings of the 19th Conference of the System Dynamics Society*, Atlanta, USA (July)
13. Jones, C. (2000) *Software Assessments, Benchmarks, and Best Practices*, Addison-Wesley Information Technology Series, Addison-Wesley Publishing Company, Reading, Massachusets
14. Wohlin, C., Runeson, P., Höst, M., Ohlsson, M.C., Regnell, B., Wesslén, A. (2000) *Experimentation in Software Engineering: an Introduction*, Kluver Academic Publishers, Norwell, Massachusets
15. Henninger, S. (1996) "Accelerating the Successful Reuse of Problem Solving Knowledge Through the Domain Lifecycle", in *Proceedings of the Fourth International Conference on Software Reuse*, Orlando, USA, pp. 124 - 133
16. Yglesias, K.P. (1998) "IBM's Reuse Programs: Knowledge Management and Software Reuse", in *Proceedings of the Fifth International Conference on Software Reuse*, Victoria, Canada, pp. 156-165
17. Althoff, K., Birk, A., Hartkopf, S., Müller, W., Nick, M., Surmann, D., Tautz, C. (1999) "Managing Software Engineering Experience for Comprehensive Reuse", in *Proceedings of the 11th International Conference on Software Engineering and Knowledge Engineering*, Heidelberg, GR

18. Williamson, K.E., Healy, M.J., Barker, R.A. (2000) "Reuse of Knowledge at an Appropriate Level of Abstraction – Case Studies Using Specware" in *Software Reuse: Advances in Software Reusability*, Proceedings of 6th International Conference on Software Reuse, Vienna, Austria, pp. 58 - 73

Adaptation of Coloured Petri Nets Models of Software Artifacts for Reuse

Kyller Costa Gorgônio and Angelo Perkusich

Electrical Engineering Department, Federal University of Paraíba,
Caixa Postal 10105, Campina Grande, Paraíba, Brasil
`perkusic@dee.ufpb.br`

Abstract. In this work we introduce an automatic adaptation approach for Coloured Petri Nets models. For this approach we define a procedure for the synthesis of a new model based on a given model and a set of behavior restrictions. This procedure was defined based on the concepts and techniques of the supervisory control theory and model checking. Moreover, we tackle the adaptation problem in the context of models reuse.

Keywords: Formal specification, Petri nets, model checking, temporal logic, supervisory control theory, models adaptation and reuse.

1 Introduction

The increasing need for more sophisticated and dependable software systems results demands higher abstraction levels and sophistication, from the design to the implementation of complex software systems [5]. One possible solution to manage such complexity is to build software artifacts that can be reused [10, 14]. Therefore, in the development process of a new system such artifacts could be used and the design would not always start from scratch.

Software reuse can be defined as the reuse of software artifacts while building new software systems. Besides code, other artifacts can be reused , such as project decisions, specifications, and documents [2, 1, 6, 19].

Reuse techniques may be applied in the design phase of software systems [18], then the objects of reuse are models instead of code. In the case that these models are described by means of a formal language, it is possible to investigate the behavior of such models based on formal analysis and simulation [5].

As defined by Krueger [10] the main software development activities that are subject of reuse are: abstraction, selection, adaptation and integration. In the context of this paper the focus is on defining an automatic approach to adapt formal models based on a set of behavioral restrictions.

The adaptation approach introduced in this paper is based on the supervisory control theory [17] and model checking [4]. Applying the approach the behavior of the resulting adapted model is maximal, that is is the one that satisfies the behavioral restrictions with minimal restrictions.

Formal methods and techniques as well as formal analysis are the basis of any mature engineering. They can be used in order to provide precise and abstract models that can

C. Gacek (Ed.): ICSR-7, LNCS 2319, pp. 240–254, 2002.

be systematically analyzed. These characteristics allow to increase the dependability on such systems. Among different formal methods, Petri Nets [15] have been successfully applied in many different phases of distributed and concurrent software developments. More specifically, Coloured Petri Nets (CPN) [8] are a very powerful tool to describe complex software models. In this paper we are concerned with the adaptation models described using CPNs.

As said before, given a model (described by a CPN) and a set of behavioral restrictions, the model is then automatically adapted. In the context of this paper the behavioral restrictions are given by temporal logic formulas. In the case on CPN models we use a temporal logic named ASK-CTL [3].

The paper is organized as follows. In Section 2 we introduce the reuse of formal models. In Section 3 the guidelines to adapt a CPN model are introduced, and in Section 4 the solution introduced and implemented is detailed. Finally in Section 6 we present conclusions and research directions.

2 Reuse of Formal Models

The reuse of software artifacts is not restricted to reuse of source code. In a similar way to what occurs with source code, formal models can also be designed considering that they can be later reused.

The formal model of a software system can be constructed in a more productive way if the designer makes use of pieces of previously constructed models that can be reused. Based on the fact that a formal models is described using a mathematical language, it is possible to investigate, and modify, its behavior in an automatic way. Therefore, the recovery and adaptation tasks for software artifacts can be done more easily.

The advantages to reuse modeling efforts are sufficiently obvious for any designer who already has reused his own efforts, and to make use of an automatic mechanism to assist him in this task can turn the reuse activity more productive.

Some works indicate the need to adopt software reuse activities during the formal modeling of software systems. Some of them suggest the adoption of object-oriented concepts and mechanisms, such as inheritance and encapsulation. In the case of Petri nets some of the efforts are reported in [11, 21, 12, 7]. Others suggest the development of a system of Petri nets patterns [16] in a similar way as for design patterns, generalizing models in Petri nets for posterior reuse.

Therefore systems are not always modeled from scratch, but existing models can also be used. The designer must think on how and where to search for pieces of models that can be directly reused, or if necessary adapted, while building a new model. Moreover, he must try to identify potential candidates for reuse and store them in a repository of models.

The following reuse activities are identified during the formal modeling of software systems:

- identification of the parts of the model of the new system;
- selection of the parts that need to be constructed and those that can be reused;
- description and recovery of the parts that can be reused;
- adaptation of the recovered models (parts);

- integration of the recovered/adapted models;
- identification of reusable (sub-)models and storing them in the repository.

A detailed discussion of these activities, excluding adaptation, in the context of Coloured Petri can be found in [13], and will be briefly introduced in Section 3.

In an informal context, where the searching for an artifact is made through the verification of its signature, the process can be frustrating. Many artifacts that satisfy the specified restrictions (signature) can be recovered, but they may not satisfy a desired behavior. There are no guarantees that a correct artifact will be recovered because a purely syntactic information (signature) is insufficient to describe what it makes. On the other hand, if the recovery process is made based on behavioral restrictions (semantic information), it is possible that the description of the artifact is equal to its implementation (the model to be recovered).

It is necessary to observe that that if the searching criteria is more restricted, close to the semantic level, the designer needs to describe the desired model more precisely. On the other hand, if the searching criteria is less restricted, more modifications in the recovered model will be needed to integrate it in the model being developed.

On the other hand, one cannot assume that the automatic recovery mechanism will always find some model satisfying completely the desired restrictions, mainly due to the computational cost to search in the state space. It is reasonable to admit that the recovered models will need some adaptation. Therefore, a mechanism to support the adaptation of recovered models becomes necessary.

In the following we present a solution for models reuse focusing in the adaptation activity.

3   Model Adaptation for Reuse

Some design practices of well established engineering disciplines consist of defining basic constructs from which complex systems can be built. These constructs are represented as mathematical models that can be analyzed, verified and/or simulated to guarantee that the behavior of a given construct satisfies a set of established requirements.

In this paper we adopt Coloured Petri Nets (CPN) [8] for the construction of software models. Models described with CPNs are considered basic constructs. It should be noted that it is possible to define basic constructs (blocks) as complex as desired, and based on these blocks it is possible to promote the construction of larger models efficiently. To do so, after the blocks are identified, it is necessary to both systematically store them for future use (reuse), and recover and adapt them when needed. Besides, it is also necessary to integrate the recovered blocks in a new design. It is important to point out that these blocks do not need to have to be defined for a specific granularity, or to be standard. Designers can recognize reusable blocks among the models they construct for specific domains.

The approach for model adaptation described in this work is based on the results of the Supervisory Control Theory (SCT) and Model Checking technique. In the SCT a model is described as finite generator given by an automata, and events are defined over an alphabet of the recognized language for the automata. The set of events are divided in controllable and uncontrollable. The basic problem solved in the context of the SCT is to find a language, with minimum restrictions, for which only the valid states of the model are reached.

One of the main results of the SCT is the definition of the algorithm of the supremal controllable sublanguage ($supC(L)$). Given a specification of a system and a set of behavior restrictions, the application of the algorithm results in a new specification satisfying the restrictions. This new specification is seen as the adapted model, or the model to be reused. The basic idea is to define a control function that observes input events, generated by the system, and disables controllable events for a certain state of the system so that illegal states cannot be reached.

The guidelines adopted to adapt models are enumerated as follows:

1. It is necessary to use of an adequate language to describe formal models, this language should have an editing and analysis tool associated. In this work we use Coloured Petri nets to describe the models, and the Design/CPN tool is used;
2. It is necessary to use an adequate language to describe the desired properties of the models, in this case we use the ASK-CTL temporal logic;
3. Verify if the behavior of the CPN model[1] satisfies the described properties. It must be observed that even if the state space does not satisfy exactly the restrictions (properties), is a model for them, it might be possible that a part of it satisfies them;
4. When necessary, restrict the model to satisfy the desired behavior. The model must be modified to inhibit the occurrence of some transitions when the reached state does not satisfies the restrictions;
5. Finally, the adapted model must be exported and integrated to the system being developed.

The repository of reusable CPNs is organized as a hierarchy described by a Hierarchical Colored Petri Nets (HCPN). It is reasonable to consider that the modeling knowledge to be generalized for latter use is well understood by a designer working with HCPN. Therefore, the models that can be reused are stored according to a classification depending on the application domain.

A model built using HCPN is indeed a collection of CPN models, named pages, a definition of colour sets (types), variables, and a hierarchical diagram defining how pages are related. A detailed discussion related to the practical and theoretical aspects of CPN and HCPN are beyond the scope of this paper, the interested reader may refer to [8].

The repository is organized as a domain hierarchy defining the number of domains, the repository is indeed a model of models. In the case that this hierarchy gets too complex it can always be broken in order to manage the complexity.

Problems related to the increase of state space were managed using programming techniques. Instead of generating the whole state space for the HCPN for the whole repository, the state spaces for the individual models for a given domain are interactively generated. As said before, the store and the recovery of models are important aspects in the context of reuse, but is out of the scope of this paper, since our emphasis is on adaptation. The reader interested in details about how to store and recover models from a repository of Coloured Petri nets models may refer to [13].

---

[1] The behavior of a CPN is given by an occurrence graph.

Based on the defined guidelines to adapt recovered CPN models, in the next section we detail the implemented solution.

4   Description of the Approach

As established previously, the main purpose of this work is to define an approach that, based on a Petri net specification and a set of behavioral restrictions written in temporal logic, generate a new specification satisfying the desired restrictions.

As discussed in the Section 3, one way to do this is to directly apply the algorithm of the supremal controllable sublanguage ($supC(L)$). However, the situation when the controllable language is empty, will be detected only when the algorithm is completely applied, and the computational cost may be quite high .

Therefore, the specifications are validated against the state space of the CPN model, and then its behavior is restricted. In this work, an approach using model checking [4] is adopted to manage this problem.

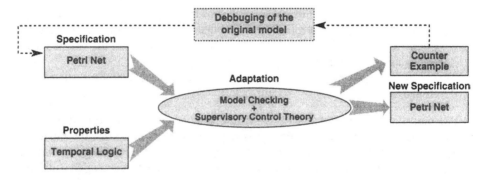

Fig. 1. Approach to the adaptation of reusable models.

In Figure 1 it is illustrated the approach. First, the occurrence graph (state space) of the CPN model is generated. The desired properties are then verified by the model checker. If it is not possible to automatically synthesize the new model from the supplied model, the designer will need to manually the supplied model or then try another one. Observe that we assume that more than one model satisfying the properties may be stored in the repository.

On the other hand, if the synthesis is possible, then the synthesis algorithm is applied, and for each undesirable state found, it is marked in order to modify the given CPN. Then we obtain a list of all the markings (states) of the occurrence graph considered undesirable. Based on this list, the given CPN net is then modified in order to satisfy the restrictions.

To get this result, the behavior of the net must be induced (controlled) to prevent that the marked states are not reached. One way to do this, it is to inhibit the occurrence of some transitions, when their occurrences may led to an undesirable state. To make this possible all nodes of the occurrence graph previously generated must be enumerated. Moreover, is necessary to add to the net new places, called control places, whose initial markings correspond to the given label for initial marking of the model, the initial state. These new places will always have to be input and output places of the CPN transitions, and every time that some of these transitions occurs, a piece of code (generated automatically) will be executed in order to determine the value of the token that will be placed in the control places. Therefore, the information contained in the token placed on the control places will always reflect the existing labels in the marked graph, or either, the current marking of the net.

Once these tokens for control places are added to the Petri net without control restrictions, the resulting model may reach states marked as undesirable. To avoid reaching these states it is necessary to inspect each transition of the model and to define the transition occurrence sequence that leads to it. If this situation occurs, and the transition is controllable, a guard must be added to this transition inhibiting its occurrence for the states leading to an undesirable state.

4.1 Implementation of the Procedure

Given an uncontrolled CPN RP_{NC}, a recovered model indeed, and a set of behavioral restrictions described in ASK-CTL, in this section we introduce a procedure to adapt a RP_{NC} to get a new CPN RP_C whose behavior satisfies the desired restrictions.

The execution of the synthesis algorithm on the state space of RP_{NC} generates a list with undesirable markings. Based on this list, the RP_{NC} is modified to prevent that the undesirable states are reached in the following way:

- Add to the set of places $P \in RP_{NC}$ control places ($Control\_Place_i$) with initial marking corresponding to the label of the initial marking of the graph previously generated.
- Add to the global declaration node of the CPN[2] a control function (called $Control\_Function$) that takes as parameter the name of a transition and the label of a marking and return the label of the next marking to be reached. The $Control\_Function$ is generated from the occurrence graph previously constructed. Based on the information contained in the occurrence graph (labeling the origin and destination nodes of each arc and the name of the transition) it is possible to easily construct such function.
- Finally, it is necessary to control the occurrence of the transitions inhibiting them when the net can reach an undesirable state. As it was established previously this can be made adding guards to the transitions. Thus, for each transition whose occurrence can cause a misbehavior the following is performed:
  1: **for all** $Control\_Place_i$ **do**
  2:    Create an arc from $Control\_Place_i$ to transition t;
  3:    Add a code to the transition t calling $Control\_Fuction$ that takes as parameters the name of t and the label of the current marking of the Petri net, which is specified by the value of the token in $Control\_Place_i$;

---

[2] The global declaration node of a CPN is used to define colour sets (types), variables, constants, and functions.

4:     Create an arc from t to $Control\_Place_i$ whose expression will be the return
       value of the code added to t;
5:     **if** t is controllable **then**
6:        **for all** Marking M in the occurrence graph of RP_{NC} that is undesirable
          do
7:           **if** Next marking reached from M is undesirable **then**
8:              Add a guard to t inhibiting its occurrence when the value of the token
                present in $Control\_Place_i$ is equivalent to the label of M
9:           **end if**
10:       **end for**
11:    **end if**
12: **end for**

It must be observed that the occurrence of an uncontrollable transition will update
the value of the token for the $Control\_Place_i$, associated to it. The fact of detecting
the occurrence of a transition does not imply, necessarily, that is possible to control it.
Note that the transitions are inhibited or not by its guard together with the the tokens
information in $Control\_Place_i$.

5   A Scenario for Reuse of Models

As said previously, there are four main aspects to consider while reusing models: abstraction, recovery, adaptation and integration. Despite that the focus of this work is on
the adaptation, it is important to discuss the other aspects. Consider the situation where
a railroad traffic control system is modeled. A system like this is composed by many
modules, and one of these modules control the locomotives maneuvers to change wagons
in a train yard.

In a model that represents this module, besides the parts that represent the pattern of
the railway and its connections, there are parts that control the changes of the compositions of the train.

In Figure 2 it is illustrated the arrival of a train with three components (a locomotive
and two wagons) to the change the composition and with the departure with only the
locomotive. In a similar way as illustrated in the Figure 2 it is possible that another
train arrives leaving or removing wagons. A designer working with this system may
notice that the control action to be taken can be modeled through a stack data structure
where the objects to be manipulated represent the wagons, and the locomotive acts as
the control.

In a similar way as illustrated in Figure 2, there are situations where the model is
a data structure of data of the type queue. For example, if a train always enter in one
section of the railway system followed, keeping a safe distance, for one another train is
natural that they leave this section in the same order that they had entered.

The models described in the above situation are strong candidates to reuse in different
contexts. Being able to promote a reduction in modeling efforts. Thus, the designer may
store them in a repository to allow its posterior recover in a systematic way.

In another situation, a designer is responsible for the modeling of part of a flexible
manufacturing system. In this case it is necessary to model the piling up and the piling

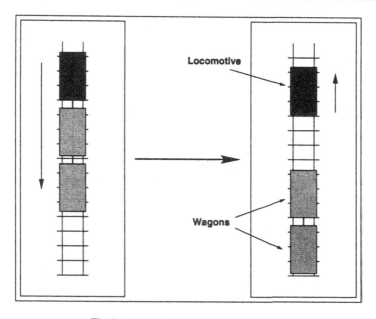

Fig. 2. System for compositions change.

down of raw material (and finished products) in the deposits of the production cells according to Figure 3. Moreover, the material enters these cells through conveyors. Again the designer needs to model a stack and a queue.

The designer does not have to construct these models from the scratch. He can search in the repository for models to reuse them. Admitting that exists an automatic method to recover these models, see [13], and that this method always finds models satisfyimg the

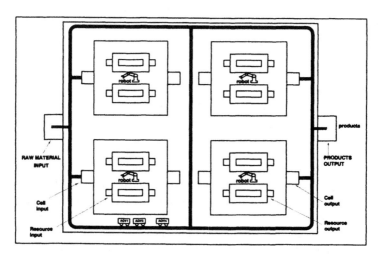

Fig. 3. Flexible manufacture system with four production cells.

criteria, the designer saves a considerable time in the activity of modeling this system, once that the models he needs are available.

Note that always when a new project is concluded, or during its development, the designer must identify potential reusable models and store them on the repository.

5.1 Storing and Recovering Models

As defined in [13] the process to store CPN models can be divided in four stages:

1. Creation of the repository, in the case that it does not exist yet. Using the Design/CPN tool a index of the repository is created for different application domains;
2. After the creation of the repository index, the global declaration node must be created. The colors (types) of the places of the index page and the application domains must be defined;
3. Later the page corresponding to the application domain must be created. In this page an environment of use for each model of the domain that will be stored must exist. In this environment one another substitution transition will lead to the model that is desired to store/recover;
4. Finally, it must be created one more page that will contain the model to be stored and eventually recovered.

A technique to recover models is detailed, and is summarized as follows:

1. First, the Design/CPN tool must be executed, then the repository model must be loaded and the occurrence graph manipulation tool must be activated;
2. After, it is necessary to describe the behavior of the model to be recovered. This description is made using the temporal logic ASK-CTL;
3. The searching procedure must be initiated. Once it was started, the designer will have to identify the application domain to be searched;
4. Each model of the domain is then automatically verified. When the models that satisfy the restrictions are found the designer is informed;
5. The model is exported.

5.2 Adaptation

As said before, in the context of reuse of models the storage and recovery of models are basic aspects. However it is important to observe that it may be necessary to customize the recovered model through the restriction of its behavior. Then, we consider in this section the application of the adaptation technique introduced in the Section 4 to synthesize models from a set of behavior restrictions. This automatic technique prevents the introduction of human errors that may occur in a manual process.

Returning to the scenario described in Section 5, the designer of the railroad system identified the stack and the queue models as potentially reusable and stored them in the repository as described in the Section 5.1. Later, when the designer needs to model the transport system between production cells of the flexible manufacturing system, he can search in the repository and recover candidates models for reuse. The recovered models are shown in Figures 4 and 5.

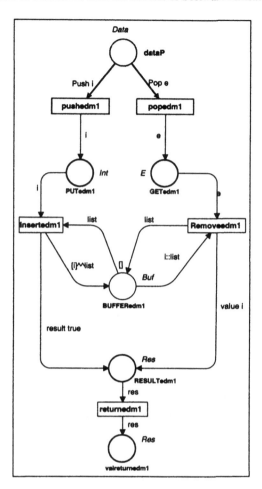

Fig. 4. CPN model of a data structure of the type stack.

In Figure 4 it is shown the CPN model for a stack. This model must be integrated to some project through substitution transitions in a HCPN (similar to function calls), and has as input and output port places **dataP** and **valreturnedm1** respectively. A token placed in place **dataP** represents a request for piling up or piling down.

If the value of the token is an integer number, we have a piling up solicitation enabling the transition **Insertedm1**. When this transition occurs, the data will be piled up. The stack is represented by the token in **BUFFEREdm1**. This token is a structure specified in CPN-ML[3] [8] of the type list, and every time that an element is added to the stack it will always be inserted in the beginning of the stack. After the insertion of an item in the stack, a token is put in place **RESULTedm1** indicating success in the operation.

---

[3] The CPN-ML language in used in CPN models to describe and manipulate colours (types) and is derived from the SML functional language [20].

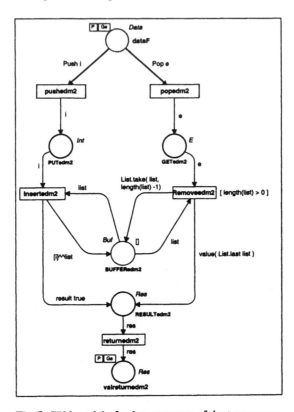

Fig. 5. CPN model of a data structure of the type queue.

On the other hand, if the value of the token in **dataP** is of the type E we have a piling down solicitation. In this in case **Removeedm1** is enabled, and, when of it occurs, the value of the head of the list in **BUFFERedm1** will be removed. Moreover, the removed value is returned for the environment in which the model is integrated.

The model shown in Figure 5 is very similar to the one shown Figure 4. The main difference, beyond the transitions and place names, is that the data are added in the beginning of the list in **BUFFERedm2** and removed of the end of it (and not from the beginning). Moreover, a guard in the transition **Removeedm2** exists inhibiting its occurrence in the case of the queue be empty.

It must be observed that for stack and queue models there is no limit for the maximum number of items that each structure holds. However, pilers and conveyors, that can be modeled by stacks and queues, have a maximum capacity that can not be exceeded. And it is desirable that the models that represent them reflect this limitation.

Then, it is necessary to adapt the recovered models before integrating them in the system being developed. The following steps are required to do that:

1. To describe the properties (behavioral restrictions) desired of the model.
2. To verify if the model can be adapted to satisfy such properties;
3. In the positive case, adapt the model.

The first step is related to the necessity of the designer to specify using the ASK-CTL language the restrictions that must be imposed to the model to be used. In the case of the transport system between production cells it is desired to limit the maximum size of the stacks and queues so that these reflect the physical capacity of the machines to be used in the construction of the real system.

The description of the desired restrictions is made in two stages. First the desired predicate must be described as a CPN-ML function that receives as parameter a node from the occurrence graph and returns a boolean value. This function must evaluate the node, determining if the desired property is satisfied or not. After that it is written an ASK-CTL formula expressing the desired behavior of the system in terms of these predicates.

The ASK-CTL predicate that express the capacity limit for the stack to maximum of two items is:

```
fun UpperLimit(n) = ( let
        val list_s = ref ''";
        val list_c = ref []
in
        list_s := (st_Mark.Stack'BUFFEREdm1 1 n);
        list_c := explode(!list_s);

        if (count(fc(!list_c, #"["), 0) < 3)
        then
                true
        else
                false
end);
```

Note that for this predicate, **BUFFEREdm1** is the place of the model of the stack that contends the stack with each inserted item. Moreover, it must be noted that this predicate is applied the stack. For the queue model t is necessary to define another predicate:

```
fun UpperLimit(n) = ( let
        val list_s = ref ''";
        val list_c = ref []
in
        list_s := (st_Mark.Queue'BUFFEREdm2 1 n);
        list_c := explode(!list_s);

        if (conta(fc(!list_c, #"["), 0) < 3)
        then
                true
        else
                false
end);
```

The ASK-CTL formula that express the property that specifies a maximum limit of two items for any one of the two structures, is:

$$POS(NOT(NF(\text{"Is it possible to limit the buffer size?"}, UpperLimit)))$$

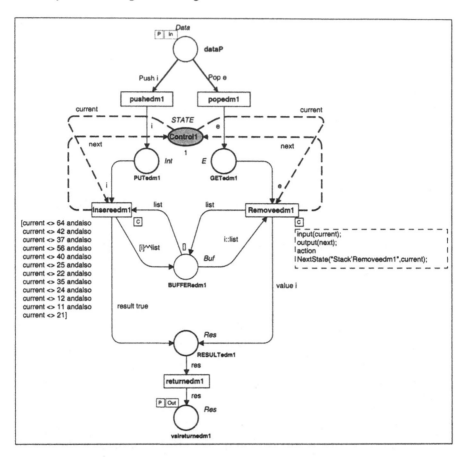

Fig. 6. CPN model of a data structure of the type stack with control restrictions.

After describing the desired behavioral restrictions, the designer must initiate the execution of the procedure to adapt the models. As result of the execution of the procedure considering the property presented above we obtain the models shown in Figures 6 and 7.

6   Conclusion

In this paper we introduced an approach to adapt Coloured Petri Nets (CPN) models for reuse based on model checking and supervisory control theory. Based on a set of temporal logic restrictions and a recovered model, a new model is then automatically built.

The introduced adaptation approach is fully implemented is is part an environment integrated as library to the Design/CPN tool. One another important aspect in the process of models reuse is how to use such models adequately.

Another important aspect is related to the compositional nature of the models. When the models were already verified, we can trust on their correct behavior. Thus, when

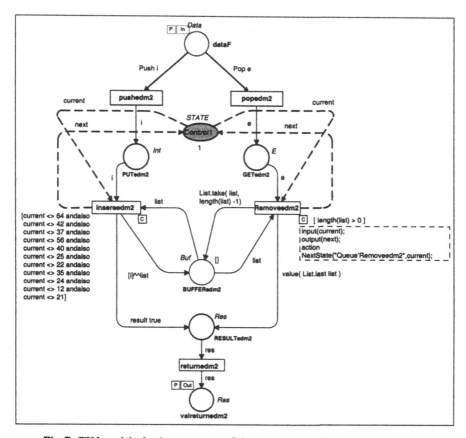

Fig. 7. CPN model of a data structure of the type queue with control restrictions.

analyzing the model being developed it is not necessary to analyze the behavior of the models that had been integrated. Therefore when generating the state space for the resulting model, the state space of the adapted models can be abstracted, resulting in a reduction for the state space of the whole model.

It is important to point out that the resulting model still needs to be verified, and therefore the state space for the whole models must be constructed. In order to deal with the state explosion problem that may occur, it is possible to define equivalence classes in order to abstract the behavior of the recovered models that were integrated to the final design [9].

We are currently working on a framework, including automatic integration, being applied do modeling flexible manufacturing systems models.

Acknowledgements

The research reported in this paper is is partially supported by grants, 465423/2000-0, 471317/2001-2 and 520944/1998-4 from CNPq (Conselho Nacional de Desenvolvimento Científico e Tecnológico), Brazil.

References

1. T. Biggerstaff and A. Perlis. *Software Reusability: Applications and Experience*, volume II of *Frontier Series*. ACM Press, New York, 1989.
2. T. Biggerstaff and A. Perlis. *Software Reusability: Concepts and Models*, volume I of *Frontier Series*. ACM Press, New York, 1989.
3. Allan Cheng, Søren Christensen, and Kjeld Høyer Mortensen. Model checking coloured petri nets exploiting strongly connected components. Technical report, Computer Science Department, Aarhus University, Aarhus C, Denmark, March 1997.
4. Edmund M. Clarke, Jr., Orna Grumberg, and Doron A. Peled. *Model Checking*. The MIT Press, Cambridge, Massachusetts, 1999.
5. Edmund M. Clarke and Jeannette M. Wing. Formal methods: State of the art and future directions. *ACM Computing Surveys*, 28, December 1996.
6. Peter Freeman. *Tutorial: Software Reusability*. IEEE Computer Society Press, Washington, D.C., 1987.
7. D.D.S. Guererro, J.C.A. de Figueiredo, and A. Perkusich. An object-based modular "cpn" approach: Its application to the specification of a cooperative editing environment. *Advances on Petri Nets: Concurrent Object-Oriented Programming and Petri Nets, Lecture Notes in Computer Science, Volume 2001*, pages 338–354, 2001.
8. Kurt Jensen. *Coloured Petri Nets: Basic Concepts, Analysis Methods and Practical Use*, volume 1 of *EACTS – Monographs on Theoretical Computer Science*. Springer-Verlag, 1992.
9. Kurt Jensen. *Coloured Petri Nets: Basic Concepts, Analysis Methods and Practical Use*, volume 2 of *EACTS – Monographs on Theoretical Computer Science*. Springer-Verlag, 1995.
10. Charles W. Krueger. Software reuse. *ACM Computing Surveys*, 24(2):131–183, June 1992.
11. C. Lakos. From coloured petri nets to object petri nets. In *Application and Theory of Petri Nets*, volume 935, pages 278–297, Torino, Italy, June 1995.
12. N. H. Lee, J. E. Hong, S. D. Cha, and D. H. Bae. Towards reusable colored petri nets. In *Proc. Int. Symp. on Software Engineering for Parallel and Distributed Systems*, pages 223–229, Kyoto, Japan, April 1998.
13. A.J.P. Lemos and A. Perkusich. Reuse of coloured petri nets software models. In *Proc. of The Eighth International Conference on Software Engineering and Knowledge Engineering, SEKE'01*, pages 145–152, Buenos Aires, Argentina, June 2001.
14. M. D. McIlroy. "mass produced" software components. In P. Naur and B. Randell, editors, *Software Engineering*, pages 138–155, Brussels, 1969. Scientific Affairs Division, NATO. Report of a conference sponsored by the NATO Science Co.
15. Tadao Murata. Petri nets: Properties, analysis and applications. *Proc. of the IEEE*, 77(4):541–580, April 1989.
16. Martin Naedele and Jorn W. Janneck. Design patterns in petri net system modeling. In *Proceedings of ICECCS'98*, pages 47–54, October 1998.
17. P. J. G. Ramadge and W. M. Wonham. The control of discrete event systems. *Proceedings of the IEEE*, 77(1):81–97, 1989.
18. D. Ribot, B. Blongard, and C. Villermain. Development life-cycle with reuse. In *ACM Symposium on Applied Computing SAC 94*, March 1994.
19. W. Tracz. *Tutorial: Software Reuse. Emerging Technology*. IEEE Computer Society Press, Los Alamitos, CA, 1988.
20. Jeffrey D. Ullman. *Elements of ML Programming*. Prentice Hall, 2 edition, 1998.
21. W. M. P. van der Aalst and T. Basten. Life-cycle inheritance: A petri-net-based approach. Computing Science Reports 96/06, Eindhoven University of Technology, Eindhoven, 1996.

Improving Hazard Classification through the Reuse of Descriptive Arguments

Shamus P. Smith and Michael D. Harrison

The Dependability Interdisciplinary Research Collaboration,
Department of Computer Science, University of York,
York YO10 5DD, United Kingdom
{Shamus.Smith, Michael.Harrison}@cs.york.ac.uk

Abstract. Descriptive arguments are an intrinsic part of the process of determining the dependability of any system, particularly in the case of safety critical systems. For such systems, safety cases are constructed to demonstrate that a system meets dependability requirements. This process includes the application of hazard analysis techniques. However, such techniques are error-prone, time consuming and apply "ad hoc" reuse. Hence, the use of systematic, exhaustive hazard analysis can lead to an illusion of high confidence in the parent dependability argument that is compromised by lack of rigour.

We have investigated the application of structure and reuse techniques to improve hazard classification arguments and their associated parent dependability arguments. A structure for hazard arguments has been presented and an example from a software hazard analysis has been exemplified using XML. Using two methods of structural reuse, hazard arguments can be improved for both argument generation and post argument construction analysis.

1 Introduction

Descriptive arguments[1] are an intrinsic part of the process of determining the dependability of any system. This is particularly the case in evaluating the dependability of safety critical systems. For such systems, safety cases are constructed to demonstrate that a system meets dependability requirements. These dependability requirements are typically verified against a system's specification via demonstrated proofs and arguments that support the development, implementation and testing of the system.

Part of this verification process is the use of techniques for systematic hazard analysis. Hazard identification, classification and mitigation techniques establish that either hazards can be avoided or that they will not affect the dependability of the system. To aid this process, descriptive arguments are commonly produced to mitigate, and therefore down play, the severity of hazards and the frequency of hazardous events/states.

---

[1] We consider descriptive arguments as informal arguments in contrast to more quantitative, numeric arguments.

C. Gacek (Ed.): ICSR-7, LNCS 2319, pp. 255–268, 2002.
© Springer-Verlag Berlin Heidelberg 2002

However, there are two main problems with reliance on hazard based safety arguments. Firstly, there is the problem of collecting and documenting all the relevant data. Commonly there are large amounts of raw data/evidence that needs to be documented. This process can be repetitive and error prone. Inconsistency over the gathered evidence can lead to casual ("sloppy") arguments.

Secondly, hazard analysis can be a lengthy process. This is particularly the case when exhaustive and systematic methods are used to consider potentially hazardous events and states. One result of this is that the analysis may be terminated prematurely. Typically, analysts justify this in two ways. Firstly, by stating that all the relevant hazards have been identified and it is presumed that no new hazards will be found in the untested areas and secondly, by making high level reuse of already completed analysis. This reuse is applied by describing the new analysis through difference/variations of the completed analysis. This can lead to inconsistencies in the application of "ad hoc", potentially unjustified, reuse as might occur in verbatim cross-referencing of evidence components for example.

We claim that the use of systematic, exhaustive hazard analysis can lead to an illusion of high confidence in the parent dependability argument that is compromised by lack of rigour in the analysis application and the associated argument definition.

We address these issues by demonstrating how dependability arguments can be improved by the systematic reuse of descriptive argument components. We propose that argument structures can be identified and reused based on the similarity of their structure and application of use. Reuse of successful arguments can augment similar new and existing arguments. We demonstrate this method on the hazard analysis of a typical safety case.

The remainder of this paper is as follows. In Section 2 we define a simple format for argument structure. Next, argument reuse is introduced and domain data dependence is considered. Also two approaches to structural reuse are presented. In Section 4 we describe our example domain that is the use of hazard arguments as part of a safety case for an industrial expert system. In this context we have explicitly examined hazard and operability studies (HAZOP) [7] as an example of a commonly used technique for hazard analysis. Next, the application of structural reuse is described in context of our example domain. Finally, we present a brief discussion, our conclusions and scope for future work.

2   Argument Structure

A common form of argument is one that is based on a triple of (claim, argument, evidence). There is a claim about some property with evidence presented to support the claim via an argument. This structure is based on a well known "standard" argument form of Toulmin [12].

Toulmin developed a notation (described in [12]) that can be used to structure a typical argument. In its initial form, it provides a link between data (evidence), claims and warrants (support)(see Figure 1).

"We may symbolise the relation between the data and the claim in support of which they are produced by an arrow, and indicate the authority for taking the step from one to the other by writing the warrant immediately below the arrow:" [12, pg99]

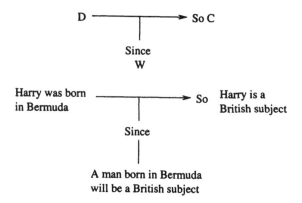

Fig. 1. Toulmin's initial argument pattern and an example

Kelly observes that Toulmin's notation can be used to express *any* argument [6, pg63]. Toulmin's arguments can be augmented with additional components, for example, qualifiers on claims and rebuttals on qualifiers, but in the context of the current work the initial definition in Figure 1 is sufficient.

What this type of argument provides is a basic structure for the definition of descriptive arguments.

3   Argument Reuse

One factor that complicates the reuse of arguments is the integration of domain specific material (e.g. data) into the argument structures. This has led to two main approaches for the reuse of arguments, one that is based on domain dependent reuse, the reuse of the data, and the other, domain independent reuse, the reuse of the argument structures and/or argument process or technique.

3.1   Domain Dependence and Independence for Reuse

For domain dependent reuse, it is the data within the domain and how it is used within an argument structure that is important. This can involve matching the current argument examples with cases in previous arguments, based on the similarity to the data/situations under discussion.

Traditional case-based reasoning (CBR) techniques can be used to determine similarity between example cases. However, this approach limits the amount of reuse that is possible. The domains under consideration would have to share fundamental characteristics if sensible results from the reuse could be obtained. An example of this is the reuse of arguments in legal cases. Libraries of previous cases can be defined and searched to find matches to the current case in terms of outcome, legal defence, scenario etc [1]. More recently, Brüninghaus and Ashley [3] have developed a classification-based approach to find abstract situations in legal texts. Their aim is to identify indexing concepts in case texts to help the construction and maintenance of CBR systems. Components of cases are indexed via the use of simple decision trees and algorithms that utilise a legal thesaurus. Therefore the reuse of the legal cases is tightly matched to the legal domain characteristics.

Similarly, if a common theme can be identified then templates of reuse can be defined. An example of this can be seen in Kelly's use of patterns for safety cases in safety critical systems [6]. In Kelly's work the overall theme is safety critical systems and the reuse of safety case patterns over a library of example argument templates. Although Kelly describes examples of domain independent and domain dependent patterns in safety cases, all the pattern examples are firmly grounded in the overall domain of safety critical systems. The reuse is at the domain level (e.g. using patterns as a reuse technique) and not necessarily at the evidence (data) level.

It is less clear how reuse in arguments can be applied in a data independent fashion. If we cannot examine the domain data explicitly (or how it is used) to determine similarity, an alternative measure of argument similarity will need to be found. This is the focus of the work presented in this paper. We have been investigating the structure of arguments and the types of claims/evidence that can enable reuse.

3.2   Approaches to Structural Reuse

We have applied the simple argument structure of Toulmin [12], as discussed in Section 2, to define argument structures via claim → argument → evidence relations. Two data independent structures are formed by this approach. Firstly, tree like parent/child relations (for direct support) and sibling relations (for diverse support). The structures can be defined using methods based on depth first and breadth first approaches, respectively. In the next two sections, we describe how these methods can define potential for reuse.

Depth first reuse. The depth first approach involves examining the sub-tree of a particular claim and determining if it can be reused to aid support of a similar claim. For example, suppose we have claim A that has two sub-levels of support. If we introduce a claim B and can determine that claims A and B are similar, is it possible to reuse the justification structure of claim A to strengthen the argument of claim B? A pictorial example of depth first reuse can be seen in Figure 2. An individual's claim of free travel through Europe is supported by a claim of general free travel for UK passport holders **and** a claim of passport ownership. The support for the passport ownership is then reused for a second claim.

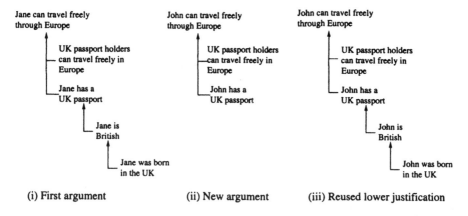

(i) First argument   (ii) New argument   (iii) Reused lower justification

Fig. 2. Depth first reuse example

Breadth first reuse. Reuse via a breadth approach involves investigating the pairings of sibling arguments. Multiple sibling arguments at the same level can provide diversity to an argument. Diversity is desirable as independent argument strands make the overall argument more robust [6, pg154], i.e. if the strength of one child argument strand is weakened, it may not have a large effect on the overall argument/claim strength. Diversity reuse involves examining claims built on diversity arguments to determine if similar claims (i.e. the diverse structure) can be applied in other argument applications. For example suppose claim A is supported by three sub-claims (A_1, A_2 and A_3). Now we introduce claim B which is currently only supported via sub-claim A_2. The question is, can we reuse the diversity structure of the claim A argument to claim B, i.e. do A_1 and A_3 also support B? (For an example, see Figure 3.) This type of reuse can also have further implications because reuse at one level of diversity may allow reuse of that claim's sub-claims, also incorporating the depth first reuse.

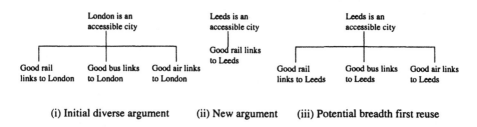

(i) Initial diverse argument   (ii) New argument   (iii) Potential breadth first reuse

Fig. 3. Breadth first reuse example

4 The Example: DUST-EXPERT

The work that is described in this paper is grounded in a real world domain. We have been using the safety case of a software package to test/examine the reuse of arguments. The package we have been using is the DUST-EXPERT expert system tool developed by Adelard [4]. In Sections 4.1-4.3 we present brief overviews of the application, the software HAZOP component of the safety case and the arguments that are used in the HAZOP.

4.1 DUST-EXPERT

DUST-EXPERT is an application that advises on the safe design and operation of plants that are subject to dust explosions. It provides general advice on preventing dust explosions. User-extensible databases on the properties of dust and construction materials are used in techniques such as decision trees to determine dust explosion reduction strategies and to calculate methods for quantitative analysis for these strategies [4].

The documentation we are using is from the DUST-EXPERT safety case developed by Adelard [4]. They state that for safety integrity requirements, the DUST-EXPERT application is classed as SIL 2[2]. The safety case focuses on the software engineering process used. In the context of the work described in this paper we are investigating the argument usage in the hazard analysis of the DUST-EXPERT safety case and more precisely, the software HAZOP.

4.2 Software HAZOP

Pumfrey [11, pg43] observes that "HAZOP is described as a technique of *imaginative anticipation* of hazards and operation problems." Although a full description of HAZOP is outside the scope of this paper (the reader is directed to [7]) we will briefly describe the HAZOP process and highlight our area of interest, namely the use of descriptive arguments.

HAZOP is a systematic technique that attempts to consider events in a system or process exhaustively. Within a particular system domain (or scenario), items (or events) are identified and a list of guide words is applied to the items. The guide words prompt consideration of deviations to item behaviour (guide word examples include LESS VALUE, MORE VALUE, NO ACTION and LATE ACTION) to elicit the potential for arriving at possible hazardous states. These guide words provide the structure of the analysis and can help to ensure complete coverage of the possible failure modes [11, pg45].

Before starting the HAZOP, a domain description, a description of the system (normally a flow diagram), a list of elements of the flow diagram called items and a group of guide words are selected. The HAZOP process is then the exhaustive application of the guide words to each item in a particular context (using the collective knowledge a multidisciplinary team).

---

[2] Safety integrity level SIL 2 implies that under a low demand mode of operation, the probability of a failure for a safety function is in the range of $>= 10^{-3}$ to $< 10^{-2}$ [2].

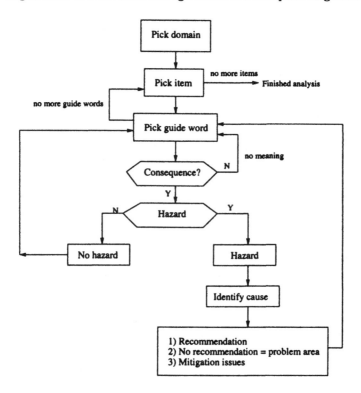

Fig. 4. Flow diagram of the HAZOP process

At each of these application steps, an implication is identified for the current item/guide word pairing. This implication has three possible results; no meaning, no hazard or hazard. This process is illustrated in Figure 4.

No meaning is used when the current guide word is not applicable for the current item. This is determined via an argument that there is no consequence for the current item/guide word pairing and such a pairing is not valid in this context (defined via expert judgement of the HAZOP team). When a *no meaning* is selected, the analysis can then move onto the next guide word.

Alternatively, a HAZOP pairing will be associated with a consequence. That consequence will either have a *no hazard* or *hazard* implication label. A *no hazard* implication is determined by there being mitigating factors (via expert judgement as understood by the HAZOP team) in the context of the consequences. These factors alter the weight of the consequences so that they fall below some threshold (also as assessed by expert judgement). For example, there may be a low impact on the system or there may a very low likelihood of it happening. Part of this process involves identifying the cause and any recommendations.

A hazard is defined when the consequence of a HAZOP pairing can not be completely mitigated. Arguments that mitigate some part of the consequence may be defined but in this case they do not change the label from *hazard* to *no hazard*. This is shown in Figure 4 by three alternatives. A hazard has some recommendation (which does not mitigate the hazard), or there is no recommendation so the hazard is marked as a problem area, or the hazard has some associated mitigating arguments.

4.3   Descriptive Arguments in HAZOP

Our interest in HAZOP is concerned with the use of arguments for hazard classification. These arguments can be used to demonstrate that the hazard classification process is accurate/valid. Typically, such classification arguments are implicitly considered in the construction of the HAZOP data. However, much of this reasoning can be extracted from the data in the form of descriptive arguments. Hence, we have reinterpreted the HAZOP data in a Toulmin style.

There are two main types of argument that we have investigated. These are the *no meaning* implications and the *consequence mitigation*. As described in Section 4.2 these types of argument are used in the classification of hazards and, in the case of *consequence mitigation*, can be used to justify hazard labels and recommendations.

We have examined arguments elicited from HAZOP analysis of the DUST-EXPERT software to determine whether reusable structures can be identified. We wish to strengthen mitigation claims with previously defined "strong" arguments. However, before this analysis process could begin, the descriptive arguments were reconstructed from the raw HAZOP data.

5   Structure and Reuse

5.1   Building a Structure in the DUST-EXPERT Example

The DUST-EXPERT HAZOP information was provided by Adelard [4] in the form of a text table. This contained 330+ individual HAZOP rows. Even though this was not the complete HAZOP, this was more than enough raw data to make manual searching for patterns impractical. This was made more complicated by the fact that the structure of the data was flat. Additionally, the arguments were not clearly marked in the text and needed to be inferred from the HAZOP consequence, implication, protection and recommendation elements. The first step in managing this data was to move it to an alternative structural representation. We have done this using XML (Extensible Markup Language)[3].

5.2   Argument Structure and Reuse in XML

In line with our desire to reuse material we have built an XML structure to house the HAZOP study data and the arguments that are implied within the data.

---

[3] There is a vast array of texts on XML including [8].

One of our overall aims is to reuse the argument structures over different domains. Therefore we have kept the raw data separate from the argument definitions. This simplifies the searching/filtering techniques that can be used on the XML structures.

Within the XML argument structures we are using the basic support hierarchy defined by Toulmin (see Section 2). As we are investigating a data independent method, claims have been classified by *type* to allow the nature of the argument structure to be defined. Initial analysis of the raw data identified seven claims types:

- *Failure claims* are claims where mitigation is determined through the inaction of some event. For example, a help window may not appear and the support for the mitigation of this issue as a hazard is that "no action is not a hazard".
- *Duplication claims* involve the determination that multiple occurrences of an issue is allowable. For example if multiple identical help screens appear in some context where "redundancy is not a hazard". Therefore the potential for redundancy to be identified as a hazard has been mitigated by this claim.
- *Testing claims* indicate that a particular consequence is not an issue (e.g. can be mitigated) as test cases can be used to determine that the fault has not been implemented.
- *User claims* involve the participation of the user in context to defend against a consequence. For example some consequence may be "obvious to the user" and hence unlikely to happen and/or corrected quickly.
- *Feedback claims* indicate that specific information has been provided to the user to allow them to avoid a hazardous situation. For example, input values may be stored in a log file and the user may be explicitly prompted to verify the data in the log. It is assumed that the feedback is at a level so that the user will definitely become aware of it.
- *System claims* are claims that are specific to system operations. Examples include internal validation of data, automated features (e.g. window updates) and operating system restrictions (e.g. modal dialogs).
- *Timing claims* negate a consequence by identifying temporal mitigations. For example, a window may be slow to cancel but this is determined as a *no hazard* as "slow operations are not a hazard" in this context.

However, it should be noted that these are not necessarily an exhaustive set of claim types. These are only the claims that were identified for this particular example/domain.

The XML structure can be translated into HTML (HyperText Markup Language) using filters, written in JavaScript, to traverse the XML tree structure searching for arguments that match set criteria. Example criteria could be (i) all the arguments that started with a failure claim or (ii) all the arguments that start with three diverse argument threads that include a user claim.

A simple visual representation of the XML tree structure for arguments of interest can be displayed to the user via HTML in a standard web browser

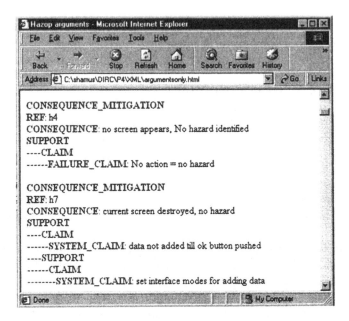

Fig. 5. XML tree representation in HTML format

(see Figure 5). It was intended that patterns of argument usage and structural similarity could then be identified for reuse purposes.

Initial experiments involved depth and breadth first filters have provided promising results on a sample of the DUST-EXPERT software HAZOP arguments.

5.3 Depth First Example

In this example, we applied a filter to the data to select all the arguments that started with a particular type of claim, e.g a duplication claim. These arguments were then examined to determine the similarity between the consequence item of the arguments and the justification of the HAZOP hazard or no hazard label. If one of the arguments has more justification (i.e. a deeper tree structure) and/or has a higher level of strength associated with it, it may be possible to reuse this arguments' justification with the other argument. This is best illustrated in a real example.

Figure 6 shows part of the output from applying the depth first filter to a subset of the HAZOP arguments. In this case, both arguments have top level duplication claims that redundancy is not a hazard. However, the second argument has further justification to this claim with diverse testing and system claims. The reuse we would be considering here would be if the same diverse pairing could be applied to the first argument in the Figure 6.

Thus we are reusing sub-trees of justification. It is hoped that this additional information will improve the overall argument mitigation.

```
CONSEQUENCE_MITIGATION
REF: h28
CONSEQUENCE: several identical help screens appear, no hazard
SUPPORT
----CLAIM
------DUPLICATION_CLAIM: redundancy = no hazard

CONSEQUENCE_MITIGATION
REF: h52
CONSEQUENCE: multiple records filled in - no hazard identified
SUPPORT
----CLAIM
------DUPLICATION_CLAIM: redundancy is not a hazzard
----SUPPORT
------CLAIM
--------TESTING_CLAIM: Test for identical records
----SUPPORT
------CLAIM
--------SYSTEM_CLAIM: System may not allow duplicates to be defined
```

Fig. 6. Example of possible reuse for a duplication claim

5.4   Breadth First Example

Using the breadth first filter, we wish to find patterns in the diverse argument threads. Ideally, there would be groupings of claims that are common over particular domains, for example if we could determine that every user claim has a sibling testing claim in each of its pairings. Therefore, we examined, over a subset of the HAZOP arguments, all the arguments that initially had two diverse claims where at least one of which started with a user claim. This generated eleven arguments of which eight comprised of user and testing diverse claims. An example of two such arguments can be seen in Figure 7.

In terms of reuse, we would be looking to augment other user claim arguments with information that supported a testing claim or to add alternative claims. For example if we had a single user argument thread, we could review other (common) testing claims to strengthen the justification for the consequence mitigation.

In this case the motivation is to strengthen the argument by adding more diverse argument threads. By identifying common threads from the existing structure, we can speed up the refinement process for arguments and also reuse the new sub-tree structures for claims which also incorporates depth first reuse.

6   Discussion

In Sections 5.3 and 5.4 we have described two approaches to descriptive argument reuse based on structural similarities. We propose that there are two main areas where such reuse will be beneficial, namely, post analysis argument refinement and "on-the-fly" argument construction.

```
CONSEQUENCE_MITIGATION
REF: h16
CONSEQUENCE: user types and nothing happens. No hazard provided user notices
SUPPORT
----CLAIM
------TESTING_CLAIM: can be picked up in testing
SUPPORT
-----CLAIM
-------USER_CLAIM: user might notice

CONSEQUENCE_MITIGATION
REF: h30
CONSEQUENCE: wrong help text displayed on top of correct text, hazard
SUPPORT
----CLAIM
------USER_CLAIM: may be obvious to user
SUPPORT
-----CLAIM
-------TESTING_CLAIM: test cases for implementation correctness
```

Fig. 7. Matching diverse argument threads using a breadth first filter

Post analysis argument refinement can be used to improve descriptive arguments. Due to the large number of arguments that may be associated with any safety case, it is unlikely that the strongest possible case will be defined on the first iteration. The methods we have discussed can be used to identify areas where argument reuse can be applied to improve the overall completed argument. Reuse in this manner would also maintain consistency between the defined arguments as similar arguments would share similar structures.

The second potential area of use would be in the construction of argument structures. As hazard arguments are being defined, previously defined arguments could be compared to see if their justification could be applied in the current situation. This "on-the-fly" analysis of the argument building process would allow reused argument components to speed up the definition process. Also consistency over the argument structure would be maintained. Common argument structures could be considered as a library of reusable parts. Expert judgement would still be required to authorise the reuse but by providing alternative candidate arguments, this process could be made systematic and semi-automated[4].

7   Conclusions and Future Work

We have investigated the development of dependability arguments and discussed the application of structure and reuse techniques to improve the resulting arguments. A basic structure for hazard arguments has been presented and an example from a software hazard analysis has been exemplified using XML to structure the data and allow the application of two methods of structural reuse.

---

[4] Therefore, the system provides the reuse candidates and the user makes the decision and applies the argument adaptation process.

Using these methods, arguments can be improved over both processes for argument generation and analysis after argument construction.

Currently, much of this work is at an early stage but we feel that it is a constructive initial step towards general argument reuse without the complications associated with explicit domain considerations. It is intended that the techniques we have discussed will be portable to new domains and other techniques that use argumentation.

However, one issue of concern is that bias may be incorporated into the reuse process. Patterns matching existing arguments may be given preference in the argument construction process. For example, new forms of arguments may be forced into the suggested structures when it is more appropriate that a new structure should be defined. In our approach, this issue is the responsibility of the user who applies expert judgement in the argument construction/adaptation process.

Another issue is the cost of the reuse process. There will be costs associated with both the organisation of the raw data into argument structures and the ease of the final reuse. Also there is the overhead of identifying appropriate reuse arguments. Such issues must be balanced against any proposed benefits. However, issues of cost and benefit typically require some form of measure to allow realistic predictions to be made. We are currently investigating a notion of confidence (and confidence in the worth of an argument) as such a measure to demonstrate that argument reuse will lead to improved arguments and consequently improved confidence in the arguments.

In regard to future work, we intend to continue with three main threads of research. Firstly, we will be adding more HAZOP definitions from the current example to enable us to identify more claim types and new clustering of claim structures. Also new criteria for searches using the depth and breadth first methods will be investigated.

Secondly, the current definition of structural similarity is quite high level. Therefore we intend to extend the structural approach to decompose consequences based on the stricter view of structural similarity as described by Plaza [9].

Finally, the current work is based on arguments used in hazard analysis and the use of HAZOP. We intend to investigate the reuse of the current XML structures and associated search methods/filters to alternative techniques which use descriptive arguments. Initially we will examine the arguments used in a technique for human error assessment, THEA [5, 10]. THEA elicits data that can be used to construct arguments for design rationale about human reliability. It is hoped that similar argument structures and search criteria will be identified that can be considered as a top level of structural and argument reuse.

Acknowledgements

This work was supported in part by the UK EPSRC DIRC project, Grant GR/N13999. The authors are grateful to Bev Littlewood for comments on a draft of this paper, to Adelard who provided the data on DUST-EXPERT and to Corin Gurr for initial discussions on the nature of arguments.

References

1. Kevin D. Ashley and Edwina L. Rissland. A case-based approach to modelling legal expertise. *IEEE Expert*, pages 70–77, Fall 1988.
2. British Standards Institution, London, UK. *Functional safety of electrical/electronic/programmable electronic safety-related systems: Part 1: General requirements*, BS IEC 61508-1:1998 edition, 1998.
3. Stefanie Brüninghaus and Kevin D. Ashley. Towards adding knowledge to learning algorithms for indexing legal cases. In *The Seventh International Conference on Artificial Intelligence and Law*, pages 9–17, The University of Oslo, Norway, June 1999. ACM.
4. Tim Clement, Ian Cottam, Peter Froome, and Claire Jones. The development of a commercial "shrink-wrapped application" to safety integrity level 2: The DUST-EXPERT^{TM} story. In *SAFECOMP 1999*, pages 216–225, 1999.
5. Bob Fields, Michael Harrison, and Peter Wright. THEA: Human error analysis for requirements definition. Technical Report YCS-97-294, The University of York, Department of Computer Science, 1997. UK.
6. Tim P. Kelly. *Arguing Safety – A Systematic Approach to Managing Safety Cases*. PhD thesis, Department of Computer Science, The University of York, 1999.
7. Trevor Kletz. *Hazop and Hazan: Identifying and Assessing Process Industrial Hazards*. Institution of Chemical Engineers, third edition, 1992. ISBN 0-85295-285-6.
8. William J. Pardi. *XML in Action: Web Technology*. IT Professional. Microsoft Press, Redmond, Washington, 1999.
9. Enric Plaza. Cases as terms: A feature term approach to the structured representation of cases. In *First International Conference on Case-based Reasoning*, pages 265–276, 1995.
10. Steven Pocock, Michael Harrison, Peter Wright, and Paul Johnson. THEA – a technique for human error assessment early in design. In Michitaka Hirose, editor, *Human-Computer Interaction: INTERACT'01*, pages 247–254. IOS Press, 2001.
11. David. J. Pumfrey. *The Principled Design of Computer System Safety Analysis*. PhD thesis, Department of Computer Science, The University of York, 2000.
12. Stephen E. Toulmin. *The uses of arguments*. Cambridge University Press, Cambridge, 1958.

Service Oriented Programming:
A New Paradigm of Software Reuse

Alberto Sillitti[1], Tullio Vernazza[1], and Giancarlo Succi[2]

[1] DIST – Università di Genova, Via Opera Pia 13, I-16145 Genova, Italy
{alberto, tullio}@dist.unige.it

[2] Libera Università di Bolzano,
Domenikaner Pl 3 P.zza Domenicani, I-39100 Bolzano, Italy
Giancarlo.Succi@unibz.it

Abstract. In recent years, web sites have evolved from simple collections of static content to suppliers of complex services to users. This evolution has allowed users to benefit from various customized services according to his needs. Currently many services are geographically-aware and they have localized features but do not communicate with systems that are complementary from a geographic of functional perspectives. However, the geographic extensity is a natural dimension on which simple services can be integrated into complex ones. This integration requires a container to provide a common and unifying view of the territory. A GIS with topological information is the ideal mapping for services that pertain to a given territory. Integration provides a way to create new services through reusing services that provide only a subset of functionality that could be used in very different integrated services. This paper analyzes the integration issues of localized services using a GIS.

1 Introduction

The current idea of software reuse was born with the Object Oriented Programming and then it evolved through components producing a set of incompatible standards. Nowadays there is a new paradigm of software reuse through services that are available online on the Internet.

The World Wide Web is a huge source of services, among them there are many geographically-aware ones: train [11] and flight [1] schedules, monitoring of the environment [18], and local information [9] are examples. Many of these services have localized features but they are too application specific ignoring the global structure of the environment. Very rarely a complete solution is available from a single source [3].

For instance, a traveler, to collect information to reach a far place, needs to split the task into many sub-task. Probably, they have to search for a bus near home to reach a railway station, then for a train to reach an airport and then for another train and/or a bus to reach the destination. Moreover these tasks are constraints dependent because the n+1 vehicle has to leave after the arrival of the n one. Introducing delays that

C. Gacek (Ed.): ICSR-7, LNCS 2319, pp. 269–280, 2002.

could affect every vehicle, this scenario could become more and more complex. A user cannot handle this complexity manually, so he, usually, supposes that most of vehicles are on time or affected by a fixed delay. This hypothesis could be fulfilled only sometimes, this means that a traveler can often experiment difficulties during a journey if delays were not predicted.

An automated system could easily handle a wider set of connections. This system has to know not only service specific information, but also further information related to the territory to relate services with each other in order to automate decisions that usually are made by human beings. Knowledge about the territory could be stored into a GIS because of the easy access and high performance that they provide. In this way an automated system can easily map services to a given territory.

Service Oriented Programming is a natural evolution of the traditional component based software development. This new technique is mainly web oriented but it allows exploitation of legacy systems that are not designed to be deployed through the Internet. In this way, a developer doesn't need to rewrite any piece of code to deploy data on the Internet or integrate information from this kind of systems with other sources. Only a translation of data is needed to establish a connection to other data sources [30].

This paper analyzes the integration issues of localized services using a GIS and its implementation through an integration architecture named AIR (Automated Information Router).

This paper is organized as follows: section 2 analyzes different way to develop applications integrating existing software; section 3 discuss service oriented programming focusing on the integration architecture, problems in service integration and AIR implementation; section 4 presents a case study; finally, section 5 draws the conclusions.

2   Integration Oriented Programming

2.1   Component-Based Programming

In the last 35 years software development has moved from extremely large and monolithic code to component base development [8] [22].

This transition creates problems related to components communication and compatibility. Many standards were developed like COM [6], CORBA [7] and EJB [15].

Usually, these components are simple and encapsulate very specific feature like statistic, graphics or e-mail functions. Once a developer chooses a component standard he can use only ones that are selected specification compliant and none of the others.

2.2   Package Oriented Programming

A way to develop new applications through integration is the package oriented programming (POP) [21].

This technique exploits mass-market applications, like Microsoft Office, as large components integrating their functionality to provide a user familiar new product with low costs. This technique is usually platform dependant because it is not possible to integrate components running on different platforms.

This is an important limit because each one provides different and specific applications that could be used as high quality components.

2.3 Service Oriented Programming

The Internet provides a large number of simple services that could be integrated to produce new and more complex ones [10]. Service integration is becoming a necessity due to specific services that are available but they are not user friendly if it is required to perform a complex task.

Web services could be considered components due to three features:
1. They are developed and deployed independently.
2. Encapsulate functionality and hide implementation details.
3. Expose interfaces.

The last point is of particular interest in the integration community. New standards, like WIDL (Web Interface Definition Language) [28] and WSDL (Web Service Description Language) [29], are emerging and play similar roles to the IDL (Interface Definition Language) in CORBA and other component technologies.

In this way component base programming could be applied to these non conventional components to develop integrated web services.

Moreover service integration solve some problems of component base programming and package oriented programming:

- It is possible and quite easy to integrate components based on different technologies using a specific adapter that converts requests from one communication protocol to another one.
- The platform used to develop and deploy services does not matter. The best platform for every single application can be chosen.

Usually, web services are very application specific and they are not able to solve wide range problems. Due to this specificity, they have a very limited knowledge of the real world. For instance, an air company service considers only airplane departures and arrivals but it cannot help users to reach the airport or the final destination. There are similar problems in every territory aware service because their knowledge is only partial.

To provide a useful integrated service, an automated system would handle nearly the whole knowledge related to the problem it has to solve. This knowledge is rarely available from a single source, but it could be available integrating many sources. This integration allows a developer to provide a new system reusing already developed and deployed services.

Service integration allow reusing not only software components but also their deployment. This is a new paradigm of software reuse that benefits by already running applications avoiding all the effort needed to build and setup the environment required by the specific software component.

Reusing service software already deployed produce two main benefits:

1. It is possible to exploit components that run inside incompatible environments (operating systems, software libraries, etc.)
2. No time and effort is required to developers to setup the working environment: it is already configured and working on a remote machine waiting for a request

These benefits allow the construction of a system without any worry about the compatibility of the execution environment, required by components, and the effort spent to build it up allowing developers to focus on the problem they have to solve.

3   Principles of Service Oriented Programming

3.1   The Integration Architecture

AIR (Figure 1) is both a client and a server: it is a client of elementary services, and a server of the complex integrated services it implements. The architecture comprises several modules, each handling a different protocol (including HTTP [13], SOAP [20], XML-RPC [26], and RMI [17]).

The architecture comprises three fundamental parts: the integration networks, the builder, and the controller.

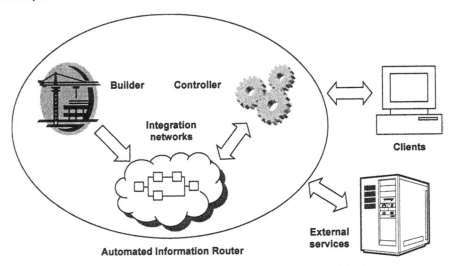

Fig. 1. AIR architecture overview

An integration network is the abstraction of an integration. It is a set of nodes and arcs (Figure 2) building a data flow diagram that routes information. Nodes perform elementary functions like access to local resources (files and database), access to external services, and transformations. Arcs connect nodes and describe the path followed by data that are coded as XML documents.

The builder initializes the system reading the configuration file and creating the integration networks in memory: it creates nodes characterized by specific parameters and connects them. After this initialization it activates the controller that manages the system at run-time.

The controller is a collection of specific protocol servers like RMI, HTTP/HTML, SOAP, etc. It is the integration server interface that manage translations from protocol specific request to a common XML format used inside integration networks.

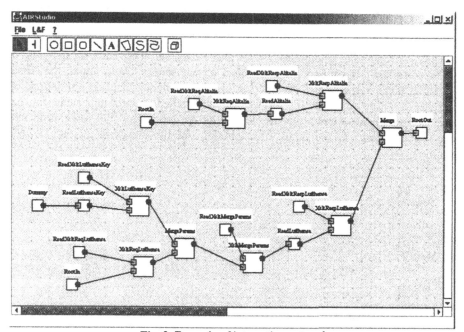

Fig. 2. Example of integration network

Inside the integration network, the information processing is managed through dataflow [14]. To simplify nodes and connections, the only data type used is XML document.

This restriction does not affect interoperability of AIR because outside the network there is the controller that handles connections with clients using different protocols and performing data format conversions through a simple syntactic translation. This translation allows AIR to reuse a wide set of already deployed services and provides an access point to different kind of clients that could not exploit services based on protocols that they do not support natively. In such cases AIR works as an interface adapter.

AIR queries the various services, converts information into a common XML [12] [25] representation and handles the information routing between the various modules. The integration is focused on web services, as this technology has developed standards that allow interoperability also between services originally not conceived for integration.

Similar services may require queries expressed in different terms, which leads to syntactic or semantic incompatibility. A syntactic incompatibility is, e.g., the difference in names of query parameters. A semantic incompatibility is, e.g., when two or more terms – that are no synonyms – addresses the same thing or partially equivalent things. In airline timetable integration one airline requires city names while another requires airport codes and there is a one-to-many relationship between cities and airports. AIR supports mappings and transformation templates to overcome such incompatibilities. Actually there is no way to generate mapping data automatically, these data are generated manually and stored into a database. Before AIR accesses a service, it queries this database to translate all terms in the request to adapt it to the specific service.

Finally, AIR handles anomalies in the elementary services, such as network or application failures. If not handled, a problem on one service could impair the whole integration. Since in most cases the services are complementary and do not depend on each other, a failure on one of the services can be handled by omitting results for that single service. In these cases the overall results are partial but the integration still works. Simple forms of redundancy are possible for the most critical parts of the integration.

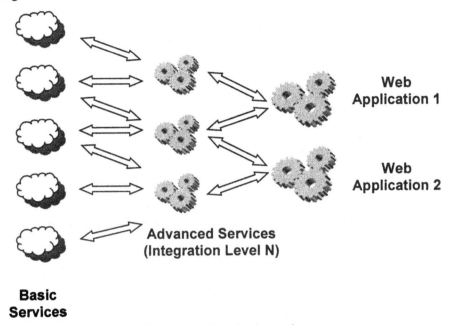

Fig. 3. Layered service integration

To construct a complex service, often many levels of integration are required. Basic services could be integrated to provide advanced services that are characterized by more complex properties. These properties could be both functional and non functional (e.g. reliability and performance). Moreover advanced services can be integrated to provide a web application or a further level of advanced service (Figure 3).

Advanced services provide a further way to reuse web services because the same basic service could be included inside many different advanced ones.

3.2 Problems in Service Integration

There are several problems when we try to integrate different services. Some of them are issues about services compatibility, others are about services non functional abilities.

Compatibility issue includes three different interrelated problems (Figure 4):
1. Protocol: the communication protocol -e.g., HTTP, FTP, ...
2. Syntax: the language used to structure the information -e.g., XML [4].
3. Semantic: the meaning of the terms used in the language [19] [16].

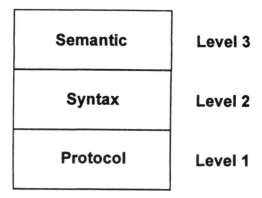

Fig. 4. Compatibility stack

Problems related to communication protocols are usually the easiest to solve. The protocols are well-defined and no subjective interpretation is allowed. It is not difficult to build an automatic translator.

In particular, the integration of different web services does not require any translations, since they all use HTTP.

Translations are often required to integrate services that are not designed for web publishing, always the case with legacy systems.

Problems related to syntax are harder, especially if a language used to code information is not machine oriented but human oriented. This is the problem of the HTML language: it is presentation oriented not content oriented. In this way an automated translator that transforms an HTML document in a more structured content oriented one, like XML, is not easy to code. Moreover, once coded it requires constant fixes due to style changes inside HTML documents. To perform these kind of data extraction XPath [27] is a useful language to make queries inside structured documents.

There are another set of problems related to service integration: non functional qualities. In service integration service level agreements (SLAs) [23] become of primary importance. Specific SLAs for basic services could allow to predict the service level of the integration. The most important non functional qualities are: response time and reliability.

The former is important because often service interrogation n+1 is performed on the basis of the result of the n one. In this way the delay of the integrated service is the sum of basic services delays. Therefore, bandwidth available is rising up [5] and it makes this problem easier to be solved.

The latter involves replaceability of basic services that could be unavailable for a while. If this is not possible integrated services are not available every time one of its component is not available. Public registers, such as UDDI [24], are working to allowing to find automatically services that fulfill desired functional and non functional qualities.

4   Sample Application of the System to GIS

The case study presented in this paper treat the integration of two kind of transportation: train and airplane.

Several airlines and train companies provide querying of time-tables through their web sites. These services allow fast and easy access to information, otherwise available only in paper form or through information-desks. In many cases, more than one company offer transportation services on the same geographic area. For users, this means that to find the best transportation solution, several services need to be browsed and compared.

An automatic system that integrates the many services for a same territory could simplify the querying and comparison. Using AIR, the authors have developed an integrated system that gives users a single access point and does - in the background - all the queries to the various services needed to fulfil the user's request (Figure 5). The requests are specified in terms of origin, destination, date of travel, and preferred transportation means.

A GIS provides position of cities, calculates distances, provides information on available train stations and airports in a city. The integration of GIS information with time-tables, fares, and optimization algorithms allows the identification of the best solutions - in terms of distance, time, or expenses - according to the user's preferences (Figure 6).

It may occur the actual transit times do not correspond with planned timetables due to, for instance, delays. Travelling users may want to be informed of such situations by the integration service through cell-phone messages (or other messaging technologies). This problem highlights another integration requirement because actual departure/arrival times of airplanes are reported on the real-time web services of airports, rather than of airlines.

In this case study all services are redundant except the GIS system, because this is the only service available from the intranet, so it could be considered reliable enough in our application. On the contrary, web available services are not under our control and we don't know their service levels, so redundancy is required.

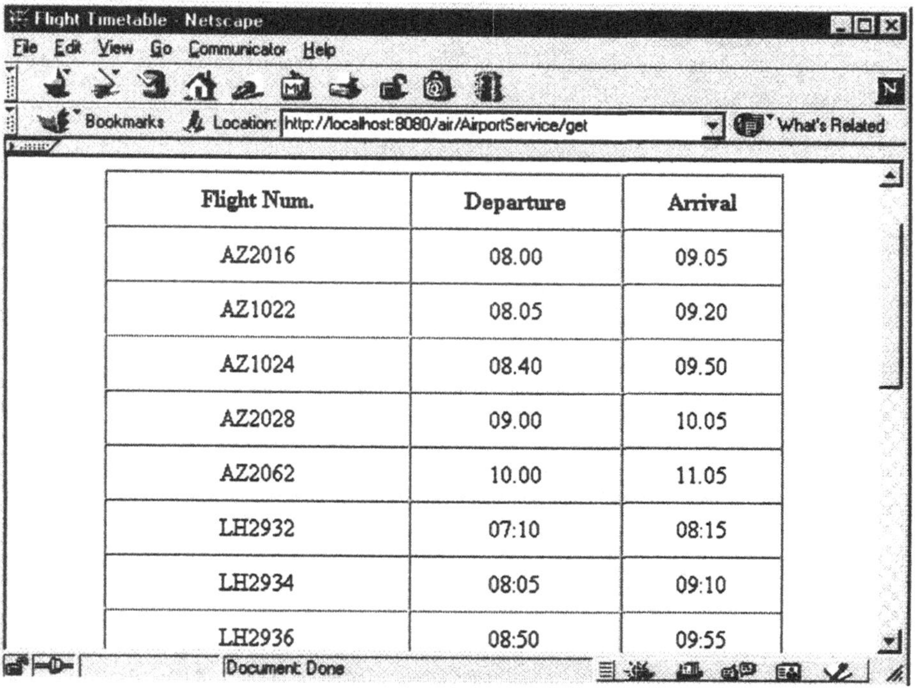

Flight Num.	Departure	Arrival
AZ2016	08.00	09.05
AZ1022	08.05	09.20
AZ1024	08.40	09.50
AZ2028	09.00	10.05
AZ2062	10.00	11.05
LH2932	07:10	08:15
LH2934	08:05	09:10
LH2936	08:50	09:55

Fig. 5. Sample of airline timetable integration

5 Conclusion and Future Work

The paper has proposed a way to integrate services that are available over the World Wide Web providing a new kind of customized services through an integration architecture called AIR. This integration is made using data-flow paradigm to route information and adapters that translate service specific data to a common representation using XML.

The web is currently designed for human oriented interfaces (HTML) without a language coded semantic interpretation that makes data hard to process by an automated system. The transition to languages that code semantic will allow the develop of more complex integrated services that are high value to users.

Public registers of services are becoming reality as languages to describe their functional and non functional qualities and their interfaces. In this way it is possible to build an integration server that not only integrates developer chosen services but it will choose the best basic services at run-time when the user request arrives, adapting its queries to interface and data translations automatically to the chosen ones.

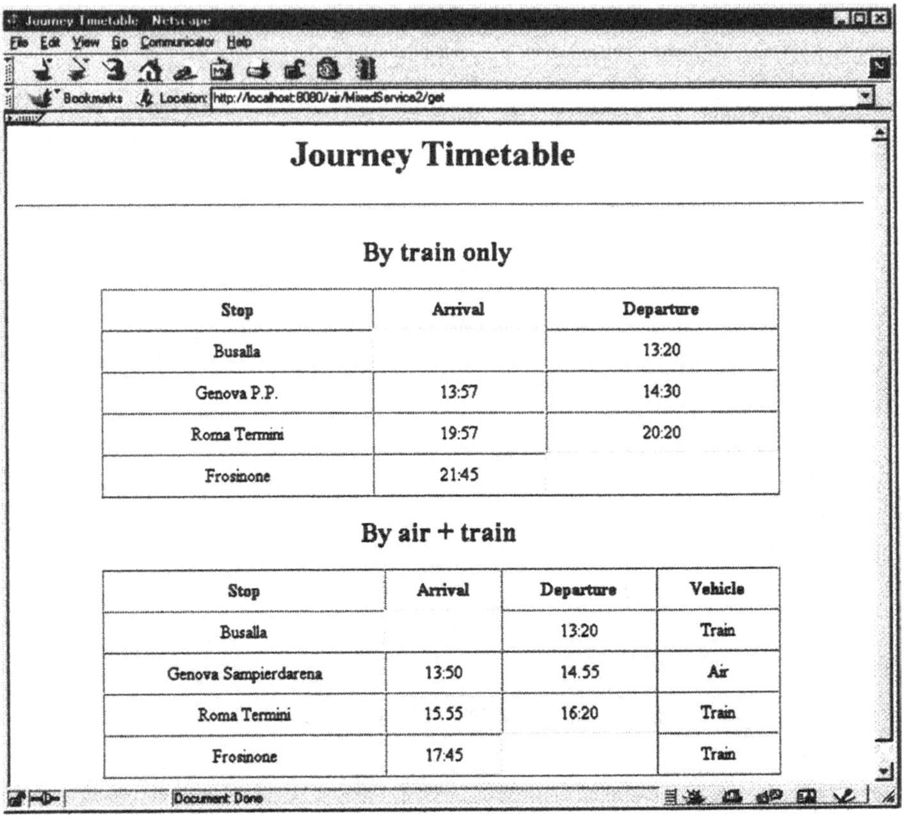

Journey Timetable

By train only

Stop	Arrival	Departure
Busalla		13:20
Genova P.P.	13:57	14:30
Roma Termini	19:57	20:20
Frosinone	21:45	

By air + train

Stop	Arrival	Departure	Vehicle
Busalla		13:20	Train
Genova Sampierdarena	13:50	14.55	Air
Roma Termini	15.55	16:20	Train
Frosinone	17:45		Train

Fig. 6. Sample query result

Acknowledgements

The first two authors thank Paolo Predonzani for his insightful comments to early versions of this work, and the European Union for partially funding this work.

The third author acknowledges the support of the Free University of Bozen, the Natural Science and Engineering Research Council of Canada, the Government of Alberta and University of Alberta.

References

1. Alitalia web site - http://www.alitalia.it/
2. Beringer D., Melloul L., Wiederhold G., "A Reuse and Composition Protocol for Services", Proceedings of the fifth symposium on Software reusability, May 1999.
3. Bouguettaya A., Benatallah B., Hendra L., Ouzzani M., Beard J., "Supporting Dynamic Interaction among Web-Based Information Sources", IEEE Transactions on Knowledge and Data Engineering, Vol. 12, No. 5, September/October 2000.
4. Ciancarini P., Vitali F., Mascolo C., "Managing Complex Documents Over the WWW: A Case Study for XML", IEEE Transactions on Knowledge and Data Engineering, Vol. 11, No. 4, July/August 1999.
5. Coffman K.G., Odlyzko A.M., "Internet growth: Is there a "Moore's Law" for data traffic?", Handbook of Massive Data Sets, J. Abello, P. M. Pardalos, and M. G. C. Resende, eds., Kluwer, 2001.
6. COM (Component Object Model) - specifications: http://www.microsoft.com/com/
7. CORBA (Common Object Request Broker Architecture) - specifications: http://www.corba.org/
8. Dahl O.J., Nygaard K., "SIMULA – An Algol Based Simulation Language." Comm. ACM, 9 (9), p. 671-678, 1966.
9. DigitalCity web site - http://www.digitalcity.com/
10. Emmerich W., Ellmer E., Fieglein H., "TIGRA – An Architectural Style for Enterprise Application Integration", Proc. 23th Int'l Conf. Software Eng., IEEE CS Press, Toronto, Ontario, Canada, 2001.
11. German railways web site - Web Site: http://www.bahn.de/
12. Goldfarb C.F., Prescod P., The XML Handbook, 3rd edition, Prentice Hall Computer Books, 2000.
13. HTTP 1.1 – specifications: http://www.ietf.org/rfc/rfc2616.txt
14. Kozar K.A., "The Technique of Data Flow Diagramming", http://spot.colorado.edu/~kozar/DFDtechnique.html, 1997.
15. Matena V., Hapner M., "Enterprise Java Beans Specification 1.1", Sun Microsystems, 1999.
16. Poo D.C.C., Toh T.K., Khoo C.S.G., "Enhancing online catalog searches with an electronic referencer", The Journal of Systems and Software, 55, 2000.
17. RMI (Remote Method Invocation) – specifications: http://java.sun.com/rmi/
18. Scorecard web site – http://www.scorecard.org/
19. Singh N., "Unifying Heterogeneous Information Models", Communications of the ACM, Vol. 41, No. 5, May 1998.
20. SOAP (Simple Object Access Protocol) – specifications: http://www.w3.org/TR/SOAP/
21. Sullivan K.J., Cockrell J., Zhang Z., Coppit D., "Package-Oriented Programming and Engineering Tools", Proc. 22th Int'l Conf. Software Eng., IEEE CS Press, Los Alamitos, CA, USA, 2000.
22. Szyperski C., "Component Software", Addison-Wesley, 1998.
23. The Service Level Management Learning Community web site: http://www.nextslm.org/
24. UDDI (Universal Description, Discovery and Integration) – web site: http://www.uddi.org/
25. XML (Extensible Markup Language) 1.0 – specifications: http://www.w3.org/TR/2000/REC-xml-20001006/
26. XML-RPC (XML Remote Procedure Call) – specifications: http://www.xmlrpc.com/
27. XPath (XML Path Language) 1.0 – specifications: http://www.w3.org/TR/xpath/

28. WIDL (Web Interface Definition Language) – specifications:
    http://www.w3.org/TR/NOTE-widl/
29. WSDL (Web Service Description Language) – specifications:
    http://www.w3.org/TR/wsdl/
30. Zhao Y., "WebEntree: A Web Service Aggregator", IBM Systems Journal, Vol. 37, No. 4,
    1998.

An Empirical User Study
of an Active Reuse Repository System

Yunwen Ye[1,2]

[1] SRA Key Technology Laboratory, Inc., 3-12 Yotsuya, Shinjuku, Tokyo, 160-004, Japan
[2] Department of Computer Science, University of Colorado, Boulder, CO80309-430, USA
yunwen@cs.colorado.edu

Abstract. This paper reports an empirical user study of an active reuse repository system. Instead of waiting passively for software developers to initiate the component location process with a well-defined reuse query, active reuse repository systems infer reuse queries from syntactic and semantic cues present in partially constructed programs in development environments, and proactively deliver components that match the inferred reuse queries. The reported empirical user study of an implemented active reuse repository system called *CodeBroker* shows that active repository systems promote reuse by motivating and enabling software developers to reuse components whose existence is not anticipated, and reducing the cost of reuse through the automation of the component location process.

1 Introduction

One factor that inhibits the widespread success of systematic software reuse is the problem of *no attempt to reuse*—software developers construct new systems from scratch rather than reusing existing software components from a reuse repository. According to previous studies [11], *no attempt to reuse* is the leading failure mode of software reuse. We are primarily concerned with the cognitive difficulties that prevent software developers from attempting to reuse: (1) the unawareness of the existence of reusable components, and (2) the lack of means to locate the wanted components [6, 21].

If software developers do not even anticipate that a component that can be reused in their current development task exists in the repository, they would not attempt to reuse. An effective reuse repository often contains numerous components (for example, the Java 1.2 core library has more than 70 packages and 2100 classes), which makes it impossible for software developers to anticipate the existence of all the components. Previous empirical studies [7] conclude that most software developers can only anticipate the existence of a limited portion of the components included in a repository, and that they would not actively seek the reuse of the components whose existence they do not know. This conclusion is corroborated by many reports [4, 5, 17] about reuse experience in companies.

Even if software developers are willing to reuse a component, they might not be able to do so if they perceive reuse costs more than developing from scratch or if they

C. Gacek (Ed.): ICSR-7, LNCS 2319, pp. 281–292, 2002.
© Springer-Verlag Berlin Heidelberg 2002

are unable to locate the component. Browsing and querying have been the principal approaches to locating components. Browsing requires that users have a fairly good understanding about the structure of the reuse repository, and it is not scalable. Querying requires that users be able to formulate a well-defined query that clearly states their information needs, which is cognitively challenging [8].

Active reuse repository systems that support information delivery mechanisms hold the potential to address the above two issues [20]. Unlike most traditional reuse repository systems that solely employ information access mechanisms (browsing and querying), which require software developers to initiate the reuse process, active reuse repository systems infer reuse queries from syntactic and semantic cues present in partially constructed programs in development environments, and proactively deliver components that match the inferred reuse queries. An active reuse repository system called *CodeBroker* has been designed and developed. This paper reports an empirical user study of the *CodeBroker* system to show how active reuse repository systems promote reuse by encouraging and enabling software developers to reuse components whose existence is not anticipated, and reducing the cost of reuse through the automation of the component location process.

2   The CodeBroker System

This section briefly describes the *CodeBroker* system, which supports Java developers by delivering *task-relevant* and *personalized* components—components that can potentially be reused in the current development task and that are not yet known to the developers (see [20, 21] for details). *CodeBroker* is seamlessly integrated with the programming environment *Emacs*. Fig. 1 shows a screen shot and the architecture of the system, which consists of an interface agent and a backend search engine. Running continuously as a background process in *Emacs*, the interface agent infers and extracts reuse queries by analyzing the partially written program in the normal editing space of *Emacs* (Figure 1a). Inferred queries are passed to the search engine, which retrieves matching components from the repository. Retrieved components are delivered by the interface agent in the delivery buffer (Fig. 1b), after it has removed the components that are contained in discourse models and user models (see below for brief discussion and [9] for details).

The reuse repository of components contains indexes created by *CodeBroker* from the standard Java documentation that *Javadoc* generates from Java source programs, and links to the Java documentation system.

CodeBroker delivers components whenever a doc comment or a signature definition is entered into the editing space. For example, in Fig. 1a, the developer wants to create a random number between two integers and writes a doc comment to indicate so. As soon as the rightmost '/' (signaling the end of a doc comment) is entered, the contents of the doc comment are extracted as a query, and components from the repository that match it are shown immediately in the delivery buffer. The similarity between a query and a component is determined by full text retrieving techniques. *CodeBroker* supports both the Latent Semantic Analysis (LSA) technique [3] and the probabilistic model [16].

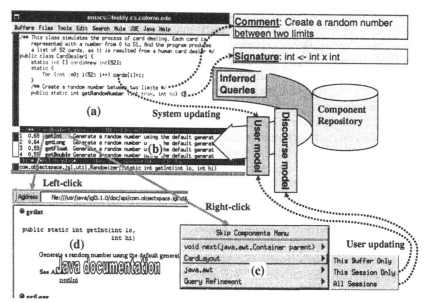

Fig. 1. The CodeBroker system

The second delivery is made at the completion of a module's signature definition. As soon as the signature definition is finished (the left bracket '{' before the cursor), *CodeBroker* extracts the signature, which is then combined with the preceding doc comment as a query to retrieve matching components. The similarity between two signatures is determined by the signature matching process [22].

CodeBroker does not deliver all components retrieved; it uses *discourse models* to filter out task-irrelevant components and *user models* to filter out user-known components [9].

Discourse models provide a way for software developers to specify which classes and packages are not of interest in the current development session. Java components are organized in packages and classes, and most programming tasks do not involve all of them. During their interactions with *CodeBroker*, if software developers find a delivered component is from a package or a class of no interest, they can add that class or package to the discourse model with the Skip Components Menu (Fig. 1c), which is activated by a right-click on a component in the delivery buffer (Fig. 1b). The Skip Components Menu has three items of different abstraction levels: The first item is the delivered method component, the second item is its class, and the third item is its package. Software developers can choose the appropriate abstraction level and then choose the This Session Only command to add it to the discourse model. If a method component is chosen, the method component will not be delivered again by *CodeBroker* in the current development session, and if a class or a package is chosen, all the components from the class or package will not be delivered again in the current session.

If software developers choose the command All Sessions instead of This Session Only in the Skip Components Menu, the component (method, class or package) goes to user models. User models contain components that individual developers know and therefore do not need to be delivered. *CodeBroker* creates initial user models for software developers by analyzing Java programs they have written and extracting all the repository components used repeatedly in the programs. During their interactions with *CodeBroker*, software developers can explicitly update their user models in the way described above.

Both discourse models and user models are used as filters by *CodeBroker* to remove unwanted components from deliveries, and are maintained through the same interface (Skip Components Menu). However, they are conceptually different. Discourse models include components that are not of interest in the *current* session no matter whether software developers know it or not, and those components need to be delivered again when a different development session starts. User models include components known to individual software developers no matter whether these components are related to the current session or not, and they persist through different development sessions.

Each delivered component is accompanied by its rank, similarity value, name, and synopsis. To avoid unwanted interruption of the normal workflow, no response to deliveries is required. Software developers can just ignore the delivery buffer if they are not interested in the deliveries. Software developers who are interested in a particular component delivered can click the component name to get the full documents for that component in an external HTML browser (Fig. 1d).

3   Structure of the Empirical User Study

The purpose of the empirical user study was to analyze how component deliveries made by *CodeBroker* promotes reuse during software development. The study attempts to answer the following questions:

(1)   Do active reuse repository systems enable software developers to reuse unknown components?

(2)   Do active reuse repository systems encourage software developers to explore the possibility of reuse?

(3)   Is the technical approach taken by *CodeBroker*—inferring reuse queries from doc comments and signatures—good enough to find components relevant to the task at hand?

(4)   Do discourse models improve the relevance of delivered components?

(5)   Do user models contribute to the personalization of component deliveries?

Five subjects, recruited from undergraduates and graduates of the Computer Science Department, University of Colorado at Boulder, voluntarily participated in the study. Two subjects had worked as professional software engineers, and the other three had been regular contributors to several open source projects. Their expertise in Java development varied, ranging from medium to expert level. All of them knew the syntax of Java very well; their expertise differed in the range of reusable components (classes and methods in Java API libraries) they knew.

Our experiments adopted both the *multi-project variation* approach, in which one subject conducted two or three different projects, and the *replicated project* approach, in which one project is conducted by two or more subjects [2]. Twelve experiments were conducted. In each experiment, the subject was asked to implement a predetermined task. Each task could be implemented with different combinations of components from the repository. The following is a sample task:

> Traditionally, Chinese write numbers with a comma inserted at each fourth number from the right. For example, 1,000,000 is written as 100,0000. Implement a program that transforms the Chinese writing format (100,0000) to the Western format (1,000,000).

Before each experiment, *CodeBroker* created initial user models for the subjects from programs they had written recently. After analyzing their user models, the subjects were assigned tasks whose best implementation would involve components they had not known. In the beginning of each experiment, the main functionality of *CodeBroker* was briefly introduced with a running example. Previous to the implementation of each task, subjects were asked to describe how they would implement the task, and at the end of each experiment, an interview was followed to capture the subjects' evaluation of the system based on their use. Subjects were told to do development in their normal way but to take advantage of the support provided by *CodeBroker*. They could use books, the Java API documentation system, and all other support as they usually did. Two subjects actually brought and consulted their favorite Java reference books.

The reuse repository used in the experiments included 673 classes and 7,338 methods from the Java 1.1.8 core API library and JGL 1.3 library (created by Objectspace, Inc.).

The automatic log mechanism of *CodeBroker* logged the reuse queries inferred, the components retrieved, and the components removed by discourse and user models. Subjects were asked to think aloud during the experiments. All experiments and interviews were videotaped and transcribed. Analyses of the experiments were based on logs and transcriptions.

4   Findings of the Empirical User Study

4.1   Reusing Unknown Components

The overall results of the empirical user study are summarized in Table 1. Subjects reused delivered components during 10 of the 12 experiments. The 12 programs created by the subjects used 57 distinct components, 20 of which were delivered by *CodeBroker*. Of the 20 reused components that were delivered, the subjects did not anticipate the existence of 9 (column 5). In other words, those 9 components could not have been reused without the support of *CodeBroker*, and the subjects would have created their own solutions instead. As two subjects commented in the interviews:

> "I would have never looked up the roll function by myself; I would have done a lot of stuff by hand. Just because it showed up in the list, I saw the Calendar provided the roll feature that allowed me to do the task."

> "I did not know the isDigit thing. I would have wasted time to design that thing."

Table 1. Overall results of the user study

1	2	3	4	Breakdown of reused components from deliveries		7	8	9	10	11
				5	6					
Subject	Experiment no.	Total no. of distinct components reused	No. of distinct components reused from deliveries	No. of components whose existence was unanticipated	No. of unknown components whose existence was anticipated	No. of reused components triggered by deliveries	Total no. of retrieved components	No. of components removed by discourse models	No. of components removed by user models	Rating on usefulness of the system (1: worst 10: best)
S1	1	10	4	2	2	0	168	45	15	7
	2	3	1	1	0	1	28	10	0	
S2	3	7	1	1	0	0	140	0	5	4
	4	4	1	1	0	0	52	0	0	
	5	5	3	0	3	1	160	0	14	
S3	6	5	2	1	1	1	60	0	0	8.5
	7	4	3	1	2	1	20	0	1	
	8	3	0	0	0	0	60	0	0	
S4	9	4	3	0	3	0	80	7	0	7
	10	3	1	1	0	2	140	68	0	
S5	11	4	1	1	0	2	100	0	1	8
	12	5	0	0	0	0	420	0	0	
Sum		57	20	9	11	8	1428	130	36	

Although the subjects anticipated the existence of the other 11 components (column 6), they had never reused them before, knowing neither the names nor the functionality. They might have reused the 11 components if they could manage to locate them by themselves. In interviews, subjects acknowledged that *CodeBroker* made locating them much easier and faster.

> "I did not have to start browsing and go through the packages, and I did not have to go through the index of methods. I could just go to the short list [in the delivery buffer], find it and click it."

> "The key benefit of this [CodeBroker] is that it gives you methods for every class, not like this one [the Java documentation system] that you have to first find which class it is in and then go to the class. Although it has index of methods, it is hard to find."

Active reuse repository systems not only supported subjects in reusing components right off the deliveries, but also triggered them to reuse other unknown components (column 7) that were not directly delivered but were needed to reuse the delivered components. To reuse one component often requires the reuse of other supplementary components that are coupled through parameter passing or accessing common class variables. In the experiments, when those supplementary components were not known, subjects used the deliveries of *CodeBroker* as the starting point and followed the hyperlinks of the documentation system to learn and reuse them.

4.2   Increasing Reuse Possibility

The relative success of ad hoc software reuse indicates that software developers tend toward constructing new systems centered on the components they know [19]. However, successful systematic reuse requires that software developers be able to create new systems centered on not only the components they know but also the components they do not yet know. Because the components timely delivered by active reuse repository systems are immediately accessible to software developers, they can create new systems with previously unknown components in a similar way as they do with known components. This claim is best illustrated with the different approaches taken by subjects S2, S3, and S5 when they implemented the task described in Section 0.

In describing his implementation plan, S3 anticipated that some methods from the `java.text.NumberFormat` class might help him read numbers in Chinese format and write it out in Western format, although he did not know exactly what those methods were. As a result, he constructed his program concisely using the methods that were delivered by *CodeBroker* and that he had anticipated. Subject S5, who did not even know the existence of the `java.text` package, described as his implementation plan that he was going "to parse the number, take out the commas and insert the commas." As S5 started programming, however, he changed his original plan after he had noticed a delivered component from the `java.text.NumberFormat` class, and created a program similar to that of S3. Subject S2, who did not know the `java.text.NumberFormat` class either, described a plan like S5's original one. Because no component from the `java.text.NumberFormat` class was delivered based on his comments, he stuck to his original plan and constructed a different program.

In the experiments, we observed several other occasions similar to the above example in which delivered components stimulated subjects to change their original plans to a new implementation approach that favored reuse.

4.3   Effectiveness of Delivering Components Based on Inferred Reuse Queries

CodeBroker infers reuse queries from doc comments and signatures contained in the program being worked in the editor. The effectiveness of delivering task-relevant components depends on the quality of doc comments written by software developers and the retrieval mechanisms used.

The more knowledge subjects had about the repository, the better were their doc comments used to retrieve relevant components. One subject described why he wrote one particular comment as:

> "I knew there should be a class called `NumberFormat` or `DecimalFormat` having the method `format`...That's why I wrote the word 'format' because I knew it would catch those."

As a result, he found what he expected from the deliveries of *CodeBroker*.

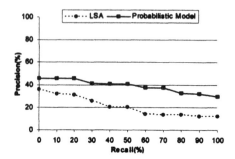

Fig. 2. Recall-precision curves

Different subjects had different styles of writing comments. Some wrote very long and elaborate comments to describe everything they wanted to do. Others wrote concise comments focusing on the major task of the program. Because descriptions of components in the repository were short and concise, the short and focused comments made the delivered components more task-relevant.

The ratio of the number of reused components to the total number of retrieved components is rather low (column 8 in Table 1 shows the total number of components retrieved in each experiment). However, this does not mean that the other retrieved components that were not reused by subjects were not relevant because subjects needed only a small subset of the retrieved relevant components to accomplish their tasks. A relatively objective way of evaluating the effectiveness of retrieval mechanisms is to compute their recall and precision [18]. Recall is the proportion of relevant material actually retrieved in answers to a query; and precision is the proportion of retrieved material that is actually relevant. Figure 2 shows the recall-precision curves for the results of executing 19 queries with the two retrieval mechanisms (LSA and probabilistic model) supported in *CodeBroker*. We created a half of the queries, and collected the other half from empirical experiments and frequently asked questions in Java-related newsgroups. Only those components that could be reused in implementing the task described by the queries were determined as relevant. Because the probabilistic model mechanism had a better performance than LSA, we used the former in the user study.

The signature matching mechanism did not play too much of a role in the experiments. Only one subject tried once to look at the change of delivery when he finished the signature declaration of a method, but the system failed to improve the task-relevance of the delivery because there was not any component in the repository that was both similar in comments and compatible in signatures to the task of the subject. In all other experiments, subjects shifted their attention to the delivery buffer immediately after they had written the comments. When they found the wanted components, they moved back to programming and did not pay any attention to the delivery buffer until they wrote the next doc comment. The original design goal of adopting the signature matching mechanism in *CodeBroker* was to help developers find components that could be reused to replace the module under development. However, in the experiments, all subjects used the system to look for components that could be reused as parts of the module implementation instead of components to replace their intended implementation. The system is apparently more effective in delivering implementation parts than delivering replacement components.

Most subjects, when asked how well the deliveries made by *CodeBroker* supported their programming, appreciated the usefulness of the system (see column 11 for their ratings).

4.4 The Role of Discourse Models

Discourse models, when created, improved the task-relevance of delivered components by filtering out components of packages and classes in which the subject was not currently interested. In four experiments, subjects added uninterested packages and classes to their discourse models, which removed about 10% percent of retrieved components from the deliveries (column 9). A careful examination of those removed components found that they could not be reused in implementing the tasks in the corresponding experiments.

4.5 The Role of User Models

The experiments, however, did not yield strong and conclusive data regarding the role of user models. Only 2% of the retrieved components were filtered by user models (column 10). That might be due to two reasons: (1) initial user models were not complete because subjects did not give us all the Java programs written by them; and (2) to observe the effectiveness of delivering unknown components, subjects were assigned the tasks that involved the part of the repository they did not know very well, and, consequently, most delivered components were unknown. In the interviews, all subjects said they did not find too many known components were delivered. Nevertheless, user models helped and were needed to reduce the number of irrelevant components to be delivered because a careful examination of components removed by user models showed they could not be reused in the tasks.

4.6 Some Problems of *CodeBroker*

The experiments also found several problems of *CodeBroker*, which include the delivery of irrelevant components and simplistic user modeling technique.

Irrelevant Components. Although the system delivered many task-relevant components, it also delivered many irrelevant components. Most subjects would have liked the deliveries of the system to be more "focused" on their tasks. However, they also acknowledged that if they could find something immediately useful from the deliveries, they would like to use the system even if the deliveries were not "focused" enough.

In the experiments, subjects were asked to implement two or three unrelated tasks; therefore, the benefits of user models and discourse models were not fully utilized. As software developers continue using the system for a relative longer time, the number of irrelevant components can be expected to be reduced.

Simplistic User Models. Current user modeling technique in *CodeBroker* is too simple. It does not have a forgetting mechanism incorporated to decide when to remove from user models those components that have not been reused by software developers for a long time because they might have forgot the components.

5 Related Work

Many reuse repository systems (for a nice survey, see [13]) have been developed, and most of them have focused on indexing and retrieval mechanisms. Active reuse repository systems focus on a new interaction style that enables software developers to reuse components without a conscientious mode change between the reuse process and the development process.

Evaluations of reuse repository systems are mostly limited to compute recall and precision of their retrieval mechanisms. Different retrieval mechanisms are compared in [12] and [14], which conclude that the full text indexing and retrieval mechanism, which is also used in *CodeBroker*, has a comparable retrieval effectiveness to other more complicated and time-consuming retrieval mechanisms, such as the multi-faceted representation mechanism [15]. Our research is unique because we do not study reuse repository systems as stand-alone systems; instead, we investigate the role of active reuse repository systems in the context of software development.

Empirical studies that are based on interview and questionnaire are another approach to understand software developers' general perspectives on reuse. Based on interviews with many developers in four companies, Fichman and Kemerer [5] identify many barriers to the success of reuse. Frakes and Fox [10] take a questionnaire-based approach to analyze the major problems in software reuse.

Research that studies how reuse influences the productivity and quality of software development [1] complements our study. We assume reuse is a desirable thing, and focus our research on how to promote reuse with active reuse repository systems.

6 Discussions and Future Research

The success of an active reuse repository system hinges on how many cues it can obtain from software developers' working environments to infer their needs for a component and retrieve that component autonomously. Currently, the performance of *CodeBroker* is affected by the quality of doc comments and documents of components. We are investigating more sophisticated mechanisms to retrieve and deliver components based on other cues in software development environments.

Reuse takes place in different phases of software development. The granularity of reusable artifacts varies in different phases, but in all phases, software developers must be able to locate the needed artifacts. The underlying design principles of

CodeBroker can be extended to other phases of software development, and similar support can be provided.

We should be careful in extrapolating our findings from the experiments with *CodeBroker*, in which the repository consisted of components that were of very high quality, carefully documented, and highly trusted by software developers. Subjects were very motivated to learn how to reuse those relevant components delivered by the system. We need to do more experiments to investigate whether the same conclusion holds with repositories that come from a less respected source.

To better understand the benefits and problems of active reuse repository systems, we plan to conduct more experiments in natural settings. We will ask interested software developers to use *CodeBroker* in their daily development practice, and conduct analysis based on automatically collected logs and routine interviews.

7 Conclusions

This paper described an empirical user study that investigated the effectiveness of promoting reuse with active reuse repository systems. The user study shows that active reuse repository systems promote reuse by supporting the reuse of unanticipated components, reducing the cost of locating components, and augmenting software developers' capability in constructing new programs with components. The inferred reuse queries and the retrieval mechanisms are not perfect in delivering all of the task-relevant components and the task-relevant components only, nonetheless, they are quite effective in helping software developers find what they want. Discourse models improve the task-relevance of delivered components, and user models help to personalize the deliveries to the background knowledge of individual software developers.

References

1. Basili, V., Briand, L., and Melo, W.: How reuse influences productivity in objectoriented systems. *Communications of the ACM*, **39**(10):104-116, 1996.
2. Basili, V.R., Selby, R.W., and Hutchen, D.H.: Experimentation in software engineering. *IEEE Transactions on Software Engineering*, **12**(7):733-743, 1986.
3. Deerwester, S., et al.: Indexing by latent semantic analysis. *Journal of the American Society for Information Science*, **41**(6):391-407, 1990.
4. Devanbu, P., et al.: LASSIE: A knowledge-based software information system. *Communications of the ACM*, **34**(5):34-49, 1991.
5. Fichman, R.G. and Kemerer, C.E.: Object technology and reuse: Lessons from early adopters. *IEEE Software*, **14**(10):47-59, 1997.
6. Fischer, G.: Cognitive view of reuse and redesign. *IEEE Software*, **4**(4):60-72, 1987.
7. Fischer, G.: User modeling in human-computer interaction. *User Modeling and User-Adapted Interaction*, **11**(1&2):65-86, 2001.
8. Fischer, G., Henninger, S., and Redmiles, D.: Cognitive tools for locating and comprehending software objects for reuse, in *Proceedings of 13th International Conference on Software Engineering*. 318-328, Austin, TX, 1991.

9. Fischer, G. and Ye, Y.: Personalizing delivered information in a software reuse environment, in *Proceedings of 8th International Conference on User Modeling*. 178-187, Sonthofen, Germany, 2001.
10. Frakes, W.B. and Fox, C.J.: Sixteen questions about software reuse. *Communications of the ACM*, **38**(6):75-87, 1995.
11. Frakes, W.B. and Fox, C.J.: Quality improvement using a software reuse failure modes model. *IEEE Transactions on Software Engineering*, **22**(4):274-279, 1996.
12. Frakes, W.B. and Pole, T.P.: An empirical study of representation methods for reusable software components. *IEEE Transactions on Software Engineering*, **20**(8):617-630, 1994.
13. Mili, A., Mili, R., and Mittermeir, R.T.: A survey of software reuse libraries, in Frakes, W., (ed.) *Systematic software reuse*. 317-347, Baltzer Science, Bussum, The Netherlands, 1998.
14. Mili, H., et al.: Another nail to the coffin of faceted controlled-vocabulary component classification and retrieval, in *Proceedings of SSR'97*. 89-98, Boston, MA, 1997.
15. Prieto-Diaz, R.: Implementing faceted classification for software reuse. *Communications of the ACM*, **34**(5):88-97, 1991.
16. Robertson, S.E. and Walker, S.: Some simple effective approximations to the 2-poisson model for probabilistic weighted retrieval, in *Proceedings of the 17th International ACM-SIGIR Conference*. 232-241, Dublin, Ireland, 1994.
17. Rosenbaum, S. and DuCastel, B.: Managing software reuse—an experience report, in *Proceedings of 17th International Conference on Software Engineering*. 105-111, Seattle, WA, 1995.
18. Salton, G. and McGill, M.J.: *Introduction to modern information retrieval*, McGraw-Hill, New York, 1983.
19. Sen, A.: The role of opportunism in the software design reuse process. *IEEE Transactions on Software Engineering*, **23**(7):418-436, 1997.
20. Ye, Y. and Fischer, G.: Promoting reuse with active reuse repository systems, in *Proceedings of the 6th ICSR*. 302-317, Vienna, Austria, 2000.
21. Ye, Y., Fischer, G., and Reeves, B.: Integrating active information delivery and reuse repository systems, in *Proceedings of ACM-SIGSOFT 8th Internationa Symposium on Foundations of Software Engineering*. 60-68, San Diego, CA, 2000.
22. Zaremski, A.M. and Wing, J.M.: Signature matching: A tool for using software libraries. *ACM Transactions on Software Engineering and Methodology*, **4**(2):146-170, 1995.

Towards the Formalization
of a Reusability Framework for Refactoring

Rodrigo E. Caballero[1] and Steven A. Demurjian, Sr.[2]

[1] United Technologies Research Center,
East Hartford, Connecticut 06108, U.S.A.
CaballRE@utrc.utc.com
[2] University of Connecticut, Department of Computer Science and Engineering,
Storrs, Connecticut 06269-3155, U.S.A.
steve@engr.uconn.edu

Abstract. As industry and academia embrace component and object-based design models, programming languages, technologies, and tools, they are outpacing our ability to formally define models and frameworks supporting organization and domain specific reuse. For software engineers to accurately assess potential and actual reuse of software artifacts, we must transition from ad-hoc reuse to a evaluative paradigm that achieves reuse of an organization's current and future products. Towards this goal, our previous work has provided a framework for reusability assessment of components and classes via metrics and refactoring guidelines. In this paper, we work towards the formalization of this reusability framework. Our objectives and contributions are: a set of properties for the assumptions of the reusability framework; the formalization of class coupling, class generality, and related class concepts which underlie reuse assessment and refactoring; a reusability improvement factor to capture refactoring gain (or loss); and a refactoring algorithm for improving reusability.

1   Introduction

The improvement of the software development process through the maintenance and utilization of large inventories of reusable software components has been advocated since the late 1960s [6]. The long articulated benefits of reducing risk, limiting development and maintenance costs, improving time to market, increasing quality and reliability, improving interoperability, supporting rapid prototyping, [1, 4, 17, 21, 23], etc., while touted, are difficult to prove in practice, despite our increased emphasis on component and object-based design models and programming languages (and associated technologies and tools). In the literature, reusable software has been characterized using two metrics [22]: *actual reuse*, the number of times that a software component has been previously used, and *reusability*, which estimates the relative applicability for reuse of a component in a future setting. This reusability, or *reuse potential*, is often targeted at *domain-and-organization-specific reuse*, which can total up to 80% of a product or application [7, 10]. Our interests are in domain-and-organization-specific

C. Gacek (Ed.): ICSR-7, LNCS 2319, pp. 293–308, 2002.
© Springer-Verlag Berlin Heidelberg 2002

reuse, which shifts costs to the earliest stages of the design/development process, and represents a long-term investment in reuse [20] to support entire product families of today and tomorrow. Towards that end, there must be a focused effort to develop, guidelines, standards, models, and metrics for reuse [11].

To support the process of improving reuse potential, we have developed an integrated reusability metric, framework, and tool [12–14]. In this work, we provide an annotation technique by which a software engineer can define related classes/components that are expected to be used together in future applications, marking them to indicate the *reusability level*, which can range from the general (able to solve problems in multiple contexts) to the specific (single use - will not be reused). For example, in a retailing application, a supplier would track a general Item (reusable in many business contexts), a auto-parts supplier would have a less general AutomotiveItem (reusable in that context only), and individual retailers would have a specific WalmartItem (useable only by that specific company). Given classes/components that have been annotated with reusability levels, our reusability metrics can be iteratively utilized to objectively classify and measure dependencies (couplings) within and among classes/components, identifying couplings that promote and hinder future reuse. For couplings that hinder reuse, ad-hoc refactoring guidelines are suggested, with a projected improvement in reusability.

Our major objective in this paper is to formalize the majority of our prior work [12–15], to yield a comprehensive framework that automates reusability assessment and refactoring. Specifically, the characteristics proposed in [15], namely, coupling between classes, and reusability level, can be modeled as *relations*, which are expressed as zero-one matrices, to facilitate their computational implementation, and provide a mathematical framework for the reusability analysis. Further, in this paper, we propose a *reusability improvement factor* that reflects the impact (positive or negative) on the application's reuse potential based on different refactoring operations that can be applied to a component/object-based application. Using this factor, we have significantly extended the analysis proposed in [15], by defining an algorithm for the improvement of the reuse potential of an object-oriented application. The proposed algorithm can be easily and efficiently implemented and integrated into the DRE tool (see [15] and http://www.engr.uconn.edu/~steve/DRE/dre.html).

The remainder of this paper is organized as follows. Section 2 mathematically expresses the basic concepts of an object-oriented application. Section 3 presents the assumptions of the reuse model, focusing on generality and related classes/components, and reviews a set of properties for the reuse framework. Section 4 contains a detailed discussion on couplings among classes, the transition from couplings that hinder reuse to ones that promote reuse, and a mathematical formulation that is the basis of the proposed reusability improvement factor. Section 5 describes the refactoring process via a formal algorithm that results in reusability improvement, as illustrated via an example. Section 6 discusses related work. Finally, Section 7 presents the conclusions, and ongoing and future research.

2   Object-Oriented Application Model

In this section, we define a model for an object-oriented application that supports the formalizations and algorithms in the remainder of the paper.

Definition 1: Let an object-oriented application S be the 3-tuple $(\mathcal{C}, \Gamma_I, \Gamma_m)$ where

- $\mathcal{C}$ is the set of classes, where each class C_p contains a set C_p^M of methods $m_i \in M$ such that each method m_i belongs to only one class
- Γ_I is the set of pair-wise inheritance relations of classes in $\mathcal{C}$

$$\Gamma_I = \{(C_p, C_q), C_p \in \mathcal{C} \wedge C_q \in \mathcal{C} \mid C_p \quad extends \quad C_q\} \qquad (1)$$

- Γ_m is the set of pair-wise coupling among methods

$$\Gamma_m = \{(m_i, m_j), m_i \in C_p^M \wedge m_j \in C_p^M \mid m_i \quad uses \quad m_j\} \qquad (2)$$

Using this definition, we define coupling relations between classes [16].

Definition 2: Two classes C_p and C_q are *pair-wise coupled*, when there is at least one method $m_i \in C_p^M$ that invokes a method $m_j \in C_q^M$, as represented by the relation Γ_C:

$$\Gamma_C = \{(C_p, C_q) \mid \exists m_i \in C_p^M \wedge \exists m_j \in C_q^M \wedge (m_i, m_j) \in \Gamma_m\} \qquad (3)$$

Note that this assumes that classes do not have direct access to attributes defined in other classes, i.e., access occurs via *get/set* methods. The relations Γ_I, Γ_C, and Γ_m can be represented using zero-one matrices, which is convenient for the computation implementation of the model. The set of classes $\mathcal{C}$ and the coupling relations Γ_C define a directed graph structure where the classes in $\mathcal{C}$ are nodes, and the ordered pairs in Γ_C are edges.

The pair-wise definitions of the relations Γ_I, Γ_C and Γ_m do not hold the property of transitivity, and for that reason such definitions might seem counter intuitive. Despite this fact, the definitions proposed here greatly facilitate the direct calculation of Γ_I, Γ_C and Γ_m from source code. This is a desirable feature of the model when it is implemented in a tool such as the one reported in [15]. Coupling and inheritance relations among groups of classes and methods are transitive relations that are modeled by the *connectivity relations* Γ_I^*, Γ_C^*, and Γ_m^*. These relations can be efficiently computed using Warshall's Algorithm [18].

3   Reuse Framework

In this section, we review the basic concepts and critical assumptions of the framework for analysis and measurement of object oriented reusability proposed in [12–14] and later extended in [15]. The reuse framework is based on two characteristics: *class reusability assessment* and *relations among classes*. As proposed in [13, 14], the *reusability* of a class can be either *general* or *specific*. A general class is one that is expected to be reused in future applications, while a specific class is only applicable in the current application. For example, in a retail application, an `Item` class to track products would be the general to all retail applications, while a `WalmartItem` class, a descendant of `Item`, would contain characteristics that are store specific. In a later publication [15], the model was extended to accommodate levels of generality, and, as such, better exploit the reuse potential of classes. For example, there could be a range of generality for classes that range from `Item` to `DeptStoreItem` to `DiscountStoreItem` to `WalmartItem`, clearly demonstrating four different reusability levels. This leads to the following:

Definition 3: The *reusability level* of a class C_i is denoted by G_{C_i}, where $G_{C_i} = 0$ when C_i is the most general class in the application, and $G_{C_i} = N$ ($N > 0$) when C_i is the most specific class in the application. Further, given a set of n classes $\mathcal{C}$, the *class generality vector* G is a vector such that the i-th component G_{C_i} is the reusability level of the class C_i.

Relations among classes is a characterization by the software engineer of classes that are expected to be reused together in future applications. For example, in the retail application, the `Item` class and `ItemCollection` class (the set of all `Item`s) may be related, if a software engineer decided that the two classes were always expected to be reused together. More often than not, related classes are coupled, as captured in Γ_C.

Definition 4: Two classes, C_p and C_q that are related can be defined by the Γ_R relation as follows:

$$\Gamma_R = \{(C_p, C_q), C_p \in \mathcal{C} \wedge C_q \in \mathcal{C} \mid C_p \quad \text{reused with} \quad C_q\} \tag{4}$$

Class reusability and relations among classes are an important part of a framework for reusability analysis. To augment these definitions, we propose a set of properties that represent the assumptions upon which the reuse framework is constructed.

Property 1. The parent of a class is equally general or more general than its children.

$$(C_p, C_q) \in \Gamma_I \Rightarrow G_{C_p} \geq G_{C_q} \tag{5}$$

By definition, the inheritance hierarchy relates classes where the children have more specific descriptions that build and extend on the parents. Since the children extend on the parents, the children have at least the reusability level of the parents, plus optional specific method(s). Consequently, the generality of the ancestors of a class has to be equally or more general than the class itself. For example, `WalmartItem`, which extends `Item`, is less general since it intended to be used by only that specific company. The levels of reusability in an inheritance hierarchy defines a *partial order* relation.

Property 2. The reusability level of a class is equal to the reusability level of the least reusable coupled class.

The reusability level of a class reflects the extent to which the class is expected to be reused in future applications. Given two classes C_p and C_q with reusability levels G_{C_p} and G_{C_q} such that $(C_p, C_q) \in \Gamma_C$, the following two situations are relevant:

- Class C_p is more specific than class C_q ($G_{C_p} > G_{C_q}$), in which case C_p is the least reusable class.
- Class C_p is more general than class C_q ($G_{C_p} < G_{C_q}$). Since there is a coupling from C_p to C_q, C_p is dependent on specific features of C_q that will condition the reusability of C_p to situations when C_q is reusable. Thus, the reusability level of C_p is equal to the reusability level of C_q, which is the least reusable class.

Property 3. Classes that do not contribute to the functionality of a component have a negative impact on reuse.

The reuse of classes that do not contribute to the functionality of the reusable component or have only a small fraction of their methods that contribute to the functionality of the reusable component, have a negative impact on the application that reuses the component. Classes that do not contribute to the functionality increase the size of the application without any real benefit. Long-term, we intend to be able to recognize such situations to alert the software engineer when they occur.

Property 4. Couplings between unrelated classes hinder reuse.

From the definition of related classes, we derive that unrelated classes are not intended to be reused together in future applications. If there are dependencies among unrelated classes, the coupled classes must be reused together in order for the system to function properly. This contradicts the intention of the software engineer not to reuse the components together. Therefore, dependencies between unrelated classes are undesirable.

4   Reusability Analysis

From the definitions of generality/related and properties in Section 3, we can draw conclusions regarding the way to assess reusability improvement by focusing on the reusability level and couplings that exist among classes. This will lead us to a methodology that is based on an initial assessment of the couplings, and a criteria to evaluate the impact on reuse of different refactoring operations to improve reusability, as we will examine in Section 5.1.

As discussed in Section 3 (see Definition 3), software engineers label or mark their classes with a reusability level, that denotes the reuse potential of the class. To simplify the discussion, assume that there are only two levels of generality,

G and S; if there are multiple reusability levels, one can focus on only two levels at a time. Between these two reusability levels there are four types of couplings: a G class can depend on another G class, a G class can depend on a S class, a S class can depend on a G class, and a S class can depend on another S class. These dependencies take the form of a method call, an instance variable reference, etc. For the purposes of this paper, we use the 8 coupling types introduced in [12–15], which are classified based on whether they are among related classes (Types 1, 3, 5, or 7) that are expected to be reused together, or among unrelated classes (Types 2, 4, 6, and 8).

Type 1: G → G among related classes. This coupling is an asset to reuse, and the objective is to increase these couplings.

Type 2: G → G among unrelated classes. This coupling is undesirable since the source and destination are not expected to be reused together. To improve reuse, one could move both the source and destination to Specific descendant classes.

Type 3: G → S among related classes. This coupling is undesirable, since the General class (to be reused) depends on a class which is not expected to be reused. To improve reuse, one could move the source to a Specific descendant or the destination to a General ancestor.

Type 4: G → S among unrelated classes. This coupling is undesirable since the source is expected to be reused while the destination is not. To improve reuse, one could move the source to its Specific descendant class.

Type 5: S → G among related classes. This coupling does not hinder reuse since the source of the coupling is not expected to be reused. However, one could improve reuse by moving the source to a General ancestor.

Type 6: S → G among unrelated classes. This coupling does not hinder reuse since the source of the coupling is not expected to be reused. There is no way to improve reuse in this case.

Type 7: S → S among related classes. This does not hinder reuse since the source of coupling is not expected to be reused. However, one could improve reuse if both the source and destination are moved to their General ancestors.

Type 8: S → S among unrelated classes. This is not a hindrance to reuse, rather, it represents the desired situation for couplings between unrelated classes; they need to be among the Specific classes.

Given the eight different coupling types, from a reusability-assessment perspective, our objective is to provide a concrete mechanism that can be utilized to automatically refactor a design in order to improve reuse. To accomplish this, it is important to track the couplings, in order to assess the impact on reuse when a coupling is moved from one coupling type to another. For example, a coupling transitioned from Type 3 to Type 1 moves a coupling that hinders reuse (Type 3) to one that promotes reuse (Type 1). To illustrate the impact on reuse of the transitions between different coupling types for related and unrelated classes, the state diagrams in Figure 1 are provided. The states in the figures represent the

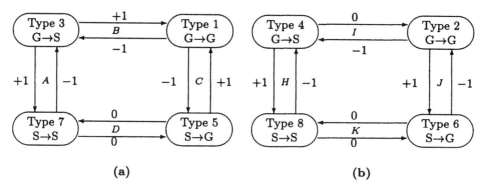

Fig. 1. Coupling Transitions for (a) Related Classes and (b) Unrelated Classes.

coupling types proposed in [13, 14], and the numbers in the transitions represent the impact on the reusability of the system when transitions occur between coupling types, +1 representing positive impact - promotes reuse, −1 representing negative impact - hinders reuse, and 0 representing no impact.

In the case of related classes, the transitions between coupling types promote and/or hinder reuse of the application as follows:

- Couplings from general to specific classes hinder the reuse of components. In the case of related classes, from Property 2, reusability of the general class is limited by the coupling to the more specific class. For this reason coupling Type 3 is undesirable for reuse, and consequently transitions to coupling Type 3 hinders reuse, as shown by the arrows labeled A/-1 and B/-1 in Figure 1 (a). In contrast, the transition in the opposite direction promotes reuse, as shown by the arrows labeled A/+1 and B/+1 in Figure 1 (a).
- Couplings between general classes that are related, represents valuable design knowledge that can be reused [15]. For this reason, transitions to couplings Type 1 promote reuse, as shown by the arrows labeled B/+1 and C/+1 in Figure 1 (a). In contrast, the transition in the opposite direction hinders reuse, as shown by the arrows labeled B/-1 and C/-1 in Figure 1 (a).
- In the case of couplings between related classes in which the source class is specific – such as Type 5 and Type 7 – from Property 2 the reusability is not affected by the coupling to another class. Coupling Type 5 and Type 7 are acceptable, but can be improved by transitioning to Type 1. For this reason, transitions between Type 5 and Type 7 have no impact on reuse, as shown by the two D arrows labeled with zeros in Figure 1 (a).

Note that in Figure 1 (a), we have not shown diagonal lines, i.e., transitions from Type 1 to/from Type 7 and Type 3 to/from Type 5. This is since these transitions can be accomplished in two steps. For example, going from Type 7 to Type 1 (change both source and destination from specific to general) can be accomplished by going from Type 7 to Type 5 to Type 1, for a net gain of +1. Note also that the process in not symmetric; from Type 7 to Type 3 to Type 1 has no gain. This was intentional, to force the path the would have a positive gain. In going from Type 7 to Type 3, there is a loss (-1). If the software engineer did not make the second move to Type 1, there would be a net loss, which doesn't occur in the other path, since Type 7 to Type 5 is a zero transition.

Correspondingly, transitions between coupling types when the classes are unrelated promote and/or hinder reuse of the application as follows:

- Based on Property 4, unrelated classes hinder reuse. Coupling types in which the source class is general are particularly undesirable. From its definition, a general class is expected to be reused in future applications, so couplings to a non-related class result in the reuse of unrelated classes every time the source class is reused. In other words, the coupling to a non-related class diminishes the reusability of the source class. Consequently, transitions from couplings Types 6 and Type 8 to couplings Types 2 and 4, respectively, hinders reuse, as shown by the arrows labeled H/-1 and J/-1 in Figure 1 (b), while transitions in the opposite direction promote reuse, as shown by the arrows labeled H/+1 and J/+1 in Figure 1 (b).
- Transitions from couplings Type 2 to Type 4 hinders reuse, as shown by the arrow labeled I/-1 in Figure 1 (b). From Property 2, coupling Type 4 not only forces the joint reuse of unrelated classes, but also diminishes the reusability of the general class. All other transitions between unrelated classes have no impact on reuse, as shown by the I/0 arrow and the two K arrows in Figure 1 (b).

Again, as with the related case, we do not at this time consider diagonal transitions, namely, Type 2 to/from Type 8 and Type 4 to/from Type 6. These diagonals and their gain or loss can be attained in a similar fashion to the previous discussion in the related case.

The *coupling type transition matrix* $\tau = [\tau_{uv}]$ is the matrix that represents the state diagrams, where:

$$\tau_{uv} = \begin{cases} +1 & \text{if the transition from coupling type } u \text{ to coupling} \\ & \text{type } v \text{ has a positive impact on reuse} \\ \\ -1 & \text{if the transition from coupling type } u \text{ to coupling} \\ & \text{type } v \text{ has a negative impact on reuse} \\ \\ 0 & \text{if the transition from coupling type } u \text{ to coupling} \\ & \text{type } v \text{ has no impact on reuse} \end{cases}$$

Then, from the state diagrams in Figure 1, $\tau = [\tau_{uv}]$ is:

$$\tau = \begin{pmatrix} 0 & 0 & -1 & 0 & -1 & 0 & 0 & 0 \\ 0 & 0 & 0 & -1 & 0 & +1 & 0 & 0 \\ +1 & 0 & 0 & 0 & 0 & 0 & +1 & 0 \\ 0 & 0 & 0 & 0 & 0 & 0 & 0 & +1 \\ +1 & 0 & 0 & 0 & 0 & 0 & 0 & 0 \\ 0 & -1 & 0 & 0 & 0 & 0 & 0 & 0 \\ 0 & 0 & -1 & 0 & 0 & 0 & 0 & 0 \\ 0 & 0 & 0 & -1 & 0 & 0 & 0 & 0 \end{pmatrix} \tag{6}$$

Note that $\tau = [\tau_{uv}]$ is used in Section 5 to evaluate the *reusability improvement factor*, $\Delta\rho$, to determine whether a refactoring operation promotes or hinders the reuse of the application.

5   Refactoring Algorithm and Example

5.1   The Refactoring Process

In this section, we present an algorithm to improve the reuse potential of an application, which is loosely based on the reusability analysis in [15]. The algorithm is comprised of a series of steps. Steps 1, 2, and 3 initialize the different vectors and matrices as defined in Sections 2 and 3, while Steps 4 through 8 represent an iterative process that is undertaken until a software engineer is satisfied with the reusability results.

1. Identify Reuse Potential
   Identify the classes that would potentially be reused in future applications. Reusable classes are characterized with varying reusability levels (see Section 3 and Definition 3), based on domain knowledge and information on the application. This process defines the class generality vector G.
2. Calculate the Couplings
   Determine the actual couplings among the methods that comprise an application. This process is done by parsing the source code and constructing the matrix M_{Γ_m}, based on the relation Γ_m (see Section 2 and Definition 2).
3. Identify the Related Classes
   Identify the groups of classes that are expected to be reused together in future applications. The classes can be related based on the couplings determined in Step 2, and/or based on domain knowledge. The relations among the classes are captured in the matrix M_{Γ_R}, based on the relation Γ_R (see Section 3 and Definition 4).
4. Determine Coupling Types
   Using the characterization of reusability for each class G, the coupling among the methods M_{Γ_m}, and the relations among the classes M_{Γ_R}, calculate $T = [t_{ij}]$, the actual couplings that are present in the entire application, using the following expression:

$$[t_{ij}] = \begin{cases} 1 & \text{if}(\ (m_i, m_j) \in \Gamma_R) \wedge (G_{C_p} = G_{C_q} \neq N) \\ 2 & \text{if}(\ (m_i, m_j) \notin \Gamma_R) \wedge (G_{C_p} = G_{C_q} \neq N) \\ 3 & \text{if}(\ (m_i, m_j) \in \Gamma_R) \wedge (G_{C_p} < G_{C_q}) \\ 4 & \text{if}(\ (m_i, m_j) \notin \Gamma_R) \wedge (G_{C_p} < G_{C_q}) \\ 5 & \text{if}(\ (m_i, m_j) \in \Gamma_R) \wedge (G_{C_p} > G_{C_q}) \\ 6 & \text{if}(\ (m_i, m_j) \notin \Gamma_R) \wedge (G_{C_p} > G_{C_q}) \\ 7 & \text{if}(\ (m_i, m_j) \in \Gamma_R) \wedge (G_{C_p} = G_{C_q} = N) \\ 8 & \text{if}(\ (m_i, m_j) \notin \Gamma_R) \wedge (G_{C_p} = G_{C_q} = N) \end{cases} \quad (7)$$

where $m_i \in C_p^M$ and $m_j \in C_q^M$, G_{C_p} and G_{C_q} are the reusability levels of the classes to which m_i and m_j belong, and N is the reusability level of the most specific class in the application.

5. Identify Undesirable Couplings

   Identify a pair of methods $m_i \in C_p^M$, $m_j \in C_q^M$ such that $[t_{ij}] \in \{2,3,4\}$, which has not been analyzed as yet. Coupling Types 2, 3 and 4 hinder the reusability of the application. The refactoring operations in Step 6 below are intended to improve them. If all of the pairs have been analyzed, identify a pair such that $[t_{ij}] \in \{5,6,7,8\}$ which has not been analyzed as yet. Coupling Types 5 and 7 can be improved to Type 1 by refactoring. Likewise, Types 2 and 4 can be improved to Types 6 and 8 respectively.

6. Refactor the Application

   Remove the undesired couplings by refactoring the application. Perform any of the following refactoring operations [3, 15]:

   (a) Move Source Method

   The source method can be moved up (case 1) or down (case 2) in the inheritance hierarchy. In the first case, remove the source method m_i from class C_p^M, and insert it in the class C_k^M, where $(C_p^M, C_k^M) \in \Gamma_I$. The two classes $\widetilde{C}_p^M = C_p^M - \{m_i\}$ and $\widetilde{C}_k^M = C_k^M \cup \{m_i\}$ result from this operation. Go to Step 7.

   In the second case, insert the method m_i, removed from the source class, in class C_l^M, where $(C_l^M, C_p^M) \in \Gamma_I$. The two classes $\widetilde{C}_p^M = C_p^M - \{m_i\}$ and $\widetilde{C}_l^M = C_l^M \cup \{m_i\}$ result from this operation. Go to Step 7.

   (b) Move Destination Method

   The destination method can be moved up (case 1) or down (case 2) in the inheritance hierarchy. In the first case, remove the destination method m_j from class C_q^M, and insert it in the class C_k^M, where $(C_q^M, C_k^M) \in \Gamma_I$. The two classes $\widetilde{C}_q^M = C_q^M - \{m_j\}$ and $\widetilde{C}_k^M = C_k^M \cup \{m_j\}$ result from this operation. Go to Step 7.

   In the second case, insert the method m_j removed from the destination class in the class C_l^M, where $(C_l^M, C_q^M) \in \Gamma_I$. The two classes $\widetilde{C}_q^M = C_q^M - \{m_j\}$ and $\widetilde{C}_l^M = C_l^M \cup \{m_j\}$ result from this operation. Go to Step 7.

   (c) Change Source Reusability Level

   Set the reusability level G_{C_p} of the class containing the source method m_i to $\widetilde{G_{C_p}} = G_{C_q} + |\delta|$, where G_{C_q} is the reusability level of the class containing the destination method m_j and $|\delta|$ is a positive integer. Go to Step 7.

   (d) Change Destination Reusability Level

   Set the reusability level G_{C_q} of the class containing the destination method m_j, to $\widetilde{G_{C_q}} = G_{C_p} - |\delta|$ where G_{C_p} is the reusability level of the class containing the source method m_i and $|\delta|$ is a positive integer. Go to Step 7.

   (e) Change Related to Unrelated

   If $[t_{ij}]$ is coupling Type 2, then consider relating the source and destination classes, resulting in a new $\widetilde{\Gamma}_R = \Gamma_R \cup \{(m_i, m_j)\}$. Go to Step 7.

7. Recalculate T

   Recalculate $[t_{ij}]$ (Eq. 7) where m_i and m_j are methods that cause the undesired coupling. If the source method m_i has been moved or its reusability level has been changed, recalculate $[t_{gi}]$ for all (g, i) such that $(m_g, m_i) \in \Gamma_m$. If the destination method m_j has been moved or its reusability level has been changed, recalculate $[t_{jh}]$ for all (j, h) such that $(m_j, m_h) \in \Gamma_m$. This operation results in $\widetilde{T}$.

8. Evaluate the Reusability Improvement Factor

   Evaluate the reusability improvement factor, $\Delta\rho$:

$$\Delta\rho = \sum_{i=0}^{n} \sum_{j=0}^{n} \tau_{[t_{ij}][\widetilde{t}_{ij}]} \tag{8}$$

The following three situations are possible:

- If $\Delta\rho > 0$, then go to Step 5 and continue the refactoring.
- If $\Delta\rho \leq 0$ and there are still refactoring operations (Steps 6a, 6b, 6c, 6d, 6e) that have not been evaluated, then return to Step 6 and apply an operation that has not been evaluated.
- If $\Delta\rho \leq 0$ and all of the refactoring operations presented in Step 6 have been evaluated, then return to Step 5 and try to eliminate a different undesirable coupling. If all of the couplings have been evaluated, terminate the process.

5.2 Applying the Refactoring Algorithm

Consider the class diagram of Figure 2, which illustrates an application that has seven classes C_1, C_2, C_3, C_4, C_5, C_6, C_7, and eight methods m_1, m_2, m_3, m_4, m_5, m_6, m_7, m_8, implemented as shown in the classes.

In order to apply the algorithm in Section 5.1, we must first identify the classes that are candidates for reuse in future applications: C_1, C_2, C_4 and C_6 as general, and C_3, C_5 and C_7 as specific, thereby setting the vector $G = (0, 0, 1, 0, 1, 0, 1)^T$, which is Step 1 of the algorithm. Next, we determine the couplings among methods, and construct the zero-one matrix M_{Γ_m}, such that

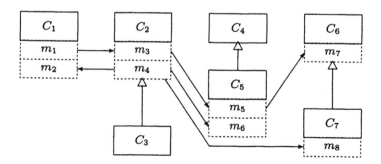

Fig. 2. Initial Class Diagram.

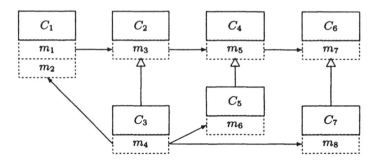

Fig. 3. Revised Class Diagram After Refactoring.

it has a 1 as its (i, j) entry when i-th method is coupled to the j-th method, and a 0 if the methods are not coupled. From the class diagram in Figure 3, we construct the matrix M_{Γ_m} shown below, which is Step 2 of the algorithm. Now, for simplicity, suppose all classes are related to one another, which leads to $\Gamma_m = \{C_1, C_2, C_3, C_4, C_5, C_6, C_7\} \times \{C_1, C_2, C_3, C_4, C_5, C_6, C_7\}$, which is Step 3 of the algorithm. Then, using the reusability level for each class G, the coupling among the methods M_{Γ_m}, and the relations among the classes Γ_R, we calculate the matrix $T = [t_{ij}]$ shown below that represents the coupling types among the methods, which is Step 4 of the algorithm. Finally, from the matrix $T = [t_{ij}]$, we can identify the undesirable couplings $\{(m_3, m_5), (m_4, m_6), (m_4, m_8)\}$, which have values of 3, 3, and 3, in the matrix, and is the first use of Step 5 of the algorithm.

$$M_{\Gamma_m} = \begin{pmatrix} 0\,0\,1\,0\,0\,0\,0\,0 \\ 0\,0\,0\,0\,0\,0\,0\,0 \\ 0\,0\,0\,0\,1\,0\,0\,0 \\ 0\,1\,0\,0\,0\,1\,0\,1 \\ 0\,0\,0\,0\,0\,0\,1\,0 \\ 0\,0\,0\,0\,0\,0\,0\,0 \\ 0\,0\,0\,0\,0\,0\,0\,0 \\ 0\,0\,0\,0\,0\,0\,0\,0 \end{pmatrix} \quad T = \begin{pmatrix} 0\,0\,1\,0\,0\,0\,0\,0 \\ 0\,0\,0\,0\,0\,0\,0\,0 \\ 0\,0\,0\,0\,3\,0\,0\,0 \\ 0\,1\,0\,0\,0\,3\,0\,3 \\ 0\,0\,0\,0\,0\,0\,5\,0 \\ 0\,0\,0\,0\,0\,0\,0\,0 \\ 0\,0\,0\,0\,0\,0\,0\,0 \\ 0\,0\,0\,0\,0\,0\,0\,0 \end{pmatrix}$$

Given all of these characteristics and assumptions, we can attempt to improve the reusability of the application via the refactoring operations presented in Steps 6, 7, and 8 of the algorithm in Section 5.1.

- Consider the coupling (m_3, m_5). Move the source method down the inheritance hierarchy, so that $\widetilde{C}_2^M = \{m_4\}$ and $\widetilde{C}_3^M = \{m_3\}$. Calculate $\widetilde{T}$, and then evaluate the reusability improvement factor, obtaining $\Delta\rho = 0$. Since this operation does not improve the reusability of the application, restore $C_2^M = \{m_3, m_4\}$ and $C_3^M = \emptyset$.
- Consider the coupling (m_4, m_6). Move the source method down the inheritance hierarchy, so that $\widetilde{C}_2^M = \{m_3\}$ and $\widetilde{C}_3^M = \{m_4\}$. Calculate $\widetilde{T}$, and then evaluate the reusability improvement factor, obtaining $\Delta\rho = +1$. Since

$\Delta\rho$ is positive, set $T = \widetilde{T}$, $C_2^M = \widetilde{C}_2^M$, and $C_3^M = \widetilde{C}_3^M$, and identify a new coupling to continue refactoring.

-   Consider the coupling (m_5, m_7). Move the source method up the inheritance hierarchy, so that $\widetilde{C}_4^M = \{m_5\}$ and $\widetilde{C}_5^M = \{m_6\}$. Calculate $\widetilde{T}$, and then evaluate the reusability improvement factor, obtaining $\Delta\rho = +2$. Given the positive impact of the refactoring operation on reuse, we set $T = \widetilde{T}$, $C_4^M = \widetilde{C}_4^M$, and $C_5^M = \widetilde{C}_5^M$.

Figure 3 illustrates the changes in the class diagram as a result of the refactoring operations, where method m_4 has moved from C_2 to C_3, and method m_5 has moved from C_5 to C_4. This has yielded a better overall software structure from a reusability perspective.

6   Related Research

There are several proposals to use formal methods in software reuse. In [8], a mathematical model based on discrete mathematics is discussed, that captures aspects of software reuse such as the representation of software components via formal specifications, the representation of user queries, the organization of software repositories, the definition of retrieval procedures, and the definition of a framework for the process of modifying software components to satisfy user queries. This effort shares our philosophy of attempting to formalize software specifications to allow software reuse, but differs since its focus is the introduction of operators that reflect semantic distance between relational specifications and our focus is on the introduction of reusability metrics intended to be iteratively applied throughout the software process.

In [5], a framework and algorithms for the maintenance problem that arises when reusing software components is presented, that addresses a way to prevent software-components-reuse defects such as logic subsumptions, redundancies, inconsistencies, and conflicts. Their solution to the reusability problem uses properties of inheritance relation such as *in copyable* and *out copyable*, as well as client-server *fan in copyable* and *fan out copyable*. Our approach shares their model of object structures as directed graphs where edges are associations and nodes are classes.

An analytical and empirical evaluation of several published reuse metrics is presented in [2], which introduces properties that should hold in any measure of time, money, and quality benefit, as a result of software reuse. Several software reuse metrics are assessed using these properties, and evaluated empirically. This effort is of interest to our own work, since in the long-term, we are interested in comparing and contrasting our metric with other metrics that have been developed.

In [9], a formal object-oriented meta-model is used for defining two measures of structural quality such as coupling and cohesion. In [19], a solution to the problem of measuring potential coupling between an application and its environment is proposed. Both of these efforts are relevant to our own work, since they focus on coupling, which is a key facet of our reuse framework, which drives both the metric calculation (see Section 3) and the reuse improvement via refactoring (see Sections 4 and 5.1).

7   Conclusions and Future Work

In this paper, we have extended the reusability framework for object-oriented design originally proposed in [12–15], through a formalization of those model concepts and the introduction of a methodology and associated processing for a refactoring algorithm that improves reuse. In our research, we identified a set of properties of the framework (see Section 3 again), formalized the representation of the characteristics proposed in [15] (see Sections 2 and 3 again), introduced the reusability improvement factor (see Section 4 again), and outlined an algorithm to improve the reusability which was demonstrated in an example application (see Section 5 again). Overall, we believe that we have taken a significant first step in establishing a formal framework for refactoring that can be the basis of continued research and development efforts.

Thus, the work herein is an important part of ongoing research on reusable components (http://www.engr.uconn.edu/~steve/DRE/dre.html). This site contains all of our research publications on reusable components, as well as the current prototype Design Reusability Evaluation (DRE) tool, which supports the original reuse model and framework [12–15]. We have a number of ongoing areas of investigation:

- We are exploring the transition weightings between coupling types (see Figure 1), to evaluate the impact on refactoring if different values are utilized (e.g., +2, -2, etc.), if diagonals are used, or if jumps across multiple levels of generality are allowed. Also, these weights may be definable, to some degree, by the software engineer who conducts reusability assessment and refactoring. Further, the current algorithm searches only in one step. Multiple steps that involve searching down bad paths (-1) for potential gain using hueristics may be possible.
- We continue to extend, refine, and reformulate the reusability model. We are also exploring formal proofs for the properties upon which the reuse framework was built, and a theoretical verification that the refactoring algorithm actually improves the reuse potential. This will include issues such as inheritance vs. composition in the refactoring process and considering the impact on maintainability.
- From a practical perspective, we have begun the process of integrating the model, metric, and refactoring algorithm into our ongoing DRE prototype. This will allow us to easily collect empirical evidence on the utility and operation of the refactoring algorithm.
- While we believe that our reusability framework is applicable to large scale projects, a more realistic example which appeared in our prior work [12–14] would not fit into the space limitations of the paper. We continue to test our

approach on other applications in order to gather empirical evidence on the utility of our algorithm vs. a human expert.

Finally, note that we have also developed a genetic algorithm that, when given a set of classes and their couplings, determines a near-optimal general/specific marking for the classes, where the software engineer can specify the distribution of general/specific classes as an input to the genetic algorithm. We are investigating using this genetic algorithm as a prelude to mark classes before applying the algorithm given in Section 5.1.

Acknowledgements

The work of S. Demurjian has been supported, in part, by a contract from the Electric Boat Corporation, Groton, CT. We also wish to thank M. Price for her insightful comments and suggestions.

References

1. Software reuse executive premier. Technical report, DOD Software Reuse Initiative Program Management Office, 1996.
2. P. Devanbu, S. Karstu, W. Melo, and W. Thomas. Analytical and empirical evaluation of software reuse metrics. In *Proceedings of 18th International Conference on Software Engineering*, pages 189–199, March 1996.
3. M. Fowler. *Refactoring, Improving the Design of Existing Code*. Addison-Wesley, February 2001.
4. P. A. Hall. Architecture-driven component reuse. *Information and Software Technology*, 41(14):963–968, November 1999.
5. Y.-F. Hwang and D. C. Rine. Verifying the reusability of software component specifications: Framework and algorithms. *Information Sciences*, 112(1-4):169–197, December 1998.
6. M. McIlroy. Mass produced software components. In *Proceedings of the NATO Software Engineering Conference*, Germany, October 1968.
7. J. Meekel, T. Horton, R. France, C. Mellone, and S. Dalvi. From domain models to architecture frameworks. In *Proceedings of the 1997 Symposium on Software Reusability*, Boston, MA, May 1997.
8. R. Mili, J. Desharnais, M. Frappier, and A. Mili. Semantic distance between specifications. *Theoretical Computer Science*, 247(1-2):257–276, September 2000.
9. S. Moser and V. B. Misic. Measuring class coupling and cohesion: A formal method approach. In *Proceedings of APSEC'97 and ICSC'97*, pages 31–40, December 1997.
10. J. S. Poulin. *Measuring Software Reuse: Principles, Practices and Economic Models*. Addison-Wesley, November 1996.
11. P. E. Presson et al. Software interoperability and reusability. *RADC-TR-83*, 1, July 1983.
12. M. W. Price. *Object-Oriented Design Methodology to Facilitate Reuse*. PhD thesis, University of Connecticut, 1998.
13. M. W. Price and S. A. Demurjian. Analyzing and measuring reusability in object-oriented designs. In *Proceedings of OOPSLA'97*, pages 22–33, Atlanta, October 1997.

14. M. W. Price, S. A. Demurjian, and D. M. Needham. Reusability measurement framework and tool for ada95. In *Proceedings of 1997 TriAda Conference*, St. Louis, November 1997.
15. M. W. Price, D. M. Needham, and S. A. Demurjian. Producing reusable object-oriented components: A domain-and-organization-specific perspective. In *Proceedings of 2001 Sympsium on Software Reusability*, Toronto, Canada, May 2001.
16. L. Reyes and D. Carver. Predicting object reuse using metrics. In *Proceedings of SEKE'98 Tenth International Conference on Software Engineering and Knowledge Engineering*, pages 156–159, San Francisco, June 1998.
17. D. C. Rine and N. Nada. Three empirical studies of a software reuse reference model. *Software - Practice and Experience*, 30(6):685–722, May 2000.
18. K. H. Rosen. *Discrete Mathematics and Its Applications*. WCB McGraw-Will, fourth edition, 1999.
19. S. Rotenstreich. Toward measuring potential coupling. *Software Engineering Journal*, 4, March 1994.
20. M. Sarshar. Reuse measurement and assessment. In *Proceedings of the International Workshop on Systematic Reuse*, pages 52–63, Germany, January 1996.
21. A. Schmietendorf, R. Dumke, and E. Foltin. Metrics based asset assessment. *Software Engineering Notes*, 25(4):51–55, July 2000.
22. G. Succi, S. Doublait, C. Uhrik, and F. Baruchelli. Reuse and reusability metrics in an object oriented paradigm. In *International Journal of Applied Software Technology*, volume 1, pages 191–202, Canada, 1995. International Academic Publishing.
23. M. Tsagias and B. Kitchenham. An evaluation of the business object approach to software development. *The Journal of Systems and Software*, 52(2-3):149–156, June 2000.

Service Facilities: Extending Abstract Factories to Decouple Advanced Dependencies

Nigamanth Sridhar, Bruce W. Weide, and Paolo Bucci

Computer and Information Science, The Ohio State University,
2015 Neil Ave., Columbus OH 43210, USA
{nsridhar,weide,bucci}@cis.ohio-state.edu

Abstract. It is widely agreed that component interactions should be based on the import and export of interface information only, not on knowledge of implementation-specific details. This can be achieved in many cases either by explicit parameterization using templates (in languages that have them) or by using some variant of the abstract factory pattern. We introduce an alternative: the use of *service facilities*. This technique is similar both to the use of templates and to the use of factories, but it is preferable to both in several important ways. Service facilities can be used to decouple design-time concrete-to-concrete component dependencies in any reasonable programming language and with any component infrastructure that is based on design-by-contract principles.

1 Introduction

Direct design-time dependencies between *concrete components* are widely recognized as undesirable because they complicate software maintenance activities. Any change in the design of a single concrete component may well entail major changes in the rest of any system that uses it – a phenomenon termed "the hairball effect" by Clemens Szyperski. The reason is that a change might affect the interaction of the component being modified with the other components that were designed to depend on it, and changes there might affect the interactions with the components that were designed to depend on them, and so on [9].

It is, therefore, commonly recommended that design-time component dependencies generally should be limited to those between a concrete component and the *abstract components* that it implements and uses (or otherwise communicates with) [5]. In fact, all popular commercial component technologies are now based on this principle – variously called "design by contract", "programming by contract", "design to interfaces", "decoupling", etc. Modern programming languages such as Java and C# support the idea by giving *interfaces* (abstract components) the same linguistic status as *classes* (concrete components). A simple rule that supports good component design in these languages is that design-time coupling should be from classes to interfaces, not from classes to classes. Common advice for easing maintenance is that new interfaces may be introduced, but existing ones should remain fixed once they are deployed in a setting

C. Gacek (Ed.): ICSR-7, LNCS 2319, pp. 309–326, 2002.

where *reuse* is expected. The internal details of classes that implement those interfaces may change even after deployment, so long as they continue to implement the same interfaces. Just as importantly, however, new implementation classes may be added for existing interfaces and thereby become available as new implementation options for clients of those interfaces.

Eventually, of course – at the latest just before code is executed – someone must select some concrete component to implement each abstract component that is used in building a larger component or final system. This means that it is helpful when discussing component-based systems to distinguish between *component design time* and *component integration (composition) time*. By the former we mean the time at which a component is considered fully designed and is entered into a component library, i.e., where it still exists out of the context of any larger component or final system in which it might be (re)used. (Design time is when concrete-to-concrete dependencies should be avoided.) By the latter, we mean the time at which the component is selected for use from the library and assembled into a larger component or final system. Integration time with respect to a library component might occur at design time, or at compile time, link time, or run time, with respect to the larger component or system in which it is used.

An important question in component-based software engineering concerns how to reconcile the desire to decouple concrete-to-concrete dependencies at component design time with the need for easy assembly of concrete components at integration time. Two basic techniques have been suggested for this. Parameterization of components using a template mechanism, a.k.a. generics, is one decoupling approach [1, 8]. As a template, a concrete component can be designed so that it depends on one or more abstract components, implementations of which are technically parameters that can be selected and bound at integration time as opposed to being fixed at design time. In languages with template support, integration time (the binding of concrete components to the abstract components they implement) means compile time because integration is achieved through template instantiation. This is relatively early integration-time binding but still much better from the maintenance standpoint than forcing such implementation commitments to occur at design time.

In modern distributed computing environments, compile time sometimes is not late enough for component integration to occur. Some information about concrete component availability or suitability simply may not be known until run time. Moreover, even where compile-time binding is appropriate, template mechanisms are not available in widely-used languages such as Java and C#, and they are not part of COM IDL, CORBA IDL, WSDL, .NET, etc., which are becoming widely used as the basis for component-based software today. So, explicit parameterization as a decoupling mechanism is effectively limited to compile-time use in C++ [7, 8].

Consequently, several design patterns have been proposed to address the decoupling problem for use in languages that do not offer linguistic support for templates. In some cases, e.g., when developing COM components, such patterns must be used even when coding in languages such as C++ that do support templates. The *abstract factory pattern* [4] is the canonical representative of these. When taken to the logical conclusion suggested by the metaphor on which it is based, the abstract factory pattern can be used rather effectively to decouple concrete-to-concrete dependencies.

But, as we will see, there remain drawbacks to both the above methods. In this paper, we introduce an alternative approach to decoupling concrete-to-concrete dependencies that is logically tantamount to using templates. This facilitates sound and modular reasoning about software behavior and has other advantages over the use of informal design patterns. However, like the abstract factory pattern, it can be employed in languages and that do not support templates but that permit component integration as late as at run time. We call the key elements of this approach **service facilities**. The name is intended to suggest a parallel to factories, because the idea is most easily explained using a service-oriented rather than a manufacturing-oriented metaphor.

Following introductions to abstract factories and service facilities (Sections 2 and 3), we present an example to illustrate how service facilities can be coded in Java (Section 4), discuss some points of comparison between service facilities and abstract factories (Section 5), and finally summarize our contributions and conclude (Section 6).

The problem of decoupling design-time concrete-to-concrete dependencies is inherent in system design (in fact, not just for software systems [9]), and it is common to all practical programming models today. The solutions presented in this paper are intended to be general enough to address the problem in distributed software systems built using component technologies such as COM, CORBA, and .NET. However, for the sake of simplicity of presentation, we use Java to illustrate service facilities. All the concepts map directly to programming constructs in commercial distributed component infrastructures.

2   The Abstract Factory Pattern

Readers who are familiar with the abstract factory pattern may wish to skim this section and proceed to Section 3. Unfortunately, the idea of a service facility is unlikely to make much sense to anyone who is not familiar with both the rationale for and some technical details of the abstract factory pattern, and the comparison between service facilities and abstract factories in Section 5 is certain to be difficult to follow without this background.

The abstract factory pattern is an approach that can dramatically reduce – but not quite eliminate – dependencies between classes (i.e., concrete components). If it is adopted uniformly, then every class has a corresponding **factory** class whose objects (class instances) can manufacture/construct/create objects of the original class, which is called the **product** class. The client program depends *almost* entirely on the interfaces (i.e., abstract components) implemented by the factory class and by the product class.

The binding of a reference to the factory object, which pins down the product's implementation class, technically happens at run time and hence can be based on information that is not known until run time. However, in most languages the set of possible implementation choices must be known at compile time. For example, Java (like most other object-oriented languages) effectively dooms any approach to decoupling concrete-to-concrete dependencies so that the strongest possible conclusion is that it "almost" works. The reason is that everywhere a constructor is invoked, Java expects to see the name of the class the object is to be an instance of – not the name of an interface. Identifying constructor names with class names is known to introduce other problems as well [6]. But the goal of design patterns is not to suggest how to change the language deficiencies we are stuck with but to record the best ways people have found to work around them [2]. The objective of the abstract factory pattern is, therefore, not to remove this language restriction but to allow us to live with it.

The result of using the abstract factory pattern is that it is possible to *localize* each concrete-to-concrete dependency to a single line of code where the factory implementation class finally *must* be chosen if the client code is to compile. Now all objects of the product class are constructed not by invoking the product class's constructor but by invoking a non-constructor method of the factory object. The lines of code that ask factory objects to construct product objects do not introduce concrete-to-concrete dependencies, and need not change when the factory and product implementation classes are replaced by different ones that implement the same interfaces (functional behavior) with different performance or other non-functional properties.

2.1   Example: A Sequence Component

This section introduces a running example that has been chosen to illustrate what we are talking about, not because it is so complex that it compellingly demonstrates either the rationale for or the advantages of any particular approach to decoupling.

Figure 1 shows the design structure of a system that uses a Sequence product interface along with a SequenceF factory interface for this product. Only one sequence implementation "R1" (for "realization (implementation) number 1"; the name is unimportant) is shown in the figure. The two implementation classes for this implementation are SequenceF_R1 and Sequence_R1. Of course, an important reason for using factories is that it is expected that there are or eventually might be other implementations of sequences with the same two interfaces that could be selected for use in the client program. For example, the Sequence interface might include methods to add, remove, and update sequence entries by position. The "R1" implementation might take best-case constant and worst-case linear time time for each of these methods, and another implementation might always take log time for each of them. Supporting easy substitution of one such implementation for another, based on the client's performance needs, is one major reason for decoupling concrete-to-concrete dependencies.

Without the abstract factory pattern, the client program would have to construct sequences as follows, spreading the name of the class throughout the code:

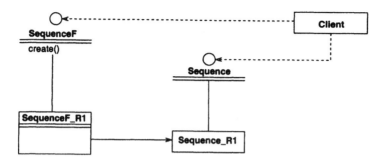

Fig. 1. Design based on the abstract factory pattern

```
Sequence s1 = new Sequence_R1 ();
...
Sequence s2 = new Sequence_R1 ();
...
s1.add (x, 3);
y = s2.remove (i);
...
```

The following code snippet shows how the client takes advantage of the abstract factory pattern:

```
SequenceF seqF = new SequenceF_R1 (); // Select implementation
...
Sequence s1 = seqF.create ();
...
Sequence s2 = seqF.create ();
...
s1.add (x, 3);
y = s2.remove (i);
...
```

This client can now easily switch to a different implementation for Sequence, the only code change being a change to the factory constructor, which appears in just one place in the code. A change from "_R1" to "_R2", for example, does not lead to a change in the client code except in this one inherently (in Java) unavoidable place. Note that the client declares both factory and product objects to have interface types.

2.2 Outsourcing

We continue by elaborating the above example a bit. Suppose the Sequence_R1 representation of sequences is built not just by using Java's built-in types, but by using other components, each of which might also have several alternative implementations. How can we design Sequence_R1 so it is possible to delay until integration time the binding of implementation classes for these components used in the sequence representation?

To be specific, suppose the representation of a sequence in Sequence_R1 consists of two stacks (call them beforeStack and afterStack) positioned so that the tops of the two stacks "face each other" in the interior of the sequence they represent. That is, the top entries of the two stacks hold consecutive elements in the sequence. All additions to and removals from a sequence can be performed by shifting entries between the two stacks until the break between them is at the appropriate position in the sequence, followed by a push or a pop on afterStack. This code depends only on the Stack interface, not on any particular implementation of it, as illustrated in Figure 2.

```
void add (Object x, int pos)
{
    this.setLengthOfBeforeStack (pos); // Shift entries between stacks
    this.afterStack.push (x); // Push x onto afterStack
}
```

Fig. 2. Sequence_R1.add (Object x, int pos)

How do factories come into play here if they are not needed in the method bodies? In a real-life factory, a factory produces a product. The typical modern factory does not manufacture its product from scratch, however. Various parts of the product are built by other factories through *outsource manufacturing*, and various parts of their products are built by still others, and so on. An automobile factory assembles engines, doors, headlights, etc., but most of these pieces are not built in the automobile factory itself but outsourced from suppliers.

Returning from physical factories to the abstract factories used in software component design, the obvious software parallel of outsourcing is that factories (or perhaps products; the metaphor is not terribly revealing here) should know about the factories that create their constituent parts. Product creation is the only place where these factories are apparent; other methods such as add above typically do not involve factories of any kind. So a reasonable approach is to have a SequenceF_R1 factory object hold a reference to a second factory object that creates stacks, which the former can use when asked to create a new Sequence_R1 object.

Outsourcing entails adding either a new method or a constructor with parameters to the SequenceF_R1 class. This permits a client program, when components are assembled, to create a factory for stacks and then give the sequence factory a reference to it. The simple integration-time code from before:

```
SequenceF seqF = new SequenceF_R1 (); // Select implementation
```

is now slightly more complex:

```
StackF stkF = new StackF_R4 ();        // Select stack implementation
SequenceF seqF = new SequenceF_R1 (); // Select sequence implementation
seqF.setStackF (stkF);                 // Set stack outsource factory
```

The advantage of the more complex code is that we have decoupled the chosen implementation of sequences from the implementation of the stacks used to represent them. Binding implementation classes together is now done at integration time, not at design time, of Sequence_R1.

In the remainder of this paper, we do not address the question of whether or how a client programmer should have any knowledge of the representation of Sequence objects, let alone enough to determine which Stack implementation should produce the best performance profile for a particular client situation. Suffice to say that there is a straightforward way to develop new implementations of the Sequence interface from a fully decoupled one, so that some or all implementation class selection decisions can be made by the component implementers or by "middlemen" with access to enough performance-related information to select reasonable subcomponent implementations for ultimate use by clients [8]. Such *partially instantiated* concrete components are no longer decoupled from other concrete components; the trade-off is between ease of implementation substitution and ease of integration for the client. Here we have simply opened up this aspect of the design to the client in order to illustrate the idea of outsourcing as directly as possible.

3   Service Facilities

The abstract factory pattern is based on a manufacturing-industry metaphor. What happens if we use a service-industry metaphor to address the decoupling problem?

Consider a safe deposit box that can be rented from a bank. The client initially needs to ask the bank for one. The bank continues to hold the box; the client merely gets a key for it. However, any change to the contents of the box can be made only at the client's behest. The bank cannot add anything to or remove anything from the box on its own. In fact, the bank cannot even open the box (except possibly under extreme legal circumstances) because it needs the other key from the client. Similarly, the client cannot change the contents of the box on his own – he needs the bank's key to open it. In short, any change to the contents of the box is initiated by the client, and the client and the bank cooperate in opening the box and changing its contents.

Notice that the bank can, if it is deemed necessary or desirable, change the physical location of the safe deposit box, as long as its contents are left unchanged. This does not affect the client's logical view of the box. The client is not concerned about where his safe deposit box is physically located, as long as he has access to it and he alone can control the contents of the box.

This situation is different from the factory metaphor is several ways. The most important is that a factory's role is limited to product creation. After that, the factory is out of the picture and the client is on his own to change the product (or, in terms of the usual OOP metaphor, to ask the product to change itself). The bank's role is significant throughout the lifetime of the safe deposit box because without the bank the client can do *nothing* to the box. The bank also controls the location of the box and is responsible for securing it so that only the client can access its contents.

We call the software analogue of a safe deposit box a **data object** because it holds information for a client but cannot manipulate that data on its own. That is, neither the data object nor the client can manipulate a data object's value unless the client explicit requests participation by the bank. We call the software analogue of the bank a **service facility object** because it must be asked to help perform all services on, i.e., manipulations of, the data objects for which it is responsible.

Here is a summary of the software design differences between service facilities and factories:

Service Facilities – There are two kinds of objects at run time: service facility objects and data objects. Each service facility object is responsible for creating certain data objects and then "keeping track of" and "protecting" all those data objects. All methods for manipulating the data objects are supplied by the service facility objects that created them. Data objects have no methods of their own.

Factories – There are two kinds of objects at run time: factory objects and product objects. Each factory object is responsible only for creating certain product objects. The client is responsible for "keeping track of" and "protecting" all the product objects that the factory objects have created for it. All methods for manipulating the product objects after their creation are supplied by the product objects themselves. Factory objects have no methods except for product creation.

3.1   A Simple Example: A Sequence Component

Figure 3(b) shows the design structure of a system that uses a SequenceSF service facility interface and a SequenceData data interface. Again, only one implementation "R1" is shown. It has two implementation classes, SequenceSF_R1 and SequenceSF_R1::SequenceData_R1. The latter is, as we code service facilities in Java, an inner class that defines the data representation used by the sequence manipulation methods that are implemented in SequenceSF_R1. Other techniques that achieve the same visibility conditions might be more appropriate in other languages. The important condition is that the data representation in SequenceSF_R1.SequenceData_R1 must be hidden from clients but visible within SequenceSF_R1.

Figure 3(a) shows the abstract factory pattern for the same situation, slightly elaborated from Figure 1 to include explicit interfaces Factory and Product. These counterparts of ServiceFacility and Data in the service facility design help make clear the similarities and differences between the two designs. They also are

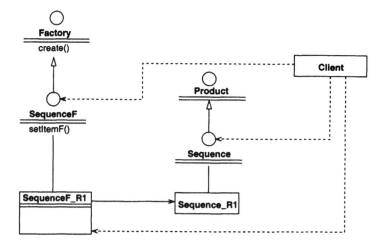

(a) Elaborated abstract factory design for sequences

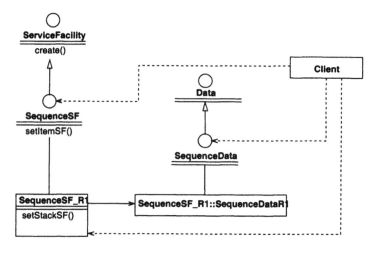

(b) Service facility design for sequences

Fig. 3. Comparison of abstract factories and service facilities

important in allowing the abstract factory solution to deal with the fact that
the sequences we have in mind are intended to be homogeneous, i.e., to contain
the same kinds of entries in all positions. We discuss this point further in the
next subsection.

The following code snippet shows how the client takes advantage of service
facilities:

```
SequenceSF seqSF = new SequenceSF_R1 (); // Select implementation
...
Sequence s1 = seqSF.create ();
...
Sequence s2 = seqSF.create ();
...
seqSF.add (s1, x, 3);
y = seqSF.remove (s2, i);
...
```

As a reminder, here again is the same code with a design based on the abstract factory pattern:

```
SequenceF seqF = new SequenceF_R1 (); // Select implementation
...
Sequence s1 = seqF.create ();
...
Sequence s2 = seqF.create ();
...
s1.add (x, 3);
y = s2.remove (i);
...
```

There is little difference in the code the client writes with these two approaches. With service facilities, the receiver object in the add and remove calls is a service facility object, so the corresponding data object is now an explicit parameter. With factories, the receiver object is a product object and the factory object is not involved. It should be noted that the same similarity is observed if outsourcing is used.

Which raises the question: What is the counterpart to outsourcing in the bank metaphor? A client with a safe deposit box may decide to store in that box the key to another safe deposit box at another bank. In other words, with service facilities, it might make metaphorical sense for the data objects to hold references to the service facilities that are responsible for their data members. This is not necessary, though, because the only code that can manipulate these data members is in the service facility that is responsible for those data objects. It is therefore more economical for service facility objects to hold references to other service facility objects (as well as to their own data objects), and for data objects to hold *only* references to other data objects. This is how we have coded service facilities in the Java example detailed in the next section.

This client can now switch to a different implementation for Sequence, the only code change being a change to the service facility constructor, which appears in just one line. A change from "_R1" to "_R2", for example, does not lead to a change in the client code except in this one unavoidable place. Note that the client declares both service facility and data objects to have interface types.

3.2 Homogeneous Containers

Since Java has no template mechanism, container or collection types are normally handled by taking advantage of the fact that Object is at the root of the class hierarchy. If we simply make sequences of Objects then everything seems fine – except for some nasty issues that are typically swept under the rug. The source of the problem is manifest *underdefinition* of the entry type. The compile-time type of entries is so "weak" that the compiler support a client programmer normally expects in finding type errors is effectively lost. One consequence is that it now becomes possible for a client program to have a container object whose entries are a heterogeneous collection of objects of different types. This complicates reasoning about client program behavior, and it usually is not what the component designer or the client had in mind in any case, but it is not caught at compile time. Another problem is that upon removal from a container, the type of an entry can be unknown to the client program and must be cast to the type the client programmer thinks (hopes) it was when it was inserted. Since inserting into a container and removal from it might take place in two distant locations in a large client program, this can be a significant problem. (We has an unpleasant first-hand experience with this situation while using a java.util.Map implementation.) Java's reflection feature can help here in principle, but the client code is an ugly mess.

Moreover, because of underdefinition of the entry type, the implementation classes for Sequence cannot do anything to entries that cannot be done to Objects. A clear symptom of this problem involves *cloning*, i.e., making a "deep copy" of a container object. The popular java.util package, for example, defines many container classes. Each has a clone method which, it might be hoped, would make a deep copy of this. It is a surprise to most potential clients of this package (at least to those who read the documentation or encounter mysterious bugs) that clone does *not* make a deep copy for these objects; it makes what the documentation calls a "shallow copy". The reason? If the declared entry type for the method that inserts an entry into a Sequence object is Object, then the compiler does not know that the actual entry type has a clone method of its own. It might seem that this problem could be avoided merely by enforcing the condition that the entries inserted must implement Java's Cloneable interface. But this does not work because Cloneable is an empty "marker" interface that merely suggests by wishful naming that any implementing class should have a clone method. When the compiler is presented with code like y = x.clone() in the clone method for a Sequence implementation class, it is unhappy because x is not known to have a clone method. There are many other possible workarounds, none of which is at all satisfactory.

The use of abstract factories reveals another symptom of the underdefinition problem. Specifically, if an implementation class for Sequence ever needs to construct a new object of the entry type by invoking its factory's create method, then it cannot do so (for essentially the same reason it cannot invoke the entry's clone method). To address this problem as well as some of the others noted above, SequenceF can demand that each implementation class have a method, say setItemF, that can be used to give each SequenceF object a reference to a factory object that can create its entry items. The new interface Factory in Figure 3(a) is now required as the type of the formal parameter to setItemF; but including this interface is a good idea in any case in order to document the details of the abstract factory pattern.

With service facilities, there is a corresponding method setItemSF in the interface SequenceSF. But the service facility for sequence items not only creates new entry objects, it is used to manipulate them. So it is possible to require that the argument to setItemSF be an implementation of some extension of ServiceFacility, e.g., one that includes a method to make a replica (clone) of its Data objects. For brevity and in order to concentrate on other points of comparison with abstract factories, we do not pursue the details of this suggestion here.

4   Example: Implementing Service Facilities in Java

In this section, we present the most important aspects of implementing the sequence example presented in Section 3.1.

4.1   The ServiceFacility and Data interfaces

The ServiceFacility interface is the root of all service facilities. This interface has the signature of one method, create(), that a client of a service facility calls to request a new object to be created. Figure 4 shows this interface.

4.2   The Data Interface

The return type of the create() method, Data, is also an interface. This interface serves as the root of all data objects that are used by a client in this model. Data is an empty interface, and serves only the purpose of enforcing some type safety. This interface is shown in Figure 5.

4.3   The SequenceSF Interface

The abstract component SequenceSF defines a generic homogeneous sequence component that could be specialized to contain items of any particular type. The SequenceSF interface therefore provides methods that a client would use to

```
package SF;

public interface ServiceFacility
{
    public Data create();
}
```

Fig. 4. The ServiceFacility interface

```
package SF;

public interface Data
{

}
```

Fig. 5. The Data interface

specialize the service facility to contain items of a certain type (in this case, just one: setItemSF). It also contains the signatures of the methods to manipulate sequences (say, for simplicity, just add, remove and length). The interface is presented in Figure 6. The SequenceData interface (not shown) extends Data but is otherwise empty.

```
package SF.Sequence;
import SF.*;

public interface SequenceSF extends ServiceFacility
{
    public void setItemSF (ServiceFacility sf);

    public void add (SequenceData s, int pos, Data x);
    public Data remove (SequenceData s, int pos);
    public int length (SequenceData s);
}
```

Fig. 6. The SequenceSF interface

4.4   SequenceSF_R1: An Implementation of SequenceSF

Figure 7 shows some parts of the SequenceSF_R1 class – an implementation of the Sequence. SequenceSF_R1 uses the two-stack representation as described in Section 2.2. For want of space, only one of the operations (add) is implemented completely here. There are similarly trivial bodies for the other operations.

The setStackSF method is used by the client to specify which implementation of the stack component is to be used in the sequence representation. This method is specific to the "_R1" implementation of sequence, which is why it is in the implementation class only, not in the SequenceSF interface. The private setLengthOfBefore operation simplifies the public method bodies. It is responsible for positioning the two stacks such that the item at position pos of the sequence is at the top of afterStack.

The structure of the SequenceSF_R1 class is the general structure of any service facility implementation in Java, as we code them. Note that the representation of the sequence, SequenceData_R1, is implemented as an inner class. The reason for this is that the service facility class needs access to the data members of that class. In C++, the same idea can be implemented using friend classes – SequenceSF_R1 must be a *friend* of SequenceData_R1.

5   Comparison to Abstract Factories

The design structures presented in Figure 3 suggest that abstract factories are very similar to service facilities. However, as we have observed earlier, there are some subtle differences between the two approaches that lead to some interesting consequences, which are described below.

```
public class SequenceSF_R1 implements SequenceSF
{
    private class SequenceData_R1 implements SequenceData
    {
        StackData beforeStack, afterStack;
        public SequenceData_R1 ()
        {
            beforeStack = (StackData) stkSF.create ();
            afterStack = (StackData) stkSF.create ();
        }
    }

    private ServiceFacility itemSF;
    private StackSF stkSF;

    public void setItemSF (ServiceFacility sf)
    { this.itemSF = sf; }
    public void setStackSF (StackSF sf)
    { this.stkSF = sf; }

    private void setLengthOfBefore (StackData before, StackData after, int len)
    {
        while (this.stkSF.length (before) < len)
        { this.stkSF.push (beforeStack, this.stkSF.pop (afterStack)); }
        while (this.stkSF.length (beforeStack) > len)
        { this.stkSF.push (afterStack, this.stkSF.pop (beforeStack)); }
    }

    public Data create ()
    { return new SequenceData_R1 (); }

    public void add (SequenceData s, int pos, Data x)
    {
        this.setLengthOfBefore (s.beforeStack, s.afterStack, pos);
        this.stkSF.push (s.beforeStack, x);
    }

    public Data remove (SequenceData s, int pos) { ... }
    public int length (SequenceData s) { ... }
}
```

Fig. 7. The SequenceSF_R1 class

5.1   Binary Operations

Consider a Point class shown in the code fragment in Figure 8. There is something different about the isEqualTo method, which tests the equality of two Point objects. Logically, equality checking is a binary operator, but as it is written in

```
class Point
{
    private int xVal;
    private int yVal;

    public int x () { ... }
    public int y () { ... }
    public bool isEqualTo (Point p)
    { return ((this.xVal == p.x ()) && (this.yVal == p.y ())); }
}
```

Fig. 8. The Point class

this class, the method takes only one parameter. The other parameter is the object on which the method is invoked; i.e., binary methods are asymmetric in standard object-oriented style. This causes several known problems with binary methods [3].

In the abstract factory approach, binary methods remain a problem, since the factory object only performs the task of creating a product object and all other operations are still associated with those product objects. With service facilities, however, the situation is different. The service facility class contains the methods used to operate on data objects, and each method takes as parameters all the data objects it has to operate upon. So, for the Point example, with a PointSF class that provides all the methods, equality checking no longer looks special with respect to the other methods. All methods in the PointSF class (shown in Figure 9) take at least one Point object as parameter. The areEqual method takes two parameters of the same type, and therefore actually looks like a binary operator. Gone with the funky asymmetric syntax are the usual problems associated with OO binary methods.

```
class PointSF_R1
{
    :
    :
    public int x (Point p) { ... }
    public int y (Point p) { ... }
    public bool areEqual (Point p, Point q)
    { return ((x (p) == x (q)) && (y (p) == y (q))); }
}
```

Fig. 9. The PointSF class

5.2 Layered Operations

Suppose that we want to implement an extension to the sequence component, to permit sorting of sequences. If designed with the abstract factory pattern, this extension is a derived class that inherits from the Sequence_R1 class. Suddenly, we have lost some of the decoupling we have gained from using abstract factories. This is because this extension only works for this particular sequence implementation. Now if the client wants to switch implementations for the underlying sequence component, the extension is no longer valid.

Another approach, one that respects decoupling, is to extend the interface (not the class) and to pass the sequence object to be sorted as an explicit parameter to the Sort operation. Such a class does not have any dependencies on other classes. Now, even if the client changes the implementation of sequences, no new implementation for the sort operation is required. This is a *layered* extension.

Layered extensions are natural to service facilities. If a sortable sequence is needed, we implement a new service facility class that holds a reference to some sequence service facility. This new class, SequenceSortSF_Ext, has the Sort method, which takes as a parameter the sequence data object to be sorted, and uses the underlying sequence service facility's methods to rearrange that sequence into sorted order.

5.3 Dynamic Relocation of Data Objects

As the safe deposit metaphor suggests, the service facility has full control of *where* a particular data object is physically located. In certain situations such as load balancing, fault recovery, etc., a service facility might decide to move the data objects it "controls" and "protects" to a different physical location. This kind of movement can be completely transparent to the client if the contents of the data objects are not altered in any way.

Such a behind-the-scenes optimization is difficult with the abstract factory pattern, because after a product object has been created, the factory no longer has any control over it. The client deals directly with the product object, and is the only party that "knows" about it, including where it is physically located. There are other ways to deal with this, but the abstract factory pattern itself does not help.

5.4 Dynamic Substitution of Implementations

It is common now for many systems – especially those for highly-available or reactive applications – to be non-terminating. They are required to run continuously, so upgrades and corrective maintenance must be done "on the fly". By way of analogy, consider one of the most important highly-available, reactive systems: humans. Replacing biological components, such as a kidney transplant, must be accomplished without killing the host! So too it should be with software: we should be able to "hot swap" components without killing the system.

We briefly allude to two kinds of scenarios where such implementation substitutions apply. One is the need to change only the algorithm used to compute something, while retaining the same data representation. This kind of substitution is extremely easy with service facilities. All we need to do is rebind the current service facility to a different service facility that provides the new algorithm. Nothing else in the client code changes if both the old and the new service facilities implement the same interface and rely on the same data representations. An example is changing the algorithm that should be used in the implementation of Sort described in Section 5.2.

On the other hand, it is often the case that different algorithms for implementing existing interfaces require different or novel data representations. For example, hashing and binary search tree algorithms for implementing a map component operate on dramatically different data structures. In this scenario, the representation of existing data needs to be converted to suit the new implementation. This is not free; but it can be done by a "representation converter". These kinds of substitutions are not supported by abstract factories, but they are readily handled with no additional complication (beyond what is obviously required in any solution) by service facilities.

6   Conclusions

The most common specific use of the abstract factory pattern is to decouple object declarations from object constructors, so that an object may be declared independently of any design-time commitment to its implementation. In general, abstract factories can be used to localize other concrete-to-concrete dependencies native to object-oriented systems. Despite their popular success in this area, though, abstract factories are insufficient for separating advanced component dependencies that arise in layered, hierarchically composed, and/or dynamically reconfigurable software.

We therefore propose the use of service facilities as a new technique that is powerful enough to address such higher-order considerations that arise in reusable component-based software. Service facilities leverage practitioner familiarity with abstract factories to address these concerns; and they solve a superset of the problems addressed by abstract factories. By uniformly replacing concrete-to-concrete dependencies with concrete-to-abstract dependencies, service facilities permit clients to assemble components independently of any design-time commitments to the implementations of their subcomponents. The commitments are deferred until integration time. Service facilities also allow familiar composition mechanisms such as parameterization to inductively propagate the benefits of abstract factories (and more) through all levels of a hierarchically composed system. Thus the decoupling problem can be solved once for each component, and the solution can be reused at all levels of a hierarchy.

We note that service facilities are offered as a design approach rather than a language mechanism. A language-neutral technique makes the benefits of using service facilities available in any OO-style implementation language or component infrastructure.

Finally, we readily admit that we do not yet have significant experience using service facilities in the design of large software systems. We offer the idea here in order to stimulate much-needed discussion of various techniques that can help decouple dependencies in such systems. Some of our current work involves building a programming environment for component-based software, including compilation of RESOLVE code [8] into Java (as the target language). This compiler generates Java code that uses service facilities as described here. It is an open question whether "real Java programmers" or "real .NET programmers" can be persuaded to embrace service facilities without significant promotion by their industrial sponsors. Our hope is that the clear similarities to abstract factories that we have emphasized will make the learning curve small for those who dare try them, encouraging others to experiment with service facilities and to assess and report on their practical effectiveness.

Acknowlegments

We gratefully acknowledge financial support from the National Science Foundation under grant CCR-0081596, and from Lucent Technologies. Any opinions, findings, and conclusions or recommendations expressed in this paper are those of the author and do not necessarily reflect the views of the National Science Foundation or Lucent.

References

1. D. Batory, V. Singhal, J. Thomas, S. Dasari, B. Geraci, and M. Sirkin. The GenVoca model of software-system generators. *IEEE Software*, 11(5):89–94, September 1994.
2. G. Baumgartner, K. Lufer, and V. Russo. On the interaction of objectoriented design patterns and programming languages. Technical Report CSD-TR-96-020, Department of Computer Science, Purdue University, 1996.
3. K. Bruce, L. Cardelli, G. Castagna, T. H. O. Group, G. T. Leavens, and B. Pierce. On binary methods. *Theory and Practice of Object-Oriented systems*, 1(3):221–242, 1995.
4. E. Gamma, R. Helm, R. Johnson, and J. Vlissides. *Design Patterns*. Addison Wesley, 1995.
5. B. Meyer. *Design by contract*, chapter 1. Prentice Hall, 1992.
6. B. Meyer. Overloading vs. object technology. *Journal of Object Oriented Programming*, October 2001.
7. D. Musser and A. Saini. *STL Tutorial and Reference Guide: C++ Programming with the Standard Template Library*. Addison-Wesley, 1996.
8. M. Sitaraman and B. W. Weide. Special feature: Component-based software using RESOLVE. *ACM SIGSOFT Software Engineering Notes*, 19(4):21–67, 1994.
9. B. W. Weide. Component-based systems. In J. J. Marciniak, editor, *Encyclopedia of Software Engineering*. John Wiley and Sons, 2002.

Software Fortresses

Roger Sessions

CEO, ObjectWatch, Inc.
roger@objectwatch.com
http://www.objectwatch.com

Abstract. Don't try to choose between J2EE and .NET, use them both! Just use a unifying architecture that recognizes the strengths and weaknesses of each platform. We propose a new model for enterprise systems called the Software Fortress Model. The Software Fortress Model treats enterprise systems as a series of self contained, mutually suspicious, marginally cooperating software fortresses (perfect for J2EE and .NET!). Each fortress makes its own choices as to software platform and data storage mechanisms and interacts with other fortresses through carefully crafted treaties. This helps enterprises focus on the critical issues of security and platform interoperability.

Biography. Roger Sessions is the author of five books and dozens of magazine articles, a columnist for Software Magazine, and the writer of the widely read and often controversial ObjectWatch Newsletter.

C. Gacek (Ed.): ICSR-7, LNCS 2319, p. 327, 2002.
© Springer-Verlag Berlin Heidelberg 2002

The Case against a Grand Unification Theory

Jayadev Misra

Dept. of Computer Sciences
Taylor Hall, University of Texas at Austin,
Austin, Texas 78712-1188, USA
misra@cs.utexas.edu
http://www.cs.utexas.edu/users/misra

Abstract. Theories and design principles of a general nature will be far too weak to be of much value to the practitioners. We should develop specialized theories that are applicable in specific domains, and we should work on binding these theories and principles much like the way we structure large systems today. Functional programming, for instance, provides impressive facilities for modularization, programming in layers and program integration. However, several important areas are not covered by the functional style of programming: non-determinism, persistent storage management, and matrix-based computations, for instance. There seem to be no easy extensions of functional-based system to include these domains.

I suggest that we abandon the idea of a Grand Unification Theory, and design specialized theories that handle a few things well. We should be studying how the capabilities of functional programming and object-based programming, for instance, can be integrated, different theories being applicable in each domain. The challenge lies in seamless integration. This proposal amounts to a strong prescription for empiricism, that we have to do a large number of experiments to understand where theories can play a role, and which kinds of theories would be most appropriate and when. Examples of a few small theories will be given and their effectiveness and limitations will be illustrated.

Biography. Jayadev Misra is a professor and holder of the Schlumberger Centennial chair in Computer Sciences at the University of Texas at Austin. He received his Ph.D. in 1972 from the Johns Hopkins University. He has been a faculty member at the University of Texas at Austin since 1974, except for a sabbatical during 1983-1984 spent at Stanford University.

His research interests are in the area of concurrent programming, with emphasis on rigorous methods to improve the programming process. He has been the past editor of several journals in this area, including: Computing Surveys, Journal of the ACM, Information Processing Letters and the Formal Aspects of Computing. He is the author of two books Parallel Program Design: A Foundation, Addison-Wesley, 1988, co-authored with Mani Chandy, and A Discipline of Multiprogramming, Springer-Verlag, 2001.

Misra is a fellow of ACM and IEEE; he held the Guggenheim fellowship during 1988-1989.

C. Gacek (Ed.): ICSR-7, LNCS 2319, p. 328, 2002.
© Springer-Verlag Berlin Heidelberg 2002

ICSR7 Young Researchers Workshop

Kai Boellert[1], Detlef Streitferdt[1], and Dirk Heuzeroth[2]

[1] Technische Universitaet Ilmenau, Germany
[2] Karlsruhe University, Germany

Abstract. The workshop aims at providing a platform for young researchers in the software reuse community to present their work. Presentations of all participants will be commented by experienced panelists and briefly discussed. As a result, all participants will get useful guidance and fresh impetus to their ongoing research. The workshop serves as a forum for the participants to get in contact with other researchers in the field and to become familiar with other approaches and future research topics.

C. Gacek (Ed.): ICSR-7, LNCS 2319, p. 329, 2002.
© Springer-Verlag Berlin Heidelberg 2002

International Workshop on Reuse Economics

John Favaro[1], Hakan Erdogmus[2], and Klaus Schmid[3]

[1] Consulenza Informatica, Via Gamerra 21, 56123 Pisa, Italy,
jfavaro@tin.it
[2] National Research Council, Montreal Rd. M-50, Ottawa, Ontario, Canada K1A 0R6,
hakan.erdogmus@nrc.ca
[3] Fraunhofer Institute for Experimental Software Engineering (IESE),
Sauerwiesen 6, D-67661 Kaiserslautern, Germany,
schmidk@iese.fhg.de

Abstract. Traditionally reuse economics has by and large concentrated on return on investment in formal, systematic reuse based on traditional cost-benefit models. Of prime importance in that context was cost savings, and more recently cost avoidance. Reuse was rationalized as a solution to minimizing wasteful consumption of resources through amortization of an artifact's development cost over multiple uses. The world has evolved since then. First, increased uncertainty in the software sector and technology in general have gradually shifted the focus from cost savings and cost avoidance to strategic issues of value generation, value management and risk. How does reuse create value in the context of strategic business decision-making? Second, the scope of reuse has evolved from type and class libraries to the entire architectural design process. Reuse economics is thus of prime concern when choosing among competing technologies and paradigms, and when applying them in a given context. How can our understanding of reuse economics leverage technical decision-making? Third, the value of software today is determined to a considerable degree by external market forces. What impact does reuse have on market perception of software value? The goal of this workshop was to bring together interested practitioners and researchers to exchange ideas and experiences, discuss current and emerging practices, and introduce next-generation concepts.

C. Gacek (Ed.): ICSR-7, LNCS 2319, p. 330, 2002.

Workshop on Generative Programming 2002 (GP2002)

Merijn de Jonge and Joost Visser

Merijn.de.Jonge@cwi.nl,Joost.Visser@cwi.nl
http://www.cwi.nl/GP2002

Background. The goal of generative programming is to replace manual search, adaptation, and assembly of components with the automatic generation of needed components on demand. Generative technology has been in practical use for decades (e.g., compiler development, application generation, automatic configuration management, preprocessing, and meta-programming). However, developing new domain-specific languages (DSLs), application generators, and component generators has been extremely hard, as it requires being knowledgeable and experienced both in language design and compiler development. Recent developments such as XML technologies and template meta-programming revived the interest in generative programming by making it more accessible to developers.

Objectives. The workshop aims to bring together practitioners, researchers, academics, and students to discuss the state-of-the-art of generative techniques and their impact on software reuse. The goal is to share experience, consolidate successful techniques, and identify the most promising application areas and open issues for future work.

Topics of interest. Impact of generative techniques on component-based development and software reuse. Assessing risks and benefits. Maintenance of generators. Reuse of generative programming assets. Styles of generative programming. Generation of code and non-code artifacts. Capturing configuration knowledge. Testing generic and generative models. Industrial applications.

Workshop format. The workshop aims to foster discussion and interaction rather than presentations. Presentations will serve to introduce a case study, provoke discussion by presenting a controversial point of view, or introduce new points of view. All participants will be given a chance to make a short presentation. The results of the workshop will be summarized in a workshop report. The workshop report and the position papers will be available form the workshop website (http://www.cwi.nl/GP2002) after the workshop.

Organizing committee. Joost Visser (CWI, The Netherlands), Merijn de Jonge (CWI, The Netherlands), Ted Biggerstaff (USA), Craig Cleaveland (independent software consultant, USA), Krzysztof Czarnecki (DaimlerChrysler Research, Germany), André van der Hoek (University of California, USA), Stan Jarzabek (National University of Singapore, Singapore), Shriram Krishnamurthi (Brown University, USA).

C. Gacek (Ed.): ICSR-7, LNCS 2319, p. 331, 2002.
© Springer-Verlag Berlin Heidelberg 2002

ICSR7 Workshop
on Component-Based Software Development Processes[1]

Christian Zeidler

ABB Corporate Research
Wallstadter Strasse 59
68526 Ladenburg, Germany
Tel.: +49 (6203) 71-6251, Fax: +49 (6203) 71-6253
Christian.Zeidler@de.abb.com

Abstract. Practitioners as well as academics claim that the component-based software development paradigm is of major importance for the field of software engineering, and expect that in the near future most software systems will be developed following from components. Software organisations, applying component-based software-development technologies, are not only better able to handle complexity but also to reduce development times and cost by the systematic reuse of in-house and standard components. Thus, component-based development offers organisations a way to quickly react on market requirements.

In practice the component-based development paradigm has only has a significant impact on the implementation phase of the software life cycle. Component technologies such as CORBA, JavaBeans/EJB, DCOM/AxtiveX and lately .NET basically allow the 'technical' cooperation of binary software building blocks of different origin. To counter this view there is a significant need to introduce the component-based development paradigm into all phases of the development life-cycle. In other words, the concept of a component should not just be seen as an implementation vehicle, but also as a central part of software design in term of concepts, methods and processes.

The goal of this workshop is to examine the process of component-based software development in all phases of the development life-cycle (i.e., specification, design, composition, testing, deployment) and to identify how this process needs to be different from traditional software development. Participation is encouraged both from practitioners to provide their experiences and help in identifying open questions, and from researches to suggest methodological support for addressing these questions. The ultimate goals is thus to enable an exchange of experience between practitioners and researches concerning the relevance and feasibility of using the component paradigm throughout the software life-cycle.

Focus

The workshop will focus on appropriate concepts, methods and applications. A non-exhaustive list of topics includes:

- Methodological foundation of component-based software development;
- Modeling of component-based systems (UML and others);

---

[1] http://www.idt.mdh.se/CBprocesses

C. Gacek (Ed.): ICSR-7, LNCS 2319, pp. 332-333, 2002.
© Springer-Verlag Berlin Heidelberg 2002

- Tools supporting component-based development;
- Integration of the component paradigm into existing environments;
- Component testing, verification, distribution, maintenance;
- Combination of heterogeneous component technologies;
- Extension of ‚standard' technologies to support component-based development (e.g., databases, languages, compiler, XML etc.);
- Industrial experience reports.

Organizing Committee

Christian Zeidler (ABB Corporate Research, Germany)
Marko Fabiunke (FhG FIRST, Berlin, Germany)
Christian Bunse (FhG IESE, Kaiserslautern, Germany)
Colin Atkinson (University of Kaiserslautern, Germany)
Ivica Crinkovic (Mälardalen University, Västerås, Sweden)

Industrial Experience with Product Line Approaches

Sholom Cohen[1]

Software Engineering Institute, Carnegie Mellon Univeristy
sqc@sei.cmu.edu

Many organizations realize that building multiple software products one product at a time is no longer viable. To retain market share in the global economy, they are pressured to introduce new products and add functionality to existing ones at a rapid pace. To address these demands, they have adopted an approach that uses software assets in the form of an architecture and components to modify, assemble, instantiate, or generate multiple products. These products, referred to as a software product line, share common features, but also provide variation points for mass customization.

This workshop will explore the state of product line practice across the software industry. It will develop a map that covers product line characteristics such as:

- Market area
- Products already fielded
- Product line practices used
- Organizational patterns

Many organizations have already experienced considerable savings in using a product line approach for software system production. Other organizations are attracted to the idea but are in varying stages of integrating product line practices into their operations. Consulting organizations and academic institutions also have valuable experiences to share in applying product line practices within industry. The workshop will attract these groups to share their experiences, positive or not, in a collaborative workshop.

Organizations may have different motivations in turning to product line approaches. We will seek out a mix of approaches including the following types of companies:

- Those that develop software derived from a common asset base for use within the enterprise
- Companies that develop a platform as a baseline for tailoring and use by other organizations
- Companies that have attempted product line practices, but that have not yet succeeded in widespread adoption

---

[1] Organizer

C. Gacek (Ed.): ICSR-7, LNCS 2319, pp. 334–335, 2002.

The workshop will look as broadly as possible to capture experiences from across a variety of business models and a spectrum of application areas. We also want to see the variety of techniques organizations are using to capture product line results.

Participants will be asked to submit in advance a brief questionnaire covering the following topics:

- How were the product lines introduced?
- Which market areas did the product lines cover?
- What practices did each group emphasize
- What organizational patterns did the organization follow?

The questionnaire will serve as a template for addressing product line concerns and will help organize the discussions. The topic areas will be the focus of subgroups that will convene during the course of the workshop.

Workshop on Software Reuse and Agile Approaches

Joseph W. Yoder

The Refactory, Inc.
yoder@refactory.com

Background. A lot of work has been done in the context of software reuse on heavyweight domain engineering methods. However there are also approaches such as Refactoring, Adaptive Object-Models, eXtreme Programming (XP), lightweight methods, domain specific languages, and evolving frameworks that put emphasize on evolution, flexibility, and responsiveness rather than proactive and preplanned generalization. These other approaches have been useful at either creating reusable components or at least made it so that systems can quickly evolve and adapt to changing user requirements.

Objectives. Our goal is to bring together practitioners, researchers, academics, and students in order to discuss the cost and benefits of these alternative methods on software reuse and compare them to the heavyweight methods. The end result is to share ideas and experiences, document what works and what doesn't, and identify when to use these alternative approaches over the heavyweight domain engineering methods.

Topics of Interest
- Reuse through Domain Specific Languages
- Reuse through Adaptive Object-Models
- Using XP to evolve Reusable Components
- Refactoring Reusable Components
- Lightweight vs. heavyweight approaches to software reuse
- Combining domain engineering and agile methods
- Evolving Components from Frameworks
- Evolving Frameworks to Domain-Specific Languages

C. Gacek (Ed.): ICSR-7, LNCS 2319, p. 336, 2002.

Software Architecture Quality Analysis Methods

Liliana Dobrica[1]and Eila Niemelä[2]

[1]University Politehnica of Bucharest,
Spl. Independentei, 313, Sect. 6, 77206 Bucharest, Romania,
liliana@ciid.pub.ro

[2]VTT Electronics,
P. O. Box 1100 FIN-90571 Oulu, Finland
Eila.Niemela@vtt.fi

Abstract. The open problem of structural methods is how to take a better advantage of software architectural concepts to analyse software systems for quality attributes in a systematic and repetitive way. Throughout the presentation we try to introduce a way of thinking founded on analysis at the architecture level of the quality attributes with the purpose to initiate and maintain a software product-line considering the quality as the main driver in product line development. This tutorial represents a study that shows the state of the research at this moment, in the quality analysis methods for software architectures, by presenting and discussing the most representative architecture analysis methods. The role of the discussion is to offer guidelines related to the use of the most suitable method for an architecture assessment process.

Summary of the Tutorial

One of the major issues in software systems development today is quality. The idea of predicting the quality of a software product from a higher-level design description is not a new one. Since 1972, when Parnas described the use of modularisation and information hiding as a means of high-level system decomposition to improve flexibility and comprehensibility until nowadays, the notion of software architecture has emerged as the appropriate level for dealing with software quality. This is because the scientific and industrial communities have recognised that software architecture sets the boundaries for the software qualities of the resulting system.

The general goal of the architecture evaluation of a software system is to analyse the architecture to identify potential risks and to verify that the quality requirements have been addressed in the design. The selection of the studied methods tries to cover as many particular views of objective reflections as possible to be derived from the general goal. Architecture is considered the first product in an architecture-based development process, and from this point of view, the analysis at this level should reveal requirement conflicts and incomplete design descriptions from a particular stakeholder perspective. The analysis could be associated with the designing of an iterative improvement of the architecture of a green software system, or with the reengineering of an existent one. Prediction methods of a single quality attribute are

C. Gacek (Ed.): ICSR-7, LNCS 2319, pp. 337–338, 2002.

meant to minimize risks (in isolation) only from that attribute perspective at a fine level. This might not be sufficient if the quality of a system is represented by a variety of quality attributes that interact with each other, and a balance between them should be established.

The beginning of this tutorial is dedicated to the definitions of the main terminology that is frequently used in the context of the methods. These are quality model and quality attributes, the definition and description from different points of view of software architectures, related styles and patterns, scenarios and other evaluation techniques performed at the architecture level. Based on these general elements and others related to methodology characterisation, we define a conceptual framework for presentation and comparison of the analysis methods. Our presentation concentrates on discovering differences and similarities between the available methods. The selection of a suitable method depends on how well each comparison element fits on a problem context. It is not the purpose of this tutorial to suggest a ranking list of analysis methods to the practitioners but give an understanding how the methods differ from each other. Only one selection criterium could be not enough to indicate the most suitable method for a defined purpose. The included evaluation techniques, the ease with which method's activities are performed and the existence of a knowledge base may represent other criteria that have to be considered in the selection process. An important element to think about is how well and in what software domain a method has been validated in practice.

During the presentation we introduce our original contributions in developing this significant and, in the same time, very new research domain. In order to be able to discuss about an analysis strategy for a product-line architecture it is a considerable advantage to have a good knowledge about the state of art and practice in the software architecture domain. One of our contributions is to extract the main concepts which are common to any software architecture and to present what specific for a product line approach in software development. The first part of the tutorial gathers together, for the first time in our knowledge, all of the important published software architecture analysis methods and attempts to compare them. The survey study represents a very important step for defining a general applicable product line architecture analysis strategy. In practice we exemplify our analysis approach and the last part of this tutorial focuses on our experiences with the product-line architecture analysis.

At the end of this tutorial, we will draw conclusions from the real level of the current research as well as the future work in this domain area defined by the presented methods. The architecture analysis is exemplified with our research experiences [1][2] on several case studies where the product line is initiated in a revolutionary style such as product-line architecture and its components are elaborated to match requirements of all expected product-line members.

References

[1] Dobrica, L., Niemelä, E. A *Strategy for Analysing Product Line Software Architectures.* VTT Publications 427, Technical Research Center of Finland, 2000.
[2] Dobrica L., E. Niemelä, *A Survey on Software Architecture Analysis Methods*, to be published IEEE Trans on Soft. Eng. 2002.

Tutorial on Practical Product Line Scoping and Modeling

Klaus Schmid and Isabel John

Fraunhofer Institute for Experimental Software Engineering (IESE),
Sauerwiesen 6, D-67661 Kaiserslautern, Germany,
{Klaus.Schmid,Isabel.John}@iese.fhg.de

1 Tutorial Overview

In order to do software reuse right, it is of key importance to make the right software reusable in the right form. This does not just happen; rather we need to identify where reuse could probably pay and what it is exactly that should be provided in terms of reusable components. This is a key idea of Product Line Engineering [3].

Traditionally, the importance of domain analysis for understanding a domain and providing requirements for reusable components in a domain is accepted in the reuse community. Especially in the product line community meanwhile an awareness has formed that adequate decision support is required to focus reusability on the functionality that provides the most payback. Recently, strong interest in these methods has developed under the name of scoping.

However, while the technologies for scoping and modeling are typically treated as independent, practical experience shows that both aspects are actually strongly interrelated. Focusing reuse requires that some sort of description of what could and should be reused is available as a basis for decision making.

On the other hand during product line modeling there is a continuous need to decide whether a certain functionality should be regarded as part of the product line / domain or as application specific and whether it should be made reusable comes up.

This observation is a key point for this tutorial: we focus on an integrated presentation of product line scoping and modeling technologies and illustrate this with the PuLSE™-method [1], which has been successfully applied in industrial practice.

2 Tutorial Goals

The key learning goals of the tutorial are:
* To understand the importance of scoping and modeling in the context of software reuse and in particular of product line development.
* To understand the range of available scoping techniques, that address the various decision making levels
  Product portfolio scoping: understanding what products should be built? How many? What aspects are impacting this decision? How can we embed our product line in a strategy?

C. Gacek (Ed.): ICSR-7, LNCS 2319, pp. 339–340, 2002.
© Springer-Verlag Berlin Heidelberg 2002

Domain Scoping: what areas of functionality are the most promising in terms of reuse? What risks may show up and how should they be addressed?

Asset Scoping: which components should really be built for reuse? Which ones promise the best return on investment?

- To understand the vast range of existing techniques for product line (domain) modeling. What are the key points of these techniques? How can we customize our techniques to a specific situation? What impacts the selection of the "right" approach? Is UML the answer?
- To understand how to find, analyze and model commonalities and variabilities within domains and between the planned products
- To understand the interrelation between the two activities scoping and modeling. This includes in what form the interactions may appear in practice and how this can be addressed by adequately integrated methods.

3 Tutorial Structure

The tutorial is structured in the following manner:
- *The importance of scoping and modeling as key factors for successful reuse*
- *Product line scoping and modeling as interacting activities*
- *Overview of product line scoping techniques*
- *Product line scoping using the PuLSE-Eco approach*
- *Overview of product line modeling techniques*
- *Product line modeling using the PuLSE-CDA approach*

References

1. J. Bayer, O. Flege, P. Knauber, R. Laqua, D. Muthig, K. Schmid, T. Widen, and J.-M. DeBaud. PuLSE: A methodology to develop software product lines. In Proceedings of Symposium on Software Reusability, SSR'99, pages 122–131, Los Angeles, USA, May 1999.
2. J. Bayer, D. Muthig, and T. Widen. Customizable domain analysis. In First International Symposium on Generative and Component-Based Software Engineering (GCSE 99), Erfurt Germany, September 1999.
3. Paul Clements and Linda Northrop. Software Product Lines : Practices and Patterns. Addison Wesley, 2001.
4. Klaus Schmid. A comprehensive product line scoping approach and its validation. In Proceedings of the 24th International Conference on Software Engineering, 2002. To appear.

Transformation Systems:
Generative Reuse for Software Generation, Maintenance and Reengineering

Ira D. Baxter

Semantic Designs, Inc.
idbaxter@semdesigns.com

Abstract. Program Transformation tools use a provided base of "transforms" (a kind of generative reuse of programming knowledge), to automate analysis, modification, and generation of software, enhancing productivity and quality over conventional methods. This tutorial provides a complete overview of Program Transformation, from theory to implementation to application. Real tools and applications are presented.

1 Transformation Systems

Transformation systems are software tools that "rewrite" constellations of concepts (characters, strings, trees, graphs) into alternative constellations. This rewriting capability is a key theoretical enabler supporting analysis, modification, and generation. Rewriting provides the basis for automation. Applying previously coded rewriting rules could provide significant additional leverage by reusing hard-won problem concepts, analysis and implementation-generating methods.

Transformation system technology has matured to the point where it is practical to apply to large scale, software systems, and offer large productivity and quality increments to engineering organizations using them [1]. Practical tools are now beginning to appear in the marketplace. The ability to make massive, reliable changes to software will fundamentally change the way organizations design and deliver software systems.

Program transformation systems provide the infrastructure to mechanize this process. *However, the actual value is derived from the capture and reuse of the generative "how-to" knowledge.* A large base of transformations can enable spectacular activities such as generating applications from specifications or translating one language to another.

The tutorial will provide the researcher and the practitioner alike with the necessary background to understand how these tools work, how to determine the capabilities and limitations of a particular system, and how to compare and therefore rationally choose among different transformation systems.

C. Gacek (Ed.): ICSR-7, LNCS 2319, pp. 341–342, 2002.

2   Technology Foundations

Practical transformation systems are extremely generalized compilers. They must:

- Parse source files and build a computer-internal-representation
- Analyze the representation for well-formedness, or interesting properties
- Modify the representation according to previous analyses, to either
  - Enhance the program (speed, space, quality)
  - Translate to another language
  - Abstract from low level concepts
- Finally, regenerate program source text from updated internal models.

The tutorial will cover these technology foundations, both in concept and in mechanism, and show how such components play together to achieve the overall effects. A conceptual vocabulary for clearly identifying transformation system components will be provided and act as basis of comparison of a number of practical systems. The author's scalable DMS Software Reengineering Toolkit will be used to illustrate a number of the foundations.

3   Applications of Transformation Systems

The tutorial will examine just a few of the many possible applications:
- Code generation from XML DTDs
- Clone Detection and Removal, which finds typically 10% redundant code in *any* system of modest scale. Code clones are often domain concepts.
- Refactoring (reorganizing object-oriented systems), and how automated tools are required to realize the promises of the refactoring/XP community
- Translating code from one language to another
Given time, we will briefly examine a theory of software change specification and automated change insertion being implemented with DMS.

References

1.   http://www.program-transformation.org

Component-Based Product-Line Engineering with the UML

Colin Atkinson and Dirk Muthig

Fraunhofer Institute for Experimental Software Engineering (IESE)
Sauerwiesen 6, D-67661 Kaiserslautern, Germany
{atkinson, muthig}@iese.fhg.de

Abstract. The software industry is pinning its hopes for future reuse and productivity gains on component-based software development. However, to date the component paradigm has only really penetrated the implementation and deployment phases of the software life-cycle, and does not yet play a major role in the earlier analysis and design activities of large software projects. This is evidenced by the fact that in today's technology being a "component" usually means being implemented as a JavaBeans, a COM object or a COBRA application. This tutorial will present a new method for component-based software engineering, known as KobrA, which supports a higher-level, model-driven representation of components and thus enables the benefits of components to be realized throughout the software life-cycle. The method thus provides a component-oriented way of developing model driven architectures (MDA).

Component and framework technologies are widely expected to dramatically increase the amount of reuse occurring in software development and maintenance, with associated improvements in time-to-market, software lifecycle costs and quality. The Gartner Group, for example, estimates that "... by 2003, 70% of new applications will be deployed as a combination of pre-assembled and newly created components integrated to form complex business-systems". However, industrial adoption of the component paradigm is failing to materialize as fast as expected due to the lack of systematic, prescriptive methods for developing, applying and reusing components. The KobrA method is a new approach for tackling this problem based on an integration of the component-based development, model driven architecture and product-line engineering paradigms.

Participants in the tutorial will receive an in depth introduction to the key characteristics of the KobrA approach [1], which include -

- Technology independence - the method is compatible with all major component implementation technologies (CORBA, JavaBeans and COM) and programming languages (e.g. Java, C++, Ada) because the essential architectural and behavioral caracteristcis of a community of components is captured in terms of UML models rather than any specific implementation language or technology.

- Architecture-centricity - in the context of a component-based system, where the architecture is dominated by the composition hierarchy, this means that the development process is oriented towards the elaboration of trees of nested components. From a top-down perspective this gives rise to a method that is recursive (i.e. hierarchical). However, the method is not exclusively top-town: at

C. Gacek (Ed.): ICSR-7, LNCS 2319, pp. 343–344, 2002.
© Springer-Verlag Berlin Heidelberg 2002

any stage in the development process preexisting components can be inserted into the component tree, providing a balancing bottom-up style of development.

- Product line support - this is achieved by means of decision models which describe the instantiation of a generic component according to the possible resolutions of the variabilities that exists in a family of related systems. A particular variant is thus identified by a concrete resolution of the decisions at a particular level of abstraction. When the decision models are combined in a hierarchic manner with the component tree, the result is a generic framework.
- Systematic COTS Component Reuse - a fundamental prerequisite for practical reuse of third-party components is a precise yet readable specification of what a component offers. KobrA's graphical UML-based specification of components is ideally suited for this purpose. Once a KobrA compliant specification of a potential reusable component has been created, the method defines a systematic strategy for integrating the component into a new system.
- Integrated quality assurance - in a tree-based product model, errors near the top of the tree can have a major impact on the lower parts of the tree. Therefore, it is important to gain as much confidence as possible that the components near the top of the tree are correct before proceeding to those lower down. In KobrA this is achieved through integrated quality modeling and inspection activities.

Biography

Colin Atkinson is a professor at the University of Kaiserslautern, and a project leader at the affiliated Fraunhofer Institute for Experimental Software Engineering (IESE) where he leads the KobrA method development team. He is also the prime author and editor of the KobrA book. His general interests are centred on object and component technology and their use in the systematic development of software systems. Colin received his Ph.D. and M.Sc. in computer science from Imperial College, London, in 1985 and 1990 respectively, and his B.Sc. in Mathematical Physics from the University of Nottingham in 1983.

Dirk Muthig has been a member of Fraunhofer IESE's Product Line department since January 1998, and is the chief author of KobrA's product line approach. He is also one of the main co-authors of the case study featured in the KobrA book. His general research is centred on strategies and methods facilitating an incremental transition towards product line engineering. Dirk received a B.S. and M.Sc. in Computer Science from the University of Kaiserslautern (Germany) and has recently submitted his Ph.D. thesis.

References

[1] C. Atkinson, J. Bayer, C. Bunse, O. Laitenberger, R. Laqua, E. Kamsties, D. Muthig, B. Paech, J. Wüst, and J. Zettel. Component-based Product Line Engineering with UML, Component Series, Addison-Wesley, 2001

Building Reusable Test Assets for a Product Line

John D. McGregor

Dept. of Computer Science
Clemson University
Clemson, SC 29634
johnmc@cs.clemson.edu

Introduction

Testing seeks to determine whether a component operates correctly or whether a system implements all of the required functionality. The artifacts produced during these activities can become assets if they are carefully designed and implemented. The assets provide opportunities to reduce the overall amount of resources needed for the test process much as product line techniques reduce the effort required for development. Careful planning and the application of statistical techniques can be used to further reduce the percentage of overall project effort devoted to testing. This paper provides an overview of a tutorial on building reusable test assets.

Test Assets

There are four categories of test assets: test plans, test cases, test data and test reports.

The test plan embodies the test strategy being used for a product. In a product line organization, a generic test plan is created and then specialized to each product. A test case is a triple including pre-conditions, the actual test stimulus and the expected results. Test cases are associated with specific product line assets. When the product line test asset is reused, the associated test cases are reused as well. Depending upon the type of system, test data can be a very expensive asset to produce. The data must be examined to determine that the conditions expected by the test case are present. Large data sets take much time to establish and to examine. A partial data set is associated with areas of commonality and other partial data sets are associated with areas of variability. The final data set is assembled for each test case. A test report associates a test case with a test data set and a test result. Test reports become assets when they are aggregated and used to consider patterns. This analysis is especially effective in a product line organization where large numbers of similar reports can be analyzed.

Comprehensive Test Process

Testing refers to a type of activity rather than to specific activities. Testing is the comparison of a manufactured piece to what was expected to be produced. Activities

C. Gacek (Ed.): ICSR-7, LNCS 2319, pp. 345–346, 2002.
© Springer-Verlag Berlin Heidelberg 2002

of this type appear at many points in a development project. In a product line organization there are two separate test processes.

Core Asset Testing Process

The core asset testing process is operated by the core asset builders. The primary goal of this process is to ensure that the components being produced as product line assets are operating correctly.

Inspections of Models – The first opportunity to examine artifacts is during the creation of analysis and design models and the software architecture. Several techniques have been developed to examine and evaluate these non-executable assets.

Component Testing – The component test process must achieve a more thorough degree of coverage since the components are intended to be reused. Component tests are based on the specifications defined in the product line architecture.

Integration Testing – Multiple components are combined into sub-assemblies and tested. Statistical techniques are used to select a set of test cases.

Product Testing Process

The product testing process is operated by the product builders. Its primary goal is to determine whether the product being produced is the product specified by the requirements.

Integration Testing – Multiple rounds of integration testing are applied as larger and larger subassemblies are constructed and tested.

System Testing – This test activity assumes that the sub-assemblies operate correctly and seeks to determine whether the product satisfies the requirements. The test cases are structured to mirror the regions of commonality and the points of variation in the product line architecture.

Post-Development Testing – A varying number of additional test phases are conducted to satisfy special concerns such as performance under load and capacity under load. The data sets for these tests are expensive to construct but easily reused across multiple products.

Architecture-Centric Software Engineering

Jan Bosch

University of Groningen, Department of Computing Science
PO Box 800, 9700 AV, Groningen, The Netherlands
Jan.Bosch@cs.rug.nl
http://www.cs.rug.nl/~bosch

1 Overview

Many software organizations are in the transition from project-centric to architecture-centric engineering of software [2]. Two typical reasons for this transition are (1) the architecture allows for a clear break-down in parts whereas a project-centric approach easily leads to a monolithic system and (2) the organization is interested in exploiting the commonalities between its products or systems. This tutorial addresses this development by providing an overview and in depth treatment of the issues around architecture-centric engineering of software. Topics include software architecture design in the presence of existing components and infrastructure (top-down versus bottom-up), architecture evaluation and assessment, software artefact variability management, software product lines and the role of the software architect. These topics are, in addition to the technical perspective, discussed from process and organizational [3] viewpoints. The topics are extensively illustrated by examples and experiences from many industrial cases (e.g. [1]).

The tutorial presents our experiences, reflections and research results concerning architecture-centric software engineering. Over the years, we have worked on this topic with a variety of companies, ranging from small and medium-sized enterprises (SMEs) to large, international organizations. Sharing our experiences and research results with the tutorial participants will allow the participants to make informed decisions about the future organization of software development in their own company (for industrial participants) or to collect additional empirical data and identify new research questions (for academic participants).

2 Contents

The tutorial contains the following parts:

- introduction to architecture-centric software engineering
  - definition of software architecture
  - software components, COTS and infrastructure
  - moving from project-centric to architecture-centric software engineering
  - different approaches to intra-organizational software reuse, e.g. software product lines

C. Gacek (Ed.): ICSR-7, LNCS 2319, pp. 347–348, 2002.
© Springer-Verlag Berlin Heidelberg 2002

- business case analysis, scoping and roadmapping
- software variability management
- software architecture design method
  - top-down versus bottom-up design
  - restrictions imposed by infrastructure, COTS and legacy components
  - functionality-based architecture design (a.o. variability analysis)
  - architecture evaluation and assessment
    scenario-based evaluation, simulation-based evaluation, evaluation using mathematical modelling and experience-based evaluation
  - architecture transformation
    imposing architectural styles, imposing architectural patterns, applying design patterns and convert quality requirements to functionality
- development of reusable components
  traditional components (provided, required and configuration interfaces)
  object-oriented frameworks (different extension models)
- architecture-centric product development
  different approaches to product development
  variability models for product derivation
- evolution processes in architecture-centric software engineering
- evolution patterns
  software artefact evolution processes: interdependence, dependence or independence
- organizing for architecture-centric software engineering
  We have identified four main organizational alternatives. In this part we discuss these alternatives, their applicability, advantages and disadvantages.
- adopting architecture-centric software engineering
  The transition from project-centric to architecture-centric software development typically requires changes at the process, organization and business level, in addition to technological changes.
- case studies: examples and experiences
- conclusion

References

[1] J. Bosch, 'Product-Line Architectures in Industry: A Case Study', Proceedings of the 21st International Conference on Software Engineering, pp. 544-554, May 1999.

[2] J. Bosch, Design & Use of Software Architectures - Adopting and Evolving a Product-Line Approach, Addison Wesley, ISBN 0-201-67494-7, 2000.

[3] J. Bosch, 'Software Product Lines: Organizational Alternatives,' Proceedings of the 23rd International Conference on Software Engineering (ICSE 2001), November 2000.

Practical Strategies and Techniques
for Adopting Software Product Lines

Charles W. Krueger

BigLever Software, Inc., 10500 Laurel Hill Cove
Austin TX 78730 USA
ckrueger@biglever.com

Abstract. This tutorial provides practical insights and guidance on lightweight strategies and techniques for adopting a software product line approach to software reuse. It will benefit practitioners and managers with responsibility for establishing software product lines and will also benefit researchers interested in learning more about the practical issues of adopting software product lines.

1. Introduction

Software product line approaches to software reuse have demonstrated great commercial value, offering order-of-magnitude reductions in time-to-market, engineering overhead, error rates, and accumulated cost when engineering a collection of similar software products. This is analogous to the advances observed in manufacturing when the emphasis moved from *hand crafting* one-of-a-kind products, to *mass production* of many identical products, to *mass customization* of many similar products. With software product lines, the emphasis shifts from strategies and techniques for hand crafting one-of-a-kind software products to strategies and techniques for the mass customization of many similar software systems.

Software product line approaches, being relatively new to the software engineering community, have often relied on intuition and pioneering spirit. As a result, the associated costs, risks, and time of adopting a product line approach can be high. This tutorial focuses on experiences and advances in *lightweight* software product line adoption strategies and techniques that lower the risks, costs, and time for establishing software product lines. The key to these lightweight approaches is to reuse and incrementally extend existing one-of-a-kind software, tools, processes, and organizations so as to minimally introduce changes to the way that software engineers currently create one-of-a-kind software systems.

2. Selecting an Adoption Strategy

Three different adoption strategies are discussed, along with the rationale an organization uses to choose one or more of these strategies in any particular software product line project.

C. Gacek (Ed.): ICSR-7, LNCS 2319, pp. 349–350, 2002.
© Springer-Verlag Berlin Heidelberg 2002

- Proactive. The organization designs and implements a complete software product line to support the full scope of products needed on the foreseeable horizon.
- Reactive. The organization incrementally grows their software product line when the demand arises for new products or new requirements on existing products.
- Extractive. The organization capitalizes on existing custom software systems by extracting the common and varying source code into a single product line.

Selecting among one or more of these adoption strategies to use for a particular software product line depends on a combination of the *initial state* and *steady state* business conditions for the software product line.

3. Variation Management Techniques

The key to effectively engineering a software product line is the ability to manage variation in both space and time throughout the life of the product line. Managing *variation in space* deals with differences among the products in the domain space of the software product line. Managing *variation in time* deals with configuration management of the product line, similar to configuration management in one-of-a-kind software systems. Collectively, managing variation in space and time is known as *variation management*.

Because variation management is at the core of software product line success, it is important to establish these techniques during the adoption of a software product line approach. However, because of the potentially complex interactions between variation in time and variation in space, designing, implementing, and deploying a variation management solution can be a daunting task. To address this problem, the tutorial illustrates how to "divide and conquer" the variation management problem as a collection of small and manageable problems.

Table 1 illustrates the variation management problem on a 3x3 grid, where each cell in the grid represents a variation management technique. The rows represent the granularity of artifacts that must be variation managed in a software product line. The columns represent variation management dimensions of space and time.

Table 1. Variation Management for Software Product Lines

	Sequential Time	Parallel Time	Domain Space
Files	version management	branch management	variation point management
Components	baseline management	branched baseline management	customization management
Products	composition management	branched composition management	customization composition management

Generative Programming: Methods, Techniques, and Applications
Tutorial Abstract

Krzysztof Czarnecki

DaimlerChrysler AG, Research and Technology,
Software Technology Lab, 89081 Ulm, Germany
czarnecki@acm.org
www.generative-programming.org

Today's software engineering practices are aimed at developing single systems. There are attempts to achieve reuse through object- and component-based technologies with two specific goals: to cut development costs, and time-to-market and to improve quality. But current research and practical experience suggest that only moving from the single system engineering to the system-family engineering approach can bring significant progress with respect to these goals [4, 8, 10].

Generative programming builds on system-family engineering and puts its focus on maximizing the automation of application development [1, 2, 7, 5]: given a system specification, generators use a set of reusable components to generate a concrete system. Both the means of application specification, the generators, and the reusable components are developed in a domain-engineering cycle.

Participants of this tutorial will learn the basic concepts of GP, and how to perform feature modeling, derive components and architectures from feature models, design domain-specific languages, and implement generators using widely available techniques such as XML and Java technologies [3] or C++ template metaprogramming [9, 5]. We will take a look at a number of case studies and round up the tutorial with an outlook on future, advanced generative technologies such as active libraries [6] and active sources [5].

References

1. D. Batory and S. O'Malley. The Design and Implementation of Hierarchical Software Systems with Reusable Components. In *ACM Transactions on Software Engineering and Methodology*, vol. 1, no. 4, October 1992, pp. 355–398.
2. J. C. Cleaveland. Building Application Generators. In *IEEE Software*, no. 4, vol. 9, July 1988, pp. 25–33.
3. J. C. Cleaveland. *Program Generators with XML and Java.* Prentice Hall 2001
4. P. Clements and L. Northrop. *Software Product Lines: Practices and Patterns.* Addison-Wesley, 2001.
5. K. Czarnecki and U. Eisenecker. *Generative Programming — Methods, Tools, and Applications.* Addison-Wesley, Boston, MA, 2000.
6. K. Czarnecki, U. Eisenecker, R. Glück, D. Vandevoorde, and T. Veldhuizen. Generative Programming and Active Libraries. In *Generic Programming: International*

C. Gacek (Ed.): ICSR-7, LNCS 2319, pp. 351–352, 2002.

Seminar on Generic Programming (Seminar 98171), Dagstuhl Castle, Germany, April 26-May 1, 1998, Selected Papers, M. Jazayeri, R.G.K. Loos, D.R. Musser, (Eds.), Lecture Notes in Computer Science 1766, Springer-Verlag, 2000, pp. 25-39

7. J. Neighbors. Software construction using components. Ph. D. Thesis, (Technical Report TR-160), University of California, Irvine, 1980.

8. D. Parnas. On the design and development of program families. In *IEEE Transactions on Software Engineering*, vol. SE-2, no. 1, 1976, pp. 1–9.

9. T. Veldhuizen. Using C++ template metaprograms. In *C++ Report*, vol. 7, no. 4, May 1995, pp. 36-43

10. D. M. Weiss and C. T. R. Lai. *Software Product-Line Engineering: A Family-Based Software Development Process*. Addison-Wesley, Reading, MA, 1999.

Author Index

Lecture Notes in Computer Science

For information about Vols. 1–2235
please contact your bookseller or Springer-Verlag